Conscription, US Intervention and the Transformation of Ireland, 1914–1918

Conscription, US Intervention and the Transformation of Ireland, 1914–1918

Divergent Destinies

Emmanuel Destenay

BLOOMSBURY ACADEMIC
LONDON • NEW YORK • OXFORD • NEW DELHI • SYDNEY

BLOOMSBURY ACADEMIC
Bloomsbury Publishing Plc
50 Bedford Square, London, WC1B 3DP, UK
1385 Broadway, New York, NY 10018, USA
29 Earlsfort Terrace, Dublin 2, Ireland

BLOOMSBURY, BLOOMSBURY ACADEMIC and the Diana logo are
trademarks of Bloomsbury Publishing Plc

First published in Great Britain 2022
Paperback edition published in 2023

Copyright © Emmanuel Destenay, 2022

Emmanuel Destenay has asserted his right under the Copyright, Designs and Patents Act, 1988, to be identified as Author of this work.

For legal purposes the Acknowledgements on pp. xiv–xv constitute an extension of this copyright page.

Cover images courtesy of the National Library of Ireland and bgblue/iStock

All rights reserved. No part of this publication may be reproduced or transmitted in any form or by any means, electronic or mechanical, including photocopying, recording, or any information storage or retrieval system, without prior permission in writing from the publishers.

Bloomsbury Publishing Plc does not have any control over, or responsibility for, any third-party websites referred to or in this book. All internet addresses given in this book were correct at the time of going to press. The author and publisher regret any inconvenience caused if addresses have changed or sites have ceased to exist, but can accept no responsibility for any such changes.

A catalogue record for this book is available from the British Library.

A catalog record for this book is available from the Library of Congress.

ISBN: HB: 978-1-3502-6658-2
       PB: 978-1-3502-6659-9
       ePDF: 978-1-3502-6660-5
       eBook: 978-1-3502-6661-2

Typeset by RefineCatch Limited, Bungay, Suffolk

To find out more about our authors and books visit www.bloomsbury.com and sign up for our newsletters.

This book is dedicated to Cornelius Crowley

Contents

List of illustrations	x
Preface	xii
Acknowledgements	xiv
Note on Translation	xvi
Biography of France's Representatives	xvii

Introduction — 1
   Echoes of Sarajevo — 1
   Conventional narratives — 5
   Plea for a new historiography of the Irish Revolution — 10
   Diplomatic sources and French narratives — 13

1 Political Crisis, British Intentions and Wartime Uncertainties (January 1913–March 1916) — 19
   Home Rule and Ulster Unionism: the impossible settlement — 19
   War breaks out: Asquith's strategy, recruitment, and the leap into the unknown — 29
   A distant war: propaganda and the war economy — 34
   Laissez-faire policy and French concerns — 40
   Conclusion — 48

2 Was the Rebellion a Turning Point? (April 1916–October 1916) — 49
   Allegiance and opportunities: US neutrality and the preparation for an insurrection — 49
   Rebellion, reactions and extrapolations? — 51
   Aftermath and executions: the transformation of Ireland? — 57
   Partition: ongoing deadlock and critical solutions — 63
   Procrastination and the end of the old administrative regime — 68
   Conclusion — 70

3 All Changed, Changed Quietly (October 1916–March 1917) — 71
   October 1916 and the threat of conscription — 71
   Opposing conscription, supporting Redmond — 76
   The decline in recruitment — 80

	The North-Roscommon by-election: the twilight of Sinn Féin	83
	Conclusion	89
4	Resisting Conscription, Redefining Ireland (March 1917–October 1917)	91
	March 1917: the Home Rule controversy	91
	Re-organizing Sinn Féin: towards the Árd Fheis	94
	The South Longford by-election: the men of Easter Week saved your sons from conscription	98
	Tightening the grip: the East-Clare election	103
	The Kilkenny by-election	113
	Árd Fheis: the Sinn Féin Convention in October 1917	118
	The shifting position of the Roman Catholic clergy	122
	The growing number of Sinn Féin sympathizers	125
	Conclusion	129
5	The Wartime Internationalization of the Irish Question (April 1917–March 1918)	131
	US intervention: a blow to the separatist movement?	131
	Colonel House and Ireland	136
	The April 1917 Irish Convention: a 'flat failure' or a 'political camouflage'?	138
	British procrastination	146
	From fear of another black '47 to fear of conscription (January–March 1918)	148
	Unholy alliances, survival and despair	154
	The goal of the Peace Conference takes hold	158
	Conclusion	163
6	Conscription, Betrayal and the Agony of the Irish Parliamentary Party (April 1918)	165
	From the Ulster 'conscription cry' to the German offensive	165
	Heated debates and some revelations	170
	A stab in the back of the dead man: a second execution of dead heroes	175
	'The miracle has been performed'	180
	Preparing the fight here and abroad	186
	An unpopular move among the British authorities in Ireland	189

	Conscription: a counter-Wilsonian move?	192
	Conclusion	195
7	Endgame (May 1918–December 1918)	197
	The German plot	197
	On the road to victory: summer 1918	201
	December 1918: the triumph of the Internationalists	211
	Conclusion	214
Epilogue		215
	How the Great War transformed Ireland	215
	Diverging destinies	218
	National minorities, post-war order and disillusions	221
Bibliography		225
Index		241

Illustrations

Figures

1.1	John Redmond and John Devlin inspecting the National Volunteers, 1915	32
2.1	Abbey Street after the Easter Rising, 1916	52
2.2	Lower Sackville Street, Dublin, after the Easter Rising, 1916	53
2.3	O'Connell Street after the Easter Rising, 1 May 1916	53
4.1	John Dillon, member of the Irish Parliamentary Party, addressing a meeting during the Longford by-election campaign in April 1917	101
4.2	Crowds on Westland Row in Dublin waiting to meet prisoners released from general amnesty, 18 June 1917	104
4.3	Crowds at Pearse Station in Dublin waiting to meet prisoners released from general amnesty, 18 June 1917	105
4.4	Handbill in support of Éamon de Valera, candidate for Sinn Féin, for the East Clare by-election, July 1917	108
4.5	Election handbill for the East-Clare by-election calling on people to vote for Éamon de Valera, July 1917	109
4.6	Éamon de Valera addressing supporters from Ennis Court House, 11 July 1917	112
4.7	Clare by-elections, July 1917. Victory parade led by pipers with Countess Markievicz	113
5.1	Election handbill issued to encourage people to vote for the Sinn Féin candidate for South Armagh, Patrick McCartan, in February 1918	156
5.2	By-election handbill for Patrick McCartan, Sinn Féin candidate for the South Armagh constituency, February 1918	157
7.1	Election and anti-conscription leaflet seeking support for Arthur Griffith, the Sinn Féin candidate in the East Cavan by-election (held on 20 June 1918)	204

7.2	Anti-conscription handbill issued by opponents of the Irish Parliamentary Party, 1918	205
7.3	Election campaign leaflet for Arthur Griffith for the East Cavan by-election in June 1918 criticizing the stance of Captain William Redmond and the Irish Party for their perceived support of conscription	206

Maps

1.1	Ireland at the outbreak of the First World War	18
4.1	Ireland and the four 1917 by-elections	90
7.1	Ireland and the 1918 general elections	211

Preface

In my first book, published in 2021 by University College Dublin Press under the title *Shadows from the Trenches. Veterans of the Great War and the Irish Revolution (1918–1923)*, I addressed the contention according to which the IRA had launched a deliberate campaign against Great War veterans during the War of Independence between 1919 and 1921. Endorsement of the hypothesis that there had been a systematic opposition between IRA members and Great War veterans had constituted a powerful psychological block to any further investigation as to the trajectories of these men. With time, the hypothesis had taken on the force of an 'agreed lie' and had imposed itself as an unchallenged historical fact.

In similar fashion, the contention that Easter Week 1916 had operated as a turning point in the history of Ireland was something that had left me perplexed. Ever since embarking on my post-graduate studies in history at the University Jules Verne in Amiens in 2006, I entertained certain reservations regarding the claim that such a short-lived rebellion could have aroused such an overwhelming memory. It was clear that the uprising, which had broken out at what was a critical moment in the Great War, had left the city centre of Dublin, and some outlying districts of the city, devastated. Furthermore, there was little doubt that the executions carried out by the British authorities in its aftermath had embittered the country's civilian populations. However, did this offer support for the presumption that the event had left an indelible impression on an Irish (and British) collective memory? Did the immediate infuriation of nationalist populations necessarily prove that they were ready to adopt a more radical political stance? More importantly, did this presumed watershed event divert nationalist civilian populations from the long-established support for the Irish Parliamentary Party, thus redirecting the course of Irish history? Arguably a piece of the puzzle seemed to be missing. I was therefore somewhat puzzled. And very keen to look at the details of the reports from France's Ambassadors and Consuls to Dublin, London and Washington during the period after Easter 1916. Most importantly, the appreciation of the situation in Ireland on the part of these diplomatic observers fortified my conviction that it was the fear of enforced military service which significantly radicalized nationalist populations in the course of the conflict.

Though historians disagree on the actual impact of the executions of the 1916 leaders, they nevertheless maintain that Easter Week 1916 (and its aftermath) did usher in a new era. But in the context of an ongoing global cataclysm, which had displaced and killed millions of people, and which led to calls for a redefinition of the borders of nation-states and paved the way for the proliferation of independence movements, worldwide, might it not be the case that it was the magnitude of this geopolitical catastrophe which could account for the transformation of Ireland? Did the indisputable political blunders of the British authorities, in the aftermath of the failed military fiasco, constitute a sufficient catalyst in the radicalization of civilian populations? Was the commitment to the goal of complete independence enough to explain the popularity of Sinn Féin and the concomitant repudiation of the Irish Parliamentary Party in the four by-elections contested in 1917? The present book seeks to advance possible answers to these questions, while challenging conventional narratives and distancing itself from (what seems to me) an artificially constructed continuity between Easter Week 1916 and the December 1918 general elections.

While the Irish Parliamentary Party (also called the Irish Party) did remain, throughout the course of the conflict, the staunch advocate of a devolution of powers within the framework of the Union, the accelerated tempo and uncertainties of wartime politics had the effect of widening the gap between the party's expectations and the aspirations of nationalist communities. It was largely the fears of being conscripted which precipitated the divorce between the Irish Party and its support base within nationalist Ireland. It was thus the set of immediate anxieties aroused by the possible introduction of conscription which decisively redirected the course of Irish history. What the global conflict thus enabled was the shift from the Irish Party's declared intention of lessening Ireland's constitutional ties with Britain to a commitment on the part of Sinn Féin to their complete severance, through the establishment of a sovereign independent Irish nation-state.

Acknowledgements

This work would not have been possible without the support of the Irish Research Council. The two-year fellowship at University College Dublin was originally planned to enable me to complete my first monograph on Irish veterans of the Great War. At some point in the research, the idea of writing my second monograph emerged from what was an unexpected discovery. In February 2019, when preparing a talk for the American Conference for Irish Studies (ACIS) in Boston, I made a visit to the Diplomatic Archives of the French Ministry for Foreign Affairs (La Courneuve). Intrigued and impressed by the considerable documentation relating to the Irish Revolution, I eventually decided to embark on a second project and to continue my research on the Irish Revolution. Here, I wish to express my fullest gratitude to Sylvie Yeomans, and all the archivists, for their time and for their support in helping me track down precious information about France's representatives to Dublin, London and Washington during the First World War.

Thanks to its financial support, the Irish Foundation of France gave me the opportunity to publish my first monograph in 2021, along with this second book. Nora Hickey (director of the Irish Cultural Centre in Paris), Pierre Joannon and the board members of the Irish Foundation of France can be assured (once again) here of my deepest gratitude.

As always, Cornelius Crowley has proved an important source of support. He read and edited numerous drafts of the book and discussed my conclusions on several occasions, in cafés in Paris over the summer of 2019. As always, his overview and insightful comments have significantly helped. When the idea of this second book was mentioned, Geneviève Hoffman urged me to publish it without hesitating, arguing that the method and scope would make a significant contribution to the historiography. Both of them kept an eye on the progress of the book, through regular discussions of my conclusions, my doubts and the various lines of inquiry that have been taken up. My colleague and friend Sarah Loom edited the last version of the book. As always, her incisive suggestions have been of considerable help.

The three anonymous reviewers who read the manuscript are to be thanked for the detailed, comprehensive and encouraging feedback which they provided.

Thanks to their minute and consistent suggestions, the manuscript has been significantly improved. They are to be assured of my entire gratitude. I equally wish to thank Emily Drewe, Abigail Lane and all the people involved in the process of editing at Bloomsbury.

Finally, I cannot forget the two most important people in the achievement of this enterprise. With the passing of time, the memory of the war songs sung by my grandmother have not disappeared. And my memory of my mother's teachings remains equally vivid.

Emmanuel Destenay
April 2021

Note on Translation

The private correspondence of France's representatives to London, Dublin and Washington have necessitated an important work of translation. All the translations have been undertaken rigorously and are my own responsibility.

Biography of France's Representatives to Dublin, London and Washington

BLANCHE, Alfred (1874–1950). Blanche was appointed Consul-General in Dublin in November 1917. In his first report to the Ministry for Foreign Affairs, Blanche explained how the US entry into the war had struck a blow to Sinn Féin. He argued that Sinn Féin was losing its grip on the pulse of nationalist Ireland and that the position which would now be adopted by Irish-Americans could force Sinn Féin to downplay its anti-British rhetoric. He even thought that US intervention could paralyse Sinn Féin in its design. However, Blanche knew that the issue of conscription could resurrect Sinn Féin. He thus positioned himself against the implementation of any military service bill to Ireland, stating his categorical disagreement with the idea that the answer to the Irish question had to be military; arguing that the solution could only be political. He considered that the British ought to take the initiative and seek an immediate solution, however defective. In his view, Home Rule, with the exclusion of a number of northern counties, had to be implemented, coupled with the establishment of a new framework for the administration of Ireland. In addition, Blanche calculated that if a policy of conscription were to be introduced, it would deprive Ireland of 100,000 men in a context where the number of agricultural workers amounted to 130,000, with the consequence that the country would quickly be deprived of its vital sector of agricultural production. Blanche forwarded a detailed account of the transformation of the political landscape that such a law would lead to in Ireland. He mentioned that civilian populations would offer their fervent support to Sinn Féin in order to avoid conscription. From Dublin, he reported in December 1917 on the first signs of incipient famine. Blanche was convinced that the prevailing misery of the population and the acute difficulty it faced in getting food were the decisive factors behind the wave of unrest.

CAMBON, Paul (1843–1924). Born in Paris, Cambon studied at Oxford, Cambridge and Edinburgh. After ten years in the administrative service in France as secretary of a *préfecture*, he was appointed prefect in the Aube administrative *département* (1872), before further postings as prefect in 1877 (Nord) and 1878 (Doubts) in eastern France. He subsequently moved to diplomatic service. In 1882, he was nominated French minister plenipotentiary at Tunis (1882–1886), before becoming Ambassador for France to Madrid. In 1890, he was sent as Ambassador for France to Constantinople, before his nomination as Ambassador to London. He played a determining and active role in the establishment of the Entente Cordiale between France and the United Kingdom in 1904. Throughout the course of the conflict, Cambon mainly wrote reports on the position of the United Kingdom, offering accounts of how the country was dealing with the conflict. However, his political correspondence also sheds light upon how the British reacted to political unrest in Ireland. From his position in London, he could receive precious and confidential information from members of the Cabinet, which played into his analysis of the situation in Ireland. In the aftermath of the executions in Dublin, he positioned himself in favour of immediate action for the settlement of the Irish question. He regarded the uprising as merely a further episode in the tumultuous history of Anglo-Irish relations. On 9 March 1917, he reported to Paris that the Irish Parliamentary Party was losing ground in Ireland. In July 1917, he alerted the Ministry for Foreign Affairs that Sinn Féin was aiming at securing the representation of Ireland at the future Peace Conference. Cambon considered that conscription was needed, and that the British were perfectly entitled to impose the measure to Ireland. He knew however that it would lead to unrest in the country. Compared to Colonel de la Panouse, Cambon always refrained from positioning himself on the issue of Home Rule and partition.

DE LA PANOUSE, Louis (1863–1945). Born in Paris, de la Panouse entered the military school Saint Cyr in 1884, from which he embarked on a successful military career. In 1886, he was appointed Second-Lieutenant in the 5th Dragoon Regiment (a cavalry unit of the French army). In 1894, he became Captain before being nominated Lieutenant-Colonel. He held several positions as military attaché to the French Republic, in Denmark, Sweden and Norway. In 1907, he was sent to the Embassy for France in Spain and subsequently to Portugal. In November 1911 he was mandated as military attaché to the Embassy of the French Republic in London and was promoted Colonel. When the 1916 insurrection broke out, he regarded it as an adventure, embarked upon with little support from the population. In October, he personally informed the Quai d'Orsay that recruitment to the army was significantly dropping in Ireland. In February 1917, he was promoted General. Throughout the First World War, de la Panouse provided detailed reports on the political situation in Ireland. After the 1916 Easter Rising, he sent a secret note to Paris explaining that the designs of the Germans were aimed at the stoking up of difficulties within Ireland, on keeping alive the threat of a possible landing, thus preventing the British from sending more troops to France. De la Panouse noted that the Rising coincided with the attacks of the German Navy and Zeppelins on the east coast of England. He deplored the sending of 18,000 men to crush the rebellion at what was a desperate moment in France, when additional British troops were needed on the Somme. From October 1916, he openly advocated the immediate implementation of Home Rule for twenty-six counties, and the creation of an Irish National Government in accordance with the Home Rule Bill. From London, he reported his conversations with British MPs, and observed the gradual accession of Sinn Féin to a position of dominance, in terms of its support within nationalist Ireland. In April 1917, he was predicting that Sinn Féin would win any election in southern and western Ireland, while also stating that the Irish question was no longer a purely domestic affair, having become an international wartime concern. When the Irish Convention was summoned, General de la Panouse anticipated it would be doomed to fail, in view of the decision of Sinn Féin not to attend. At the beginning of 1918, he reported that British public opinion played a decisive role in convincing the Prime Minister to include Ireland in the new Military Service Act. While he agreed that Ireland ought to be conscripted, he esteemed the British had made a terrible blunder in pushing for a vote on conscription in April 1918, without simultaneously granting Ireland a large measure of autonomy. Throughout the conflict, he consistently advocated conscription for Ireland, not however without granting Home Rule first to the south of the island. He believed the partition of the island was inevitable. In May 1918, General de la Panouse confidentially wrote that the British had never been serious in their declared intentions to implement Home Rule, even for twenty-six counties. He wrote that such a project would have had implications for the United Kingdom as a whole and would have redefined the relation between Westminster and the three kingdoms.

DES LONGCHAMPS, Jean (1872–1967). By the time the First World War broke out, des Longchamps was Consul-General for France in Dublin. In February 1915, realizing that British wartime propaganda was inefficient, he suggested a delegation of French Catholic priests be sent to Ireland to help recruitment and thwart German propaganda. From Dublin, as early as January 1916, he expressed his serious concerns about the open drilling of Irish Volunteers, voicing his worries at their adoption of an openly pro-German rhetoric. Des Longchamps warned this could potentially turn into a war issue, if Sinn Féiners continued to demonstrate openly. On 18 April 1916, a few days before the 1916 uprising, he sent a detailed report on the situation of Ireland to the Quai d'Orsay in Paris. He agreed that a campaign of repression carried out against the agitators could jeopardize the country's political stability, while nonetheless stating his belief that Ireland could not endorse pro-German seditious propaganda in wartime. He concluded that the 1916 rebellion had occurred due to lack of clear-sightedness and energy on the part of the British Government. He seems not to have been aware that a rising was being planned and was subsequently dismissed in June 1916 and sent to Paraguay. Seventeen months passed before he was replaced by Alfred Blanche. Between June 1916 and November 1917, Mr Armany, in charge of the Consulate in Dublin, was responsible for sending reports to the French Ministry for Foreign Affairs.

JUSSERAND, Jean Jules (1885–1932). Born in Lyon (France), Jusserand started his diplomatic career as Consul of the French Republic to London in 1878, before being appointed minister plenipotentiary in Copenhagen in 1890. In 1910, he became Ambassador to Washington. A few days before the insurrection of Easter Week 1916, he received confidential information that a landing was in preparation in Ireland and would take place at the same time as an attack by the German navy. Following the executions of the 1916 ringleaders, he reported that the Irish national cause was being compared to that of the thirteen colonies in the proclamation of their independence from Britain in 1776. Though his correspondence was mainly focused on the United States, he sent a detailed report, dated 26 April 1918, in which he explained the extent to which the Irish question was becoming a vexed issue for Woodrow Wilson, the receiver of numerous letters from leading Irish-Americans begging him to personally intervene against the introduction of conscription in Ireland. Jusserand met privately with Lord Reading, British envoy to Washington, who explained to him that it appeared more and more urgent to grant Home Rule to the Irish before the full implementation of conscription. His reports and his personal correspondence allow for a detailed comprehension of how Irish-Americans reacted to the 1916 uprising and to the conscription crisis.

Introduction

Echoes of Sarajevo

Edward Grey, Britain's Foreign Secretary, had guaranteed Paul Cambon, France's Ambassador to London, that Britain would assist France if it were to come under threat. Cambon had played a determining role during the negotiations of the Entente Cordiale in 1904.[1] A series of agreements between the two imperial powers had significantly normalized Anglo-French relations, while also helping clarify their respective colonial demarcations in Africa, and ensuring France the substantial support of the British in the event of an attack. An agreement promoting mutual recognition of imperial possessions stipulated that France was in full control of Morocco and that Britain would maintain its grasp on Egypt. By 1904, Paris had grown increasingly suspicious of Germany's system of alliances, notably the 1882 Triple Alliance, which threatened its vital interests. Otto von Bismarck, Chancellor of the German Reich at the time, had managed to enlist the support of both Austria-Hungary and Italy against any potential French inclination to regain the territories of Alsace-Lorraine (which France had lost to the Reich as a result of its decisive defeat in 1871). As it sought to recover from the calamitous experience of the 1870–71 Franco-Prussian War, France found itself up against an ironclad alliance that was in a position to marshal vast numbers of troops all along its borders. The 1904 Entente Cordiale thus represented an agreement offering some strategic assurance to France. The pact was also a source of bitter political frustration for the Reich, which sought to contest French imperial control of Morocco the following year, leading to

---

[1] Christopher Andrew, 'France and the Making of the Entente Cordiale', *Historical Journal* 10, no. 1 (1967): 89–105.

the Tangier Incident in 1905 and the Agadir Crisis in 1911.² The stakes of European rivalries and imperial mistrust were being ratcheted up through the play between various strategic alliances and international crises in the period leading up to 1914.

There was another country where the 1904 Entente Cordiale was a cause for dismay and stupefaction. When, on 6 April 1904, the agreements between France and Great Britain were signed, the Irish realized that they could no longer rely on their presumed ally. For more than a century, revolutionary Ireland had consistently looked to France, in a posture of a somewhat sentimental expectation.³ From 1792 onwards, France had exported revolution to the rest of Europe and had fostered the inclination of stateless peoples to rise up against their imperial masters.⁴ Thanks to its expansive military imperialism, France conquered territories and imposed the French model of citizenship and sovereignty. After a first unsuccessful expedition to Ireland in 1796,⁵ France made advance preparations for a second, again unsuccessful, invasion of the island in 1798.⁶ From what had been a position as messianic liberator plotting a landing through which the Irish were to be set free, France had now, at the start of the twentieth century, become the closest ally of Britain in Europe, the two former enemies brought together by their shared political and security concerns. When the Entente Cordiale was eventually signed, revolutionaries in Ireland were thus faced with a distinctly unpromising fact: the French would no longer be there to assist them.⁷ Consequently, republican dissidents in Ireland looked towards Germany for help, even before the beginning of the conflict. As the international situation worsened in Europe, the British frowned at Germany's

---

[2] Ima Christina Barlow, *The Agadir Crisis* (Chapel Hill: University of North Carolina Press, 1940); Geoffrey Barraclough, *From Agadir to Armageddon: Anatomy of a Crisis* (New York: Holmes and Mier, 1982); Christopher Clark, *Sleepwalkers: How Europe Went to War in 1914* (London: Allen Lane, 2012), 204–214; Keith Wilson, 'The Agadir Crisis, the Mansion House Speech, and the Double-Edgedness of Agreements', *Historical Journal* 15, no. 3 (1972): 513–532.
[3] Robert Kee, *The Green Flag. A History of Irish Nationalism* (London: Weidenfeld & Nicolson, 1972), 41–148.
[4] T. C. W. Blanning, *The French Revolutionary Wars, 1787–1802* (London: Hodder, 1996); Alexander Grab, *Napoleon and the Transformation of Europe* (New York: Palgrave Macmillan, 2003); Raymond Kubben, *Regeneration and Hegemony. Franco-Batavian Relations in the Revolutionary Era, 1795-1803* (Leiden, Boston: Martinus Nijhoff, 2011); Connelly Owen, *The Wars of the French Revolution and Napoleon, 1792–1815* (London: Routledge, 2006); Edward James Kolla, *Sovereignty, International Law and the French Revolution* (Cambridge: Cambridge University Press, 2017).
[5] John A. Murphy, *The Expedition to Bantry Bay, 1796* (Cork: Mercier Press, 1997). See also Donald R. Come, 'French Threat to British Shores, 1793–1798', *Military Affairs* 16, no. 4 (1952): 174–188.
[6] Thomas Pakenham, *The Year of Liberty: The Story of the Great Irish Rebellion of 1798* (London: Abacus, 2000), Part IV, Chapter II.
[7] Jérôme aan de Wiel, *The Irish Factor, 1899–1919; Ireland's Strategic and Diplomatic Importance for Foreign Powers* (Dublin: Irish Academic Press, 2008), 33–44.

interference in Irish affairs. Germany's repositioning as the champion of Irish sovereignty baffled the French.[8] But the succession of crises unfolding in the years before 1914 proved that the French were unquestionably right, in strategic terms, in abandoning their century-old support for the Irish as the price to pay for a vital alliance with Britain.

On 28 June 1914, in Sarajevo, Gavrilo Princip, a 19-year-old Bosnian Serb, shot and killed the heir to the throne of the Austro-Hungarian Empire, Archduke Franz Ferdinand, and his wife. Throughout Europe, the assassination of Ferdinand spurred the hopes and expectations of a host of ethnic minorities within the rival European empires. In the short term of the summer of 1914, it led to a 37-day crisis. Infuriated by the death of the man who had been designated successor to the emperor Franz Joseph (1830–1916), Vienna issued an ultimatum to Serbia on 23 July, having previously secured political support from Berlin for the state goal of dampening Serbian nationalism and the protection of its multi-ethnic empire. Princip's momentous act risked precipitating the break-up of the Austro-Hungarian Empire, if the ethnic minorities were to invoke principles of national sovereignty and demand political autonomy. From Saint-Petersburg, the Russian Tsar warned Vienna against any attack directed at the Serbs, pledging Russian support for their little Orthodox brother. The decision of Nicholas II to mobilize his army alarmed Berlin, while the mass mobilization of Russian soldiers on its eastern flank aroused widespread concern, ultimately causing Kaiser Wilhelm II to declare war on the Russian Empire on 1 August 1914. On 3 August, Germany declared war on France and, the following day, on Belgium. In the longer span, this was to unleash a four-year Armageddon and the mobilization of sixty-five million troops worldwide.[9]

While Britain's Prime Minister, Herbert Asquith, was certainly puzzled as to the immediate and longer term implications of the assassination of Ferdinand, he could at least find in the international crisis a modicum of unexpected solace: the European crisis provided an unexpected resolution to, or at least suspension of, the political stalemate over Irish Home Rule. From Downing Street, the outbreak of the war offered him an opportunity to alleviate tensions caused by the unresolved constitutional impasse in Ireland. The British declaration of war on Germany on 4 August 1914 averted the immediate threat of a civil war in Ireland between die-hard unionist paramilitary organizations (UVF) and fervent nationalist followers (Irish Volunteers). As a fully-fledged part of the United

---

[8] Ibid, 158–209.
[9] Clarke, *The Sleepwalkers*, xxi.

Kingdom since the Act of Union of 1801, Ireland nevertheless remained divided by its century-old cultural, political and religious tensions. Since William of Orange's conquest of Ireland at the Battle of the Boyne in 1690, the proudly loyal descendants of the socially dominant Protestant majority had ruled the country, imposing English as the national language, reducing the Irish language to cultural and social marginality and dispossessing Catholics of their lands, while simultaneously maintaining control, both local and national, on the administrative and civic institutions of the country. A series of rebellions broke out during the late eighteenth and nineteenth centuries, with the declared intention of lessening, or entirely severing, Ireland's ties with Britain and achieving political autonomy; but in vain. Gradually, in the context of a more democratic suffrage and political culture, a movement of constitutional nationalism came to eclipse the ideology of armed insurrection. Under the leadership of Charles Stewart Parnell, a Protestant from a family of landowners,[10] constitutional nationalism (a political movement initiated in the 1870s) brought about a profound mutation in both the goals and the methods of Irish nationalism through his gradual and cautious navigation between the magnetism of the 'physical force' or 'advanced' nationalist tradition and the pursuit of constitutional change for Ireland within the existing legislative order. Far away from powder and guns, Parnell opened up a space for a nationalist politics that would be dedicated to the same achievement of autonomy (Home Rule) within the United Kingdom, but through constitutional and electoral channels. Since 1870, 'the promise or threat of Home Rule [had been] the driving force behind every substantial faction in Irish politics',[11] and so, by the time the Germans were engaged in the business of provoking the French in Morocco, nationalist Ireland was closer than ever before to the goal of achieving political autonomy. But that was to reckon without the determined opposition of Ulster and its armed loyalists, who solemnly pledged their readiness to forfeit their lives to defend their birth-right allegiance to Crown and Parliament, rather than consent to the administration of Ireland from a parliament in Dublin. Britain was faced with the immediate threat of civil war inside Ireland.

By August 1914, the British Government thus found itself trying to read the course of events on the European continent while also looking anxiously to the

---

[10] F. S. L. Lyons, *Charles Stewart Parnell* (London: Gill & Macmillan, 1977); F. S. L. Lyons, *The Fall of Parnell* (London: Routledge & Kegan Paul, 1960); Joep Leerssen, ed., *Parnell and his Times* (Cambridge: Cambridge University Press, 2020).

[11] David Fitzpatrick, *Politics and Irish Life, 1913–1921; Provincial Experiences of War and Revolution* (Cork: Cork University Press, 1998), 77.

smaller island of Ireland to the west. France's representatives to Dublin and London predicted, somewhat ominously, that the outbreak of war would precipitate violent conflict between loyalist populations and nationalist communities in Ireland. Through its consular emissaries, the Quai d'Orsay had sufficient information on the state of the country to justify its fears that certain factions within Ireland might create a diversionary 'Irish' conflict, the effect of which would be to weaken Great Britain in wartime, and which were seen as a direct consequence of the political strategies, public miscalculations, and internal rivalries that had blighted its administration of Ireland. Colonel de la Panouse, French military attaché to London, and Paul Cambon, Ambassador to London, sent regular dispatches to the French Minister for War and Minister for Foreign Affairs about the evolving Irish political situation. From their vantage-points in Dublin and London, they provided a meticulous recording of the internal upheavals that were to transform Ireland, forwarding weekly dispatches about its political climate.

Conventional narratives

In both Irish and British collective memories, the 1916 Easter Rising is regarded as a turning point, a watershed which irreversibly transformed the history of Ireland and led to the fall of the Irish Parliamentary Party.[12] The abortive one-week military insurrection, it is generally argued, paved the way for the 'magical transformation'[13] and 'political resurrection for Ireland'.[14] Ireland's Military Governor arguably 'played a pivotal role in the transformation [of the rebels] into a host of heroes'.[15] Following the executions of the rebels, the British

---

[12] F. S. L. Lyons, 'The Passing of the Irish Parliamentary Party (1916–1918)', in *The Irish Struggle, 1916–1926*, ed. Desmond Williams (London: Routledge & Kegan Paul, 1966), 95–196; Charles Townshend, *Easter 1916, The Irish Revolution* (London: Penguin Books, 2005), 300–323; Michael Wheatley, *Nationalism and the Irish Party: Provincial Ireland 1910–1916* (Oxford: Oxford University Press, 2005), 224–249; Conor Mulvagh, *The Irish Parliamentary Party at Westminster, 1900–1918* (Dublin: University College Dublin Press, 2016), 129–169. Lyons, Mulvagh, Townshend and Wheatley (among others) argue that Easter Week operated as a watershed event and that the fall of the Irish Party seemed almost inevitable after the 1916 insurrection.

[13] F. S. L. Lyons, *Ireland since the Famine* (Dublin: Fontana Press, 1973), 381.

[14] Charles Tansill, *America and the Fight for Irish Freedom, 1866–1922* (New York: The Devin-Adair Co., 1957), 196.

[15] Thomas Hennessey, *Dividing Ireland: World War I and Partition* (London: Routledge 1998), 237. Some historians have asserted that the remarkable change was not so much the consequence of the rebellion itself as of the subsequent executions of the leaders, thus acknowledging capital punishment as another factor, along with the uprising, in the radicalization of Irish nationalist populations. Historians disagree on the importance of the executions even though they assert that Easter Week 1916 transformed the course of Irish history.

Government made a series of political decisions that directly contributed to the radicalization of opinion in nationalist Ireland.[16] During summer 1916, it has been contended, the partition crisis brought about a radical change and gradually triggered a split within the Catholic Church and among Irish Nationalists.[17] The transformation of Irish politics from nationalism to republicanism between Easter Week 1916 and the December 1918 general elections testified to the surge of anti-government violence after the insurrection, and to the intensity of anti-government sentiments in nationalist Ireland, both with a climate of general mistrust and resentment provoked by the coercive measures of the British administration in the country. The immediate consequence of Easter Week 1916 was to spark off a political upheaval leading to the emergence of a united separatist party, Sinn Féin.[18] In 1917 alone, Sinn Féin won the four by-elections that were organized in the country. It defeated the Irish Parliamentary Party (also called the Irish Party) and imposed itself as the newly dominant driving force in nationalist Ireland. By the end of 1917, it had developed an effective and winning narrative of self-determination. Sinn Féin activists purported they would secure a seat for Ireland at the future Peace Conference. After Easter Week 1916, anti-British sentiments and the demand for full independence came to merge, rallying all sections of nationalist Ireland. Home Rule no longer matched the aspirations of younger nationalists, it is thus argued: a more radical political line had now emerged. In April 1918, the introduction of the Military Service Act for Ireland added to the infuriation of nationalist Ireland and

---

[16] Fearghal McGarry, *The Rising Ireland: Easter 1916* (Oxford: Oxford University Press, 2010), 277. Recently, a new generation of academics have challenged the conviction that Easter Week 1916 was the determining factor in triggering the Irish revolution. Fearghal McGarry has argued that the decisions made by the British in administrating Ireland in the eighteen months following the uprising contributed to radicalizing nationalist Ireland, thus nuancing the claim that the executions were the only tipping point. His research supports the conclusions of David Fitzpatrick who has insisted that 'the revolutionary impact of the Rising on Irish politics cannot simply be explained by latent hatred for Britain, or for that matter by admiration for the brave rebels and indignation at their long-drawn-out punishment'. David Fitzpatrick, *Politics and Irish Life*, 108.

[17] Jérôme aan de Wiel, *The Catholic Church in Ireland, 1914–1918: War and Politics* (Dublin: Irish Academic Press, 2003), 122.

[18] Michael Laffan, *The Resurrection of Ireland. The Sinn Féin Party, 1916–1923* (Cambridge: Cambridge University Press, 1999), 75. Drawing on extensive archival material, Michael Laffan has claimed that the period from April to December 1916 was one of transition. In his view, the most important development in the months following the uprising was the emergence of a united Sinn Féin, which gradually gained hold over the loyalties of nationalist Ireland. He attributes this shift to 'an emotional reaction against what was seen as the excessive scale of the arrests and executions after the rising'. The absence of a 'well-organized alternative' explains why, according to Alvin Jackson, 'there was no avalanche-like collapse of the [Irish Parliamentary] party until mid-1917'. Alvin Jackson, *Home Rule: An Irish History, 1800–2000* (London: Weidenfeld & Nicolson, 2003), 171.

eventually brought about the demise and extinction of the Irish Party.[19] Talk of the introduction of conscription had been nothing but a deplorable blunder.[20] By the time the Armistice was signed on 11 November 1918, Sinn Féin had become the sole plausible, hegemonic vehicle for the aspirations of nationalist Ireland. A few weeks later, the party gained 65 percent of the popular vote in the general elections. Another, more local, conflict was now looming for the British.

Several considerations compounded the decisive advantage achieved by Sinn Féin during the four by-elections of 1917, whose routing of the Irish Party cannot be explained by any one single factor. Domestic events in the country unquestionably shaped the reconfiguration of Irish politics, offering solid leverage to Irish separatists in their political designs. However, these domestic aspects should not be disconnected from the range of international wartime concerns, which also, with varying degrees of visibility, accounted for the transformation of republicanism into a nationwide demand.

In the light of these various narratives, it is staggering to realize that the First World War and the political evolution of Ireland have been charted by way of a set of parallel histories, which do not interconnect. While historians do agree that in the aftermath of the rebellion, a series of external events accounted for the political success of Sinn Féin, they have neglected or failed to explore fully the dynamics of geopolitical interactions between the First World War and the Irish Revolution.[21] And histories of the First World War that are written outside Ireland have tended to replicate nationalist Irish historiographies, foregrounding the Rising as a transformative moment without going beyond the conventional and cursory reference to 1916 when making a glancing reference to Ireland during the period.[22] Even more striking is the insufficient engagement with the most divisive wartime issue Ireland had experienced since the 1913 Home Rule crisis: conscription. By deliberately engaging with the issue of

---

[19] Adrian Gregory, '"You might as well recruit Germans": British public opinion and the decision to conscript the Irish in 1918', in *Ireland and the Great War: 'A War to Unite Us All?'*, ed. Adrian Gregory and Senia Pašeta (Manchester: Manchester University Press, 2002), 129. On the basis of a comprehensive study of the debates in the House of Commons prior to the passing of conscription for Ireland in April 1918, Adrian Gregory has concluded that 'the constitutional nationalists were sacrificed to appease the British public demanding a sacrifice'.

[20] Malcom Thomson, *David Lloyd George* (London: Hutchinson, 1948), 292.

[21] Keith Jeffery, *Ireland and the Great War* (Cambridge: Cambridge University Press, 2000), 2.

[22] Francis M. Carroll, *America and the Making of an Independent Ireland. A History* (New York: New York University Press, 2021), 1. In accordance with the well-entrenched conviction that the Easter Rising was the turning point for Ireland, Francis M. Carroll opens his exhaustively researched and impressive *magnum opus* in 1916, with the uprising in Dublin. He contends that the failed insurrection profoundly transformed Irish society.

conscription *solely* from April 1918 onwards,[23] historiography has overplayed the claim that Easter Week 1916 was the major determining factor in twentieth-century Irish history. Even the claim that the conscription crisis of April 1918 impacted Irish history more than the Easter Rising[24] strikes a note that is somewhat disconnected from the dynamics of the First World War, insomuch as the contention gives too much credit to a single moment of unrest, without charting the gradual shift of nationalist populations towards Sinn Féin. Throughout the war, the possible implementation of conscription had a fearful resonance throughout Ireland, generating a climate of mistrust and anxiety among civilian populations.[25] By engaging fully with the issue of conscription from August 1914, the present book endeavours to show that the dynamics of interaction between the Irish Revolution and the conscription scares have been downplayed, to the point of being almost entirely neglected in terms of its unfolding over time.

Arguably, though the primary purpose of this book is to revisit the transformation of Ireland, focusing on how fears of compulsory military service radicalized civilian populations and paved the way for the accession of Sinn Féin to a position of hegemony in nationalist Ireland, the analysis presented here will (inevitably, albeit indirectly) compel historians to (re)engage with the way Ireland supported the war effort. Recent research has been able to provide ample demonstration that the Great War was 'an all-Irish effort',[26] convincingly questioning the mantra according to which the Irish had adopted a 'mental neutrality'[27] during the conflict. If the latter contention, grounded in a sense of bitterness stemming from centuries of Anglo-Irish relations, has been subjected to much needed scrutiny, the first mentioned hypothesis can also come in for

---

[23] Adrian Gregory, 'You might as well recruit Germans', 113–132.
[24] Aan de Wiel, *The Catholic Church in Ireland*, 203–255. Aan de Wiel maintains that the 1918 conscription crisis was politically speaking more important than the Rising in the transformation of Ireland.
[25] Aan de Wiel, *The Catholic Church in Ireland*, 117; Timothy Bowman, William Butler and Michael Wheatley, *The Disparity of Sacrifice. Irish Recruitment to the British Armed Forces, 1914–1918* (Liverpool: Liverpool University Press, 2020), 58. Aan de Wiel has argued that 'from the summer of 1916 onwards, the threat of conscription would be like a sword of Damocles over Ireland', without demonstrating the importance of conscription during the four by-elections in 1917 and the extent to which conscription intervened in the radicalization of Irish nationalist public opinion (this not being the subject of his study). Bowman, Butler and Wheatley are, to this day, the first historians to discover what they call a series of 'conscription scares' in Ireland from August 1914 onwards. Through a detailed analysis, the three authors have shown that sporadic, but highly efficient, anti-conscription episodes resonated throughout Ireland before Easter Week 1916 and until the 1918 conscription crisis.
[26] Niamh Gallagher, *Ireland and the Great War. A Social and Political History* (London: Bloomsbury, 2019), 172.
[27] Charles Townshend, *Easter 1916, the Irish Rebellion*, 60.

criticism, for its tendency to generalize or exaggerate Irish support for the war effort. To argue that during the conflict 'at no point did most people lose support for the Allied cause and the international effort to defeat Germany'[28] is correct, in the sense that people's support was certainly consistent throughout the conflict (in spite of the uprising and British political blunders in its aftermath). Yet it does not mean that *all* sections of Irish society backed the war. France's representatives to Dublin and London repeatedly underlined the fact that rural populations were largely indifferent regarding the conflict. This would seem to suggest (if an attempt to reconcile these two viewpoints is to be attempted) that Irish society was indeed seriously divided. Beyond Catholic/Protestant, Nationalist/Unionist and rural/urban divides (and beyond the sterile obsession with the attempt to arrive at a quantified assessment of the attitudes within the country's various confessional groups) scholars have managed to shed light upon the mobilization of different sections of Irish society, arguing that the conflict did enjoy popular support and legitimacy.[29] Since the late 1990s, the memory of the Great War has acted as a vehicle for reconciliation between the Republic of Ireland and the United Kingdom.[30] The centenary of the First World War eventually brought an end to what has been qualified as a pervasive 'national amnesia'[31] surrounding Ireland's participation in the conflict. But this might, in turn, have triggered a potentially sweeping generalization, to the effect that *all* the Irish (with the exception of a marginal group of extremist or 'advanced' republicans) actually backed the war.

If all these narratives are to be woven into a broad historical picture, in order to come to terms with what really happened between 1914 and 1918, then the accounts of foreign diplomats tend to frustrate somewhat the quest for a clear and settled picture regarding attitudes within Ireland (and their shifts over time), to be found in the existing literature on the period. Opposition between support for Britain's engagement in the conflict and greater support for Sinn Féin in December 1918 might (after all) not be as clear-cut as it may seem, especially when a distinction between voluntary war effort and protest against enforced military service is drawn.[32] But this (paradoxically) would mean (and to such an

---

[28] Gallagher, *Ireland and the Great War* 159.
[29] Jeffery, *Ireland and the Great War*, 10; John Horne, 'Our war, our history', in *Our War: Ireland and the Great War*, ed. John Horne (Dublin: Royal Irish Academy, 2008), 1–34; Catriona Pennell, *A Kingdom United: Popular Responses to the Outbreak of the First World War in Britain and Ireland* (Oxford: Oxford University Press, 2012), 231.
[30] Horne, 'Our war, our history', 3.
[31] Francis Xavier Martin, '1916 – Myth, Fact and Mystery', *Studia Hibernica*, 7 (1967); 68.
[32] Gallagher, *Ireland and the Great War*, 151.

extent would tend to bear out the conclusions of France's representatives) that fears of enforced military service had the effect of radicalizing and alienating populations that were indifferent to the war (or who at least supported the war only because they would not have to fight it!).

Plea for a new historiography of the Irish Revolution

The present book examines the period from August 1914 to December 1918 in relation to the international situation and wartime concerns. It aims to re-address – and at times redress – the well-entrenched, but somewhat inaccurate, conclusion that Easter Week 1916 was the *most important* factor in the radicalization and reshaping of all allegiances in nationalist Ireland. In its place, the intention is to propose a more nuanced and gradualist account of how fears of conscription played into the anxieties and mistrust of civilian populations, from August 1914 onwards. Concerns about military service have been largely ignored by historians of Ireland. That the rise of Sinn Féin was compounded by fears of conscription and the ability of the party to shape a new rhetoric which was in line with international wartime expectations has not been given sufficient recognition in the historiography of the Irish Revolution.[33] This book therefore seeks to enlarge and diversify the scope of previous research, focusing on diplomacy and international relations and how they conditioned the growing popularity of Sinn Féin. While shedding light on the Irish Revolution in its relation to wartime diplomacy, the book also seeks to provide insight into some of the features that were at play in the dynamics of Anglo-American relations of the period, and how both powers, separately, had repercussions on the Irish Revolution.

I shall argue that the triumph of Sinn Féin in December 1918, following a series of victories during the 1917 and 1918 by-elections, cannot be dissociated from the larger stage of wartime politics, and that it cannot be seen solely as the spectacular after-effect of the executions of the 1916 leaders. In order to properly understand whether and how the failed military insurrection fortified Sinn Féin, a detailed analysis must be undertaken as to the popular mood within Ireland in the aftermath of the executions. Above all, historians must acknowledge that the immediate reaction to the executions might not have been sufficient to overthrow

---

[33] Laffan, *The Resurrection of Ireland*, 77–121.

the Irish Parliamentary Party. It is necessary to distinguish between popular consternation (in the immediate aftermath of the rebellion) and the gradual, longer-term transformation of Sinn Féin into a mighty political machine. These two questions tend to be analysed together, whereas they might be more effectively assessed in terms of their specific factors and their distinct timescales. Existing scholarship tends to suggest that these two episodes are linked, or that they are in effect indistinguishable. My intention here is to question this approach. Such a conventional narrative is grounded in the conviction that Sinn Féin support was fortified by an attritionary process of frustration and anger, and by declining allegiance to the country's constitutional nationalist party. Sinn Féin did indeed forge a new narrative, aimed at capturing popular support and routing the Home Rule party. But between April 1916 and April 1918, two major events appeared to have been largely underestimated; the threat of conscription and the US intervention in the First World War.[34]

The present book seeks to challenge traditional narratives according to which the 1916 Rising directly or indirectly led to the Irish Revolution. Easter Week 1916 retains its status as a turning point in twentieth-century Irish history, a watershed not only in the nationalist mythology, but also in the unionist and northern Irish collective memory. Similarly, it is still being portrayed as 'the turning point for Ireland, as well as for Britain'[35] in American collective memory. I argue here that the real turning point in Ireland's history came about when Sinn Féin captured the anti-conscription movement and exploited a rhetoric of self-determination for its own specific ends, thus forging a narrative which could proclaim its compatibility with Wilsonian ideals. I maintain that while the reorganization of Sinn Féin by the end of 1916 ensured the party enhanced visibility, there remained nevertheless an ongoing dispute over the loyalties of nationalist Ireland, an issue which cannot be ignored. In order to fully differentiate itself from the Irish Party, Sinn Féin portrayed itself as the only viable opposition to conscription in the country. From there, they could further undermine John Redmond's leadership through the refashioning of an ideological project for nationalist Ireland, in which Home Rule could be cast as the goal of a now obsolete narrative. The threat of conscription enabled Sinn Féin to revive its

---

[34] Carroll, *America and the Making of an Independent Ireland*, 13–35. In chapter 2, Carroll reveals how Wilson, through his Secretary of State, Robert Lansing, and the US Ambassador to London, Walter Hines Page, insisted that Lloyd George should settle the Irish question, doing so only five days after the US had entered the global conflict. In directly appealing to Congress, Irish-Americans had turned the Irish question from a purely British domestic concern into an American issue in wartime.

[35] Carroll, *America and the Making of an Independent Ireland*, ix.

attractiveness in the ongoing competition for the allegiances of Irish nationalist opinion. A renewed rhetoric was however needed in order to bring about the ideological eclipse of the Irish Parliamentary Party, insofar as John Redmond had clearly and consistently voiced the constitutional nationalist opposition to conscription, from January 1916 onwards, and throughout the whole course of the war. Once Sinn Féin had launched its rallying cry for self-determination, the party was in a position to offer nationalist Ireland a new direction, in total opposition to the goal which the Irish Parliamentary Party had striven to achieve in the period culminating in the summer of 1914.

My intention is to fuse international and diplomatic perspectives with the concerns of social and cultural history, in order to demonstrate how American and British foreign and domestic policies variously thwarted or fed into, whether directly or indirectly, the dynamic of the Irish Revolution. As was noted by France's representatives, the US intervention in the conflict had the effect of stifling the wave of seditious anti-British speeches prevalent in Ireland. Following the US entry into the war on the side of the British and French in April 1917,[36] Sinn Féin realized that they needed to tone down their (anti-British) rhetorical opposition to the Great War and the party successfully managed to appropriate the Wilsonian rhetoric. US intervention thus operated as a double-edged sword. Even though conscription acted as a trigger for Sinn Féin support, it is to be remembered that the Irish Parliamentary Party had been consistent in its objection to its implementation. The fight for the hearts and minds of nationalist Ireland that played out between Sinn Féin and the Irish Parliamentary Party from 1917 onwards was above all ideological. An effective and explicit anti-conscription movement needed to materialize, outside the framework of Home Rule. And it needed to operate outside the political frame of UK constitutional order. It required advocating total independence. Sinn Féin thus formulated its aspirations in terms of what it now seemed possible to obtain, through the changed geopolitical perspective of which the US appeared the harbinger. Wilson's principles, both through their substance and their (American) origin, had deep and immediate resonance in Ireland, and came at a time when the Irish Parliamentary Party remained caught up in its efforts to work out the terms of a Home Rule compromise agreement with the Ulster Unionists and the British Government. Sinn Féin could feed on this less compromising and more inspiring narrative of self-determination. Colonel de la Panouse, France's military attaché

---

[36] Ross Kennedy, *The Will to Believe: Woodrow Wilson, World War I, and America's Strategy for Peace and Security* (Kent (Ohio): Kent University State Press, 2009).

to London, quickly grasped the fact that the party was resorting to Wilsonian rhetoric to appeal to its audience. As the US pressed the British to resolve the Irish question, and it became clear that US foreign policy was beginning to have an impact on British domestic affairs through the interventions of an Irish-American diaspora, the introduction of conscription, a policy which the British authorities in Ireland had consistently objected to, was approved in April 1918.

Diplomatic sources and French narratives

It has been customary for the history of the Irish Revolution (1913–1923) to be written by way of the archival material that is available primarily in Great Britain and in Ireland (most historians in Ireland being monolingual). Weekly and monthly reports from Inspectors of the Royal Irish Constabulary (RIC), along with other series of documents from the Colonial Office at The National Archives in London, enable researchers to achieve a better comprehension of the dynamic of the revolution and the changing political situation as it was playing out, county by county.[37] Going through these detailed accounts, a broader picture of Anglo-Irish relations appears. Cabinet Papers, Colonial Office Papers, and War Office Papers (all conserved in London) are crucial sources in assessing the state of public opinion at the outbreak of the First World War. They are also vital for the subsequent monitoring of the increasing popularity of Sinn Féin in the period leading up to the December 1918 general elections. In Dublin, the files recording the testimonies of former republican activists which are part of the Military Archives offer a comprehensive account of how the War of Independence (1919–1921) was conducted against the British. The same files also enable

---

[37] Joost Augusteijn, *Mayo. The Irish Revolution, 1912–1923* (Dublin: Four Courts Press, 2022); John Burke, *Roscommon. The Irish Revolution, 1912–1923* (Dublin: Four Courts Press, 2022); Marie Coleman, *County Longford and the Irish Revolution* (Dublin: Irish Academic Press, 2003); Seamus Cullen, *Kildare. The Irish Revolution, 1912–1923* (Dublin: Four Courts Press, 2021); Terence Dooley, *Monaghan. The Irish Revolution, 1912–1923* (Dublin: Four Courts Press, 2017); Michael Farry, *Sligo. The Irish Revolution, 1912–1923* (Dublin: Four Courts Press, 2012); Brian Feeney, *Antrim. The Irish Revolution, 1912–1923* (Dublin: Four Courts Press, 2021); Adrian Grant, *Derry. The Irish Revolution, 1912–1923* (Dublin: Four Courts Press, 2018); Donald Hall and Martin Maguire. *County Louth and the Irish Revolution, 1912–1923* (Dublin: Irish Academic Press, 2019); Donald Hall, *Louth. The Irish Revolution, 1912–1923* (Dublin: Four Courts Press, 2019); Patrick McCarthy, *Waterford. The Irish Revolution, 1912–1923* (Dublin: Four Courts Press, 2015); Fergal McCluskey, *Tyrone. The Irish Revolution, 1912–1923* (Dublin: Four Courts Press, 2014); Patrick McGarty, *Leitrim. The Irish Revolution, 1912–1923* (Dublin: Four Courts Press, 2020); John O'Callaghan, *Limerick. The Irish Revolution, 1912–1923* (Dublin: Four Courts Press, 2018); Daniel Purcell, *Fermanagh. The Irish Revolution, 1912–1923* (Dublin: Four Courts Press, 2022); Pauric Travers, *Donegal. The Irish Revolution, 1912–1923* (Dublin: Four Courts Press, 2022).

historians to apprehend how the Irish Volunteers (and later on, Irish Republican Army) and the civilian populations lived through and reacted to the conflict. Also in the Military Archives of Ireland, the Michael Collins Papers (1918–1922) and the Truce Liaison and Evacuation Papers (1921–1922) offer historians an opportunity to explore further certain aspects of the Anglo-Irish War, building on the traditional historiographies that have drawn on the archive material in London. Between 1947 and 1957, the Republic of Ireland embarked on the collection of primary source material and the recording of oral testimonies of former activists who had participated in the Irish War of Independence, creating the Bureau of Military History (1913–1921) which comprises a collection of 1,733 witness statements, contemporary documents, photographs of the period and voice recordings. With the purpose of assembling and coordinating material that would form the basis for the historical record of the movement of independence, the Military Archives compiled one of the most significant databases for the study of the Irish Revolution. The National and Military Archives tend to orientate research almost exclusively towards material preserved in Dublin and London, neglecting County Council Archives or the archives of academic institutions, such as University College Dublin.

While relying on the above-mentioned documents, a supplementary range of archival material, rarely solicited by historians of the Irish Revolution, has also been consulted, namely the diplomatic archives of the French Ministry for Foreign Affairs in Paris. The conception of this monograph in fact emerged from the consultation of a series of reports written by France's representatives to Dublin, London and Washington, the effect of which was to reshape my understanding of Easter Week 1916 and its aftermath. My original willingness to carry out research in French archives, and to compare them with the abundant historiography of the Irish Revolution written by way of British and Irish sources, stemmed from the need to portray the Irish Revolution from an outsider's point of view, at a certain distance therefore from the recurrent and traditional Irish or British perspectives. But the idea for triangulating the narrative in this way and for engaging with the material of the Quai d'Orsay was also compounded by the position of the French during the conflict. In the general light of French anxieties about a possible defeat in the Great War, especially between 1916 (battles of the Somme and Verdun) and 1918, France's concern was to ensure that her ally, Great Britain, would not be weakened by domestic unrest in Ireland.[38]

---

[38] Aan de Wiel, *The Catholic Church in Ireland*, 79.

Throughout the conflict, Paris furthermore desperately needed to enlist American public opinion, which had not been secured at the outbreak of the war partly because of the influential Irish-American diaspora. From the moment the first shots rang out in August 1914, French military strategy was aimed at halting the march of the Germans. And this involved keeping an anxious and interested eye on affairs in Ireland. Without interfering in Britain's domestic affairs, the French repeatedly offered to help in the efforts to recruit Irishmen.[39] France's representatives to Dublin and London observed the evolution of the political situation in Ireland, knowing only too well that an armed movement would compel London to levy troops for Ireland, who would consequently not be available for the Western Front.

What do French diplomatic archives reveal about the Irish Revolution? What is there to be seen through these accounts that might not be in evidence from an exploration of the sources in London, Dublin or Washington? Material drawn from French diplomatic and military archives represents an unquestionably valuable contribution to our understanding of the period and offers a relatively neutral account of the rapid disintegration of British governance in Ireland. Throughout the conflict, Paul Cambon, Ambassador for France to London; Colonel de la Panouse, France's military attaché to London, Alfred Blanche, Consul-General for France to Dublin, and his predecessor Jean des Longchamps, repeatedly argued that the introduction of conscription in Ireland would be a political blunder. Most important, in this respect, is the fact that these observers were unanimous in their contention that the rise of Sinn Féin in 1917 was correlated to fears of being drafted into the British Army. The conclusions reached by the French consular commentators are supported by the abundant additional evidence (the private papers of activists, newspaper cuttings, conversation with British officials, secret reports from police inspectors). These consular onlookers tended to discount any suggestion that the 1916 Rising was a watershed event, and their dispatches lent little support to the contention that Easter Week 1916 transformed the course of Irish history. What radicalized nationalist populations and redirected the course of Irish history was the immediate, tangible and material fear of being forced to fight, the fear of being railed into the inter-imperial Great War through conscription. By the end of 1917, references to self-determination had come to prominence in Sinn Féin rhetoric, representing an increasingly vital component of the programme put

---

[39] Ibid., 128–152.

forward during the four 1917 by-elections. US entry into the war had put a damper on anti-British seditious propaganda in Ireland, but it also enabled Sinn Féin to renew the message broadcast in electoral campaign speeches. Indeed, American entry into the war enabled the party to lay claim to what was now a geopolitical rhetoric of self-determination. It could hold out to its electorate the promise of a seat at the future Peace Conference in Paris. Anti-conscription rhetoric and the demand for self-determination thus merged, the conjunction contributing directly to the terminal eclipse of the Irish Parliamentary Party and to the transformation of Ireland.

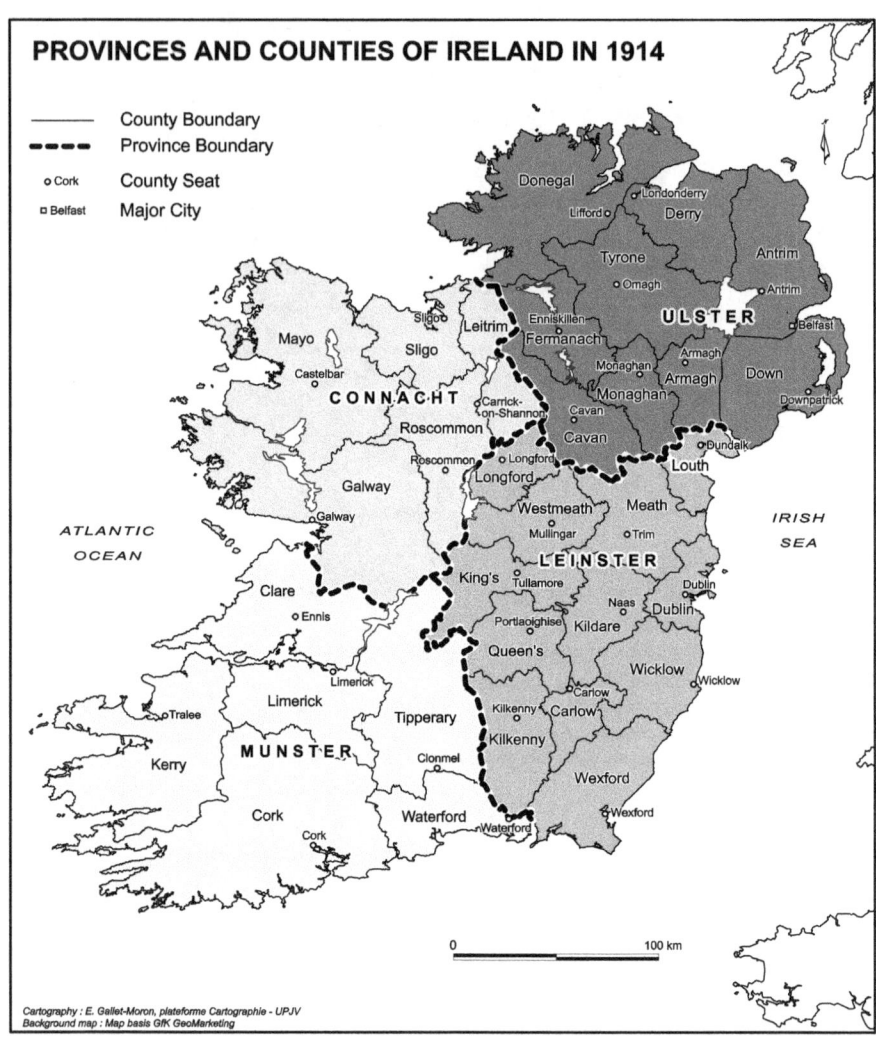

Map 1.1 Ireland at the outbreak of the First World War. Courtesy of Emilie Gallet-Moron.

1

Political Crisis, British Intentions and Wartime Uncertainties (January 1913–March 1916)

At the beginning of the twentieth century, constitutional nationalism had progressively imposed itself as a viable political alternative to a more radical and separatist republicanism. Instead of relying on armed insurrection and direct confrontation, members of the Irish Parliamentary Party (IPP) had re-imagined a political strategy that consisted in securing Ireland's claims through legislative channels. With an overall population of 4,374,500,[1] the island appeared to be a single territory on which two peoples coexisted.[2] More than a mere geographical and economic divide between the industrialized north and the agricultural south, the 'polarisation between the protestant north and catholic south'[3] both structured and separated the expectations of nationalist and unionist populations. Ulster remained predominantly loyal to the British Crown whereas, in the rest of the country, the majority hoped for the establishment of a parliament in Dublin as advocated by the Home Rule project. Devolution and a certain degree of autonomy spearheaded the manifesto of Irish MPs who, as representatives of Ireland, participated in the elaboration of British domestic policy at Westminster where they sat in the same chamber as the unionist MPs from Ulster.

Home Rule and Ulster Unionism: the impossible settlement

During the 1910 general elections, the Liberals and the Conservatives (with strong unionist sympathies) secured 279 seats each.[4] Out of political necessity,

---

[1] *Statistics of Military Effort of the British Empire during the Great War* (London: HMSO, 1922), 363.
[2] F. S. L. Lyons, *Ireland since the Famine* (Dublin: Fontana Press, 1973), 224.
[3] L. P. Curtis, 'Ireland in 1914', in *A New History of Ireland, VI, Ireland Under the Union, II, 1870–1921*, ed. W. E. Vaughan (Oxford: Oxford University Press, 1996), 175.
[4] Lyons, *Ireland since the Famine*, 269.

the leader of the Liberal Party, Herbert Asquith, offered an alliance to the eighty-four Irish MPs.[5] In order to attain a resounding defeat of the Conservative Party candidate, Arthur Balfour (the Liberal candidate), agreed to support the devolution project in exchange for the support of these eighty-four Irish MPs. The Home Rule project stipulated that Ireland would remain a fully-fledged part of the United Kingdom but would benefit from a certain autonomy in domestic affairs. Irish Nationalists therefore sided with the Liberal Party in the hope of achieving their century-long project.[6] Asquith's strategy guaranteed him a convincing victory.

Nevertheless, in order to be able to keep his word, the newly-elected Prime Minister needed to counter the powers of the House of Lords. British constitutional precedent granted the Upper House an unrestricted power of veto on any legislation approved by the Lower House. Even though the House of Commons agreed on the provisions for the proposed devolution of powers to a subordinate Irish legislature, the House of Lords retained its absolute power to veto any Home Rule Bill. This is precisely what had occurred in 1893, when a Home Rule Bill had been presented before the House of Commons and approved, only to be subsequently vetoed by the Upper House which insisted on maintaining Ireland in the United Kingdom. Constitutional Nationalists deplored the systematic opposition of the Lords, while Ulster Unionists relied heavily on the Chamber to protect their existing constitutional position. From a purely legislative point of view, Asquith needed first to silence the House of Lords. He therefore drew up a piece of legislation that would prevent the Lords from vetoing any bill beyond three sessions of parliament.

A few months after his election, the Prime Minister introduced the Parliament Act. The proposed bill stipulated that 'any measure that had passed in three successive years through the House of Commons would thus automatically become law'.[7] When the House of Commons voted the law in 1911, this strategic manoeuvre stirred up vehement protest in Ulster.[8] Overnight, the loyalist community found itself deprived of its traditional political support in the Lords and Ulster had no choice but to look on, powerless, as the British Government rewarded constitutional Nationalists with a future status of devolution for the

---

[5] David Fitzpatrick, *Politics and Irish Life, 1913-1921; Provincial Experiences of War and Revolution* (Cork: Cork University Press, 1998), 72.
[6] Alvin Jackson, *Home Rule: An Irish History, 1800-2000* (London: Weidenfeld & Nicolson, 2003), 107.
[7] Lyons, *Ireland since the Famine*, 277.
[8] Patricia Jalland and John Stubbs, 'The Irish Question after the Outbreak of War in 1914: Some Unfinished Party Business', *The English Historical Review* 96, no. 381 (1981): 805.

island. Appalled by what they regarded as open treason, Ulster Unionists observed the evolution of the situation with deepening anxiety. In April 1912, the British Government finally introduced the Home Rule Bill before Parliament for the third time. When the House of Commons agreed to offer a degree of autonomy to Ireland, the House of Lords was no longer in a position to counter the Government's intention. As the Ambassador for France to London, Paul Cambon, observed, 'Home Rule was the outcome of a parliamentary combination that guaranteed the survival of the Asquith Cabinet'.[9]

By April 1912, the deal secured between British Liberals and Irish Nationalists was progressively transforming the course of Ireland's history. This third Home Rule Bill offered a constitutionalized response to the century-long expectations of nationalist Ireland.[10] The bill stunned the unionist community and triggered the armed revolt of Ulster. Before the official adoption of the Home Rule project, Ulster Unionists mobilized opposition to what they regarded as treason by the Liberals. In September 1912, 400,000 Unionists signed the Ulster's Solemn League and Covenant, vowing in the eventuality of the establishment of an autonomous parliament in Dublin to which the north would have to pledge allegiance, to rise against the British Government, and pledging to resist by all necessary means.[11] Under the leadership of Sir Edward Carson, loyalist populations pledged their unconditional support to the Crown but openly defied the British Government. Although nationalism had been slowly shifting from a revolutionary strategy to a constitutional agenda, Ulster Unionists nonetheless considered themselves to have little option but to resort to a posture of violent defiance in order to secure their place in the United Kingdom. However, the British Parliament eventually adopted the Home Rule project in January 1913.

All over the province of Ulster, the vote at Westminster crystallized a sense of outrage and led to the immediate foundation of the anti-Home Rule Ulster Volunteer Force (UVF), a paramilitary organization whose avowed aim was to resist any introduction of Home Rule. 'Under no circumstances does Protestant Ulster want to depend on a government in Dublin',[12] explained Colonel de la Panouse to the French Minister for War. In his capacity as France's military

---

[9] Archives Diplomatiques du Ministère des Affaires Étrangères, La Courneuve (hereafter AD), Political and Commercial Correspondence, Great War, 1914–1918, Ireland, 1CPCOM/545, telegram from Paul Cambon to the Minister for Foreign Affairs, 3 May 1916.
[10] Jackson, *Home Rule: An Irish History*, 110.
[11] Lyons, *Ireland since the Famine*, 305.
[12] Service Historique de la Défense, Vincennes (hereafter SHD), Third Republic (1870–1940), Army Staff, 7N700, telegram from Colonel de la Panouse to the Minister for War, 8 January 1914.

attaché in London, he reported that Ulster's militarized response to the passing of the bill was reviving armed violence on the island and that this could potentially cripple the British Cabinet. Colonel de la Panouse did not in the least sympathise with Ulster Unionists, and was not surprised to hear that the south of the country had denounced the undemocratic and rebellious rhetoric of Ulster, before responding through the creation of its pro-Home Rule paramilitary group, the Irish Volunteers, in November 1913. By then, the UVF already numbered 76,757 officers and men.[13]

Had it not been for the vigour of this militarized reaction in Ulster, Irish constitutional nationalism could be deemed to have secured an historical victory. From the alliance with the Liberals in 1910 to the Parliament Act in 1911 and the subsequent passing of Home Rule in 1913, John Redmond could rightly claim to have offered nationalist Ireland a lasting victory and could hope to have his name enshrined in the genealogy of politicians whose leadership had advanced the cause for autonomy. Nevertheless, protest in Ulster, at once resolute and widespread, somewhat undermined this constitutional achievement. All over the island, the Home Rule crisis effected a shift from constitutional to paramilitary or revolutionary strategies. By 1913, the divide between the north and the south had widened. On 8 January 1914, Colonel de la Panouse confessed that the Home Rule crisis could, 'from a military point of view, lead to disastrous consequences, was the army summoned to repress agitation in the north of Ireland'.[14] France's military attaché anticipated that the British Cabinet would be compelled to take action in order to restore law and order and foresaw that the British Army in Ireland would resent having to march against northern unionist populations if such an order was given to them. Little did he know how right he was. Only two months later, what was to be known as the Curragh incident proved him right.

On 14 March 1914, the British War Office officially demanded that all measures be taken with the object of giving adequate protection to depots, arms and ammunition stores in Ulster. A telegraph was sent to Sir Arthur Paget to this

---

[13] The National Archives (hereafter TNA), Colonial Office (hereafter CO), CO 903/17, Chief Secretary's Office, Judicial Division, Intelligence Notes, 1913, p. 35. Following the passing of the 1912 Home Rule Bill, women from the Ulster Women's Unionist Council (UWUC) organized first aid, established medical training schemes and secured medical equipment in anticipation of a civil war in Ireland. On that point see Diane Urquhart, 'Unionism, Orangeism and War,' in *Irish Women and the Vote: Becoming Citizens*, ed. Louise Ryan and Margaret Ward (London: Routledge, 2019), 139–141.

[14] SHD, Third Republic (1870–1940), Army Staff, 7N700, telegram from Colonel de la Panouse to the Minister for War, 8 January 1914.

effect. London feared that the UVF would seek to capture arms and ammunition in military barracks and ordered the protection of the depots. As *The Irish Times* would report later on, this was a purely precautionary decision.[15] However, Paget feared that 'these moves would provoke bloodshed, and that officers with Ulster family connections would be placed in a uniquely impossible situation'.[16] In his capacity as Commander-in-Chief of the Irish Command, he inquired of General Gough, Commander-in-Chief of the 3rd Cavalry Brigade, how British troops would react if they were ordered to march in Ulster. Loyalist soldiers and officers categorically rejected the eventuality of taking up arms against loyalist populations in the north. Confrontation between loyalist populations and the British Government further intensified when some officers and men of the British Army stationed at the Curragh maintained they would refuse to march against the rebellious north. As staunch followers of British rule in Ireland, they explicitly defied the Government. General Gough officially resigned and his decision was repeated by an important number of British officers stationed in the south of the country, at the Curragh (County Kildare).[17]

In the immediate aftermath, the British Government ordered both the former Commander-in-Chief and all outgoing officers to hand over full command. In order to appease the discontent among the troops, Asquith categorically declared that British troops in Ireland would never be required to engage physically with the Ulster Volunteers.[18] In fact, the British Government 'had no intention of mounting any coercive assault on Ulster'.[19] On 23 March 1914, the Prime Minister publicly intervened in person, declaring categorically to *The Times* that no unionist leaders would be arrested.[20] Paget had made approaches to the British Government, insisting that in the eventuality of military action being taken against the north, men and officers ought to be allowed to 'be absent from duty during the period of operations',[21] and that an even larger number of resignations from the military staff would ensue if this was not the case. It would appear that Colonel de la Panouse had foreseen the crisis that would result if the army was ordered to march against the north; he further envisaged that, should military

---

[15] *The Irish Times*, 23 March 1914.
[16] Jackson, *Home Rule: An Irish History*, 129.
[17] Ian Beckett, ed., *The Army and the Curragh Incident, 1914* (London: Bodley Head for the Army Records Society, 1986), 79.
[18] George Paget, *A History of the British Cavalry, 1816–1919, vol. 7, The Curragh Incident and the Western Front, 1914–18* (London: Leon Cooper, 1996), 9.
[19] Jackson, *Home Rule: An Irish History*, 130.
[20] *The Times*, 23 March 1914.
[21] Beckett, *The Army and the Curragh Incident*, 81.

manoeuvres take place, the figure of 110,000 Ulster Volunteers 'would considerably increase',[22] as civilian populations were bound to enrol in the paramilitary battalions in order to support the UVF.

British public opinion split over the attitude adopted by British troops. Unionist daily newspapers openly approved of the British officers' resignations, condemning the position of the Asquith Government:

> We accuse the Government of handling over their power to the Army. We accuse them of trying to hoodwink honest officers, with lawyers' pettifoggery, and we accuse them of failing on that attempt. We accuse them of proceeding with the Home Rule Bill when they know as a matter of fact that they have not the power to put it in force. They have destroyed the Second Chamber and put the army in its place. [...] Ulster refused to be coerced, the army refuses to be coerced. What power remains to the Government to carry through the Home Rule Bill?[23]

The *Morning Post* castigated the obsessive attempts of the Government to placate Irish MPs at the expense of northern Unionists by continuing to envisage the implementation of the Home Rule Bill. General Gough soon came to be compared to the 'Whigs' in America who had refused to march against the colonists.[24] On the other side of the political spectrum, the country's most popular daily newspaper underlined that a very serious responsibility rested upon the Curragh officers, even though no order had technically been disobeyed since none had yet been given. Quoting Sir Edward Carson, *The Times* concluded that the Curragh incident was but the consequence of 'driving loyal and peaceful subjects to extremities'.[25] However, voices in the left-wing and liberal press raised their concern: 'Will British officers tell the Parliament the laws they need not to vote? From the answer to this question will depend the future of English liberties!'[26] The *Daily News* called the rebellious officers 'crofters', who 'either had to obey or go to prison'. Appalled by what they regarded as 'a military dictation', they appealed to the opposition in the House of Commons to retreat from 'the yawning precipice of social chaos to which step by step reactionary and seditious influences ha[d] led the Army'.[27] Another daily newspaper spoke of 'an

---

[22] SHD, Third Republic (1870–1940), Army Staff, 7N700, telegram from Colonel de la Panouse to the Minister for War, 23 March 1914.
[23] *Morning Post*, 26 March 1914.
[24] *The Times*, 23 March 1914.
[25] *The Times*, 27 March 1914.
[26] *Daily Chronicle*, 25 March 1914.
[27] *Daily News*, 27 March 1914.

unprecedented political situation in British politics'²⁸ and demanded that firm action be taken against the dissident officers. Meanwhile, wiring from Washington, the correspondent of *The Irish Times* reported that US public opinion believed in Home Rule and regarded the whole situation as the result of 'bad management' and 'short-sighted procrastination' by Asquith.²⁹

Such debates surrounding the legitimacy of British officers in Ireland took precedence over what was in fact the real crux of the issue: the cultural and political implications of the Curragh incident. On the territory of the island, two nations/civilizations coexisted, side by side, with their conflicting cultures, political expectations, and distinct collective memories.³⁰ The Curragh incident was, before all else, a cultural and political crisis, but de la Panouse maintained it was undeniably a military blunder attributable to Paget and to the British Government. France's military attaché to London particularly resented the Curragh incident and his concerns were largely shared in Paris. He scathingly argued that 'the Government had not taken the UVF seriously; they were laughed at, but nothing was done to prevent this insurrectional movement from expanding'.³¹ Little did he know that it was indeed 'Asquith's delaying tactics'³² that were to blame. Asquith failed to treat the Unionists with sufficient seriousness, as he remained convinced that they 'were bluffing'³³ and would never engage in any action capable of compromising a parliamentary decision. Such an interpretation does indeed appear justified when we examine the Curragh incident. France's military attaché asserted that the War Office had made a dramatic mistake in inquiring about the possible reaction of the army. They indirectly gave the impression that British troops in Ireland would soon be compelled to shoot some of their own and that the military had a choice: that of refusing to march against Ulster. That the argument consisting in allowing officers and men to 'disappear'³⁴ was a mere pretext to legitimise a counter-revolution fomented by the army in Ireland came as no surprise to the French attaché. London's handling of the incident conditioned the escalation of a violent rhetoric among Ulster Unionists. It thus gave public notice to Irish (and also British) public opinion that the army in Ireland would go against any democratic

---

28 *The Nation*, 28 March 1914.
29 *The Irish Times*, 23 March 1914.
30 Lyons, *Ireland since the Famine*, 224–248.
31 SHD, Third Republic (1870–1940), Army Staff, 7N700, telegram from Colonel de la Panouse to the Minister for War, 23 March 1914.
32 Jackson, *Home Rule: An Irish History*, 140.
33 Ibid.
34 Beckett, *The Army and the Curragh Incident*, 81.

process that might undermine the interests of loyalist communities. 'For an impartial spectator, it seems that the demands of Ulster are unacceptable. Ulster has always been the master of Ireland. They cannot resign themselves to become a minority in the future Parliament in Dublin. In short, they fight not to be governed by those they have dominated historically',[35] wrote de la Panouse.

In pursuit of a political advantage, the Liberals were ready to sacrifice the loyalist minority of Ulster. De la Panouse pointed to the legislative channel through which Asquith intended to solve the Irish question, while emphasizing that Ulster had been sacrificed and side-lined in the negotiations. More problematically, the very resistance of Ulster to Home Rule had been largely underestimated by the Asquith Cabinet. Colonel de la Panouse blamed the British Government for allowing the army in Ireland openly to threaten and challenge both constitutional nationalism and the authority of the British Government. He blamed Paget for being at the origin of the crisis and was somehow puzzled to hear that the Commander-in-Chief of the Irish Command had asked for the advice of British officers: 'if they had been given orders instead of being asked for their advice, no incident would have happened',[36] he concluded with some degree of confidence. The Curragh incident did not only highlight the cultural and political links between army officers and Ulster Unionists, it also brought to light the fact that Paget had exceeded his prerogatives and publicly compromised the Government. 'What was the point of asking for their advice', wondered de la Panouse, 'if not to create more agitation in Ireland?'[37] Jean des Longchamps, France's Consul-General in Ireland, expressed concern at the overt weakness of the British Government during the Curragh incident; according to him, this issue had created a vacuum.[38]

A series of political measures adopted between 1910 and 1914 further accentuated the polarization between Nationalists and Ulster Unionists, as the British authorities faced a serious political crisis. As long as Ulster Unionists benefited from legislative protection and could rely on the sympathy of the Conservatives, they abided by the rules. However, the rise of constitutional nationalism significantly undermined their privileges and forced unionist

---

[35] SHD, Third Republic (1870–1940), Army Staff, 7N700, telegram from Colonel de la Panouse to the Minister for War, 23 March 1914.
[36] SHD, Third Republic (1870–1940), Army Staff, 7N700, telegram from Colonel de la Panouse to the Minister for War, 29 March 1914.
[37] Ibid.
[38] AD, Political and Commercial Correspondence, Great War, 1914–1918, Ireland, 1CPCOM/545, telegram from Jean des Longchamps to the Minister for Foreign Affairs, 6 May 1916.

leaders to radicalize their action. On 25 April 1914, with the assistance of senior British military figures to boot, the UVF managed to smuggle 35,000 rifles from Germany into Ireland.[39] Ulster Unionists appeared determined to 'resist Home Rule, if needed, by a civil war'.[40] Paul Cambon, Ambassador for France to London, asserted that Germany 'tried to provoke a civil war over Home Rule'[41] and to interfere in British domestic affairs. On 27 April, when asked by a member of Parliament whether large quantities of rifles and ammunition had been surreptitiously landed in the north of Ireland and whether it was true that cordons of armed persons had prevented free entrance to the harbour, Asquith answered that, 'in view of this grave and unprecedented outrage, the House [could] be assured that His Majesty's Government [would] take, without delay, appropriate steps to vindicate the authority of the law'.[42] However, the Prime Minister added that His Majesty's Government would vow to 'protect officers and servants of the King and His Majesty's subjects in the exercise of their duties and in the enjoyment of their legal rights'.[43] Such a formulation could only raise questions in the House, and Asquith reasserted the commitment of the Government not to punish loyal members of the army who objected to coercing their fellow countrymen. What lay behind the term 'legal rights' appeared to be more the desire to turn a blind eye to the present situation, something France's military attaché noted at that time. In spite of the assurance that the Government would vindicate the authority of the law, 'no movement of troops has been ordered yet',[44] de la Panouse reported. Unable to take further action against the UVF, the British Government nonetheless took action against the Irish Volunteers. A few weeks later, in July 1914, the British authorities intercepted 2,500 rifles and 176,000 rounds of ammunition from Hamburg (Germany) at Howth (Dublin), destined for the Irish Volunteers.[45] After tense verbal exchanges with the Volunteers, soldiers of the King's Own Scottish Borderers opened fire on the unarmed crowd, killing three people and injuring thirty. What would

---

[39] Henry Harris, *The Irish Regiments in the First World War* (Cork: Mercier Press, 1968), 8–9.
[40] AD, Political and Commercial Correspondence, Great War, 1914–1918, Ireland, 1CPCOM/545, telegram from Jean des Longchamps to the Minister for Foreign Affairs, 6 May 1916.
[41] AD, Political and Commercial Correspondence, Great War, 1914–1918, Ireland, 1CPCOM545, telegram from Paul Cambon to the Minister for Foreign Affairs, 3 May 1916.
[42] Hansard, House of Commons Debates, series 5, vol. 61, cc1347, Asquith to House of Commons, 27 April 1914.
[43] Ibid.
[44] SHD, Third Republic (1870–1940), Army Staff, 7N700, telegram from Colonel de la Panouse to the Minister for War, 30 April 1914.
[45] TNA, CO 904/29/2, Dublin Castle Records, Importation and supply of arms to the National Volunteers; 1914–1917, report from the RIC regarding the landing at Larne, 24 April 1914, pp. 92–115.

come to be known in Irish collective memory as the shooting of Bachelor's Walk highlighted 'a sharp difference in the treatment meted out to hostile nationalists in Dublin'.[46] Had the British Army in Ireland momentarily and officiously taken control of Irish domestic affairs? Or was the reaction of the Government a sign that they could only restore order in the south, where they could counter the Irish Volunteers, but that nothing could be done against the rebellious north? Diplomatic obligations required that de la Panouse refrain from too overt a criticism of the decisions of the Asquith Cabinet. However, when it came to military issues, the military attaché maintained that the laissez-faire policy of Asquith was only worsening the situation, an argument that would later reappear in his correspondence during the conflict.

As early as June 1914, the House of Lords had proposed an amendment to the Home Rule Bill that would permanently exclude the nine Ulster counties.[47] Asquith had originally introduced an Amending Bill to the House of Lords, on 23 May 1914, devised on the basis of an optional six-year exclusion for the province. At that time, Carson and the other Unionist MPs had comprehensively rejected it, even if Carson's will to compromise was in evidence when he eventually accepted the permanent exclusion of six counties only. Between 21 and 24 July 1914, an inter-party conference took place at Buckingham Palace to determine which counties in Ulster would be excluded from the Home Rule Bill. However the Buckingham Palace Conference failed, as temporary exclusion was abandoned.[48] Partition would thus be on the basis of a permanent exclusion, something to which John Redmond could not consent. The British had accepted the Home Rule Bill without taking into account the cultural and political expectations of Ulster Unionists. They now hoped to appease the embittered tension between Redmond's followers and those of Carson. This indirectly suggested that the third Home Rule Bill, which had envisaged devolution for the whole of Ireland, was now irrelevant, as Ulster counties could opt out. What appeared salutary to Carson entirely discredited Redmond. At that time, de la Panouse expressed his dismay and incomprehension. The inter-party conference reinforced this impression that even though the Home Rule Bill had been voted, Ulster could always hope to opt out. Partition appeared to be a solution envisaged both by the British Cabinet and Ulster Unionists.

---

[46] Jackson, *Home Rule: An Irish History*, 136.
[47] Joseph Lee, *Ireland 1912–1985: Politics and Society* (Cambridge: Cambridge University Press, 1989), 7.
[48] Jackson, *Home Rule; An Irish History*, 140.

By August 1914, the question of Home Rule had 'monopolised the mind of the nation',[49] as public Irish opinion scrutinized every single declaration by British officials. Both the Irish Volunteers and the Ulster Volunteer Force seemed prepared for a potential armed conflict in Ireland and, as one Unionist volunteer recalled, 'little did [they] think [they] were drilling to fight not [their] countrymen, but the Germans'.[50]

War breaks out: Asquith's strategy, recruitment, and the leap into the unknown

When Britain declared war on Germany on 4 August 1914, the decision completely redefined Irish political rhetoric, momentarily curtailing the political enmities between John Redmond and Edward Carson. When the First World War broke out, Carson controlled 84,865 Ulster Volunteers,[51] but the 171,890 Irish Volunteers[52] operated independently of Redmond. In order to take full advantage of the Irish domestic situation, Asquith adopted an approach that was emollient and, perhaps inevitably, duplicitous, consisting in reassuring both the Nationalists and the Ulster Unionists as to the outcome of the Home Rule Bill.

Shortly after the outbreak of the war, a number of nationalist newspapers reported (wrongly) that the British Government planned to revive the 1793 Militia Act. It was rumoured that any man belonging to the Irish Volunteers would be more likely to be conscripted.[53] Such lies originated from a fallacious article published in *The Independent* on 13 October 1914.[54] The *Sligo Champion* reported that they 'had just heard that the Militia Ballot Act [was] to be put into force at once (…) and to apply to Great Britain and Ireland'.[55] Titled 'An "Independent" Bogey Officially Exposed', the article humiliated *The Independent* and set forth Redmond's immediate reaction to what was regarded as overt conspiracy. Underlining that 'seldom in the history of the British Empire was there such unanimity of sentiment at the opening of a Parliamentary Session', the

---

[49] León Ó Broin, *Revolutionary Underground: The Story of the Irish Republican Brotherhood, 1858–1924* (London: Gill & Macmillan, 1976), 151.
[50] Imperial War Museum, 79/35/1, War diary of David Starrett (1914–1918), p. 1.
[51] TNA, CO 903/18, Chief Secretary's Office, Judicial Division, Intelligence Notes, 1914, p. 39.
[52] TNA, CO 903/19, Chief Secretary's Office, Judicial Division, Intelligence Notes, 1914, p. 49.
[53] Timothy Bowman, William Butler and Michael Wheatley, *The Disparity of Sacrifice. Irish Recruitment to the British Armed Forces, 1914–1918* (Liverpool: Liverpool University Press, 2020), 217.
[54] *The Independent*, 13 October 1914.
[55] *Sligo Champion*, 24 October 1914.

tribune lambasted the 'scare-mongers who, on their own responsibility, ha[d] been threatening conscription for some time'.[56] In an article titled 'Militia Ballot Act: A Complete Denial',[57] the *Freeman's Journal* quoted the long address of Redmond discrediting those 'absurd and ridiculous lies'. A few days later, the same newspaper demanded public apologies from *The Independent* for what was called 'the circulation of the malignant concoction about conscription'.[58] Given the number of daily newspapers circulating and relaying the news,[59] it is certain that the article published in *The Independent* had given rise to widespread concern and alarm.[60] They were nonetheless publicly ridiculed and discredited by members of the Irish Parliamentary Party and nationalist newspapers. Furthermore, it must be noticed that threats of conscription were not only ignited by press speculation and anti-British seditious propaganda.[61] In order to recruit more men into the British Army, the Irish were often reminded of the possibility that if men 'were not forthcoming, the Government [would] exercise the powers vested in them to get them'.[62] While those rumours were discredited, the possibility of conscription was agitated as a future threat in order to levy more troops. Following the first 'conscription scare', across Ireland, police inspectors reported that hundreds of young men had fled to the United States in order to avoid being taken.[63] Fears of being conscripted into the British Army had deep and immediate resonance in rural districts.[64] However, they generated little unrest and the reports of the police inspectors were fast to acknowledge that they had but a limited impact.

On 15 September 1914, the Prime Minister delivered a passionate speech in the House of Commons, in which he 'recognise[d] the atmosphere which this great patriotic spirit of union ha[d] created in the country'.[65] A few days later, on 18 September 1914, the Home Rule Bill received royal assent, but its enactment was simultaneously postponed for the duration of the conflict. Nationalist

[56] *Sligo Champion*, 14 November 1914.
[57] *Freeman's Journal*, 24 October 1914.
[58] *Freeman's Journal*, 26 October 1914.
[59] *Evening Herald* (Dublin), 20 October 1914; *Leitrim Advertiser*, 22 October 1914; *Longford Leader*, 24 October 1914.
[60] *Freeman's Journal*, 11 October 1916.
[61] Bowman, Butler and Wheatley, *The Disparity of Sacrifice*, 58.
[62] *The Daily Express* (Dublin), 13 November 1914.
[63] Bowman, Butler and Wheatley, *The Disparity of Sacrifice*, 59.
[64] TNA, CO 904/95, Report of the RIC Inspector General, October 1914; TNA, CO 904/120, Crime Special Branch, October 1914. *Leitrim Advertiser*, 11 November 1915.
[65] Hansard, House of Commons Debates, series 5, vol. 66, cc892, Asquith to House of Commons, 15 September 1914.

populations were overjoyed by this political victory and sent congratulatory telegrams to the Irish Party. Widespread rejoicing and popular demonstrations took place across the country with large concourses of people parading the streets.[66] However, the issue of the geographical areas in Ulster to be excluded from the implementation of the act was to remain unsolved, for the duration of the European conflict.

Asquith promised Carson that the Home Rule Bill would be amended.[67] Carson then delivered a fiercely passionate speech in which he vowed that Ulster would protect unconditionally the British Empire and the motherland.[68] Redmond, who had previously hoped the British would consent to allowing the Irish Volunteers to remain in Ireland as a defensive force, was politically trapped by the passing of Home Rule, coupled with its immediate postponement.[69] On 20 September 1914, at Woodenbridge, he urged the Irish Volunteers to fight for 'the sacred rights and liberties of small nations and the respect and enlargement of the great principle of nationality'.[70] Following Redmond's endorsement of volunteer engagement in the imperial war effort, in September 1914, the Irish Volunteers, the pro-Home Rule and pro-IPP militia, that had been created in response to the creation of the anti-Home Rule UVF, split.[71] Even though he had no form of control over the paramilitary organization in his capacity as leader of the Irish Parliamentary Party, Redmond succeeded in securing the consent of the overwhelming majority of the Irish Volunteers. Those who transferred their loyalty to Redmond and agreed to enrol in the British Army became subsequently known as the National Volunteers. Irish Volunteers who refused to pledge allegiance to Redmond remained known as the Irish Volunteers. As is evident in the declaration of the Committee of the Galway City Volunteers, while Volunteers

---

[66] Gallagher, *Ireland and the Great War*, 140–148.
[67] David Howie and Josephine Howie, 'Irish Recruiting and the Home Rule Crisis of August–September 1914', in *Strategy and Intelligence: British Policy during the First World War*, ed. Michael Dockrill and David French (London: Bloomsbury Academic, 1996), 15.
[68] *Belfast Evening Telegraph*, 14 August 1914.
[69] Hansard, House of Commons Debates, series 5, vol. 65, cc1029, John Redmond to House of Commons, 3 August 1914. It must be highlighted that not all of Redmond's followers and Irish MPs backed the war effort. Some, such as John O'Dowd, disavowed recruiting, accusing the leader of the Irish Parliamentary Party of sacrificing Irishmen at the altar of British imperialism. For an analysis of divisions within the Nationalist movement see James McConnel, 'Recruiting Sergeants for John Bull? Irish Nationalists, MPs and Enlistment during the Early Months of the Great War', *War in History* 14 (2007); 408–428.
[70] *Freeman's Journal*, 21 September 1914.
[71] Other political organizations such as Cumann na mBan split over the question whether to support the war effort. See Senia Pašeta, 'New Issues and Old: Women and Politics in Ireland, 1914–1918', in *Irish Women in the First World War Era. Irish Women's Lives, 1914–1918*, ed. Jennifer Redmond and Elaine Farrell (London: Routledge, 2019), 113–114.

could possibly 'endorse the statesmanlike speech of Mr Redmond when he [had] offered the services of the Irish Volunteers for home defence',[72] they objected to being enrolled in the British Army. By adjusting his rhetoric in order to adapt to the political necessities of wartime, and thus accommodate Asquith's strategy, Redmond had isolated himself from a good part of the Irish Volunteers. Yet while revolutionary ideology possibly deprived Redmond of a bigger reservoir of nationalist recruits, it certainly did not immediately weaken the Irish Parliamentary Party. The immediate split within the organization revealed the parallel and conflicting expectations of constitutional and revolutionary Nationalists.

Between 4 August 1914 and 1 February 1915, over 50,000 volunteers enrolled in the British Army.[73] Among them were the members of the two paramilitary organizations, meaning that recruitment significantly weakened the composition

Figure 1.1 John Redmond and John Devlin inspecting the National Volunteers, 1915. Cashman Collection. Courtesy of RTÉ Ireland.

---

[72] Galway County Council Archives, GS/1/3, Minutes of Meetings of the Irish Volunteers Galway City, 12 August 1914.
[73] Patrick Callan, 'British recruitment in Ireland, 1914–1918', *Revue Internationale d'Histoire Militaire* 63 (1987); 49.

of the UVF and Irish Volunteers alike. In February 1915, the UVF registered 61,982 members (a loss of 22,883 members),[74] while the strength of the Irish Volunteers dropped from 171,890[75] to 143,210.[76] Between 15 December 1914 and the end of 1915, the Colonial Office reported that 10,794 National Volunteers and 8,203 Ulster Volunteers had enlisted in the British Army, alongside 23,144 recruits not known to belong to the paramilitary forces.[77] By 1916, 95,143 Irishmen had enlisted in the British Army since the outbreak of the conflict.[78] Both unionist and nationalist paramilitary organizations accounted for 45 per cent of all the recruits during the entire European conflict.[79] However, recruits were not all driven by political (and economical) incentives. News of atrocities committed against Belgium civilians by the German Army, along with extensive coverage of mass displacements of populations following the invasion of Serbia by the Austrian Army also alarmed civilian populations. Men enlisted because, to a certain extent, they regarded the conflict as nothing but a 'democratic crusade'.[80] Furthermore, loyalty to friends and collective pressures accounted for the enlistment of thousands of civilians.[81] Barristers, solicitors, civil engineers, merchants, doctors, along with skilled and semi-skilled workers, enrolled *en masse*,[82] which supports the contention that enlistment was not always related to economic concerns. Across the country, and especially in Dublin, people mobilized on a large scale.[83]

Although the whole of nationalist Ireland did not back the British in the war against Germany, the large number of recruits is evidence of the fact that the European situation and domestic political issues proved vital enough to generate what was an unexpectedly high number of volunteers.[84] Their manifold and

---

[74] TNA, CO 903/19, Chief Secretary's Office, Judicial Division, Intelligence Notes, 1915, p. 51.
[75] Ibid., p. 49.
[76] Ibid.
[77] Ibid., p. 53.
[78] Patrick Callan, 'Recruiting for the British Army in Ireland during the First World War', *The Irish Sword* 66 (1987); 42.
[79] Ibid., 52.
[80] John Horne, 'Our war, our history', in *Our War: Ireland and the Great War*, ed. John Horne (Dublin: Royal Irish Academy, 2008), 8.
[81] David Fitzpatrick, 'The logic of collective sacrifice: Ireland and the British army, 1914–1918', *Historical Journal* 38, no. 4 (1995); 1023.
[82] Emmanuel Destenay, *Shadows from the Trenches. Veterans of the Great War and the Irish Revolution (1918–1923)* (Dublin: University College Dublin Press, 2021), 5–11.
[83] Richard Grayson, *Dublin's Great Wars. The First World War, the Easter Rising and the Irish Revolution* (Cambridge: Cambridge University Press, 2018), 23–48.
[84] Catriona Pennell, *A Kingdom United: Popular Responses to the Outbreak of the First World War in Britain and Ireland* (Oxford: Oxford University Press, 2012), 83.

antagonistic expectations led to the raising of three distinct Irish divisions; the 10th (Irish) Division, the 16th (Irish) Division, and the 36th (Ulster) Division. From the outbreak of the war, the three newly-raised Irish corps trained in Ireland, before departing for England to complete their training. On 1 July 1915, Sir Bryan Mahon, commanding officer of the 10th (Irish) Division, received the order to prepare his men to embark for the Dardanelles.[85] On 10 July 1914, at 3am, the men marched to Basingstoke station *en route* to Devonport, where they set out to sea at 5am, amidst loud cheers from the shore.[86] A few weeks later, in October 1915, the 36th (Ulster) Division crossed the Channel and moved to its position north of Amiens, on the Somme.[87] Two brigades of the 16th (Irish) Division embarked for France on 19 December 1915,[88] while the third, the 49th Brigade, remained in England to complete its training. The unit eventually reached France in March 1916.[89]

In August 1914, *The Irish Times* reported that 'Unionists and Nationalists have ranged themselves together against the invader of their common liberties'.[90] The Irish understood the common requirement to make sacrifices as 'people from all social backgrounds, were strongly committed to the Allied war effort from the outset and supported this Alliance until the conflict had ended'.[91] While effectively demonstrating strong support for Britain's war effort, and insisting that social pressure enforced a new moral order in 1914, Irish civilian populations, as well as their political representatives, remained nonetheless primarily focused on the future administration of the island.

A distant war: propaganda and the war economy

In rural districts, the so-called European War appeared disconnected from the everyday life of civilian populations. While it is generally acknowledged that 'urban Southern Ireland was heavily bound up in the war effort',[92] a gap between rural and urban areas seemed to persist. After all, recruitment was predominantly

---

[85] Bryan Cooper, *The 10th (Irish) Division in Gallipoli* (Dublin: Irish Academic Press, 1918), 32.
[86] Grayson, *Dublin's Great Wars*, 85–112.
[87] Tom Johnstone, *Orange, Green and Khaki: The Story of the Irish Regiments in the Great War, 1914–18* (Dublin: Gill & Macmillan, 1992), 221.
[88] TNA, War Office (hereafter WO), WO 95/1955, Operations of the 16th Division, December 1915.
[89] Johnstone, *Orange, Green and Khaki*, 206.
[90] *The Irish Times*, 5 August 1914.
[91] Gallagher, *Ireland and the Great War*, 8
[92] Ibid., 48.

an urban experience.[93] In June 1915, the Ambassador for France, Paul Cambon, regretted that the Irish people 'consider that Home Rule, the autonomy of their country, as well as the national question, [were] far more important than the European war'.[94] By August 1914, Home Rule had monopolized all the minds on the island, and by June 1915, in his view, the situation had not changed significantly. This, however, did not mean that in some localities the conflict did not heavily impact on local life. Indeed, the global conflict touched every aspect of Irish life.[95] The sinking of the RMS *Lusitania* on 7 May 1915, for instance, infuriated local communities in the south of Ireland and, as dead bodies continued to wash up on the Irish shore for several months, the Irish realized to what extent Germany could threaten Irish life.[96]

A few days before the 1916 Rising broke out in Dublin, Jean des Longchamps believed that the British Government ought to design propaganda that would clearly explain to the Irish 'what [was] really at stake during the conflict',[97] instead of only looking to incorporate Irishmen in the British Army for their war effort. 'Incurable defiance', 'hypnotised by local concerns', 'stubborn'; the Consul-General deplored that the Irish had forgotten that 'their nation [was] situated in Europe'.[98] The decision to postpone the application of Home Rule had somehow fortified the conviction among staunch republicans that the British Government never intended to grant Ireland any degree of autonomy. Cambon noted that the postponement of the bill had sufficed to raise doubts among the most anti-British sections of the population. That situation had begun to crystallize from September 1914 and even though Cambon had been confidently assured by some British officials that 'because the Irish refused to enrol in the British Army they did not deserve Home Rule and shall not be granted Home Rule',[99] the bill had nonetheless been given royal assent and in all likelihood, Home Rule was only a matter of time.

---

[93] Bowman, Butler and Wheatley, *The Disparity of Sacrifice*, 41.
[94] AD, Political and Commercial Correspondence, Great War, 1914–1918, Ireland, 1CPCOM/545, telegram from Paul Cambon to the Minister for Foreign Affairs, 14 June 1915.
[95] David Fitzpatrick, 'Home front and everyday life', in *Our War: Ireland and the Great War*, ed. John Horne, 133.
[96] Gallagher, *Ireland and the Great War*, 61–73.
[97] AD, Political and Commercial Correspondence, Great War, 1914–1918, Ireland, 1CPCOM/545, telegram from Jean des Longchamps to the Minister for Foreign Affairs, 18 April 1916.
[98] Ibid.
[99] AD, Political and Commercial Correspondence, Great War, 1914–1918, Ireland, 1CPCOM/545, letter from Paul Cambon to the Minister for Foreign Affairs, 14 June 1915.

From the outbreak of the conflict, anti-British propaganda had been widespread throughout the country.[100] The heavy losses suffered by front-line Irish troops on the Somme and in the Dardanelles revived the old accusation that England had deliberately exposed the Irish troops more than hers.[101] Cambon knew enough of the tumultuous Anglo-Irish history not to pay too much attention to such charges. Anything could be interpreted in the light of conflicting Anglo-Irish relations: one could easily portray recruitment as a cynical method used to destroy a whole generation of young Irishmen,[102] accuse the British Cabinet of giving positions of command to Protestant and Unionist officers,[103] or blame the British for the losses suffered by Irish regiments during the Gallipoli landing in 1915.[104] Narratives, propaganda, and individual events all fuelled resentment. Nonetheless, they could not however plausibly eclipse the well-entrenched certainty that Ireland had never been so close to a new administrative and governmental order. This is the reason why propaganda adjusted its own particular rhetoric in order to take account of political expectations.

In August 1915, the landing at Gallipoli 'operated a complete switch in the attitudes held by advanced nationalist propagandists towards Irish soldiers in the British Army'.[105] Indeed, Gallipoli was 'the first instance in which Irish civilians, who had joined up as volunteers, were killed in large numbers at once'.[106] Civilians recalled that 'Dublin was full of mourning, and on the faces one met there was a hard brightness of pain'.[107] Localities were faced with collective mourning as newspapers and official correspondence revealed the names of Ireland's dead. From scorn, mockery, and accusations of betrayal, the dramatic destruction of the 10th (Irish) Division at Gallipoli forced republican propaganda to re-think its position. Once Irish Volunteers in the British Army began to suffer casualties, 'the worst that was said of them was that they were

---

[100] Bowman, Butler and Wheatley, *The Disparity of Sacrifice*, 40. For a complete and detailed account of anti-recruitment campaigns during the First World War see Ben Novick, *Conceiving Revolution: Irish Nationalist Propaganda during the First World War* (Dublin: Four Courts Press, 2001).
[101] AD, Political and Commercial Correspondence, Great War, 1914–1918, Ireland, 1CPCOM/545, letter from Paul Cambon to the Minister for Foreign Affairs, 14 June 1915.
[102] *Sinn Féin*, 22 August 1914.
[103] Jesuit Archives of Ireland, Dublin (hereafter IJA), CHP 1/63, Father Joseph Wrafter, Chaplain in the 8th Royal Munster Fusiliers, to the Irish Fr Provincial Thomas V. Nolan SJ Archbishop, 2 November 1915.
[104] *Weekly Freeman's Journal*, 11 September 1915.
[105] Novick, *Conceiving Revolution*, 56.
[106] Gallagher, *Ireland and the Great War*, 137. Gallagher acknowledges the limits in establishing the extent to which the Gallipoli campaign impacted public opinion and its commitment to the war effort.
[107] Katharine Tynan, *The Years of Shadow* (London: Constable, 1919), 178.

misguided fools who had been tricked into volunteering for certain death by recruiters'.[108] As Irish casualties piled up, staunch republicans elaborated a new rhetoric that consisted in portraying the recruits as dupes.[109] Those opposed to recruitment could not possibly, through their words, metaphorically trample on the bodies of Irishmen lying dead in the Dardanelles and on the Somme. After all, they were sons of Ireland and had enrolled in specific circumstances. In February 1916, one of the most prominent opponents to recruitment felt more or less compelled to nuance the contemptuous accusations levelled against recruits of the 10th and 16th Divisions: 'Let me say plainly that if any Irishman is convinced that he will serve Ireland by becoming a British soldier, and if he acts on that conviction, he is a patriotic and a brave man.'[110] The summer of 1915 saw the downplaying of derogatory descriptions of Irish recruits, but this did not modify the portrayal of John Redmond, who was still being nicknamed the 'obedient servant of every Government official desirous of exploiting Ireland in the English interest'[111] as late as 1916. This testifies of a continuity among propagandists in their targeting of the representative of the Irish Party, regardless of the losses suffered by Irish units. The young Irishmen who had volunteered remained 'these poor misguided brothers [who] ha[d] been tricked and deluded into giving battle for England'.[112] Counter-recruiting campaigns attacked the Irish authorities, portraying speakers on recruiting platforms as 'men who, in 1914, [had] met together day by day to tell of their plans to murder [. . .] women and children by starvation',[113] while cynically protesting their profound respect for the children of Erin lying on the battlefields.

Divisions were not confined to the political sphere, but were also poison affecting private circles and at times the enrolment of a son in the British Army could bitterly divide families. When one volunteer from a republican family told his parents he had decided to enlist, the recruit from County Tipperary was regarded as 'a red coat' by his own father.[114] When Mark Kenna sought to explain why he would go and fight on the Somme, he only met with the despair of his parents: 'This is how you treat us after all we've done for you?!', asked his

---

[108] Novick, *Conceiving Revolution*, 58.
[109] *Worker's Republic*, 5 September 1914.
[110] *Irish Volunteer*, 12 February 1916.
[111] *The Dundalk Examiner and Louth Advertiser*, 22 January 1916.
[112] *Worker's Republic*, 26 February 1916.
[113] Ibid.
[114] Military Archives of Ireland (hereafter MAI), Liaison and Evacuation Papers (hereafter LE), 24, War Service Officers, Accession of 1919–1921, Ex-members of British Army who joined the IRA, letter from Bishop to Colonel O'Connell, 20 February 1936.

mother.¹¹⁵ However insignificant or anecdotal such examples may have been, they were nonetheless evidence of the widening divide provoked by the enlistment of a son, a father, or a relative. In order to counter any perfidious accusations from republican newspapers and to silence any suspicious comments in their neighbourhood, soldiers would publicly declare that 'they had fought for France and for Belgium – not for England – but [. . .] would be happy one day to fight for their country in order to get independence'.¹¹⁶ Even though bitter nationalist propaganda called for young men not to volunteer for the war effort, that narrative did not capture any more support than would be expected.¹¹⁷ On the contrary, it was recognized that fighting in the British Army during the world conflict was significantly different from enrolling for economic considerations during peace-time. These young men were Ireland's children, and the sorrow felt by their families echoed through the most aggressively nationalist newspapers all through the war.¹¹⁸ Once a parent had received the dreaded letter giving notice that a son had been lost on the battlefields of Gallipoli or the Dardanelles, they were clearly less inclined to embrace an aggressive nationalist propaganda. Clearly, Ireland supported her children fighting in the trenches of the Somme and in the Gallipoli peninsula.

In short, the Irish had to be left alone, if only out of fear that Ulster Unionists would compromise Home Rule, and this is something that is clearly reflected in the correspondence of Ambassador Paul Cambon. By September 1914, the political situation had been placed in limbo for the duration of the war, having ended in deadlock during the summer. However, the Home Rule Bill had already been entered on the statute book. There was one political move which further complicated the situation for the Irish Parliamentary Party. When Carson entered the new Government, 'it revived all the concerns of the Nationalists regarding the application of the Home Rule'.¹¹⁹ By June 1915, even though the Home Rule Bill had been enacted legislatively, it could be overthrown and suppressed with pressure from Ulster Unionists. A close analysis of the enrolments in the Irish

---

[115] *Irish Volunteer*, 24 October 1914.
[116] AD, Political and Commercial Correspondence, Great War, 1914–1918, Ireland, 1CPCOM/545, letter from Paul Cambon to the Minister for Foreign Affairs, 14 June 1915.
[117] Gallagher, *Ireland and the Great War*, 5. Gallagher argues that the activities of vocal and demonstrative radicals have often been highlighted as evidence to support the contention that an anti-war sentiment prevailed within Catholic Irish society at large. Indeed, it is debatable to minimize the role of Catholic Ireland in supporting the war effort only because extreme nationalist and separatist elements objected to supporting the Allies.
[118] *Nationality*, 2 October 1915.
[119] AD, Political and Commercial Correspondence, Great War, 1914–1918, Ireland, 1CPCOM/545, letter from Paul Cambon to the Minister for Foreign Affairs, 14 June 1915.

Volunteers at that period does not support the idea that Carson's entry into the Government and Redmond's eviction fortified the revolutionary paramilitary organization. On 5 May 1915, some 11,070 men belonged to the anti-recruitment Irish Volunteers.[120] At the end of July 1915, the number had scarcely changed, with a total of 11,365 members.[121] While such inconsistency toughened anti-British feelings, and raised concerns among the Irish Parliamentary Party, in all fairness, it must be admitted that the Irish did not react violently against the British Government. Paul Cambon and Jean des Longchamps, as well as Colonel de la Panouse, would all send detailed reports to their respective ministers in 1914. However, in 1915, their correspondence remained almost non-existent. Apart from the letter from Paul Cambon to the Minister for Foreign Affairs, dated 14 June 1915,[122] dealing with the Irish question, and the letter from Colonel de la Panouse to the Minister for War, dated 1 June 1915, highlighting the possible introduction of conscription to Great Britain,[123] the overall number of reports from these three representatives of the French Republic testified to the quiet and steady political situation in Ireland.

Such stability derived in part from the relatively satisfactory economic conditions in wartime and it is often forgotten that Ireland benefited from the war in this respect. Although wartime inflation of prices and wages had an impact on the everyday life of civilian communities,[124] in the south, farmers profited from the conflict.[125] From the beginning of the war, rural populations 'became rich thanks to the demand for agricultural goods'.[126] While the industrial north benefited more from the British war economy, the south also received lucrative contracts and agriculture reaped immediate benefits.[127] Economic benefits were 'concentrated in certain geographical areas and industrial sectors',[128] such as the industrial north-east of the country with its shipyards in Belfast. Five state-run national factories were eventually established in Dublin, Waterford, Cork and Galway, employing 2,148 people.[129] The Irish economy did well during the war, as

---

[120] TNA, CO 903/19, Chief Secretary's Office, Judicial Division, Intelligence Notes, 1914, p. 49.
[121] Ibid., p. 50.
[122] AD, Political and Commercial Correspondence, Great War, 1914–1918, Ireland, 1CPCOM/545, letter from Paul Cambon to the Minister for Foreign Affairs, 14 June 1915.
[123] SHD, Third Republic (1870–1940), Army Staff, 7N700, telegram from Colonel de la Panouse to the Minister for War, 1 June 1915.
[124] Padraig Yeates, *A City in Wartime, Dublin 1914–1918* (Dublin: Gill & Macmillan, 2012), 62–65.
[125] Keith Jeffery, *Ireland and the Great War* (Cambridge: Cambridge University Press, 2000), 31.
[126] SHD, Third Republic (1870–1940), Army Staff, 7N1254, letter from Colonel de la Panouse to the Minister for War, 15 December 1916.
[127] Niamh Puirséil, 'War, work and labour', in *Our War: Ireland and the Great War*, ed. John Horne, 184.
[128] H. D. Gribbon, 'Economic and Social History', in *A New History of Ireland*, ed. W. E. Vaughan, 346.
[129] Ibid., 347.

'shipbuilding, engineering and textile industries responded to the expanded wartime demand for their products'.[130] As an Inspector of the Royal Irish Constabulary (RIC) reported, farmers and shopkeepers 'felt their interests were strongly bound up with the British'.[131] In addition, Irish workers could obtain a job through the labour exchange system.[132] Women from different political and religious affiliations actively supported the war effort. They participated in voluntary work and wartime charitable activities in order to demonstrate their loyalty to the Allies.[133] Middle- and upper-class women, both Catholics and Protestants, engaged in activities such as nursing, ambulance driving, fund raising and were active in other war-relief associations.[134] They wholeheartedly offered moral and humanitarian support throughout the conflict, providing comfort to disabled servicemen and relief to front-line troops. When Belgium refugees began to land on Irish shores following the German invasion of their country, voluntary associations were established and women volunteered to provide accommodation for these civilian victims of the conflict.[135]

Economic prosperity and political concerns explained why the British authorities in Ireland refused to take drastic measures to crush overt armed demonstrations that occurred in Ireland, albeit in relatively insignificant numbers from August 1914 and April 1916. Without going so far as to predict that an insurrection would break out in Dublin, Jean des Longchamps was nonetheless sufficiently concerned with the seditious attitude of the Irish Volunteers that on 18 April 1916 he wrote a report on the situation of Ireland.

Laissez-faire policy and French concerns

The unrest which erupted sporadically on the island between August 1914 and April 1916 was largely aimed at stopping recruitment for the army.[136] At that

---

[130] Jeffery, *Ireland and the Great War*, 30.
[131] TNA, CO 904/157/1, Reports of the State of the Country, 1916–1918, Item 65, Midlands and Connaught District, February 1918.
[132] Yeates, *A City in Wartime*, 298–299.
[133] Maeve O'Riordan, 'Titled Women and Voluntary War Work in Ireland during the First World War: a case study of Ethel, Lady Inchiquin', in *Irish Women in the First World War Era*, ed. Redmond and Farrell, 32–51; Deborah Tom, 'Women, War Work, and the State in Ireland, 1914–1918', in *Irish Women in the First World War Era*, 122–137; Fionnuala Walsh, *Irish Women and the Great War* (Cambridge: Cambridge University Press, 2020), 125–163.
[134] Gallagher, *Ireland and the Great War*, 31–60. Gallagher contends that 'their services have been understated, treated as an addendum to the military effort' and reveals the important contribution of upper- and middle-class women in mobilizing for the war effort and in encouraging recruitment.
[135] Gallagher, *Ireland and the Great War*, 36.
[136] Bowman, Butler and Wheatley, *The Disparity of Sacrifice*, 40.

time, anti-British sympathies contributed to fuelling century-long resentment. However, 'the majority of the Irish laughed at the revolutionaries and still believed in constitutional nationalism',[137] according to the Consul-General for France. In 1914, following the outbreak of the war, 'dissidence in Ireland was constrained by the degree of support for the war demonstrated by nationalist Ireland'.[138] However, France's diplomatic consuls worried at Germany's subtle and ongoing propaganda towards Ireland and frowned at the insufficient recruitment figures. In order to boost recruitment, halt anti-war activities and counter anti-British sentiments, the Quai d'Orsay received an Irish delegation in Paris at the end of April 1915 and agreed to the sending of a French mission to Ireland.[139] Where the British failed, the French hoped to succeed in moving the hearts and minds of the Irish people. If the Quai d'Orsay knew that bitter and century-long Anglo-Irish conflicts had crystallized suspicion towards the Crown, they nonetheless disagreed with how the British were handling anti-war and anti-Allies sentiments.

On 7 September 1914, the Dublin Metropolitan Police had warned the Government of the danger to be expected in Dublin,[140] while on 26 October 1914, the Detective Department of the Dublin Metropolitan Police submitted a full report to the Under-Secretary. The Irish Volunteers had recently marched to a meeting nearly 1,000 strong, with 230 of their number armed with rifles.[141] Several reports were received by Dublin Castle during the year 1915. During the summer of the same year, the question of the implementation of compulsory service gave a considerable stimulus to the Irish Volunteers.[142] Following the collapse of the Liberal Government,[143] the creation of a wartime coalition triggered a second 'conscription scare'. Its direct impact on recruitment is striking; out of fear of being drafted overnight 'some [men] joined up with friends and family and got into units of their choice'.[144] Fears of conscription ran parallel to the political debates in Westminster. Members of the United Irish League in Ballinaglera (County Leitrim) reassured rural populations: 'there is no danger of conscription and the young men should remain at home and put

---

[137] AD, Political and Commercial Correspondence, Great War, 1914–1918, Ireland, Home Affairs (1918–1922), 95CPCOM/1, report on the situation of Ireland, 25 April 1918.
[138] Pennell, *A Kingdom United*, 229.
[139] Jérôme aan de Wiel, *The Catholic Church in Ireland, 1914–1918: War and Politics* (Dublin: Irish Academic Press, 2003), 132–144.
[140] *Royal Commission on the Rebellion in Ireland. Report of the Commission* (London: HMSO, 1916), p. 8.
[141] Ibid.
[142] Ibid., p. 7.
[143] *Sligo Champion*, 24 July 1915.
[144] Bowman, Butler and Wheatley, *The Disparity of Sacrifice*, 66.

down their crops'.¹⁴⁵ If newspapers like the *Freeman's Journal* vehemently criticized *The Independent* in October 1914, by the end of 1915 they had adopted a different approach when conscription gradually came to be seen as a possibility. On 26 October 1915, the paper published that several Irish MPs had given a motion to the Government the day before. It was clearly stated that conscription would be a deplorable blunder if it were to be applied in Ireland.¹⁴⁶ Perhaps out of neutrality, the paper refrained from expressing individual views and merely relayed the motion. Rural populations learnt that the United Irish League wholeheartedly supported John Redmond and that they could be assured that conscription would never apply to Ireland, for the simple reason that '[there was] not even a sufficient number [of men] to till the land, and there was, therefore, no danger of any man being brought into the army against his will'.¹⁴⁷

Rural populations were indeed desperately needed during the conflict given that agricultural production was vital for the war effort. This is actually the reason why farmers were less likely to join the armed forces because they greatly benefited from the war economy.¹⁴⁸ No conscription would be enforced, 'but men must volunteer'¹⁴⁹ in order to alleviate the shortage of manpower in the Irish regiments, explained one recruiting sergeant. During recruiting meetings, sergeants hammered home that if Ireland wanted to avoid conscription, 'the men of Ireland should come forward voluntarily to take the places of their fellow countrymen who were falling in battle'.¹⁵⁰ It represented a way to spur the men on and to incite them to enlist. In a meeting at Ballymote, John O'Dowd (MP and representative chairman of the United Irish League) calmed the temper of his fellow countrymen, declaring that 'no matter how the Irish Parliamentary Party were talked of, and no matter how they were criticised, they were all against conscription'.¹⁵¹ He reminded the audience that 'they all knew that the Home Rule Bill was on the Statute Book, and they could take it from him that it could never be taken off (applause). The war was a terrible thing, but it would eventually end in favour of the Allies.'¹⁵² By then, within revolutionary and labour circles, activists kept campaigning against recruitment.¹⁵³

---

145   *Sligo Champion*, 24 July 1915.
146   *Freeman's Journal*, 26 October 1915.
147   *Sligo Champion*, 27 November 1915.
148   Bowman, Butler and Wheatley, *The Disparity of Sacrifice*, 70.
149   *Daily Express* (Dublin), 22 November 1915.
150   *Kilkenny Moderator and Leinster Advertiser*, 13 November 1915.
151   *Sligo Champion*, 4 December 1915.
152   Ibid.
153   Yeates, *A City in Wartime*, 143–144.

Ireland was in a state of great prosperity throughout the whole of 1915, meaning that Irish discontent could not be attributed to economic conditions. When conscription was introduced in January 1916, to be followed in May 1916 by the Military Service Act,[154] it applied to Great Britain alone, and Ireland was not made subject to the provisions. Cautious British politicians wanted to avoid unnecessary unrest in Ireland, knowing only too well that the Irish people would not stand for it. On 5 January 1916, in the House of Commons, John Redmond delivered a speech against compulsory service in Ireland, in which he emphasized that the Irish had answered the call, but could not be compelled by coercion to support the British war effort against their will:

> Ireland has thoroughly identified herself with the Empire in this War. We in Ireland regard this as our War in a way that was never true of any war in which the Empire was engaged in the past, and we in Ireland have been determined, so far as our poor resources allowed it, to prove that we were willing to make any sacrifice necessary in order to bring this War to a speedy and successful issue. And if we were convinced – if I personally were convinced that the passage of this Bill was in the remotest degree necessary to end this War, or I go even further – if it were in my sober judgment really calculated to promote the speedy and successful ending of this War, the position which I would take up would be entirely different from my attitude to-day.[155]

James Chambers, a Unionist MP, insisted on the inclusion of Ireland in the measure, but the leader of the Irish Party warned of the disastrous consequences this would lead to.[156] At that time, Augustine Birrell, Chief Secretary for Ireland, had reported that men between 19 and 41 in each of the provinces of Ireland were numbered as follow: 174,597 in Leinster, 169,489 in Ulster, 136,637 in Munster and 81,392 in Connaught.[157] As early as January 1916, the ambivalent position of nationalist Ireland was becoming evident. Voluntary enlistment would not damage Anglo-Irish relations. Compulsion would in contrast be regarded as another British attempt to coerce Ireland and punish the Irish. Redmond's unfaltering determination and opposition to conscription in the

---

[154] Dittmar Dahlmann, 'Parliaments', in *The Cambridge History of the First World War, Volume II, The State*, ed. Jay Winter (Cambridge: Cambridge University Press, 2014), 57.
[155] Hansard, House of Commons Debates, series 5, vol. 77, cc1006, John Redmond to House of Commons, 5 January 1916.
[156] Hansard, House of Commons Debates, series 5, vol. 78, cc67, John Redmond to House of Commons, 17 January 1916.
[157] Hansard, House of Commons Debates, series 5, vol. 77, cc1270, Birrell to House of Commons, 10 January 1916.

House of Commons was echoed in local and national newspapers. The Irish Parliamentary Party was said to be '[Ireland's] only safeguard against conscription'.[158] On 18 January 1916, the *Freeman's Journal* reassured the Irish population and put an end to ongoing hearsay: 'The threat of conscription in Ireland is now definitely at an end.'[159] Retracing the heated political debates in the House of Commons during which conscription was voted for Great Britain, the daily newspaper praised the action of the Irish Party and explained to its readers that 'it was owing to the opposition of the Irish Party, to their statesmanlike attitude throughout, to their declaration of the opinion of Ireland in favour of the war but against coercive measures, and to their commanding Parliamentary position, that Ireland [was] free from conscription'.[160] By January 1916, numerous organizations and local city councils had already passed resolutions against conscription, while never questioning the intentions of the Irish Party which was still portrayed as the only viable force capable of defeating it.[161] Local authorities such as the Kerry County Council issued motions against conscription while pledging their entire trust and allegiance to the Irish Party.[162]

As reported by France's representatives to London and Dublin, as long as the British Cabinet gave a choice to the Irish, that was the best that could be hoped for. Therefore, while 'nationalist Ireland did enter the war in 1914',[163] they entered the war for political reasons, and could not account for the whole of nationalist public opinion. While representatives of the Irish Party unconditionally backed the British war effort, the representatives of the French Government testified to the fact that the war did not register in the conscience of all nationalist circles. To some civilians, the conflict was nothing but a distant event, completely disconnected from the concerns of everyday life.

Confidential information reported that in January 1916, 'the fear of the Military Service Bill being applied to Ireland'[164] gave a new impetus to the Irish Volunteers. At that point, the RIC was still consistently reporting to the Under-Secretary, and Lord Middleton had had an interview with the Prime Minister on 26 January 1916, during which he had expressed his concerns about seditious

---

[158] *The Kilkenny Moderator and Leinster Advertiser*, 13 January 1916.
[159] *Freeman's Journal*, 18 January 1916.
[160] Ibid.
[161] Jackson, *Home Rule: An Irish History*, 172.
[162] *Kerry Evening Post*, 5 January 1916.
[163] Catriona Pennell, 'More than a "Curious Footnote": Irish Voluntary Participation in the First World War and British Popular Memory', in *Towards Commemoration. Ireland in War and Revolution, 1912-1923*, ed. John Horne and Edward Madigan (Dublin: Royal Irish Academy Press, 2013), 42.
[164] *Royal Commission on the Rebellion in Ireland. Minutes of Evidence* (London: HMSO, 1916).

newspapers and unauthorized drillings.[165] The Prime Minister requested a memorandum, which Birrell submitted. On 26 February, he saw Sir Matthew Nathan, and on 6 March Lord Wimborne. Both men were anxious regarding recent developments but, as Lord Middleton reported, they were 'unable to move further owing to the general attitude of the Government which it was impossible to disturb'.[166] A few days before the 1916 uprising broke out, France's Consul-General to Dublin had summed up the position of Sinn Féin since the outbreak of the Great War. He spoke of 'its hatred for England [and of] its complete disinterest for the conflict'.[167] Des Longchamps was unable to understand why no action was taken to forbid Sinn Féin meetings. At that time, the insurrection had not yet broken out, but the agitation on the part of Sinn Féin activists bewildered him and he openly condemned the passivity of the British Government: 'It would have been better to crush the evil from the beginning at the time when the organization Sinn Féin and its influence were still innocent.'[168] The Consul-General insisted on the conviction that apart from carrying out a few search operations, the attitude of the British had merely consolidated the belief within Sinn Féin that they benefited from considerable impunity. On St Patrick's Day, 17 March 1916, 1,100 armed Irish Volunteers had demonstrated in the streets of Cork, while in Dublin, 1,600 armed men had gathered. All over Ireland, the British authorities reported that 5,955 Irish Volunteers had paraded and it was estimated that they possessed 2,637 rifles and shotguns.[169] (The *Royal Commission on the Rebellion in Ireland* would later report that on 24 April 1916, there were approximately 16,000 Irish Volunteers in the country.)[170] The Inspector-General of the RIC remarked that 'the Irish Volunteer leaders [were] a pack of rebels who would proclaim their independence, in the event of any favourable opportunity, but with their present resources and without substantial reinforcements it [was] difficult to imagine that they [would] make even a brief stand'.[171]

These distinct and individual actions remained somewhat isolated and did not in the least reflect the state of public opinion as a whole. Military marches occurred in Cork and in other cities all over Ireland, but 'the provocative attitude

---

[165] *Royal Commission on the Rebellion in Ireland. Report of the Commission*, 10.
[166] *Royal Commission on the Rebellion in Ireland. Minutes of Evidence*, 31.
[167] AD, Political and Commercial Correspondence, Great War, 1914–1918, Ireland, 1CPCOM/545, telegram from Jean des Longchamps to the Minister for Foreign Affairs, 18 April 1916.
[168] Ibid.
[169] TNA, CO 904/23/2, Sinn Féin Volunteers Parades, St Patrick's Day, 17 March 1916.
[170] *Royal Commission on the Rebellion in Ireland. Minutes of Evidence*, 3.
[171] *Royal Commission on the Rebellion in Ireland. Report of the Commission*, 10.

of the Sinn Féiners ended up by exasperating the population devoted to the Irish Parliamentary Party'.[172] Civilian populations still backed the Irish Parliamentary Party, even intervening directly in order to suppress meetings. As local resistance to the overt display of force by Sinn Féin spread, civilian populations acted as shields against armed revolutionary nationalism. In order to properly gauge the limits of the importance and the popularity of Sinn Féin and the Irish Volunteers before the 1916 insurrection, one needs to understand that local populations responded by way of demonstrating their hostility to these provocations. That the French hoped for the adoption of more drastic measures against these meetings is undeniable. However, the reluctance to impose sanctions spoke for the willingness of the British authorities not to undermine voluntary recruitment.

While railing against the British authorities for their refusal to neutralize dissident movements, Jean des Longchamps was not specifically concerned with Sinn Féin as such, but he was worried by their adoption of an openly pro-German rhetoric. More than a possible nuisance to British domestic affairs in Ireland, this could potentially turn into a war issue if Sinn Féin continued to demonstrate openly without any immediate response from the British authorities in Ireland. The Quai d'Orsay 'knew that British policy in Ireland was far from successful and that it could have important repercussions: the possible destabilization of their main ally, Britain, and the complete failure of recruitment'.[173] By the beginning of April 1916, the French authorities had already measured 'the dangers which the British Government, and therefore France, could face from hostile elements'.[174] John Redmond and Edward Carson had called for the enrolment of Irishmen in the British Army and 95,143 Irishmen had already enlisted by January 1916.[175] Overt armed demonstrations by Sinn Féin were in no sense representative of a climate characterized by the support of the vast majority of local populations. Across the country, 'many people were convinced by the Allied cause and believed that Germany was in the wrong'.[176] Furthermore, any hostile demonstration could not eclipse the well-entrenched certainty that Ireland had never been so close to achieving a new constitutional order of government. One could argue that these open displays of armed republicanism actively sought to eclipse the heroism of Irish units. This in turn accounted for

---

[172] AD, Political and Commercial Correspondence, Great War, 1914–1918, Ireland, 1CPCOM/545, telegram from Jean des Longchamps to the Minister for Foreign Affairs, 18 April 1916.
[173] Aan de Wiel, *The Catholic Church in Ireland*, 79.
[174] AD, Political and Commercial Correspondence, Great War, 1914–1918, Ireland, 1CPCOM/545, telegram from Jean des Longchamps to the Minister for Foreign Affairs, 18 April 1916.
[175] Callan, 'Recruiting for the British Army', 42.
[176] Gallagher, *Ireland and the Great War*, 157.

the violent reaction on the part of the supporters of the Irish Parliamentary Party, who swore they would expunge the affront to the memory of the martyrs lying in Gallipoli and on the Somme. Nonetheless, the displays of hostility appeared sufficiently significant to be a cause of worry for the Consul-General for France.

Before the rebellion broke out on 24 April 1916, the British authorities in Ireland reported that, in spite of anti-recruitment propaganda and seditious speeches, 'after the war broke out, there was a considerable wave of feeling in Ireland in favour of the Allies'.[177] The British knew too well that seditious feelings on the island could always re-emerge at the slightest opportunity. However, they had also learnt that repression would only play into the hands of the rebels. Surveillance remained the preferred option, instead of foolishly trying to arrest any single agitator. A section of nationalist Ireland, hostile to the Irish Parliamentary Party and morally opposed to the participation of Irishmen in the British Army, had gradually started to orchestrate anti-recruitment campaigns all over Ireland, with the aim of deterring Irishmen from supporting the war effort.[178] However, what the French singularly failed to appreciate were the reasons why the British authorities in Ireland were turning a blind eye to these openly seditious demonstrations.

Among the Irish Parliamentary Party and the British authorities in Ireland, there prevailed a reassuring confidence that 'Sinn Féiners were incompetent intellectuals unable to take action except for their wordy speeches, that they had absolutely no support from the population and that all prosecution against them would just make them appear more sympathetic and more powerful'.[179] While des Longchamps agreed that repressing the agitators could damage political stability, he nonetheless believed that Ireland could not possibly accept pro-German seditious propaganda in wartime. When the rebellion started on 24 April 1916, the Consul-General for France concluded that 'out of lack of clear-sightedness and energy from the British Government and the Nationalists, the insurrection did happen'.[180] What had begun as a purely domestic issue for the British before the Great War would gradually turn into an international affair.

---

[177] *Royal Commission on the Rebellion in Ireland. Report of the Commission*, 6.
[178] Novick, *Conceiving Revolution*, 51–71.
[179] AD, Political and Commercial Correspondence, Great War, 1914–1918, Ireland, 1CPCOM/545, telegram from Jean des Longchamps to the Minister for Foreign Affairs, 6 May 1916.
[180] Ibid.

Conclusion

In 1914, 'Irish people, whether unionist or nationalist, on the whole opted to support the war'.[181] Indeed, a significant number of nationalist recruits and former members of the Irish Volunteers enrolled in the British Army – alongside Irish Unionists – as soon as the conflict broke out. Ireland's ability to raise three distinct divisions accounted for the large number of nationalist and unionist volunteers who were ready to assist the British Empire in its hour of need. Counter-recruitment campaigns and anti-British propaganda spoke for the minority of Irish people who, far from downplaying their centuries-old bitterness against the British, maintained the same political line, regardless of the international implications of the war. Representatives from France nonetheless nuanced the conviction that nationalist Ireland unconditionally backed Britain. In addition, from a purely political angle, they did not comprehend why the British turned a blind eye in the face of pro-German propaganda and seditious literature. On 18 April 1916, only a few short days before the 1916 uprising broke out, Jean des Longchamps wrote his personal account of the situation in Ireland. Without interfering in the way the British handled these overt displays of German support, des Longchamps urged a policy of coercion, albeit not for the disarming of the Irish Volunteers. Nothing indicates that he had received any confidential information as to what was being planned by the future rebels. However, he remained sufficiently concerned with the open displays of military drilling and armed demonstrations to alert the Quai d'Orsay, only a few days before the first shots of the insurrection echoed in the corridors of London and Paris.

---

[181] Pennell, *A Kingdom United*, 231.

2

Was the Rebellion a Turning Point? (April 1916–October 1916)

A part of nationalist Ireland, hostile to the Irish Parliamentary Party and morally opposed to the participation of Irishmen in the British Army, could not countenance the possibility of wearing the British uniform. From this section of nationalist Ireland there was a gradual orchestration of anti-recruitment campaigns, aimed at deterring Irishmen from enlisting in the army. While thousands of members of the Irish Volunteers dropped their weapons in order to put on the British khaki, others continued to drill, waiting for the conflict to be over, while keeping in mind the unresolved issues of how far actual power would be devolved and how hard Ulster would resist it. Before John Redmond launched a call for recruits at Woodenbridge on 21 September 1914, at the beginning of the same month a handful of rebels had gathered in the headquarters of the Gaelic League in Dublin and sworn to strike a blow at England during the conflict.[1] Fortified by America's neutrality, the future leaders of the 1916 uprising looked towards Germany in order to achieve their political goal by rising against the British in wartime.

Allegiance and opportunities: US neutrality and the preparation for an insurrection

A few weeks after the war had broken out, a handful of dissidents had gathered in the Mansion House, in Dublin, and sworn to rise against Great Britain.[2] They, not surprisingly, mentioned the possibility of calling on Germany for help.

---

[1] L. P. Curtis, 'Ireland in 1914', in *A New History of Ireland, VI, Ireland Under the Union, II, 1870–1921*, ed. W. E. Vaughan (Oxford: Oxford University Press, 1996), 180.

[2] León Ó Broin, *Revolutionary Underground: The Story of the Irish Republican Brotherhood, 1858–1924* (London: Gill & Macmillan, 1976), 160; Curtis, 'Ireland in 1914', 180.

While Edward Carson and John Redmond called on Unionists and Nationalists to back the British authorities, republicans took advantage of America's neutrality in order to travel to the United States and meet Germany's representatives. Sir Roger Casement took passage on the Norwegian steamer *Oskar II* and travelled to New York, where he met Captain Franz von Papen at the German Embassy in Washington.[3] US neutrality permitted Irish-American organizations to provide support for rebellious movements in Ireland, thus allowing the Irish rebels and representatives of the German authorities to meet in America in order to discuss the possibility of a rebellion in Dublin.[4] Casement presented himself at the German embassy for an interview with von Papen, Germany's military attaché.[5] During the meeting, both agreed on the need to strengthen cooperation between their two countries. Von Papen then planned a meeting between Casement and the State Secretary for Foreign Affairs, Arthur Zimmerman, in Berlin. On 2 November 1914, Casement went to Germany at Zimmerman's invitation and the two signed a pact according to which Germany would financially support an uprising in Ireland.[6]

From August 1914, Irish-American communities benefited from the neutrality of the United States and thus offered economic and political support to rebels in Ireland. US neutrality helped Irish rebels to challenge the British Government in wartime, network with the German authorities in the US, and create a congenial breeding ground for a future rebellion in Dublin. Before the insurrection, France's representatives were warned by the American authorities that 'the Irish communities in the United States ha[d] clearly sided with the Germans'.[7] One week before the Easter Rising, American intelligence services

---

[3] Jérôme aan de Wiel, *The Irish Factor, 1899–1919: Ireland's Strategic and Diplomatic Importance for Foreign Powers* (Dublin: Irish Academic Press, 2008), 165.

[4] Francis M. Carroll, *America and the Making of an Independent Ireland. A History* (New York: New York University Press, 2021), 7.

[5] Aan de Wiel, *The Irish Factor*, 165.

[6] Charles Tansill, *America and the Fight for Irish Freedom, 1866–1922* (New York: The Devin-Adair Co., 1957), 178. This officious pact would also alter the conditions of detention for Irish prisoners of war in Germany given Casement and Zimmerman also agreed on the creation of an 'Irish Brigade', a term traditionally given to Irishmen who had enrolled in the French Army. As a direct consequence of this agreement, from December 1914 onwards, the Germans separated Irish POWs from their British comrades in the hope of encouraging desertions. Irish POWs were grouped in a special camp, Limburg an der Lahn, where they were treated much better than their British brothers-in-arms. At the beginning of 1915, Casement visited the prisoners in person and encouraged them to transfer their allegiance to the Kaiser. As POWs in German camps many of these men understandably hesitated between allegiance and the possibility of transferring their loyalty. On that point see Emmanuel Destenay, 'La captivité des prisonniers de guerre irlandais dans les camps allemands: répressions, résistances et transferts de loyauté', *Revue historique* 678 (2016): 59–80.

[7] Archives Diplomatiques du Ministère des Affaires Étrangères, La Courneuve (hereafter AD), Political and Commercial Correspondence, Great War, 1914–1918, Ireland, 1CPCOM/545, telegram from Jean des Longchamps to the Minister for Foreign Affairs, 18 April 1916.

had raided the office of a member of the German Embassy in Washington and seized compromising documents revealing the involvement of Irish-Americans in arms deals and negotiations with German representatives.[8] From London, Colonel de la Panouse received confirmation that 'Irish-Americans knew of what their brothers in Ireland were preparing for'.[9] A few days before the rebellion broke out, Jean Jusserand, Ambassador for France in Washington, had received confidential information that a landing was being prepared in Ireland and would take place at the same moment as an attack by the German navy.[10] On 22 April 1916, the Dublin Metropolitan Police sent a secret report to London in which it was clearly pointed out that a party of 'Sinn Féiners [would go] out on Sunday next, 23 instant at 4pm'.[11] That very same day, the *Gaelic American* published an article in which it was estimated that $46,000 had already been sent from the US to Ireland in order to arm the Irish Volunteers.[12]

Rebellion, reactions and extrapolations?

On Easter Monday 1916, a handful of rebels marched down the streets of the city centre of Dublin and proclaimed the Irish Republic.[13] When the insurrection broke out, the French authorities concluded that the rebellion would oblige the British to maintain troops in Dublin. 'Germany seeks to compel the British

---

[8] Michael Doorley, *Irish-American Diaspora Nationalism. The Friends of Irish Freedom, 1916–1935* (Dublin: Four Courts Press, 2005), 44; Francis M. Carroll, *America and the Making of an Independent Ireland*, 10. Carroll contends that 'in the weeks following the Rising' the British requested from the US State Department any relevant communications but that the Secretary of State refused the request. According to Carroll, the US did not pass sensitive information to the British in the aftermath of the Rising. However, the real question (and Carroll remains silent about it) is to know whether the Wilson administration informed the British of a possible rebellion in Ireland after raiding the office of the German military attaché in New York on 18 April 1916. Carroll claims that the British were able to 'decode the German codes'; what seems to be suggested, here, is that out of neutrality the US Government deliberately refrained from alerting the British of the upcoming rebellion in Dublin. This tends to suggest that Wilson, and the US Government, were ready to go as far as allowing a rebellion to stun British society in wartime. But the Ambassador for France in Washington was provided with this piece of information.

[9] Service Historique de la Défense, Vincennes (hereafter SHD), Third Republic (1870–1940), Army Staff, 7N1253, telegram from Colonel de la Panouse to the Minister for War, 1 May 1916.

[10] SHD, Third Republic (1870–1940), Army Staff, 7N1253, telegram from Colonel de la Panouse to the Minister for War, 1 May 1916.

[11] The National Archives (hereafter TNA), Colonial Office (hereafter CO), CO 904/23/3, Sinn Féin activities, meetings in 1916, secret Report from Dublin Metropolitan Police, 22 April 1916.

[12] *Gaelic American*, 22 April 1916.

[13] Richard Grayson, *Dublin's Great Wars. The First World War, the Easter Rising and the Irish Revolution* (Cambridge: Cambridge University Press 2018), 113–176.

Government to maintain troops in Ireland',[14] wrote Colonel de la Panouse. He went on: 'the real undertaking of the Germans is to create internal difficulties, maintain the threat of a possible landing, and prevent our Allies from sending more troops to France to fight alongside our army'.[15] France's military attaché had foreseen the direct consequences of the insurrection: the British people would this time be required to dispatch units to Ireland in order to quell the insurrection.

No more than 1,500 rebels had taken up arms against the British on 24 April 1916.[16] The fighting took place almost exclusively in the capital, with some sporadic shots exchanged in local places.[17] Nonetheless, the authorities called for

Figure 2.1 Abbey Street after the Easter Rising, 1916. Keogh Photographic Collection. Courtesy of the National Library of Ireland.

---

[14] SHD, Third Republic (1870–1940), Army Staff, 7N1254, letter from Colonel de la Panouse to the Minister for War, 28 April 1916.
[15] Ibid.
[16] Laurence McCaffrey, *Ireland: From Colony to Nation State* (Englewood Cliffs: Prentice-Hall, 1979), 139–140.
[17] TNA, War Office (hereafter WO), WO 32/9510, Summaries of events and communiqués of the rebellion in Ireland, secret report, 27 April 1916. For additional information regarding the mobilization of Irish Volunteers in cities such as Cork, Limerick or Mayo see Charles Townshend, *Easter 1916: The Irish Rebellion* (London: Penguin Books, 2005), 214–242.

Figure 2.2 Lower Sackville Street, Dublin, after the Easter Rising, 1916. Murtagh Collection. Courtesy of RTÉ Ireland.

Figure 2.3 O'Connell Street after the Easter Rising, 1 May 1916. Cashman Collection. Courtesy of RTÉ Ireland.

reinforcements as they were unable to dislodge the insurgents in Dublin. On Easter Monday 1916, the force of nearly 5,000 men was, contrary to expectations, insufficient to deal with the situation.[18] In the evening, the British Cabinet ordered additional reinforcements: 2,500 men arrived from the Curragh that evening and night, and over 1,000 men from Belfast and three machine-guns from Athlone arrived in the capital on the following day.[19] Further reinforcements from England arrived two days later. The 7th Sherwood Foresters left England and were sent to Ireland to quell the rebellion[20] while a battalion of the Lincolnshire Regiment departed from Liverpool to restore law and order.[21] 'Ireland was the first fighting that we had', remembered an English private who had expected to fight on the Western Front against the Germans. As more troops sailed from Great Britain,[22] casualties piled up in the streets of Dublin. The increasing number of dead bodies lying in the streets of the capital accounted for the warm welcome which Dubliners gave to the newly-dispatched British battalions. Troops from England rejoiced at the attitude of the civilian populations: 'people were coming and giving you a cup of tea, a few sandwiches or something like that'.[23] Irish women wandered the streets of Dublin to offer them milk, food and cigarettes.[24] Local populations were amused to find the troops trying to talk French to them, thinking they were in France.[25] By 28 April 1916, the British had sent 14,000 men to Ireland to restore order.[26] When the rebels eventually surrendered after five days of fighting, Colonel de la Panouse reported that overall 18,000 men had been sent to crush the Irish rebellion.[27]

The casualties and damage to properties horrified civilians, and in the immediate aftermath of the uprising, the capital is reported to have looked like 'a

---

[18] *Royal Commission on the Rebellion in Ireland, Minutes of Evidence and Documents Relative to the Sinn Féin Movement*, Parliamentary Papers (London: HMSO, 1916), p. 9.
[19] Ibid.
[20] University of Leeds Library (hereafter ULL), Peter Liddle Collection (First World War) (1914–1918), Domestic Front (1914–1918), tape 1349, interview of J. Rogers, 2 February 1998.
[21] ULL, Peter Liddle Collection (First World War) (1914–1918), Domestic Front (1914–1918), Ireland, file 15, interview with F. Lingwood, January 1971.
[22] ULL, Peter Liddle Collection, (First World War) (1914–1918), General Aspects (1914–1918), GS 1387, letter from Captain Round to his aunt, 11 May 1916
[23] ULL, Peter Liddle Collection, (First World War) (1914–1918), Domestic Front (1914–1918), Ireland, file 15, interview with F. Lingwood, January 1971.
[24] National Library of Ireland, Diary of Mary Martin, 5 May 1916.
[25] ULL, Peter Liddle Collection, (First World War) (1914–1918), General Aspects (1914–1918), G403, G.H. Crowe, Recollections, p. 6.
[26] SHD, Third Republic (1870–1940), Army Staff, 7N1254, letter from Colonel de la Panouse to the Minister for War, 28 April 1916.
[27] SHD, Third Republic (1870–1940), Army Staff, 7N1261, telegram from Colonel de la Panouse to the Minister for War, 1 May 1916.

scene of a tremendous holocaust of flames and smoke bellowing into the air'.[28] Casualties arising out of the rebellion amounted to a total of 116 officers and soldiers killed, 13 RIC officers and men shot, and 318 casualties among civilians and insurgents.[29] Investigations carried out in the aftermath of the Rising would subsequently lead to the dismissal of 25 public servants in connection with the insurrection.[30] Throughout Ireland, the rebellion initially met with little sympathy.[31] In the middle of the First World War, families of front-line soldiers fighting in the trenches of the Somme strongly resented an insurrection that was perceived as a stab in the back for all the Irish troops involved in the conflict. Civilians were highly critical of an uprising which was an indirect insult to the sacrifice of all front-line Irish officers and men who had lost their lives in Belgium, France and Gallipoli since the outbreak of the conflict. Out of the 1,082 men from the area who served in the British Army during the Great War, 528 were already serving in April 1916, 121 of whom had already been killed when the rebellion occurred.[32] This accounted for the violent reactions on the part of civilians who had already lost a loved one.

As they surrendered and marched past the smouldering ruins of Dublin, the rebels were booed and insulted by Dubliners: 'we passed through a number of hostile groups of people who shouted all sorts of things at us, including calling us "murderers" and "starvers of the people"'.[33] Crowds of women waited for the prisoners to pass by to insult them.[34] 'We would have been torn to pieces by the "separation" women who followed us shouting out abuse and obscene language. They were kept at bay by the soldiers',[35] recalled one prisoner. Widows, sisters or mothers of the dead shouted and spat at the prisoners. Women whose husbands were away fighting in the British Army lambasted the insurgents.[36] Writing from Dublin, on 6 May 1916, Jean des Longchamps never evoked any expression of popular support from local populations for the rebellion.[37] Constitutional

---

[28] Max Caulfield, *The Easter Rebellion* (Dublin: Gill & Macmillan Ltd, 1995), 230.
[29] TNA, CO 903/19, Chief Secretary's Office, Judicial Division, Intelligence Notes, 1916, p. 35.
[30] TNA, CO 904/25/1, Wilson-Byrne Committee on Sinn Féin Rebellion, 18 July 1917.
[31] Fearghal McGarry, *The Rising Ireland: Easter 1916* (Oxford: Oxford University Press, 2010), 277.
[32] Grayson, *Dublin's Great Wars*, 163.
[33] Military Archives of Ireland (hereafter MAI), Bureau of Military History, 1913–1921 (hereafter BMH), BMH, WS340, witness statement from Oscar Traynor, 24 January 1950, p. 24.
[34] MIA, BMH, WS388, witness statement from Joe Good, member of the Irish Volunteers, 19 May 1950, p. 20.
[35] MAI, BMH, WS805, witness statement from Lilly Curran, 3 May 1963, p. 10.
[36] Padraig Yeates, *A City in Wartime, Dublin 1914–1918* (Dublin: Gill & Macmillan, 2012), 233–234; Grayson, *Dublin's Great Wars*, 123–124.
[37] AD, Political and Commercial Correspondence, Great War, 1914–1918, Ireland, 1CPCOM/545, letter from Jean des Longchamps to the Minister for Foreign Affairs, 6 May 1916.

nationalism had offered the Irish a viable framework for their aspirations, and even though the 1916 rebels sought to counter the achievements of the Irish Parliamentary Party, esteeming that devolution was nothing less than an imperial policy, during Easter Week 1916 nationalist Ireland remained loyal to John Redmond.

On the Western Front and on the Somme, the response of the Irish battalions varied enormously.[38] Irish troops condemned the rising, their reaction to the insurrection mirroring both that of Dubliners and civilian populations in Ireland as a whole. Irish soldiers stationed on the Somme 'would [have] like[d] nothing better than to see the rebels sent to the front'.[39] 'Shoot the lot of them straight off!',[40] screamed a private. 'Exterminate the blighters',[41] shouted regular soldiers. Nationalist volunteers who had enrolled in the British Army to fight against Germany also lamented the rebellion. 'I will never forget the men's indignation. They felt they had been stabbed in the back',[42] confessed one fervent supporter of Redmond with the Connaught Rangers. William Redmond, brother of the leader of the Irish Parliamentary Party, collapsed on hearing news of the Rising, 'sobbing bitterly like a child'.[43] On the Somme, regular Irish troops of the British Expeditionary Corps and volunteers from the 16th (Irish Division) and 36th (Ulster) Division worried for their relatives.[44] Although Home Rule had been granted royal assent in September 1914, many nationalist followers feared that a direct consequence of the rebellion would be to jeopardize the tense negotiations between the Irish Parliamentary Party and the British Government. As far as the Unionists were concerned, the rebellion represented a further act of treason on the part of the south, at a time when the British Empire was engaged in a vital struggle. Nonetheless, the executions of the ringleaders brought about a split among Irish units, as men reacted differently to the repression.

---

[38] For some details on the diverse responses of Irish units to the Easter Rising see Timothy Bowman, *Irish Regiments in the Great War. Discipline and Morale* (Manchester: Manchester University Press, 2003), 127–131; Grayson, *Dublin's Great Wars*, 164; Yeates, *A City in Wartime*, 236–238.

[39] Dublin City Library and Archives (hereafter DCLA), Monica Roberts Collection, Vol. I, RDFA/001/01, Joseph Clarke to Monica Roberts, 11 May 1916.

[40] DCLA, Monica Roberts Collection, Vol. IV, RDFA/001/2, George Soper to Monica Roberts, 20 May 1916.

[41] ULL, Liddle Collection (First World War) (1914–1918), General Aspects (1914–1918), GS 0253, Memoirs of Second Lieutenant Butler, 27 April 1916.

[42] Jane Leonard, 'The reaction of Irish officers in the British army to the Easter Rising of 1916', in *Facing Armageddon: The First World War Experienced*, ed. Cecil Hugh and Peter Liddle (London: L. Cooper, 1996), 263.

[43] Terence Denman, *A Lonely Grave: The Life and Death of William Redmond* (Dublin: Irish Academic Press, 1995), 97.

[44] DCLA, Monica Roberts Collection, Vol. II, RDFA/001/14, Christopher Fox to Monica Roberts, 31 May 1916.

On the Somme, loyalist troops rejoiced when they learned of the executions of the ringleaders.[45] However, for some Irish battalions, the news of the sentence passed on the rebels revolted them. Faithful followers of the Irish Parliamentary Party condemned the executions. One sergeant with the 2nd Royal Irish Rifles disagreed with the harshness of the sentences.[46] Harry Loughlin, an Irish soldier with a British Expeditionary Force unit, confessed: 'I did not in the least sympathize with the sentences passed upon the Sinn Féiners.'[47] Several volunteers went as far as to call into question their part in the war effort on the British side: 'It was a rude awakening, guns being fired at the people of my own race by soldiers of the same army with which I was serving.'[48] In this respect, the reactions of nationalist front-line soldiers to the executions of the 1916 ringleaders mirrored the transformation over time of Irish public opinion. Despite their conflicting responses to Easter Week, the unfaltering loyalty towards the Crown and honour of the Irish troops did not weaken the internal organization of the battalions. '[N]o acts of indiscipline occurred in the Irish regiments as a result of the Rising',[49] which was enough to reassure the British Government.

Aftermath and executions: the transformation of Ireland?

It is often argued that the failed military insurrection paved the way for the transformation of the country.[50] There is indeed 'a consensus that the suppression of the rebellion was the key factor in the transformation of public opinion after the Rising'[51] and that the Rising radicalized Irish nationalist communities. When British authorities responded with coercive measures and executed the ringleaders, it operated a shift in popular opinion.[52] Even though historians have disagreed on the importance of the executions, they nonetheless agree in considering that Easter Week 1916 paved the way for the political accession of Sinn Féin.[53]

---

[45] Emmanuel Destenay, 'The Impact of Political Unrest in Ireland on Irish soldiers in the British army, 1916–1918: a re-evaluation', *Irish Historical Studies* 161, no. 2 (2018): 58.
[46] John Lucy, *There's a Devil in the Drum* (London: Faber & Faber, 1938), 352.
[47] DCLA, Monica Roberts Collection, Vol. I, RDFA/001/02, Harry Loughlin to Monica Roberts, 17 June 1917.
[48] Tom Barry, *Guerrilla Days in Ireland* (Dublin: Irish Academic Press, 1949), 1.
[49] Bowman, *Irish Regiments in the Great War*, 131.
[50] F. S. L. Lyons, *Ireland since the Famine* (Dublin: Fontana Press, 1973), 381.
[51] McGarry, *The Rising Ireland*, 264.
[52] Thomas Hennessey, *Dividing Ireland: World War I and Partition* (London: Routledge, 1998), 237.
[53] Tansill, *America and the Fight for Irish Freedom*, 196.

'In all fairness', wrote Paul Cambon, when the insurrection broke out, 'English public opinion did not really worry. Everyone knew the Sinn Féin attempt could not succeed and the history of Ireland has unfortunately accustomed England to consider with cold blood the violence that breaks out periodically in the island.'[54] Given that the rebellion took place while Great Britain and the British Empire were fighting a vital war, General Maxwell, Ireland's Military Governor, responded with an unprecedented level of violence and ordered the execution of fifteen prisoners.[55] Between 3 and 12 May, prominent rebels were executed in Dublin. On 3 May 1916, three were shot at dawn in a yard at Kilmainham Gaol.[56] On 4 May, more executions were carried out. All the condemned men were allowed to see priests shortly before their execution, and one of them, Joseph Plunkett, even married his fiancée in the chapel of the prison. All of them died facing British firing-squads. Seventeen other court-martials were commuted to penal servitude. Redmond's determination to prevent further bloodshed did not deter Maxwell from executing another man, John MacBride, on 5 May and on 8 May, four more rebels were executed.[57]

Meanwhile, representatives of the Irish Parliamentary Party sensed that untold damage had already been done and begged the House of Commons to prevent Maxwell from carrying out further atrocities. That did not prevent Sir John Lonsdale, a staunch Unionist, to request the immediate implementation of conscription to Ireland.[58] On 11 May 1916, Dillon warned the Prime Minister that more executions would infuriate civilian populations.[59] He sought to undermine the authority of the Prime Minister, arguing that prisoners were being executed without trial: 'You are doing everything conceivable to madden the Irish people and to spread insurrection – perhaps not insurrection, because if you disarm the country there cannot be insurrection – but to spread disaffection and bitterness from one end of the country to the other.'[60]

Laurence Ginnell, an Independent Nationalist MP, speaking in the House of Commons, was scathing in his comments about the Prime Minister, arguing

---

[54] AD, Political and Commercial Correspondence, Great War, 1914–1918, Ireland, 1CPCOM/545, telegram from Paul Cambon, Ambassador of France to England, to the Minister for Foreign Affairs, 12 May 1916.
[55] Grayson, *Dublin's Great Wars*, 163–176; Townshend, *Easter 1916*, 269–299.
[56] Townshend, *Easter 1916*, 279.
[57] Lyons, *Ireland since the Famine*, 377.
[58] Jérôme aan de Wiel, *The Catholic Church in Ireland, 1914–1918: War and Politics* (Dublin: Irish Academic Press, 2003), 116.
[59] Hansard, House of Commons Debates, series 5, vol. 82, cc935, Dillon to House of Commons, 11 May 1916.
[60] Ibid.

that recruitment in Ireland and the unnatural alliance between John Redmond and Edward Carson had not undermined the thirst to avenge Ireland of its past sufferings:

> You wanted our young men to remember the German atrocities – they prefer to remember yours in our country. You wanted our young men to remember Belgium – they prefer to remember Ireland. They remember how time and again in the past you decimated them by fire and sword, pitch-cap, and gibbet, and coffin ships.[61]

Dillon lamented that the British were gradually alienating the Irish from the war effort.[62] The following day, in Dublin, on 12 May 1916, another rebel, James Connolly, received Holy Communion before being executed. By then, General Maxwell had refused the right of burial in consecrated ground for the body of Patrick Pearse.[63]

From Washington, the Consul for France reported that 'many people believe[d] the English would be well advised if they could benefit from the present situation and avoid increasing the number of martyrs'.[64] Initially, there was little sympathy for the leaders of the Easter Rebellion in the United States.[65] Broadly speaking, the American papers regarded the Rising as 'foolish and misguided'.[66] *The New York Times* criticized the 'treacherous and perfidious'[67] conduct of the rebels in wartime. More moderate, but nevertheless opposed to the uprising, the *Washington Star* concluded that 'every friend of Ireland and the Irish people must deeply deplore the lamentable blunder of revolution'.[68] The *Chicago Tribune* refrained for being too openly vehement, simply expressing the viewpoint that the rebels were not advancing the cause of Ireland.[69] Nevertheless,

---

[61] Hansard, House of Commons Debates, series 5, vol. 82, cc969, Ginnell to House of Commons, 11 May 1916.
[62] Hansard, House of Common Debates, series 5, vol. 82, cc940, Dillon to House of Commons, 11 May 1916.
[63] Robert Kee, *The Green Flag. A History of Irish Nationalism* (London: Weidenfeld & Nicolson, 1972), 574.
[64] AD, Political and Commercial Correspondence, Great War, 1914–1918, Ireland, 1CPCOM/545, telegram from Jean des Longchamps to the Minister for Foreign Affairs, 25 May 1916.
[65] Tansill, *America and the Fight for Irish Freedom*, 202. For recent work on the diverse responses to Easter Week among Irish-American circles see Michael Doorley, *Irish-American Diaspora Nationalism. The Friends of Irish Freedom, 1916–1935* (Dublin: Four Courts Press, 2005) and his recent monograph *Justice Daniel Cohalan, 1946–1965. American Patriot and Irish-American Nationalist* (Cork: Cork University Press, 2019).
[66] Francis M. Carroll, *American Opinion and the Irish Question, 1910–1923. A Study in Opinion and Policy* (Dublin: Gill & MacMillan, 1978), 57; Alan J. Ward, *Ireland and Anglo-American Relations, 1899–1921* (Toronto: University of Toronto Press, 1969), 101–125; Stephen Hartley, *The Irish Question as a Problem in British Foreign Policy, 1914–1918* (New York: St Martin's Press, 1987), 50–78.
[67] *The New York Times*, 26 April 1916.
[68] *Washington Star*, 1 May 1916.
[69] *Chicago Tribune*, 2 May 1916.

Maxwell's unflinching determination to execute fifteen rebels had not only generated strong protest within Ireland, it had also aroused the dismay of Irish-American communities.[70] The profound transformation of Irish-American public opinion mirrored the evolution of public opinion in Ireland.[71] Stephen MacFarland, President of the Irish League of New York, immediately sent a cable to John Redmond, on 4 May 1916, in which he expressed his entire support.[72] Senator James D. Phelan sent a letter to Joseph P. Tumulty, Secretary to President Wilson, in which he protested against the executions of Irish rebels and demanded that Wilson intervene.[73] Senators and Congressmen framed resolutions and called on the British to recognize the rebels as prisoners of war, rather than criminals, which was sufficient to indicate that the US Senate regarded the executions as excessive.[74]

On 14 May 1916, 4,000 people gathered in Carnegie Hall in New York City to pay their respect to the fallen.[75] The following day, from Philadelphia, Michael J. Ryan, President of the United Irish League of America, warned Redmond that the executions had alienated every Irish-American.[76] On 16 May 1916, Shane Leslie, one of the editors of the weekly periodical entitled *Ireland*, a strong advocate of Home Rule and follower of the Irish Party, reported to Redmond that the 'present wave of fury sweeping through Irish-America originated with the executions and not with the rising. The rising only called out sympathy for you, except in a small circle. The executions enabled that circle to spread their ripples further than they had hoped or dreamed.'[77] Even though Wilson was hindered/underpinned by 'diplomatic protocol from speaking out publicly about Ireland',[78] he nonetheless lectured British representatives in private, urging them to refrain from shedding more Irish blood. Similarly, the fate of three Americans who had participated in the rebellion and been sent to jail in Wales permitted the US President to appeal to the British Government.

---

[70] Elizabeth McKillen, 'Ethnicity, Class and Wilsonian Internationalism Reconsidered: The Mexican-American Immigrant Left and U.S. Foreign Relations, 1914–1922', *Diplomatic History* 25, no. 4 (2001): 573.
[71] Carroll, *America and the Making of an Independent Ireland*, 12.
[72] MacFarland to John Redmond, quoted in Denis Gwynn, *The Life of John Redmond* (London: Harrap, 1932), 485.
[73] Library of Congress (hereafter LC), Woodrow Wilson Papers (1786–1957), letter from Senator James D. Phelan to Joseph P. Tumulty, 22 May 1916.
[74] Carroll, *America and the Making of an Independent Ireland*, 16.
[75] *The New York Times*, 15 May 1916.
[76] Michael J. Ryan to John Redmond, quoted in Denis Gwynn, *The Life of John Redmond*, 500.
[77] Shane Leslie to John Redmond, quoted in Denis Gwynn, *The Life of John Redmond*, 500.
[78] Carroll, *American Opinion and the Irish Question*, 18.

Benefit concerts were organized to 'raise money to assist in rebuilding portions of Dublin and provide support to families who had lost loved ones'.[79] The Wilson administration lent its full support to the Irish National Aid Association and 'intervened positively in Irish affairs' in the aftermath of the uprising.[80] However, while Wilson backed relief for Ireland, this should not be interpreted as a disguised support for the rebels. Indeed, relief for Ireland could as well be interpreted as a condemnation of the destruction of the city, and who were to blame if not the 1916 rebels? In addition, Wilson had roots in Ulster, had always refrained from joining any Irish-American association and firmly believed in sustainable Anglo-American diplomatic relations.[81] Wilson's determination to help needs to be seen as a political, as well as strategic, move: so-to-speak to make sure Wilson could 'retain the loyalty of the Irish American community, a crucial element of the Democratic Party coalition in 1912'.[82]

The Ambassador for the United Kingdom to the United States reported this change in American public opinion. On 19 May 1916, Sir Cecil Spring-Rice wrote to Sir Edward Grey: 'I fear that recent events have alienated from us almost the entire Irish Party.'[83] From Washington, Jusserand noted that the 1916 insurrection, and the Irish national cause generally, was being compared to that of the thirteen colonies in the proclamation of their independence from Britain in 1776.[84] Ambassadors Cambon and Jusserand, along with Colonel de la Panouse, maintained that the executions had triggered a shift in Irish public opinion. (However, they did not highlight the fact that the repression of the leaders had brought about a reconfiguration of the Irish political landscape.) France's representatives tended to focus their comments on the role of General Maxwell. Notwithstanding the brutal mishandling of the rebellion, the uprising itself did not appear to come in for any considerable degree of support.[85] The executions of the ringleaders and the numerous deportations caused popular agitation and, in the immediate aftermath of the rebellion, the crux of the matter

---

[79] Carroll, *America and the Making of an Independent Ireland*, 20.
[80] Bernadette Whelan, *United States Foreign Policy and Ireland: From Empire to Independence, 1913–1929* (Dublin: Four Courts Press, 2006), 119.
[81] Robert Schmuhl, *Ireland's Exiled Children. America and the Easter Rising* (Oxford: Oxford University Press, 2016), 74–117.
[82] Carroll, *America and the Making of an Independent Ireland*, 21.
[83] Denis Gwynn, ed., *The Letters and Friendships of Sir Cecil Spring-Rice: A Record* (Boston: Houghton Mifflin Co., 1929), Vol. 2, 331.
[84] AD, Political and Commercial Correspondence, Great War, 1914–1918, Ireland, 1CPCOM/545, telegram from Jean Jusserand to the Minister for Foreign Affairs, 18 May 1916.
[85] SHD, Third Republic (1870–1940), Military Headquarters (1914–1918), 16N2968, telegram from Colonel de la Panouse to General Joffre, Commander-in-Chief of French Forces, 19 June 1916.

was in fact the manner in which the British Government had dealt with the situation.

In June 1916, Colonel de la Panouse described Sinn Féin as a latent element of agitation in the country, identifying it as a focus for all the underlying discontent throughout the island. 'At this moment in time, all the Irish youth, most of Irish women, and almost all the intellectuals have pledged allegiance to Sinn Féin',[86] he wrote. A delegation of French bishops visited Ireland between 3 and 20 June 1916 and received a warm welcome from their Irish counterparts in Maynooth, Dublin and Cork.[87] The idea originated from Jean des Longchamps.[88] In April 1916, a few days before the uprising, he had suggested a plan aimed at helping recruitment and countering German propaganda in Ireland.[89] The Quai d'Orsay, concerned with a possible rising in Ireland, adopted his plan in the hope that it would encourage the Irish to contribute to the war effort. The Quai d'Orsay had decided to rely upon the clergy to organize a campaign of propaganda in favour of recruitment, knowing full well that France was closely associated with the British and that only through religion could the French approach and convince Irish public opinion. A comprehensive memorandum was sent to the French Minister for Foreign Affairs, with detailed accounts of their encounters with the Irish clergy:

> The proclamation of the Irish Republic had provoked sarcasm and protest from the immense majority of the Irish. The executions of the fifteen ringleaders, followed by a large campaign of house searches [...] turned the rebellion into a sympathetic event for a large number of people. [...] A Professor from University College Cork admitted: "Before the shooting, my students did not bother with politics. Today, they are all Sinn Féiners". Anderson, President of University College Galway, admitted: "Not even two of my students are not Sinn Féiners. And women are worse!"[90]

Hearsay, rumour and gossip nourished the post-1916 collective imagination. As is borne out by the correspondence from representatives of the United States and France, the executions clearly inflamed nationalist Ireland. In the aftermath of the rebellion, the Consul for France in Dublin and France's military attaché to

---

[86] Ibid.
[87] Aan de Wiel, *The Catholic Church in Ireland*, 144–152.
[88] AD, Political and Commercial Correspondence, Great War, 1914–1918, Great Britain, 1CPCOM/546, telegram from Jean des Longchamps to the Minister for Foreign Affairs, 30 September 1915.
[89] AD, Political and Commercial Correspondence, Great War, 1914–1918, Ireland, 1CPCOM/545, telegram from Jean des Longchamps to the Minister for Foreign Affairs, 18 April 1916.
[90] AD, Political and Commercial Correspondence, Great War, 1914–1918, Ireland, 1CPCOM/545, French Mission to Ireland, 3–20 June 1916.

London even went as far as concluding that 'Easter Week 1916 had ruined the hopes of the Irish Parliamentary Party'.[91] 'It is no longer a question of Home Rule. One could rightly argue Ireland has stepped back 50 years and is now back to the old Fénian times',[92] added Cambon. However, the immediate reaction of civilian populations in the aftermath of the uprising did not (and Cambon would later on indirectly admit having been too categorical on this point) necessarily mean that people had sided or would side with Sinn Féin. Anger and bitterness resulting from the executions of the 1916 ringleaders were equally shared by supporters of the Irish Party. And even though the executions inflamed nationalist public opinion, there was no tangible evidence to show that they had strengthened Sinn Féin.

Partition: ongoing deadlock and critical solutions

The idea that the 1916 insurrection and the subsequent executions had swung Irish opinion away from constitutional nationalism in favour of a republican separatist agenda was described by one historian as 'a most misleading oversimplification'.[93] What proved to be damaging for the Irish Parliamentary Party's future was ultimately neither popular agitation nor the handling of the martyrs of Easter Week, but a growing suspicion that even though Home Rule had been placed on the statute book, the British had never had the intention of implementing it and if they did, that partition would follow.

What the rebellion did give was 'a new and desperate urgency'[94] to the question of Home Rule. By 1914, the Home Rule Act had been signed by the British monarch and suspended for the duration of the entire conflict. At that time, Home Rule had been acknowledged without any mention of partition, for any part of Ulster. While the raising of the unionist paramilitary organization (the UVF) clearly illustrated the categorical refusal of the loyalist populations to pledge their allegiance to a parliament in Dublin controlled by the Irish Parliamentary Party, in 1914, the Home Rule Act still provided assurance for the expectations of the constitutional nationalist MPs.

---

[91] SHD, Third Republic (1870–1940), Military Headquarters (1914–1918), 16N2968, telegram from Colonel de la Panouse to General Joffre, Commander-in-Chief of French Forces, 22 June 1916.
[92] AD, Political and Commercial Correspondence, Great War, 1914–1918, Ireland, 1CPCOM/545, telegram from Paul Cambon to the Minister for Foreign Affairs, 3 May 1916.
[93] Kee, *The Green Flag*, 591.
[94] Ibid.

On his return from Ireland on 25 May 1916, the Prime Minister announced in the House of Commons that

> the present system of government in that country had hopelessly broken down, and that the Cabinet had unanimously requested the Minister of Munitions, to bring about, if possible, a provisional settlement of the Irish question by consent, everyone I think of all parties in this country was thrilled by the hope that in the interests not only of Ireland, but of the Empire, the Irish question might be put out of the way, at any rate until the War had concluded.[95]

In the aftermath of the insurrection, in June 1916, the country witnessed the first attempt to reach a political compromise between Ulster Unionists and Irish Nationalists. John Redmond committed himself whole-heartedly to this venture. A proposition was then drafted, calling for the immediate application of Home Rule for Ireland. Lloyd George (Minister for Ammunitions), in an effort to mediate between Nationalists and Unionists, sought to devise a Janus-faced rhetorical compromise that could accommodate both sides. By deliberately holding separate meetings with Carson and Redmond,[96] Lloyd George developed a narrative that could match the expectations of both Ulster Unionists and the members of the Irish Parliamentary Party. Out of 'pre-meditated duplicity',[97] the British Prime Minister gave written assurances to Carson that the border would be permanent while simultaneously giving his word to Redmond that partition would be on a temporary nature. At some point, clarifications would be needed. Ulster Unionists held out for the exclusion of their entire province, composed of nine counties, while the Nationalists objected and pressed for the entire island to be granted political autonomy. In the end, Carson felt the need for political reasons to concede that three of the nine Ulster counties where an important Catholic population lived, would be better left out. Carson believed that the exclusion of the six northern counties would be permanent, while Redmond was led to think exclusion was to be temporary. On 23 June 1916, at the Ulster National Convention in St. Mary's Hall Belfast, MP Joseph Devlin delivered a speech in support of Lloyd George's proposals: 475 delegates voted in favour and 265 against.[98] A protest

---

[95] Hansard, House of Commons Debates, series 5, vol. 84, cc1428, John Redmond to House of Commons, 24 July 1916.
[96] Michael Laffan, *The Resurrection of Ireland. The Sinn Féin Party, 1916-1923* (Cambridge: Cambridge University Press, 1999), 58.
[97] Éamon Phoenix, *Northern Nationalism: Nationalist Politics, Partition and the Catholic Minority in Northern Ireland, 1890-1940* (Belfast: Ulster Historical Foundation, 1994), 22.
[98] Anthony Hepburn, *Catholic Belfast and Nationalist Ireland in the Era of Joe Devlin, 1871-1934* (Oxford: Oxford University Press, 2008), 179.

meeting took place in Derry on 20 July 1916 and opposition rapidly spread through other counties, such as Tyrone and Fermanagh.[99] Delegates from Fermanagh, Tyrone and Derry City overwhelmingly (68 per cent) voted against the proposals.[100] That day, the anti-partition league (to be known as the Irish National League)[101] was created as the clergy mobilized against partition.[102] Even though there was much and angry opposition to partition, even on a temporary basis, Redmond and Devlin eventually persuaded a majority of northern nationalists to accept, for now, the latest British proposals.[103]

On 22 July 1916, Lloyd George eventually informed Redmond of the Cabinet's decision that the proposed partition of the island was to be permanent.[104] In his address to the House of Commons on 24 July 1916, the representative of the Irish Parliamentary Party reminded the House that 'the agreement was, in the words of the Prime Minister himself, for what he called a provisional settlement which would last until the War was over, or until a final and permanent settlement was arrived at within a limited period after the War'.[105] Redmond deplored the duplicitous rhetoric of the British Government, which had informed him, a few days earlier, that 'another Cabinet Council had been held, and that it had been decided [...] to insert in the Bill two entirely new provisions, one providing for the permanent exclusion of Ulster, of the six Ulster counties'.[106] Redmond publicly accused the government of endangering the future of Home Rule and putting at risk the security of the British Empire.[107]

The same political shift infuriated Nationalists as well as Unionists, gravely damaging Asquith's policy of compromise. While Carson consented to partition, dissonant voices arose among the unionist community. *The Irish Times*, the organ of unionism in Ireland, objected to partition, arguing that 'Ireland must be a self-governing unit'.[108] The *Irish Independent*, the leading newspaper for nationalist opinion, wrote that the prospect of partition had stirred up 'a thrill of horror and amazement'.[109] It even invited the leader of the Irish Parliamentary

---

[99] Laffan, *The Resurrection of Ireland*, 58.
[100] R. B. McDowell, *The Irish Convention, 1917–18* (London: Routledge & Kegan Paul, 1970), 53–54.
[101] David Miller, *Church, State and Nation in Ireland, 1898–1921* (Dublin: Gill & Macmillan, 1973), 342–343.
[102] Aan de Wiel, *The Catholic Church in Ireland*, 118–119.
[103] Phoenix, *Northern Nationalism*, 29.
[104] Aan de Wiel, *The Catholic Church in Ireland*, 121.
[105] Hansard, House of Commons Debates, series 5, vol. 84, cc1429, John Redmond to House of Commons, 24 July 1916.
[106] Ibid.
[107] Ibid.
[108] *The Irish Times*, 27 June 1916.
[109] *Irish Independent*, 6 July 1916.

Party to resign: 'there are men enough left in Ireland still to carry on the constitutional fight'.[110] That comment brought to light the unprecedented disappointment and rage which the question of partition aroused. It has been argued that following the July 1916 crisis over the permanent or temporary exclusion of the six Ulster counties,[111] the issue of partition brought about a radical change in Ireland and paved the way for the political accession of Irish radical nationalism precisely because the Irish Party 'was losing touch with the grass roots'.[112] It is indeed perfectly true that leading churchmen (such as Edward O'Dwyer and William Walsh) adopted a more radical stance, and looked towards Sinn Féin as a future political alternative. It made perfect sense that northern MPs belonging to the Irish Party deplored that the party did not seem to find credible solutions to several crises. However, the provocative suggestion that Redmond needed to step down in no sense implied any switch to endorsing of revolutionary methods; 'the constitutional fight' had to be carried on. Throughout the country, it was alleged that, in order to please Ulster Unionists, Redmond was actively and secretly signing the future dismemberment of Ireland. The negotiations in the summer of 1916 testified to the inability of the Irish Party to reach a settlement and subsequently 'had important long-term effects'.[113] As late as December 1916, the RIC Inspector-General reported that the Irish party 'ha[d] not got over the feeling of distrust occasioned by the failure of the Home Rule Conversations'.[114] While nationalist Ireland could reasonably hope for the implementation of Home Rule, public opinion realized, overnight, that Home Rule now implied a divided Ireland and that six counties were to be sacrificed. The original Home Rule Bill never referred to partition or to the possibility of having two distinct and separate constitutional entities on the island. However, the reaction of Ulster Unionists in 1913, followed by the creation of a paramilitary organization, had given clear notice of the need to acknowledge that the north would object by all necessary means to Home Rule.[115] As soon as the negotiations started, Jean des Longchamps received confidential information that Carson had succeeded in protecting northern loyalist populations and that Redmond needed to accept a temporary partition of the country.

Des Longchamps insisted that 'the separation of Ulster from the rest of the country constituted a serious disadvantage for Ireland which would then be

[110] Ibid.
[111] Hepburn, *Catholic Belfast and Nationalist Ireland*, 179.
[112] Aan de Wiel, *The Catholic Church in Ireland*, 114.
[113] Laffan, *The Resurrection of Ireland*, 61.
[114] TNA, CO, 904/101, Inspector General's report, December 1916.
[115] Lyons, *Ireland since the Famine*, 305.

deprived of its most industrialised region'.[116] From a northern Irish point of view, Ulster depended strongly on agricultural produce from the south and in the eventuality of a partition, the six counties would still remain acutely dependent on southern Ireland. Furthermore, taxation and economic policies would entirely be conditioned to the establishment of a parliament in Dublin. The situation would remain provisory, which would offer nationalist deputies the possibility of claiming that partition would only be temporary, until the end of the European war. Most importantly, 'would Sinn Féin keep on offering a breathing space to nationalist leaders?'[117] By June 1916, Jean des Longchamps already anticipated future heated disputes between constitutional Nationalists and Sinn Féin leaders. In pondering the future move of Sinn Féin, the Consul foresaw that the issue of partition would possibly revive Sinn Féin and turn it into a significant platform for political opposition.

Overnight, the British Government crystallized popular resentment. Redmond was left trapped in a pincer movement. The Irish MPs faced the same dilemma if they were to avoid losing their followers to Sinn Féin, while at the same time ensuring they managed to reach an acceptable settlement with the British.[118] As soon as a settlement seemed plausible, two major issues arose. From now on, extreme elements in the country supported by the turbulent part of the population would systematically oppose the Irish Parliamentary Party. All dissatisfied and ambitious factions of the Irish population were waiting to swoop down on Redmond at the first occasion.[119] On the other side, unionist representatives feared losing the support of their anti-Home Rule population in Ulster. 'That abrupt shift'[120] illustrated the intransigent position of unionist members of the Cabinet who, out of fear of losing the support of their party in Ulster, refused to endorse the Asquith project. A few days after the meeting in the House of Commons, on 3 August 1916, Roger Casement was hanged in Pentonville Prison in London.

In the US, Wilson was being publicly attacked for not interceding in British domestic policy. On 30 September 1916, Jeremiah A. O'Leary, a New York-based Irish American, president of the American Truth Society, published a diatribe

---

[116] AD, Political and Commercial Correspondence, Great War, 1914–1918, Ireland, 1CPCOM/545, telegram from Jean des Longchamps to the Minister for Foreign Affairs, 24 June 1916.
[117] Ibid.
[118] AD, Political and Commercial Correspondence, Great War, 1914–1918, Ireland, 1CPCOM/545, telegram from Paul Cambon to the Minister for Foreign Affairs, 12 May 1916.
[119] SHD, Third Republic (1870–1940), Army Staff, 7N1253, telegram from Colonel de la Panouse to the Minister for War, 13 July 1916.
[120] AD, Political and Commercial Correspondence, Great War, 1914–1918, Ireland, 1CPCOM/545, telegram from M. Comert to M. Berthelot, 27 July 1916.

against Wilson.[121] Aware that 'hyphenated groups', among them Irish-Americans and German-Americans, hoped to question his legitimacy as President of the US, Wilson answered back that he 'would feel deeply mortified to have [them] or anyone like [them] vote for [him]'. He went on: 'Since you have access to many disloyal Americans and I have not, I will ask you to convey this message to them.'[122] Wilson's public denunciation of O'Leary operated as a turning point in the campaign, and helped Wilson get re-elected. He was nonetheless 'reminded that the Irish question had not gone away'.[123]

Procrastination and the end of the old administrative regime

Paul Cambon, Colonel de la Panouse and Jean des Longchamps all insisted that immediate action was required. De la Panouse maintained that the old administrative governance of Ireland had tumbled down and needed to be replaced by a provisional government until the definite creation of a new government in accordance with the Home Rule Bill.[124] He believed the problem could only be solved through the reshaping of the framework for British rule in Ireland. The Consul for France to Dublin agreed in his assessment with that of France's military attaché to London, blaming the British Government for its laissez-faire approach to the Irish question. According to the Consul, the uprising had stemmed from the 1913 crisis, and he argued that there was a continuity between the raising of the Ulster Volunteer Force, the manner in which the British had been crippled by the reaction of Ulster to the Home Rule Bill, and the subsequent outbreak of the rebellion in Dublin. By 1913, the diplomat contended that the British had shown their weakness – and had done so publicly. Coupled with the laissez-faire policy, it could be no surprise that a minority of activists had seized the opportunity to rise against the Empire. Carson was believed to be entirely responsible for the evolution of the events in Ireland. He had been the first to import weapons to Ireland to arm the Ulster Volunteer Force. Ulster's violent reaction to the imminence of Home Rule had in turn led to the creation of the Irish Volunteers. Des Longchamps pointed to the responsibility of both the UVF and the Irish Volunteers in the insurrection,

---

[121] *The New York Times*, 30 September 1916.
[122] Ibid.
[123] Carroll, *America and the Making of an Independent Ireland*, 22.
[124] SHD, Third Republic (1870–1940), Military Headquarters (1914–1918), 16N2968, telegram from Colonel de la Panouse to General Joffre, Commander-in-Chief of French Forces, 22 June 1916.

arguing that, had it not been for the insurrectional unrest in Ulster in 1913, and the insurrectional paramilitary organization on the part of the Irish Volunteers, Easter Week 1916 might not have witnessed a rising.[125] Reading between the lines, the implication is that two political blunders had been made by the British. First of all, they had been unable to silence Ulster refusal of Home Rule, showing unmistakable signs of weakness in dealing with the Curragh mutiny. Secondly, they had not been able to disarm either the Irish Volunteers or the UVF.

When the June negotiations collapsed, the French regretted the fact that the solution presented to both nationalist and unionist leaders had not been drafted far earlier: 'after three months of procrastination, the British Government ended up adopting a solution they could have applied to Ireland from the very first day'.[126] As the situation worsened, France's representatives to London and Dublin gradually witnessed the weakening of the authority of the Prime Minister. The Irish question had weakened Asquith and completely undermined the British Government. Critiques of the Irish Parliamentary Party sprang up almost everywhere. However, the recrudescence of Sinn Féin in its most aggressive form was matched by the determined pugnacity of John Redmond.[127] Following the revelation by Asquith that the British Government was contemplating a permanent partition of the island, Redmond had immediately shaped a narrative that was intended to counter such a decision. At that time, Sinn Féin offered nothing more than what the Irish Parliamentary Party had fought for. Redmond publicly declared he would be opposed to a permanent partition of the island. A few months later, in October 1916, the British authorities released Sinn Féin prisoners who had been jailed for their participation in the rebellion. As soon as they returned to Ireland, some of them began to orchestrate large meetings throughout the island, delivering seditious speeches which publicly advocated a German victory. 'Out of the 1800 arrested Sinn Féiners, more than 1000 have been released. They behave poorly',[128] wrote a French Catholic bishop. The nature of their speeches was an illustration of the fact that in October 1916, any patent opposition to the British Government's position (with the exception of that

---

[125] AD, Political and Commercial Correspondence, Great War, 1914–1918, Ireland, 1CPCOM/545, telegram from Jean des Longchamps to the Minister for Foreign Affairs, 2 June 1916.
[126] AD, Political and Commercial Correspondence, Great War, 1914–1918, Ireland, 1CPCOM/545, telegram from Paul Cambon to the President of the Council, 7 August 1916.
[127] SHD, Third Republic (1870–1940), Army Staff, 7N1253, telegram from Colonel de la Panouse to the Minister for War, 9 August 1916.
[128] AD, Political and Commercial Correspondence, Great War, 1914–1918, Ireland, 1CPCOM/545, mission of the French bishops to Ireland, 7–14 October 1916.

voiced by the Irish Parliamentary Party) was a channel for sentiments and alignments that were anti-British, anti-Allies, and pro-German.

Conclusion

In October 1916, Colonel de la Panouse had advocated the immediate implementation of Home Rule for the twenty-six counties. In this, he was displaying a complete disregard for the position of the Irish Parliamentary Party, stemming from the conviction, in the light of all the efforts deployed by Ulster Unionists to resist Home Rule, that the loyalist north would never be coerced to consent to the authority of a parliament in Dublin. While they did fully understand the need to secure the agreement of the Irish Parliamentary Party, France's representatives reckoned that the British Government had no choice but to go forward with the immediate implementation of Home Rule (albeit in an imperfect form). In October 1916, the British could decide to do nothing, or they could decide to establish a new administrative regime for the twenty-six counties. As the negotiations had reached a deadlock and it appeared Asquith was refusing to take any further action, the British Government agitated the threat of conscription for Ireland. It thus offered Sinn Féin its first possibility through which it could gradually politically challenge the Irish Parliamentary Party. Such a move gave a further impetus to Sinn Féin. As will now be argued, the blurring distinction between Sinn Féin and the Irish Parliamentary Party occurred a few weeks later, not because of Easter Week 1916 and a possible partition of Ireland, but because of conscription.

3

All Changed, Changed Quietly (October 1916–March 1917)

Traditional frameworks of interpretation have been effective in mystifying the uprising, foregrounded as the determining factor in the radicalization of nationalist Ireland during the war, and portraying it as the pivotal and irreversible turning point in twentieth-century Irish history. Reports drafted by France's representatives did not however depict the rebellion as a decisive moment in the shifting mood of nationalist Ireland during the period. While a climate of unrest did exist in the aftermath of the insurrection it did not necessarily testify to a willingness to support Sinn Féin. Open unrest did not necessarily mean that the people involved had sided or would side with Sinn Féin. Everything indicated that after the executions of the ringleaders, the temper of the country had gradually cooled down, only to be inflamed once again in October 1916 when conscription emerged as a serious topic in debates at the House of Commons. France's representatives pointed to evidence of the growing popularity of Sinn Féin from October 1916 onwards. While they noted the spread of unrest throughout the country, they were more circumspect in pinpointing of the reasons for the growing discontent among civilian populations. The conviction of French observers was that the mood of unrest and apprehension within Ireland had twofold sources: the incapacity of the British Government to take action, along with the threat of conscription.

October 1916 and the threat of conscription

In October 1916, the question of conscription was beginning to transform the course of Irish history.[1] On 18 October 1916, during a meeting at the House of

---

[1] Michael Laffan, *The Resurrection of Ireland. The Sinn Féin Party, 1916–1923* (Cambridge: Cambridge University Press, 1999), 128. Michael Laffan has claimed that widespread fears that Irishmen would be conscripted had appeared from the very beginning of the war. While he provides compelling

Commons, John Redmond warned the British that the situation of the country was serious and required nothing less than the immediate overhaul of the existing provision for the government of Ireland.[2] He insisted that conscription would be unthinkable without the formal and explicit consent of the Irish people.[3] Overnight, whereas Ireland had been spared from the Military Service Bill a few months earlier, substantive grounds for mistrusting the position of the Irish Parliamentary Party was now emerging throughout Ireland. The threat of conscription would gradually condition a swing in the popular mood among rural communities predominantly made up of landowners, farmers and labourers, and all those who were dependent on the predominantly agrarian economy of nationalist Ireland.

From the beginning of the war, economic prosperity had ensured tacit support for the British war effort. A few days after the 1916 uprising, Jean des Longchamps had reported that 'the income of the farmers had increased significantly and contributed to make them more pacific'.[4] He had nonetheless warned that a growing anti-British mentality remained, an undercurrent there to be revived in the countryside at the first opportunity.[5] In December 1916, the Consul Manager for France in Dublin, who was replacing Jean des Longchamps, drew up a report on the socioeconomic situation of Ireland since the beginning of the Great War. Underlining first the geographical isolation of the island that had spared the country's civilian populations from the atrocities, displacements and starvation endured elsewhere, he maintained that the years 1915 and 1916 were a period of prosperity for Ireland.[6] Cattle-rearing increased by 2.6 per cent, sheep-farming by 4.5 per cent and horse-breeding by 6.8 per cent. Irish agricultural production commanded high prices on the British market. In 1911, 1912 and 1913, the total annual value of all agricultural goods exported from

---

details in charting the way activists from various backgrounds joined Sinn Féin and successfully defeated the Irish Party in by-elections, his three-page sub-section dealing with conscription provides no evidence, in spite of the author's impressive marshalling of archival sources, that conscription did indeed arouse widespread concerns from the beginning of the war.
[2] Hansard, House of Commons Debates, series 5, vol. 86, cc581, John Redmond to House of Commons, 18 October 1916.
[3] Hansard, House of Commons Debates, series 5, vol. 86, cc590–591, John Redmond to House of Commons, 18 October 1916.
[4] Archives Diplomatiques du Ministère des Affaires Étrangères, La Courneuve (hereafter AD), Political and Commercial Correspondence, Great War, 1914–1918, Ireland, 1CPCOM/545, telegram from Jean des Longchamps to the Minister for Foreign Affairs, 6 May 1916.
[5] AD, Political and Commercial Correspondence, Great War, 1914–1918, Ireland, 1CPCOM/545, telegram from Jean des Longchamps to the Minister for Foreign Affairs, 6 May 1916.
[6] AD, Political and Commercial Correspondence, Great War, 1914–1918, Ireland, 1CPCOM/546, telegram from Armany, Consul Manager of France to Dublin, to the Minister for Foreign Affairs, 18 December 1916.

Ireland amounted to £28,500,000. By 1914, it reached £30,000,000. In 1915, the overall value of Irish agricultural production for the British market amounted to £39,000,000 and for the first half of 1916 alone, the value of these exports to Britain totalled to £20,000,000. By December 1916, the British Government had already bought up the entire 1917 production of linen. 'Overall', concluded the Consul, 'the prosperity of the farmers was such that they did not need to resort to banks to obtain loans.'[7]

However, when portraying the socioeconomic situation in Ireland, the Consul distinguished between the agricultural sector and the working classes. While factories in Belfast and Londonderry had registered orders from the British Government, in some parts of the country charities had to provide assistance to low-income workers and to women who were awaiting the end of their training period in order to be approved for work in ammunition factories. From his correspondence, it appears that workers tended to look to revolutionary paramilitary movements (and the Consul recalled the support of the working classes for the lock-out in Dublin in 1913) whereas rural populations reaped the benefits of the conflict. France's Consul pointed to the fact that farmers and other members of Ireland' agricultural communities could overnight be turned into a reservoir for the country's revolutionary movements. Hence the need, for the duration of the war, to ensure that they should not be provoked into discontent. Even though isolated elements did manage to stage demonstrations and defy the British Government openly by the end of 1916, such initiatives were, in the opinion of the Consul, sporadic and isolated, under no circumstances the embodiment of the prevailing popular mood in Ireland. During the war, exports of Irish goods to Great Britain improved the standard of living of agrarian populations. Compared to an average £40,000,000 of deposits in Irish banks in the period prior to the war, the total value now amounted to £64,000,000, a sign that 'money ha[d] been circulating among rural populations as never before.'[8]

In many sections of the population, economic prosperity, the absence of compulsory service and the promise of Home Rule were all factors contributing to the widespread climate of indifference to the political climate in the country. Sergeant Burke, Intelligence Officer of the Midlands and Connaught, offered the following, prudent assessment of the social repercussions of the war, contending that the outbreak of the conflict had in no sense stirred up any degree of

---

[7] Ibid.
[8] AD, Political and Commercial Correspondence, Great War, 1914–1918, Ireland, 1CPCOM/546, telegram from Alfred Blanche to the Minister for Foreign Affairs, 26 January 1918.

'enthusiasm for the Allied cause among the farming and shop keeping class, and in fact, except to make money as long as the War last[ed], many profess[ed] they [did] not care who wins the war'.[9] He went on: 'Most of the farmers do not care if Home Rule is passed; they only want to make money, avoid serving in the army and be left to their own devices.'[10] Six months after the 1916 rebellion, these communities were still enjoying buoyant incomes. However, the prospect of conscription was gradually leading to a climate of mistrust and opposition. When the British authorities started to seriously consider how conscription could be implemented in Ireland, the war, from being a far-away and almost imaginary event, began to loom as an ominous – and imminent – possibility. Overnight, the fear of being drafted began to lend substance to the risk of violent protest in Ireland.

Opposition to conscription first manifested itself in the form of passive resistance. Local populations openly declared their objection to conscription, without however making a definite move towards supporting Sinn Féin. Resistance to conscription remained a matter for verbal misgivings. This in turn led to a revival of anti-British sentiment, offering another pretext for some young men 'to spend their time hatching mischief or brooding over old wrongs which their forefathers [had] suffered under English rule'.[11] Agitation mainly came from young men 'who in ordinary times would emigrate to the USA.'[12] Faced with the impossibility of emigrating, these young men dreaded being forcibly enrolled in the British Army. The impossibility of emigrating left the country host to a population of 'steaming young men',[13] who were causing continual unrest, admitted one constable.

Before the House of Commons met on 18 October 1916, the climate of widespread and growing apprehension that conscription would soon apply to the island was brought to the attention of the British authorities. In September 1916, the RIC Inspector in Kilkenny reported that young farmers, shop assistants, and artisans 'dread[ed] the idea of conscription'.[14] His counterpart in West

---

[9] The National Archives (hereafter TNA), Colonial Office (hereafter CO), CO 904/157/1, Reports of the State of the Country, 1916–1918, Report from Sergeant Burke, Intelligence Officer, Midlands and Connaught District, 28 February 1917.
[10] TNA, CO 904/157/1, Reports of the State of the Country, 1916–1918, Report from Sergeant Burke, Intelligence Officer, Midlands and Connaught District, 30 January 1917.
[11] TNA, CO 904/157/1, Reports of the State of the Country, 1916–1918, Items 224–225, Midlands and Connaught District, October 1916.
[12] Ibid.
[13] TNA, CO 904/157/1, Reports of the State of the Country, 1916–1918, Item 50, Southern Command, March 1918.
[14] TNA, CO 904/101, Inspector's report, Kilkenny, September 1916.

Galway admitted that local populations feared being drafted overnight to serve in the British Army.[15] The Intelligence Officer of the Southern District reported that the national press 'remained friendly but [was] carrying on active opposition against conscription'.[16] To quote just one of a significant ranges of examples, *The Longford Leader*, in its 30 September 1916 issue, devoted an entire article to the question of compulsory service:

> England is now out in full cry for the Conscription of the remnant of the Irish Race left in Ireland. Great Britain is now in full cry like a pack of ravenous wolves to sweep the few thousands of young men left here into the military maw and send them to be slaughtered. They want the flower of the Irish manhood wholly exterminated in order that later on they may more easily rule Ireland.[17]

Captain Whitfield, Intelligence Officer for the Northern District, warned the British Government that 'the feeling against conscription [was] strong, and there [was] a real fear of it'.[18] In more rural and agricultural districts, discontent and disloyalty was 'limited almost entirely in the country to the sons of farmers, and in the towns to shop assistants; the former largely through fear of conscription'.[19] Popular unrest arose from 'the fear of being taken from comfortable homes to fight under any flag',[20] wrote one RIC Inspector from Connaught, where the peasantry and other civilian populations dreaded being drafted into the British Army. A shift in the attitude of local civilian populations thus did unquestionably occur, something that had not been experienced in the immediate aftermath of the rebellion. In September 1916, Captain Dickie, in his capacity as Intelligence Officer of the Southern District, had already alerted the authorities that 'if universal service [was] enforced, it [would] meet with considerable opposition. The Roman Catholic clergy, the local members of parliament, the press, the Gaelic Societies and the Volunteer Bodies [would] oppose it strongly'.[21]

Between 7 and 14 October 1916, a delegation of French bishops visited Ireland and fraternized with Roman Catholic priests there. Additional evidence

---

[15] TNA, CO 904/101, Inspector's report, West Galway, October 1916.
[16] TNA, CO 904/157/1, Reports of the State of the Country, 1916–1918, Report from Captain Dickie, Intelligence Officer, Headquarters, Southern District, Cork, 30 October 1916.
[17] *Longford Leader*, 30 September 1916.
[18] TNA, CO 904/157/1, Reports of the State of the Country, 1916–1918, Report from Captain Whitfield, Intelligence Officer, Headquarters, Northern District, 30 October 1916.
[19] TNA, CO 904/157/1, Reports of the State of the Country, 1916–1918, Report from Sergeant Sandbach, Intelligence Officer, Midlands and Connaught District, 3 October 1916.
[20] TNA, CO 904/157/1, Reports of the State of the Country, 1916–1918, Report from Sergeant Burke, Intelligence Officer, Midlands and Connaught District, 31 October 1916.
[21] TNA, CO 904/157/1, Reports of the State of the Country, 1916–1918, Report from Captain Dickie, Intelligence Officer, Headquarters, Southern District, Cork, 30 October 1916.

from the bishops following their stay supports the claim that October 1916 operated as a turning point. They came to the same conclusions: the fear of conscription had aroused unrest all over the island. Monseigneur Touvet (Bishop of Orleans), Monseigneur Lenfant (Bishop of Digne), M. Batiffol (Chanoine of Notre-Dame) and Patrice Flynn (curé de Suresnes), all acknowledged that civilian populations and the Roman Catholic clergy had taken a strong stand against any military service act. The bishops noted the threat of conscription provided a significant boost to Sinn Féin. 'For the moment,' wrote the representative of the French bishops, 'England is reluctant to impose conscription, as it would give rise to widespread resistance.'[22]

The anti-conscription unrest was at times tainted by a whiff of pro-German propaganda. On 7 October, a meeting took place in Tullamore during which the organizers enjoined people to shout 'Long Live the Kaiser.'[23] Anti-conscription agitation thus merged with pro-German feelings, something also reported by Colonel de la Panouse: 'I was told that women deliberately insult soldiers in the streets and that in movie theatres people clap their hands for the enemy and boo the Allies, King George, his ministers and the military.'[24] According to the testimony of the French bishops and France's military attaché to London, British soldiers came to be singled out and frequently had to face a barrage of verbal insults from civilians. Nevertheless, such sporadic acts of hostility and pro-German sympathies were not characteristic of the overall climate in nationalist circles. Organizations within local communities, along with the Catholic clergy, who since the outbreak of the war, had remained faithful to the Irish Parliamentary Party, still pledged their support to John Redmond.

Opposing conscription, supporting Redmond

Concerns about conscription arose throughout Ireland among shopkeepers, workers, and labourers. However, this did not throw the Irish into the arms of Sinn Féin. Roman Catholic priests were active in countering Sinn Féin propaganda and remained loyal to the Irish Parliamentary Party (the Irish Party). In October 1916, the RIC Inspector of the Midlands and Connaught

---

[22] AD, Political and Commercial Correspondence, Great War, 1914–1918, Ireland, 1CPCOM/545, mission of the French bishops to Ireland, 7–14 October 1916.
[23] Ibid.
[24] Service Historique de la Défense, Vincennes (hereafter SHD), Third Republic (1870–1940), Army Staff, 7N1253, telegram from Colonel de la Panouse to the Minister for War, 30 October 1916.

underlined that in many places, 'the priests came out and aided the RIC in keeping the rebels in check'.[25] Even though the vast majority of the Irish people were hostile to conscription, that did not mean they agreed with the strategy of armed demonstrations endorsed by the Irish Volunteers.

Organizations such as the United Irish League pledged their unconditional support for John Redmond and vowed to help the Irish Party to resist forced enrolment. At the beginning of October 1916, 270 people gathered to oppose conscription in Parke (County Roscommon).[26] On 15 October, in Drumcong (County Leitrim), 230 civilians attended a meeting of the United Irish League during which support for the Irish Parliamentary Party was advocated and conscription condemned. On 10 November, in Kilkerrin (County Galway), a similar demonstration was held, during which members of the United Irish League reiterated their support for the Irish Parliamentary Party. In Cortoon, the local branch of the United Irish League urged support for Redmond and condemned conscription.[27] During these meetings, backing for the Irish Parliamentary Party was clearly aligned with the issue of opposing conscription. While the aim of the United Irish League was clearly to make a display of its support for the Irish Parliamentary Party, the topic addressed in such meetings was nonetheless a patent sign that conscription represented a potential threat.

In September, October and November 1916, the usual daily newspapers relayed ongoing debates about a possible compulsory military service, while insisting on the need to send more men to the front. When another conscription scare plagued the island, the newspapers that usually supported the Irish Party displayed an unaltered loyalty towards the party. One MP fought publicly at a meeting to reassure local populations that 'there [would] be no conscription, owing to the Irish Party'. He swore he would lose his life before allowing 'a man to be taken'[28] while acknowledging that John Redmond had always supported recruitment since the outbreak of the war. In East Galway, an important resolution was passed by the Mount Bellew District Council, asking John Redmond to ensure that men would not be conscripted because the few people now remaining were needed to 'till the land and produce food for the nation'.[29] The *Donegal Independent* preferred to publish a letter to the editor entitled 'The Conscription Menace' in which it was stated that in England people were

---

[25] TNA, CO 904/157/1, Reports of the State of the Country, 1916–1918, Items 224–225, Midlands and Connaught District, October 1916.
[26] TNA, CO 904/21/3, Ireland: Dublin Castle Record, National Organizations, 9 November 1916.
[27] TNA, CO 904/21/3, Ireland: Dublin Castle Record, National Organizations, 12 November 1916.
[28] *Kilkenny Moderator and Leinster Advertiser*, 14 October 1916.
[29] *Roscommon Messenger*, 30 December 1916.

infuriated by the fact that Irishmen were treated differently while 'their sons and brothers ha[d] been already taken, and their fathers, the older men, [were] threatened'.[30] Several 'conscription scares' agitated rural populations but the Irish Party was always regarded as the saviour, the one that would protect farmers' sons and labourers from forced enrolment. Even after the Rising, the press relayed speeches and resolutions from MPs against conscription. Clearly the Irish Party between August 1914 and the end of 1916 was positioned as the only political opposition to conscription, while openly advocating recruitment. A thorough analysis of France's representatives and of the private reports of police inspectors clearly reveal that the question over conscription alarmed local populations. This is the reason why a distinction must be drawn between political concerns over partition (likely to embitter the Irish Party, Sinn Féin and the élites in general) and the dread to be forced to serve in the British Army (likely to infuriate rural and other civilian populations).

In November 1916, the first by-election since Easter Week 1916 took place in West Cork. In spite of the aggressive rhetoric of the anti-Redmond Home Rule candidate, the Redmondite candidate won. Bearing in mind the outcome of the first by-election after the rebellion, at a time when Redmond and the Irish Parliamentary Party found themselves in a delicate position as a result of the fall-out from the discussions on the possible introduction of conscription in Ireland, it can be better understood that discontent, protest and popular unrest had not (yet) managed to boost popular support for Sinn Féin. Not only did their candidate not secure victory, he actually came last in the poll.[31] In September 1916, one member of the Irish Parliamentary Party bitterly regretted that 'enthusiasm and trust in Redmond and the party [was] dead so far as the mass of the people [was] concerned'.[32] However, this peremptory judgement on the part of John Dillon was arguably motivated by the latter's rivalry with John Redmond. The indications at the end of 1916 were that it was clearly wrong. The Irish Parliamentary Party secured a victory a few weeks later. Neither Easter Week 1916 and its aftermath, nor the fears of conscription were enough to compromise the party's position as the political channel for the demands and aspirations of nationalist Ireland.

In December 1916, Lloyd George became Prime Minister of the United Kingdom and decided to free all 1916 prisoners. It has been claimed that this was

---

[30] *Donegal Independent*, 2 December 1916.
[31] *Irish Independent*, 15 November 1916.
[32] F. S. L. Lyons, *John Dillon: A Biography* (London: Routledge & Keagan Paul, 1968), 403.

the 'first step in the revival of the separatist movement'.[33] However, it did not cause great enthusiasm in Ireland 'even though there were some cheers for them at the quayside and on arrival at their homes'.[34] Certainly conscription was an ominous issue and a source of bitterness in nationalist Ireland. However Redmond, voice of nationalist Ireland, voiced his clear condemnation. He did not however dispose of any great political leeway to contest and oppose a possible decision by the British Government in this regard. Indeed if he were to save Home Rule, he had no alternative but to reiterate his opposition to conscription. Even in the eventuality of a Dublin parliament in accordance with the provisions of the Home Rule Act, conscription could still be applied to Ireland. When it was envisaged to grant Home Rule to Ireland immediately, this meant that conscription would inevitably follow. Home Rule then appeared contingent to conscription. Politically speaking, the Asquith Cabinet expected to grant Home Rule only to impose conscription on the Irish. In short, voluntary recruitment since August 1914 was no longer enough and the British were accused, and rightly so, of adding another condition to the Home Rule project.

This being said, by January 1917, civilian populations still regarded the Irish Party as the only viable opposition to conscription. On 1 January, in Kiltyferrigle (County Donegal), Rev. A. Gallagher strongly advocated support for the Irish Party and protested against conscription. So as to resist the introduction of a military service act, the Irish population was urged to back John Redmond and his party. On 14 January, in Kilbannon (County Galway), Rev. Father Waldron exhorted local people to form a committee for the purpose of agreeing on the most effective means for increasing the amount of land allocated to tillage in the coming spring. While the initial goal of the speech was to reassure farmers and labourers as to the next harvest, the vexed issue of conscription coloured the discussions. Father Waldron warned his flocks not to do anything that would be unlawful, suggesting that 'the government would never pass conscription'. Conscription, in his view as a member of the Catholic clergy, spoke for the willingness of the British to punish the Irish people, in the eventuality of there being unrest. Agitation, unrest, and any other threats to public order would, he warned, be dealt with through the introduction of military service in Ireland. In an attempt to assuage the fears of the members of the United Irish League, Father Waldron recalled 'the Irish had given a good deal of recruits' and if recruitment continued, England would not implement

---

[33] Laffan, *The Resurrection of Ireland*, 77.
[34] Robert Kee, *The Green Flag. A History of Irish Nationalism* (London: Weidenfeld & Nicolson, 1972), 595.

conscription. That very same month, in Drumkeeran (County Leitrim), Reverend P. McMorrow and F. E. Meehan, MP, appealed to the people to support the United Irish League, advising them to till as much as possible, thus making a contribution to the war effort to defeat Germany. Agricultural issues in particular relating to harvests did not however eclipse the persistent question as to whether the British would consider introducing conscription. During this meeting, in front of 300 people, Reverend McMorrow moved a motion of confidence in the Irish Parliamentary Party and called on Redmond to resist conscription.[35] As strong supporters of Redmond, the Catholic hierarchy adopted a line of argument according to which conscription was a disciplinary measure that would be envisaged by the British authorities should unlawfulness prevail in the country.

The decline in recruitment

In the eventuality of the introduction of conscription, religious, military and political authorities in Ireland all knew that widespread resistance was bound to follow. As early as June 1916, Jean des Longchamps had warned the French Minister for Foreign Affairs that 'its application in Ireland would certainly lead to a general uprising'.[36] From October 1916 onwards, conscription became a recurrent concern. By that time, 57,583 Catholic and 47,147 Protestant recruits had already enrolled in the British Army to take part in the war.[37] Due to the losses after the terrible battles on the Somme, approximately 40,000 men were needed in order to preserve the existing Irish divisions.[38] At that time, 300 volunteers were joining the British Army every week. The British authorities considered that a figure of 1,100 recruits per week, 4,400 each month, were required in order to offset the shortage of manpower. At that time, many RIC Inspectors stated that few recruits were being obtained,[39] and Colonel de la Panouse personally informed the Quai d'Orsay that recruitment was not satisfactory.[40] In January 1917, police inspectors submitted reports regarding the

[35] TNA, CO 904/21/3, Ireland: Dublin Castle Record, National Organizations, 8 January 1917.
[36] AD, Political and Commercial Correspondence, Great War, 1914–1918, Ireland, 1CPCOM/545, telegram from Jean des Longchamps to the Minister for Foreign Affairs, 2 June 1916.
[37] SHD, Third Republic (1870–1940), Army Staff, 7N1254, letter from Colonel de la Panouse to the Minister for War, 13 October 1916.
[38] AD, Political and Commercial Correspondence, Great War, 1914–1918, Ireland, 1CPCOM/545, mission of the French bishops to Ireland, 7–14 October 1916.
[39] TNA, CO 904/157/1, Reports of the State of the Country, 1916–1918, Report from Captain Whitfield, Intelligence Officer, Northern District, Irish Command, 30 October 1916.
[40] SHD, Third Republic (1870–1940), Army Staff, 7N1253, letter from Colonel de la Panouse to the Minister for War, 13 October 1916.

trends for recruitment in their respective counties. In County Carlow, since the outbreak of the conflict, recruitment had, overall, 'been very bad' and 'was now almost nil'.[41] In County Cavan, recruitment had fairly been satisfactory up to the outbreak of the 1916 insurrection, 'but since then it had been practically at a standstill'.[42] In County Cork, recruitment was 'practically dead'.[43] The executions of the 1916 leaders coupled with allegations in the press concerning the excessive use of force by the military in reprisal had aroused 'a great amount of sympathy with the rebels amongst people' and directly weakened the spirit of volunteering. 'Up to the date of the rebellion recruiting was fair, but since then very few recruits have joined, and there is no sign of matters improving in this respect',[44] admitted the RIC Inspector. The County Kilkenny RIC Inspector reached the same conclusion. In his view, the number of recruits registering had been excellent prior to the rebellion; since April their number had gradually diminished.[45]

By December 1916, there were 100,000 objectors who could be drafted into the army. 'The British Government hesitates in adopting a measure that would solve the situation', wrote France's military attaché, 'but they are willing to save Ireland and they acknowledge that to end protest and agitation conscription would not necessarily be the most violent means and could be an advantageous remedy'.[46] Even though the Irish had answered the call to arms in large numbers since the outbreak of the conflict, the British hoped to recruit a further contingent of volunteers. Between August 1914 and February 1915, over 50,000 volunteers had enrolled in the British Army.[47] By 1916, 95,143 Irishmen had enlisted.[48] During the entire conflict, 134,202 recruits volunteered for the war (approximately 6 per cent of the entire male population of the island).[49] While bearing in mind that in 1916 the British Government imposed conscription in Great Britain, it is nonetheless worth pointing out that during the course of the First World War 24

---

[41] TNA, CO 904/120/11, Reports on the State of Counties as January 1917, Report of Crime Special Branch (County Carlow), 21 February 1917.
[42] TNA, CO 904/120/11, Reports on the State of Counties as January 1917, Report of Crime Special Branch (County Cavan), 16 January 1917.
[43] TNA, CO 904/120/11, Reports on the State of Counties as January 1917, Report of Crime Special Branch (County Cork), 24 January 1917.
[44] TNA, CO 904/120/11, Reports on the State of Counties as January 1917, Report of Crime Special Branch (County Galway), 24 January 1917.
[45] TNA, CO 904/120/11, Reports on the State of Counties as January 1917, Report of Crime Special Branch (County Kilkenny), 23 January 1917.
[46] SHD, Third Republic (1870–1940), Army Staff, 7N1254, letter from Colonel de la Panouse to the Minister for War, 15 December 1916.
[47] Fergus Campbell, *Land and Revolution: Nationalist Politics in the West of Ireland, 1891–1921* (Oxford: Oxford University Press, 2005), 196.
[48] Patrick Callan, 'Recruiting for the British Army in Ireland during the First World War', *The Irish Sword* 66 (1987): 42.
[49] *Statistics of Military Effort of the British Empire during the Great War* (London: HMSO, 1922), 363.

per cent of the male population of England went to war, 23.7 per cent of Scots fought in the conflict while 21.5 per cent of the Welsh male population experienced fighting. Compared to the overall population of the three nations, this represented 11.5 per cent of the population of England, 11.5 per cent of the Scottish population and 10.9 per cent for Wales.[50]

The end of 1916 and the first weeks of 1917 were not marked by any notable differences compared to the previous months. While the threat of conscription continued to infuriate the Irish, RIC Constables did not deplore an increase in the number of seditious incidents in their reports, some evidence of passive resistance notwithstanding. On 31 December 1916, Sergeant Burke, Intelligence Officer of the Midlands and Connaught, pointed out that 'the dread of conscription [was] the only cause of discontent the people have'.[51] In January 1917, the Northern District remained 'in a peaceful state'.[52] One RIC Inspector even underlined that there were 'symptoms that the wild wave of enthusiasm which came into being after the rebellion [was] passing away to some extent'.[53] While acknowledging the difficulties encountered in recruiting volunteers, RIC Inspectors went on to note that relations between the military and civilians were satisfactory. In February 1917, in County Kerry, the RIC Inspector underlined that the attitude of people towards injured men who returned from the front was friendly.[54] At that time, in County Kilkenny, wounded demobilized men and discharged soldiers maintained good relations with local civilians. Relations between loyal sections of the community, nationalist sympathisers and the military 'was all that could be desired'.[55]

Far from being challenged, by 1917 the Irish Party enjoyed popular legitimacy. When the German unrestricted submarine warfare began to threaten everyday agricultural production, the Irish Parliamentary Party strongly encouraged farmers and labourers to cultivate more food in order to preserve Ireland from starvation.[56] Indeed, it was no longer possible to rely upon imports in order to compensate potential crop failures and food shortage. By January 1917, rural

---

[50] Ibid.
[51] TNA, CO 904/157/1, Reports of the State of the Country, 1916–1918, Report from Sergeant Burke, Intelligence Officer, Midlands and Connaught District, 31 December 1916.
[52] TNA, CO 904/157/1, Reports of the State of the Country, 1916–1918, Report from Captain Whitfield, Intelligence Officer, Northern District, 29 January 1917.
[53] Ibid.
[54] TNA, CO 904/120/11, Reports on the State of Counties as January 1917, Report of Crime Special Branch (County Kerry), 22 January 1917.
[55] TNA, CO 904/120/11, Reports on the State of Counties as January 1917, Report of Crime Special Branch (County Kilkenny), 23 January 1917.
[56] Gallagher, *Ireland and the Great War*, 73–82.

communities dreaded the possibility of food shortage but trusted the Irish Party and expanded food production as requested, another evidence of the ability of the Irish Party to reach out to rural populations.[57]

The North-Roscommon by-election: the twilight of Sinn Féin

By the beginning of 1917, in order to properly distance itself from the Irish Parliamentary Party, Sinn Féin devised a new narrative according to which Easter Week 1916 was not only a rising against British rule in Ireland, but a protest against conscription. By deliberately suggesting that the 1916 rebels had deterred the British Government from imposing conscription on Ireland in 1916, Sinn Féin legitimized the rebellion as a bloody protest against a military service bill.

A sense of cohesion and common purpose among disparate groups and organizations emerged during the North-Roscommon by-election campaign, thus reviving the fortunes of the separatist party.[58] While this may be the case, the presence in communities of the released 1916 prisoners, the reorganization of Sinn Féin, and the unrest within a predominantly agrarian community required some additional and tangible bogeyman to be fought against. As early as January 1917, a tactical ploy adopted by Sinn Féin was to associate the Irish Parliamentary Party with conscription. A vote for Redmond's nominee 'was a vote for conscription and for handing over the best of Ulster to Carson and his pets'.[59] Candidates of the Irish Parliamentary Party were impugned as 'England's faithful garrison'.[60] During the campaign for the North-Roscommon constituency, conscription represented a determining argument for Sinn Féin. At Strokestown, on 19 January 1917, Laurence Ginnell, MP, called upon the people of North-Roscommon to support Count George Plunkett.[61] Three of Plunkett's sons had participated in the 1916 rebellion; one (Joseph) had been executed, and the two others had been imprisoned in its aftermath. Anyone opposing him would do so

---

[57] John Horne, 'Our war, our history', in *Our War: Ireland and the Great War*, ed. John Horne (Dublin: Royal Irish Academy, 2008), 9.
[58] Laffan, *The Resurrection of Ireland*, 82.
[59] *Irish Independent*, 31 January 1917.
[60] Ibid.
[61] Descended from a prominent Old English family, which included Sir Oliver Plunkett, George's relatives included the earls of Fingall and the barons of Dunsany. His title of 'Count' did not come from his ancestry, however, but from the Vatican. In 1884 Pope Leo XIII created him a papal count for donating money and property to the Sisters of the Little Company of Mary, a Catholic nursing order.

'under cover of the Union Jack, Dublin Castle, and Martial Law'.[62] Beyond this implicit attack upon the Irish Parliamentary Party, the speaker certified that 'if elected Count Plunkett would prevent the young men of Ireland from becoming forced into the English Army'.[63] What the October 1916 debates in the House of Commons had made room for was the possibility for Sinn Féin to rekindle its attraction by presenting itself as the only plausible channel through which to oppose conscription. Most, not to say all, of the speakers in favour of Plunkett insisted that Redmond and the Irish Party 'were traitors and job hunters'.[64]

At Tarmonbarry, on 25 January 1917, Fr O'Flanaghan, C. C., denounced Redmond and the Irish Party. He went as far as to confess that 'the rebels of Easter Week had saved the country from conscription, and had it not been for them the young men he saw to-day would be shedding their blood in France and in Flanders'.[65] He pointed out that changes had been made in various commands since the outbreak of the war, and asked the audience 'was Ireland the only country which would continue riding the same old saw-bones?'[66] He focused on the fate of Irishmen from the 16th (Irish) and 36th (Ulster) Divisions who had lost their lives in France in order to prove to his audience that this could soon be the fate of every single male civilian in Ireland. What is particularly striking here is the new rhetoric consisting in the portrayal of Easter Week 1916 as a determining moment in the postponement of the implementation of conscription in Ireland. A few days later, at Elphin, Ginnell revived this same myth, reminding his audience that

> conscription applied elsewhere [and] would have been applied to Ireland but for the Irish Volunteers. If the Irish Party had had the manhood to insist upon complete self-government when John Bull was in a right place and could not afford to refuse it, they would have got it. As the result of Mr Redmond's actions thousands of Irishmen are buried to-day at the bottom of the Dardanelles, in Sulva Bay, and in the trenches of Flanders who ought to be at home breaking up the trenches of Roscommon.[67]

Here Redmond was explicitly portrayed as the politician who had not even been granted devolution for Ireland, despite sacrificing thousands of Irishmen. During the Battle of the Somme in 1916, armies on the Western Front had

---

[62] TNA, CO 904/23/3, Sinn Féin meetings, Report 'The Sinn Féin Movement', 1917, p. 4.
[63] Ibid.
[64] Ibid., p. 6.
[65] Padraig Yeates, *A City in Wartime, Dublin 1914–1918* (Dublin: Gill & Macmillan, 2012), 357.
[66] *Irish Independent*, 31 January 1917.
[67] TNA, CO 904/23/3, Sinn Féin meetings, Report 'The Sinn Féin Movement', 1917, p. 7.

suffered heavy losses. However, the military fiasco of the Dardanelles and the landing at Gallipoli in which the 10th Irish Division was involved occurred in 1915. The Irish had already come to terms with the sacrifices of their division abroad, and the casualties had not resulted in any significant growing surge for Sinn Féin. As Irish troops began to see action and casualties piled up following the landing at Gallipoli and the destruction of the 10th (Irish) Division, 'propagandists began to pity and mourn the loss of young Irishmen',[68] describing army volunteers as 'misguided fools who had been tricked into volunteering for certain death by recruiters'.[69] To portray them as the children of Ireland who had been misled was therefore not a new narrative in 1917. What changed was to claim that Easter Week 1916 had delayed conscription in Ireland, whereas by January 1916, Asquith had already decided *not* to include Ireland in the January 1916 Military Service Act. However, when coupled with the foregrounding of the martyrs of the battlefields of Belgium, France or Gallipoli, the denunciation of Redmond was not enough. What justifies our reservations as to our questioning the claim that it was the brutality of the repression in the aftermath of Easter Week 1916 which strengthened Sinn Féin is that there was virtually no mention of General Maxwell's unflinching resolution to execute the ringleaders during the course of the by-election campaign. The keynote of all the election meetings was the trenchant criticism of the Irish Parliamentary Party. And in this respect, the burning subject of conscription was what served to catch the attention of local populations. In Boyle, on 1 February 1917, Father O'Flanagan delivered an impassioned speech in which he asserted that 'the action of Count Plunkett's son and the other young men of Easter Week kindled a fire on the hills of Ireland which saved the young men from being conscripts'.[70] Easter Week 1916 had therefore, to his mind, saved the country from the threat of conscription. Numerous speakers argued that 'Sinn Féin Volunteers [had] saved [the Irish] from conscription!',[71] in what amounted to a loose and inaccurate association between the Irish Volunteers and the Sinn Féin party. In an area described as one that at any time 'experienced more agrarian unrest than almost any other part of the country',[72] conscription appeared a compelling question, capable of striking fear into farmers, labourers and peasants alike.

---

[68] Ben Novick, *Conceiving Revolution: Irish Nationalist Propaganda during the First World War* (Dublin: Four Courts Press, 2001), 51.
[69] Ibid., p. 58.
[70] TNA, CO 904/23/3, Sinn Féin meetings, Report 'The Sinn Féin Movement', 1917, p. 11.
[71] Ibid., p. 13.
[72] Laffan, *The Resurrection of Ireland*, 77.

In addition to opposing conscription, George N. Plunkett and his followers anticipated the end of the conflict and the shaping of a new post-war order. Plunkett, now running for election as a Sinn Féin candidate, put before the Roscommon electors the outlines of a choice. It hinged on the growing divergence between the original objectives of Sinn Féin and those of the Irish Parliamentary Party, and on the ideological conception of what the country was to become after the Great War. Plunkett was described as someone 'capable of representing Ireland at the International Peace Conference'.[73] A letter from a clergyman to the editor endorsed his viewpoint. In this and in other correspondence, Plunkett was referred to as 'Ireland's First Gentleman', who stood 'for Ireland and clearness in Irish political life'.[74] The clergyman (who wished to remain anonymous) recalled the visit to his prison in Richmond Barracks, a few days after his eldest son, Joseph, was executed. 'I said to him: "you surely have suffered for your country". His answer was a noble one: "Ah, yes, Father; but my country is well worth suffering for."'[75]

During the North-Roscommon election, members of the United Irish League (UIL) overwhelmingly supported the nominee of the Irish Party and published articles in which they re-asserted their trust in the Irish Party and in its capacity to oppose conscription.[76] In West Cork, the UIL tendered their thanks and gratitude to the Irish Party in preserving the country from conscription[77] while T. J. Devine, President of the North-Roscommon branch of the League, honoured the late M. O'Kelly, MP for North-Roscommon, in a tribute.[78] Galvanized by the support of the League, the Irish Party did not wait idly by and offered resistance to every fallacious accusation. In Swinford (County Mayo), John Dillon publicly challenged Sinn Féin propaganda: 'I tell you that neither the insurrection nor Sinn Féin could have saved Ireland from conscription if it had not been for the Parliamentary Party (cheers). We saved Ireland from Conscription in spite of all the difficulties.'[79] At another public meeting, another MP maintained that 'the Irish Party had defeated conscription'.[80] A largely attended meeting of the Young Ireland Branch of the United Irish League was held in Limerick to condemn the attack against the Irish Party and to remind the people of Ireland that that they

[73] *Irish Independent*, 31 January 1917.
[74] Ibid.
[75] Ibid.
[76] *The Roscommon Messenger*, 13 January 1917.
[77] *Weekly Freeman's Journal* (Dublin), 6 January 1917.
[78] *Freeman's Journal*, 2 January 1917.
[79] *Freeman's Journal*, 17 January 1917.
[80] *Irish Independent*, 7 February 1917.

did not know 'all that had been done by the Irish Party in opposing conscription'.[81] One of the most interesting tributes was written with the intention of humiliating Sinn Féin and its nominee: 'If Ireland stands firmly by the Irish Party it is quite possible that Ireland will be at least a self-governing nation before the end of the war (hear, hear).' The tribune ridiculed George N. Plunkett expressing the hope that 'not one elector in North Roscommon [...] would be carried away by fudge'.[82] Daily newspapers constantly relayed (and commented on the reactions) of the Irish Party, allowing its members to rebuke any accusations from Sinn Féin. The Irish Parliamentary Party restlessly published addresses in the press to discredit Sinn Féin.

Plunkett received 3,022 votes to 1,708 for Devine and 687 for Tully, and such result inspired other districts, also revealing how the election redirected and channelled aspirations throughout the whole of Ireland. 'What Roscommon did yesterday, Kilkenny would do to-morrow, if it got the chance',[83] promised one local newspaper. After the declaration of the poll, Plunkett announced that he would not sit in the House of Commons but would fight 'for the Irish people in Ireland'.[84]

A few days after his victory, on 12 March 1917, Plunkett arrived in Kilkenny where he was met at the railway station by the mayor and numerous civilians. A procession was then formed and about 1,800 people followed them to the hotel where Plunkett and Father O'Flanagan addressed the crowd from the windows of the hostel. In his capacity as newly-elected MP, Plunkett swore that he would not go to Westminster but would remain in Ireland. The following day, at a public meeting, he vowed to help capture the other eighty-two Irish seats in Parliament. Plunkett did not refer to the Irish Parliamentary Party, to the martyrs of Easter Week 1916, or to the dead soldiers buried on the Western Front or in Gallipoli. His speech focused entirely on the international recognition of Ireland's right to be independent:

> We want to make a good case for Ireland so that the cause of Ireland, as one of the small nations of the world, will get due hearing at the great peace conference which is to take place after the war. If we do not take the necessary steps and let the cause of Ireland be treated as a domestic question by an English parliament,

---

[81] *Freeman's Journal*, 1 February 1917.
[82] *Weekly Freeman's Journal* (Dublin), 8 February 1917.
[83] *Irishman*, 31 March 1917.
[84] Military Archives of Ireland (hereafter MAI), Bureau of Military History, 1913–1921 (hereafter BMH), WS722, witness statement from Dan McCarthy, former member of 'D' Company, 4th Battalion, Dublin Brigade, Irish Volunteers, 8 September 1952, p. 10.

when we seek admittance at the door of the Peace Conference we will be told that we have come to the wrong door.[85]

The issue of the oath of allegiance fused with the pledge to the goal of independence. There then followed an acknowledgement of the need for an international solution to the Irish question. And that was precisely the fault line between Sinn Féin and the Irish Parliamentary Party. Both formations objected to conscription (although compared to Redmond, Sinn Féin managed to channel the opposition to compulsory military service more successfully, so that it was not so closely associated with the British Government). However, Redmond had never imagined an independent Ireland and remained loyal to the framework of intra-UK devolution, and to Home Rule. Plunkett offered an alternative to the Irish. In addition to preserving their sons from the threat of forced incorporation into the British Army, Sinn Féin was holding out the promise of securing a seat at the future Peace Conference, where the demand for independence through self-determination would be granted through diplomatic means. The fact that Plunkett excluded the option of another military insurrection must not be neglected; with international peace would come independence for the Irish. Furthermore, even if the British backed off and offered an immediate implementation of Home Rule, devolution was now an old-fashioned and irrelevant framework of self-government. By March 1917, it was clear that anti-conscription rhetoric and narratives of self-determination at the Peace Conference were providing Sinn Féin with a strong platform on which they could build a new agenda.

On St Patrick's Day, in front of 2,800 people, after he had been presented the Freedom of the Borough of Sligo, Plunkett pledged that he would 'not accept anything short of a complete independence for Ireland'.[86] The argument that England had 'tried to enforce conscription upon Ireland, and were it not for the resolution of the Irish people, [Irishmen] would all be in the English Army to-day' was the crucial point to which Plunkett returned to (time and again) in his address to the audience. Indirectly referring to the martyrs of 1916, his speech sought to convince the crowd that conscription had been avoided through the action of the 1916 rebels. 'Now remember it was not the Parliamentary Party that saved you, it was the people of Ireland that saved themselves', he hammered home. At the same time, England was 'still hankering after the idea of still driving

---

[85] TNA, CO 904/23/3, Sinn Féin meetings, Report 'The Sinn Féin Movement', 1917, p. 16.
[86] Ibid.

the Irish people into the English army'. In order to illustrate England's thirst for additional manpower, Plunkett mentioned those who had gone to England to be employed at munition works but had subsequently been conscripted. Redmond had not been in a position to avoid this, nor would he have been in a position to mount a plausible opposition to conscription. And for this reason, Plunkett argued the Irish Parliamentary Party was nothing but a decomposing corpse. Most importantly, wrongs and mischiefs had been done to the Irish. There was nothing which could ever change that. However, the future of the Irish nation was not carved in stone. Redmond was painted as desperately clutching at the straw of Home Rule at a time when Sinn Féin was moulding its discourse and fashioning its goals in order to match the realities and the possibilities of the future post-war international order.

Conclusion

The North-Roscommon by-election has been described as a turning-point, one of 'the most important in modern Irish political history'.[87] In order to compete with the Irish Party, Sinn Féin developed a narrative according to which the Irish Parliamentary Party was the covert supporter of conscription for Ireland. Sinn Féin rekindled its attraction by presenting itself as the only plausible channel through which to oppose conscription, arguing that Easter Week 1916 was nothing but a counter-conscription rebellion which had saved the Irish youth from being drafted. This helped Sinn Féin attract the sympathy and active support of rural populations. While the issue of conscription explained why younger generations of Irishmen turned to Sinn Féin, the mistrust of the old constitutional party also needs to be taken into account. The political success of Sinn Féin lay in its ability to present conscription not only as a perfidious British strategy, but also as a policy which enjoyed the unofficial support of the Irish Parliamentary Party. However, it was not enough for Sinn Féin simply to oppose conscription. They needed to develop a new political manifesto. Sinn Féin held out the promise of a seat at the future Peace Conference. By doing so, they managed to make Home Rule appear an old-fashioned or obsolete project for the Government.

---

[87] Laffan, *The Resurrection of Ireland*, 77.

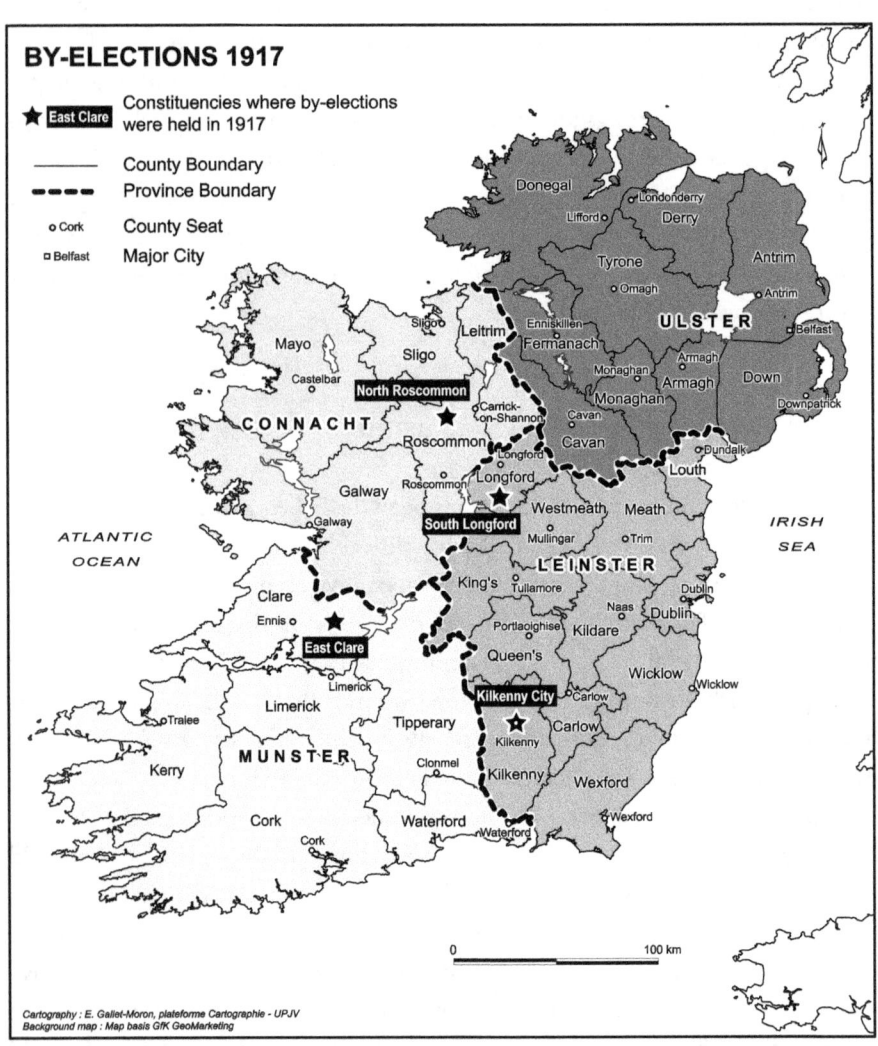

Map 4.1 Ireland and the four 1917 by-elections. Courtesy of Emilie Gallet-Moron.

4

Resisting Conscription, Redefining Ireland (March 1917–October 1917)

As previously seen (Chapter 3), debates over conscription aroused vehement opposition throughout the island. By March 1917, Sinn Féin increasingly fed on the popular opposition to conscription to discredit the Irish Party and portray its leader as the advocate of compulsion. Redmond and his followers left no stone unturned to counter these fallacious accusations but they did not succeed in preventing the seditious party from capturing the majority of votes during the North-Roscommon contest. During this election, Sinn Féin adapted its rhetoric in order to distance itself more clearly from the stance of Irish constitutional nationalism at the time. In advocating self-determination, they clearly gave an alternative to the Home Rule project. When the British organized the Irish Convention in July 1917, the initiative had the effect of further sealing the exclusive association between Redmond and the goal of Home Rule, allowing Sinn Féin to refashion its rhetoric to ensure its compatibility with Woodrow Wilson's call for the independence of stateless people. Once again, the real question remains to know what was likely to lead civilian populations to cast a vote for Sinn Féin. Were promises for complete independence the real incentives? Or were supporters of Sinn Féin primarily voting for the party to avoid conscription?

March 1917: the Home Rule controversy

As early as March 1917, it was being argued that 'the sudden resurrection of the Home Rule controversy ha[d] quickened interest in political matters amongst people of all shades of opinion and the nationalist press devote[d] most of their space to this subject. The Nationalist party ha[d] recovered a good deal of prestige by the truculent attitude they ha[d] assumed in the House of Commons.'[1]

---

[1] The National Archives (hereafter TNA), Colonial Office (hereafter CO), CO 904/157/1, Reports of the State of the Country, 1916–1918, Item 166, Southern District, March 1917.

While the Inspector of the Southern District insisted upon the ability of the constitutional party to make a stand against conscription, France's representatives remained dubious. They concluded that the noisy demonstration of the parliamentarians in the House of Commons on 7 March 1917 was a clear symptom of the threat which the Irish Parliamentary Party was now facing.

On 7 March 1917, William Redmond pleaded with the House of Commons to grant Ireland Home Rule 'in the name of men who [were] doing their duty; in the name of men who ha[d] died; in the name of men who [could] die, and who at this very moment [could] be dying'.[2] Irritated by the reluctance of the Prime Minister and the resistance of Ulster Unionists, John Redmond's brother pointed out that at the present time, Ireland remained the only country within the British Empire that had not been granted devolution.[3] Fully aware of the objections of the Unionist Party, he had prepared a speech in which he sought to isolate Carson and his followers, insisting that all over Great Britain people were demanding that a settlement be reached for the Irish:

> In God's name, why cannot you do it? I do not believe there is an Englishman in Europe who would not this very night agree to a full and free measure of Home Rule if the Irish people themselves would demand it. What stands in the way of a settlement? The attitude of a section of our countrymen in the North of Ireland! If you ask an Englishman, be he Liberal or Conservative, why Home Rule is not granted, the reply will be, "Home Rule we are ready to grant – every journal in England says so – if only you and your countrymen, North and South, can agree about it."[4]

While Lloyd George (now Prime Minister) acknowledged the call of the Irish Parliamentary Party and recognized the commitment of all the Irish who had volunteered for the war effort, he nonetheless maintained that a settlement had to be 'acceptable to both sections in Ireland'.[5] Lloyd George responded to the demands of the Irish MP by stating that it would be impossible to impose by force on any part of Ireland a form of government which Ulster did not want. Recalling the determination of Ulster to resist in 1914, and the refusal of his predecessor, Herbert Asquith, to use military force to coerce the North, the

---

[2] Hansard, House of Commons Debates, series 5, vol. 91, cc445, William Redmond to House of Commons, 7 March 1917.
[3] Hansard, House of Commons Debates, series 5, vol. 91, cc446, William Redmond to House of Commons, 7 March 1917.
[4] Hansard, House of Commons Debates, series 5, vol. 91, cc444, William Redmond to House of Commons, 7 March 1917.
[5] Hansard, House of Commons Debates, series 5, vol. 91, cc456, Lloyd George to House of Commons, 7 March 1917.

British Prime Minister repeated that they would by no means compel, physically or politically, Ulster Unionists to accept a settlement against their will. Lloyd George even brought to the attention of the Irish MPs that none of them was ready to leave out the six counties.[6] William Redmond foresaw that this situation would play into the hands of the revolutionaries (and even openly warned the British Cabinet about the eventuality). Based on the underlying and tacit conviction, in March 1917, that Ulster Unionists would always deter the British from implementing Home Rule, the dilemma of the British Cabinet was brought out into the open: Home Rule could never happen unless Carson consented to it.

Members of the Irish Parliamentary Party thus accused the British Government of undermining constitutional nationalism. During the debate in the House of Commons, the apprehensions of the Irish Party came to be voiced more and more explicitly. Out of pride and despair, John Redmond violently condemned the position of the British Government and went as far as to state that he was entirely convinced that the British were seeking to destroy the constitutional party.

> If by your action to-day you are undoubtedly making the constitutional movement more difficult, and if the constitutional movement disappears, I beg the Prime Minister to take note that he will find himself face to face with a revolutionary movement, and he will find it impossible to preserve.... He will have to govern Ireland by the naked sword.[7]

M. T. P. O'Connor intervened, stressing that 'with a view to strengthening the hands of the Allies in achieving the recognition of the equal rights of small nations and the principle of nationality against the opposite German principle of military domination and government without the consent of the governed, it [was] essential without further delay to confer upon Ireland the free institutions long promised to her'.[8] O'Connor sought to capture the idea of equal rights for stateless peoples. However, the Home Rule project implied only devolution, not full independence. Therefore, O'Connor's somewhat uncertain intervention did not correspond to the stated goals of the Irish Party. Clearly, full independence could not be advocated in support of what was in fact a project for devolution.

---

[6] Ibid.
[7] Hansard, House of Commons Debates, series 5, vol. 91, cc478, John Redmond to House of Commons, 7 March 1917.
[8] Hansard, House of Commons Debates, series 5, vol. 91, cc425, O'Connor to House of Commons, 7 March 1917.

Colonel de la Panouse concluded that the Irish MPs had opted for a dangerous game in remaining in London in order to seize any occasion to fight the Government line.⁹ Indeed, the less they managed to articulate the demands of the Irish, the more Sinn Féin gained strength.

The following day, the constitutional party reluctantly published a manifesto in which it denounced the policy of the Government, going as far as to accuse London of deliberately handing over Ireland to the revolutionaries. Asquith had sought to keep up a Janus-like rhetoric that was aimed at ensuring the support of both Ulster Unionists and constitutional Nationalists for the war effort. Asquith's strategy had put an end (or at least postponed) the eventuality of civil war in Ireland, conveying the impression that the island would, in due time, come to be governed according to the will of its majority. In March 1917, the declaration made by Lloyd George vindicated those who had suspected Asquith's dual commitment of being duplicitous and ultimately untenable.

In the period leading up to the Sinn Féin Árd Fheis in the autumn of 1917, the domestic situation in Ireland was taking the form of a burgeoning rivalry between the Irish Parliamentary Party and Sinn Féin. For the first time since the outbreak of the war, Ambassador Paul Cambon underlined that 'Irish nationalist deputies [were] losing ground every day because Sinn Féin competed to become the official opposition to England'.¹⁰ He regretted that the Irish question had not been solved and that 'Ireland remained an open scar in the side of the English Empire'.¹¹ One strategy available to Sinn Féin was to portray the Irish Party as the natural ally of the British Government. Sinn Féin activists continuously and fallaciously portrayed Redmond and the Irish Parliamentary Party as advocates of conscription, thus undermining the authority of the Irish Party, and drawing a stark ideological distinction between devolution and complete independence for Ireland.

Re-organizing Sinn Féin: towards Árd Fheis

In October 1916, in the middle of anti-conscription agitation, the RIC Inspector of the Midlands and Connaught reported that the lack of support for Sinn Féin

---

⁹ Archives Diplomatiques du Ministère des Affaires Étrangères, La Courneuve (hereafter AD), Political and Commercial Correspondence, Great War, 1914–1918, Ireland, 1CPCOM/546, telegram from General de la Panouse to the Minister for Foreign Affairs, 17 March 1917.
¹⁰ AD, Political and Commercial Correspondence, Great War, 1914–1918, Ireland, 1CPCOM/546, telegram from Paul Cambon to the President of the Council, 9 March 1917.
¹¹ Ibid.

was partly due to its poor organization.¹² At that time, the separatist movement was still disorganized and, by the end of the year, 'little had been done to channel or organize the change in public opinion'.¹³ So Sinn Féin reorganized itself into a machinery capable of presenting candidates and unifying all sections of revolutionary Ireland. Separatist activists were given the sobriquet Sinn Féin, thus reinforcing the popularity and the visibility of the party, while any association with the rebellion permitted Sinn Féin 'to exert a strong influence on the structure of the new separatist movement'.¹⁴ However, a unified front was needed if the Irish Party was to be deprived of its dominant position in Irish nationalist opinion and allegiances.

George N. Plunkett, scathingly portrayed by Paul Cambon as 'thirsty for honours, even-tempered bourgeois',¹⁵ proved to be a decisive actor in the internationalization of the Irish question in wartime, when in February 1917 he won the first electoral contest on a Sinn Féin platform. Before the Sinn Féin Convention that was to take place on 19 April 1917, the Ambassador for France in London wrote that Sinn Féin was now beginning to gain more and more support all over the island. A confidential report submitted to the French Minister for Foreign Affairs underlined that Plunkett's electoral victory had opened a new era for Ireland.¹⁶ Pointing to the moment when Sinn Féin had begun to organize as a coherent political structure, the secret report stated that from March 1917, the Irish question shifted from being a purely domestic issue to an international concern, through the ability of Sinn Féin to reshape its rhetoric.

It has been argued that if the Irish Party 'were going to be challenged on a nation-wide scale and if that mass opinion which had shown itself ready to be wooed away at the Roscommon by-election was to be successfully wooed all over Ireland, something much more effective and politically mature than this sort of activity had to be devised'.¹⁷ In February 1917, the Irish Parliamentary Party was not dead. John Redmond was indeed in a difficult position, with Home

---

[12] TNA, CO 904/157/1, Reports of the State of the Country, 1916–1918, Items 224–225, Midlands and Connaught District, October 1916.
[13] Michael Laffan, *The Resurrection of Ireland. The Sinn Féin Party, 1916–1923* (Cambridge: Cambridge University Press, 1999), 72.
[14] Ibid., p. 69.
[15] AD, Political and Commercial Correspondence, Great War, 1914–1918, Ireland, 1CPCOM4, telegram from Paul Cambon to the President of the Council, 15 May 1917.
[16] AD, Political and Commercial Correspondence, Great War, 1914–1918, Ireland, Home Affairs (1918–1922), 95CPCOM/1, report on the situation of Ireland, 25 April 1918.
[17] Robert Kee, *The Green Flag. A History of Irish Nationalism* (London: Weidenfeld & Nicolson, 1972), 597.

Rule and conscription appearing to be mutually conditional, but the rhetoric of Sinn Féin only consisted in voicing the movement's opposition to conscription. Furthermore, there were ongoing bitter quarrels within the separatist movement, as Sinn Féin clearly remained lacking in its organizational structures. Tensions between various anti-British elements accentuated that lack of cohesion in the immediate aftermath of the Roscommon by-election.[18]

On 19 April 1917, in the Mansion House Dublin, the Sinn Féin Convention took place under the presidency of Plunkett. Over a thousand representatives of various organizations from all over Ireland attended.[19] 'A striking feature', recalled the former secretary to Archbishop Walsh, 'was the number of young priests there'.[20] The Convention opposed conscription and demanded that Ireland be represented at the future Peace Conference.[21] Ideological claims that had appeared during the North-Roscommon by-election were now being taken up on a national scale. When Sinn Féin incorporated self-determination *and* a seat at the Peace Conference into its political agenda, it was becoming clear that Sinn Féin demands were in a position to supersede anything that had been imagined for Ireland within the terms of the Irish Party agenda. Compared to the Irish Party, Sinn Féin completely disregarded a dominion status for Ireland. Their demand was for immediate and absolute independence. Sinn Féin had reinvented its programme, thus disregarding the hitherto almighty Home Rule scenario.

When Plunkett summoned the Convention in the Mansion House in Dublin, the resolute affirmation that Ireland was a separate nation was clearly articulated. Sinn Féin rhetoric had undeniably evolved beyond the demand for Home Rule. As stated in a secret report issued to the French Minister for Foreign Affairs, by now Sinn Féin was channelling all its energies into the by-election campaigns, having devised a strategy aimed at the electoral defeat of the Irish Parliamentary Party.[22] In light of the scope for an internationalization of the terms in which the Irish question might now be resolved, Sinn Féin was astute in its appropriation of such wartime rhetoric of self-determination. Its real coup was not to impose itself as the defender of a united Ireland but to channel post-war ideals and gain

---

[18] Laffan, *The Resurrection of Ireland*, 86.
[19] Padraig Yeates, *A City in Wartime, Dublin 1914–1918* (Dublin: Gill & Macmillan, 2012), 386–388.
[20] Military Archives of Ireland (hereafter MAI), Bureau of Military History, 1913–1921 (hereafter BMH), WS687, witness statement from Rev. Monsignor M. Curran, former Secretary to Archbishop Walsh, 17 June 1952, p. 204.
[21] Ibid.
[22] AD, Political and Commercial Correspondence, Great War, 1914–1918, Ireland, Home Affairs (1918–1922), 95CPCOM/1, report on the situation of Ireland, 25 April 1918.

credibility by its espousal of the Wilsonian vision of an international post-war order of sovereign nation-states. The real danger for John Redmond did *not only* stem from the resistance of Ulster Unionists to Home Rule or from popular unrest generated by the threat of conscription, it also emanated from the aspirational potential of the goal which Sinn Féin could now exploit in its rhetoric.

General de la Panouse wrote, on 24 April 1917, that 'if elections were to happen, it [was] possible the Nationalists from M. Redmond's party would, in numerous districts, be replaced by Sinn Féiners'.[23] Whereas, one RIC Inspector had vowed in February 1917 that 'were a general election to take place, Sinn Féin would be returned in most constituencies in Connaught',[24] it now appeared that not only would Sinn Féin candidates be returned, they would decisively take over from constitutional candidates. Two demands appeared interwoven and both were to be pursued during the Peace Conference: the refusal to have the Irish conscripted, and Ireland's claim to total independence. Even if a constitutional solution to the Home Rule stalemate were to be achieved (however unlikely that now seemed), Sinn Féin were presently in a position to offer a broader set of ideas, thus disregarding the earlier demand for Home Rule as an irrelevant claim. What characterized the transformation of Sinn Féin was not only their success in opposing partition: John Redmond and the Irish Parliamentary Party had been promised Home Rule for the whole of Ireland in 1914. And even though they could, with some justification, appear to have been tricked by the British in the latter's efforts to pacify Ulster Unionists, the Irish people knew only too well the determination of Redmond and of all the political achievements of the Irish Party over the previous ten years. Sinn Féin captured growing support because through its insistence on the intended international post-war Peace Conference, they could dangle before Irish opinion the conviction that the settlement of Ireland's demands was no longer to be sought in the corridors of Westminster, but in the chambers of the future Peace Conference. In short, Sinn Féin managed to intensify its call for total independence and sovereignty by having it resonate in a profoundly changed, more international echo chamber.[25] From March 1917, every single speech delivered by Sinn Féin candidates incorporated the concepts of independence and self-determination, combined with the imperative need to

---

[23] AD, Political and Commercial Correspondence, Great War, 1914–1918, Ireland, 1CPCOM/546, telegram from General de la Panouse to the Minister for Foreign Affairs, 24 April 1917.
[24] TNA, CO 904/157/1, Reports of the State of the Country, 1916–1918, Item 180, Midlands and Connaught District, February 1917.
[25] Kee, *The Green Flag*, 604.

fight conscription. Anti-conscription rhetoric merged with claims for self-determination as a successful tactic of bringing all the various revolutionary factions together under the umbrella of Sinn Féin.

The South Longford by-election: the men of Easter Week saved your sons from conscription

The Longford by-election provided the ideal setting for the deployment of the new Sinn Féin narrative.[26] It claimed to be the only party capable of protecting the Irish from compulsory military service, arguing that the Irish question was no longer a merely domestic issue but now an international concern. From that followed the need to secure a seat at the future Peace Conference. Abstention from Westminster and Easter Week 1916 merged with a perennial anti-British rhetoric as a focus for channelling popular discontent. The issue of compulsory military service dominated debate during the election campaign and was relied upon by speakers to further discredit the Irish Parliamentary Party. Far from being merely another argument, there is ample evidence to support the case that conscription decisively modified the course of the electoral contest and imposed itself as a determining factor in nationalist public opinion.

On 29 April 1917, Plunkett delivered a talk at a meeting in Ballymahon on behalf of Joseph McGuinness. At the time, the Sinn Féin candidate was still in Lewes Prison in England for the part he had played during Easter Week 1916. Plunkett warned the crowd that 'John Redmond would have allowed the young men and the middle-aged men to be conscripted for a sham Home Rule'. He went on: 'The Party I represent would not sell their country like this, but would insist on being represented at the Peace Conference which would assemble after the war.'[27] Portraying the Irish Parliamentary Party as incapable of resisting conscription was a way to ensure that the young men in rural districts would refuse to support it. A narrative focused on the ominous possibility of compulsory service caught the attention of those young men most liable to be conscripted, while the ideological principle of representation at the Peace Conference enlarged the scope of Sinn Féin's agenda. In the confrontation with the political line of Redmond, what was therefore at stake was not merely the opposition to

---

[26] Marie Coleman's account of County Longford during the Irish Revolution is the most comprehensive study to this day. Marie Coleman, *County Longford and the Irish Revolution* (Dublin: Irish Academic Press, 2003).
[27] TNA, CO 904/23/3, Sinn Féin meetings, Report 'The Sinn Féin Movement', 1917, p. 21.

conscription but a new vision of Ireland, in line with the principles being outlined for a transformed post-war international order. John Milroy, a prominent Sinn Féin activist, also campaigned for McGuinness. On 29 April 1917, at a meeting in Abbeyshrule, he claimed that the Irish Party would 'allow conscription to be passed',[28] in effect lying to the audience with his distorted presentation of what Redmond and his followers were seeking to achieve. Defamation and misinformation contributed markedly to tarnishing the reputation of the Irish Party.

Interestingly enough, references to Easter Week 1916 thus merged with the immediate relevance of the anti-conscription argument. Soon, Easter Week 1916 was being portrayed (once again) as a military insurrection aimed at avoiding conscription. In Carrickedmond, on 22 April 1917, Milroy spoke of the heroic participation of McGuinness during the 1916 uprising and added that 'only for that rebellion, some of the men now listening would be lying rotting in the soil of Flanders as conscription would have surely been passed only for that rising'. At another meeting, he described the cell in which McGuinness was confined and gave a minute description of the appalling conditions of his detention. He ended by referring to the 1916 rebellion: 'Only for that fight every young man listening to me would be lying dead in Flanders or some of the other war zones.'[29] It was 'due to the Sinn Féiners'[30] that conscription was prevented, concluded another Sinn Féin orator. During another meeting, one republican claimed that 'the men of Easter Week [had] saved Ireland from conscription'. Another activist said he had been a convert to the Sinn Féin movement since he had realized that 'the Irish Party were a corrupt body, and would have had conscription in Ireland only for Easter Week'.[31] Redmond and the Irish Party were said to have cheered in Parliament when the men were executed in Dublin, another fallacious (yet recurrent) accusation. At a meeting in Ballymahon, on 6 May 1917, someone proclaimed that the members of the House were 'all enemies of Ireland'[32] who had stood up and cheered at the executions of the 1916 rebels, waving hats and handkerchiefs. These groundless accusations fuelled the resentment of those who were listening. The *Longford Leader* covered the campaign in a special editorial and addressed the issue of an Irish Republic, as advocated by Plunkett. It reminded the electorate that having sent men to the

[28] Ibid., p. 26.
[29] Ibid., p. 23.
[30] Ibid., p. 24.
[31] Ibid., p. 29.
[32] Ibid., p. 28.

British Parliament for the last 116 years, it appeared to them that 'it would be nothing but play-acting to withdraw them on principle after all those years of acquiescence'.[33]

As was revealed by the *Irish Independent* during the Longford by-election, what was said to civilians in the street mattered as much as what was printed in the press.[34] The gap was widening between what was covered by the press (generally in sympathy with the Irish Party) compared to what could be found in pamphlets and speeches from platforms. In a tribune entitled 'Priests and People Rally Round Mr McKenna', the Irish Party claimed: 'It was a lie that the Irish members cheered the execution of any rebel leaders. It was a lie that Mr Redmond ever dreamt of allowing conscription to be introduced in Ireland.' Stressing all the legislative reforms and political accomplishments achieved by the Irish Party since Parnell, Irish MPs reminded the people of Longford that 'land reform, labour reform, education, local government – all came without [Sinn Féin] assistance'. In electrifying speeches, many Irish MPs took the floor to defend their political line: 'the stock-in-trade of Sinn Féin was the conscription bogey and the abominable charge that the Irish Party cheered at the executions of the leaders of the rebellion. Long before the rebellion the Irish Party had defeated conscription, and it was the presence in the House of Commons of a united and determined Irish Party that saved Ireland from the Military Service Act (cheers).'[35] Local newspapers continued to support the Irish Party, reminding the Longford electorate what they owed to constitutional nationalism. 'What was it that gave the labourer a plot of land and a cottage he could call his own – was it Sinn Féin?',[36] a journalist provokingly asked. A staunch supporter of the Irish Party, the *Longford Leader* published a speech by Canon Corcoran, in which he reminded the electorate that 'the Irish Party and the constitutional movement [had] done much for Ireland'[37] and that the Irish needed to remain united behind the Irish Party in order to achieve devolution. Speaking immediately after him, Reverend Conefry warned the crowd that 'the only persons who wanted them to forsake the constitutional movement and turn away from the Irish Party were the men who never did an honest day's work'.[38] He went on to ask whether the Irish were ready to turn against a constitutional movement which had won

---

[33] *Longford Leader*, 28 April 1917.
[34] *Irish Independent*, 1 May 1917.
[35] Ibid.
[36] *Longford Leader*, 28 April 1917.
[37] *Longford Leader*, 5 May 1917.
[38] Ibid.

Figure 4.1 John Dillon, member of the Irish Parliamentary Party, addressing a meeting during the Longford by-election campaign in April 1917. Cashman Collection. Courtesy of RTÉ Ireland.

practically everything for the people of Ireland. At Drumlish, during a meeting in support of the Irish Party candidate, one Irish MP 'asked whether the electors were prepared to turn South Longford into another O'Connell street'.[39]

Families of servicemen in Longford, as a garrison town, represented a strong anti-Sinn Féin element during the election. As the attendance grew at Sinn Féin meetings, 'tensions abounded in relation to soldiers' wives'.[40] On 22 April 1917, a number of women and girls belonging to the town turned out with a Union Jack and started a counter-demonstration to the Sinn Féin meeting held after the return of the forces from Clondra.[41] Members of the Sinn Féin committee were attacked by a crowd of women on their way back from Ballymahon, where a meeting in support of Joseph McGuinness had been held.[42] All in vain.

---

[39] *Irish Independent*, 1 May 1917.
[40] Diarmaid Ferriter, *A Nation and Not a Rabble* (London: Profile Books, 2015), 172.
[41] *Longford Leader*, 28 April 1917.
[42] MAI, BMH, WS722, witness statement from Dan McCarthy, former member of 'D' Company, 4th Battalion, Dublin Brigade, Irish Volunteers, 8 September 1952, p. 11.

On 9 May 1917, the Sinn Féin candidate won against the candidate of the constitutional party by just thirty-eight votes. Joseph McGuinness, still in jail in England for his participation in the 1916 uprising, secured 1,498 votes against 1,461 for his opponent. While the narrow outcome testified to the growing popularity of Sinn Féin, it also showed that the Irish Parliamentary Party had certainly not been ousted altogether. With reference to the narrow margin of his victory, it has also been argued that McGuinness would in all likelihood have been defeated had it not been for the support of the Catholic Archbishop of Dublin.[43] On 8 May 1917, eighteen Catholic bishops and three Protestant prelates had issued a circular in which they called on the Irish people to reject 'the dismemberment of [their] country'.[44] The Irish Party could still rely upon the unaltered support of the Archbishop of Armagh and the Catholic hierarchy,[45] but a number of priests had openly supported Sinn Féin,[46] thus supporting the claim that if the majority of the bishops still backed the Irish Party, 'the Catholic Church was little by little adapting to a new political environment'.[47] While their appeal never directly invited local populations to cast a vote for Sinn Féin, a heavy blow was struck against the Irish Parliamentary Party and its candidate when Archbishop Walsh declared that the Irish needed to 'show to the Government and to the world that the country [was] unresolvedly opposed to Partition'.[48] Electoral campaign leaflets in support of Joseph McGuinness directly quoted Archbishop Walsh, who had deplored that 'the country [was] practically sold'.[49]

General de la Panouse regarded this victory as the 'triumph of Sinn Féin and the most formidable blow struck against Mr Redmond and his party',[50] an assessment shared by other commentators. The constituency had always been regarded as 'a west-British garrison town' where 'wives and dependents (of British soldiers) formed the most prominent and noisiest element of the party'.[51]

---

[43] Laffan, *The Resurrection of Ireland*, 102.
[44] *Irish Independent*, 8 May 1917.
[45] *Freeman's Journal*, 1 May 1917.
[46] *Kerry Evening Post*, 16 June 1917.
[47] Jérôme aan de Wiel, *The Catholic Church in Ireland, 1914–1918: War and Politics* (Dublin: Irish Academic Press, 2003), 127.
[48] Service Historique de la Défense, Vincennes (hereafter SHD), Third Republic (1870–1940), Military Headquarters (1914–1918), 16N3007, telegram from General de la Panouse to the General Commander-in-Chief of the French Armies in the North and North East of France, 14 May 1917.
[49] National Library of Ireland (hereafter NLI), EPH C88, handbill used as part of an election campaign leaflet to support McGuinness, 1917.
[50] SHD, Third Republic (1870–1940), Military Headquarters (1914–1918), 16N3007, telegram from General de la Panouse to the General Commander-in-Chief of the French Armies in the North and North East of France, 14 May 1917.
[51] MAI, BMH, WS687, witness statement from Reverend Monsignor M. Curran, Secretary to Archbishop Walsh, 17 June 1952, p. 200.

Reverend Curran, Secretary to Archbishop Walsh, asserted that 'outside Ulster and South Dublin, there was hardly a constituency in all Ireland with such a pro-British, pro-ally and reactionary outlook. Its loss to the Parliamentary Party proved that they could no longer count on any constituency.'[52] The victory of McGuinness amounted to a further break in the hold of the Irish Parliamentary Party on nationalist Ireland and a further step in the transformation of Sinn Féin, rendered possible through its insistence on the threat of conscription.

Tightening the grip: the East-Clare election

In its preparation of the Irish Convention (see following chapter), the British Government granted amnesty to all individuals jailed in England who had been arrested for their participation in the 1916 rebellion. Lloyd George thus sought to placate American opinion and facilitate the work of the Irish Convention. When the British released the 117 remaining prisoners of Easter Week, among them Éamon de Valera who would later run for the East-Clare by-election, 'the released prisoners received a rapturous welcome in Ireland. They were escorted through the streets of Dublin by enthusiastic crowds, cheering and waving small orange, white and green tricolours.'[53] Their release contrasted sharply with that of political prisoners in December 1916. It illustrated how, in the mind of local populations, prisoners and 1916 rebels were now immediately associated with Sinn Féin.

In Enniscorthy (County Wexford), 2,000 people accompanied by a band greeted the released prisoners. Nothing seditious or disloyal was noticed by the police, with the exception of the singing of 'Easter Week'. In Wexford, a crowd of 1,000 assembled and accompanied the prisoners shouting 'Up the Rebels' and singing 'Easter Week'.[54] At 11pm on 6 June 1917, in Ballina (County Mayo), a large crowd gathered near the Post Office. Two Sinn Féin flags were unfurled and a parade marched through the principal streets of the town. During the procession there were some cries of 'Up Dublin', 'Up the Rebels', and 'Up Sinn Féin'.[55] Easter Week 1916 and its martyrs were by now fully associated with Sinn Féin. On 16 June 1917, in Glin (County Limerick), a small crowd of young men and women marched through the streets singing 'Easter Week' and other rebel songs, shouting

---

[52] Ibid., p. 201.
[53] Kee, *The Green Flag*, 601.
[54] TNA, CO 904/23/3, Sinn Féin meetings, Report 'The Sinn Féin Movement', 1917, p. 33.
[55] Ibid., p. 34.

'Up the Rebels', and carrying Sinn Féin flags. Everything occurred very quickly however, and these demonstrations did not generate any unrest or outrages, nor any unlawful acts. The RIC Inspector of County Galway reported that in Atherny, the return of the detainees 'passed off quietly when the crowd afterwards dispersed'.[56] In Tralee (County Kerry), on 20 June 1917, a crowd of 4,000 people assembled to welcome the three released martyrs on their return home.[57] Three days later, on 23 June 1917, about 10,000 people and three bands welcomed freed prisoners on their arrival in Cork City. The local Irish Volunteers took possession of the railway station and formed a guard of honour to receive them. After their arrival, a procession numbering about 2,000 marched to the Grand Parade where a public meeting was held, at which about 5,000 people were present.[58] That same day, in Limerick, over 1,000 local Sinn Féiners turned out to welcome two released prisoners.[59] All these prisoners 'were the natural leaders of

Figure 4.2 Crowds on Westland Row in Dublin waiting to meet prisoners released from general amnesty, 18 June 1917. Keogh Photographic Collection. Courtesy of the National Library of Ireland.

[56] Ibid., p. 35.
[57] Ibid., p. 36.
[58] Ibid., p. 37.
[59] Ibid., p. 39.

Figure 4.3 Crowds at Pearse Station in Dublin waiting to meet prisoners released from general amnesty, 18 June 1917. Keogh Photographic Collection. Courtesy of the National Library of Ireland.

the movement which had flourished as a result of the rebellion'.[60] However, in order to tighten the ties between the newly-released detainees and the Sinn Féin cause, it was essential that a narrative be fashioned according to which their action in April 1916 had contributed to the deferral of conscription.

When he decided to run for the East-Clare by-election, Éamon de Valera and the other imprisoned leaders 'found a united, efficient and energetic party awaiting them'.[61] On 24 June 1917, Arthur Griffith delivered a speech at a Westmeath convention in which he made clear that the independence of Ireland was now the first objective of the party.[62] On his release from jail, Éamon de Valera repeatedly swore allegiance to the Irish Republic.[63] On 30 June 1917, on his arrival at Ennis, he delivered a speech in which he read out the 1916 Proclamation of the Irish Republic from the meeting platform.[64] When running

---

[60] Laffan, *The Resurrection of Ireland*, 107.
[61] Ibid.
[62] *Irish Independent*, 25 June 1917.
[63] *Irish Independent*, 16 July 1917.
[64] Maurice Moynihan, ed., *Speeches and Statements by Éamon de Valera 1917–1973* (Dublin: Gill & Macmillan, 1980), 6.

for election, Sinn Féin candidates were careful to enshrine their political action within the legacy of the architects of 1916.[65] For the leaders who were still alive, their association with the martyrs of the Rising 'was a guarantee to the public of their *bona fides*'.[66] But the main objective of Sinn Féin was to establish an independent republic, not through revolutionary violence, as had been the intention of the 1916 rebels, but through participation in a future Peace Conference. What Sinn Féin candidates such as de Valera hoped to draw from the 1916 Proclamation was certainly not the need to foment another military insurrection, but above all the idea of national sovereignty.

A few days before the election of Éamon de Valera, Paul Cambon alerted the French Government that 'the extremist party clearly [sought], before anything else, to demand the representation of Ireland at the Peace Conference'.[67] From London, Cambon had heard of the intentions of Sinn Féin regarding the internationalization of the Irish question. When he campaigned for the East-Clare by-election, de Valera fused anti-conscription rhetoric with a vision of a totally independent Ireland. Opposition to an immediate and very concrete fight (conscription) was needed, alongside the grander international perspective of the Peace Conference. Electoral material for the by-election addressed a wide range of concerns among the local population. In one pamphlet dealing with land taxation, conscription was only mentioned at the very end. It was clearly indicated that 'England would enforce conscription in Ireland',[68] thus ostensibly demonstrating yet again that the way to avoid conscription was to support Sinn Féin. Another poster reminded people that 'every vote for de Valera [was] a vote against conscription'.[69] A black and white drawing portraying de Valera marching towards the Peace Conference indicated that Sinn Féin sought to achieve full independence for Ireland and to prevent land taxation. However, at the bottom of the cartoon, the electorate was reminded it was to 'vote for De Valera who [had] saved [Their] Sons from Conscription'.[70] Another leaflet was entirely dedicated to the conscription issue. It explained that a vote for de Valera was 'A

---

[65] Joseph Lee, *The Modernization of Irish Society, 1848–1918* (Dublin: Gill & Macmillan, 1973), 157.
[66] Dudley Edwards, 'The Achievement of 1916', in *1916: The Easter Rising*, ed. Dudley Edwards and Fergus Pyle (London: MacGibbon and Kee, 1968), 211.
[67] AD, Political and Commercial Correspondence, Great War, 1914–1918, Ireland, 1CPCOM/546, telegram from Paul Cambon to the Minister for Foreign Affairs, 7 July 1917.
[68] University College Dublin Archives (hereafter UCDA), Éamon de Valera Papers (1882–1985), P150/550, electoral poster in support of De Valera, 'Threatening A Land Tax', July 1917.
[69] UCDA, Éamon de Valera Papers (1882–1985), P150/550, electoral poster in support of De Valera, 'Vote for De Valera!', July 1917.
[70] UCDA, Éamon de Valera Papers (1882–1985), P150/550, electoral poster in support of De Valera, 'Vote for De Valera who saved Your Sons from Conscription', July 1917.

Vote against Conscription'.[71] Another carried the slogan: 'Vote for De Valera who saved your sons from conscription',[72] thus reiterating the myth of the 1916 Rising as a counter-conscription rebellion. In a district where young men could be drafted overnight into the army, the prospect of being conscripted, in all likelihood, acted as another (if not as the main) determining factor. Sinn Féin even received donations from private individuals who hoped 'to counteract conscription'.[73] At the time of the East-Clare by-election, a secret report from an RIC Inspector argued that the fear of conscription 'prevailed over the South of Ireland'[74] and had been an important factor in the sweeping victory of Éamon de Valera, who defeated the candidate of the Irish Parliamentary Party by nearly 3,000 votes.[75]

That conscription appeared a determining factor in the sweeping victory of the former 1916 martyr comes as no surprise, as the issue was monopolizing the attention of all sections of society in Ireland at the time. A few days before the polls, a journalist of *The Kilkenny People* wrote a diatribe against the Irish Parliamentary Party, in which he explicitly warned that a vote for the Irish Party would bring Ireland closer to conscription. Only Éamon de Valera could avoid compulsory service and prevent Irishmen from being sent abroad to die in foreign lands.

> If the young men of Clare are willing to accept Conscription – if the Clare farmers are anxious to see their sons transported to Bagdad, or Salonika, or shipped to "somewhere East of Suez", then their course is clear and their man is Crown Prosecutor Lynch. If, on the other end, they are not going to have conscription if they are prepared to fight against it and want a leader who, in their case and in the cause of Ireland, will look death in the face without flinching, then their course is no less clear and their man is Éamon de Valera.[76]

In reviving the memories of the Irish public, who had heard of the heavy casualties which Irish troops had faced in Gallipoli and on the Western Front, the editor knew he was touching a sore point. How important conscription remained in the by-election campaign can best be understood through a pamphlet in support of the Irish Party. Lynch was running against de Valera.

---

[71] NLI, Ephemera Collection, EPH B148, election handbill issued in support of Éamon de Valera, 1917.
[72] NLI, Ephemera Collection, EPH C474, election handbill issued in support of Éamon de Valera, 1917.
[73] NLI, Manuscript Section, MS 10,494 (3), Sinn Féin Provincial Correspondence, County Wexford, 1917–1918, letter from a Sinn Féin member, 17 June 1917.
[74] TNA, CO 904/157/1, Reports of the State of the Country, 1916–1918, Item 147, Southern Districts, July 1917.
[75] Laffan, *The Resurrection of Ireland*, 112.
[76] *The Kilkenny People*, 23 June 1917.

VOTE

FOR

DE VALERA!

EVERY VOTE FOR DE VALERA is a **CALL FOR JUSTICE** to the Council of the Nations.

EVERY VOTE FOR DE VALERA is a Vote for Ireland a Nation.

EVERY VOTE FOR DE VALERA is a Vote **Against Conscription.**

EVERY VOTE FOR DE VALERA is a Vote **Against Partition**

EVERY VOTE FOR DE VALERA is a Vote for Ireland's Language and for Ireland's Ideals and Civilization.

UP De VALERA!

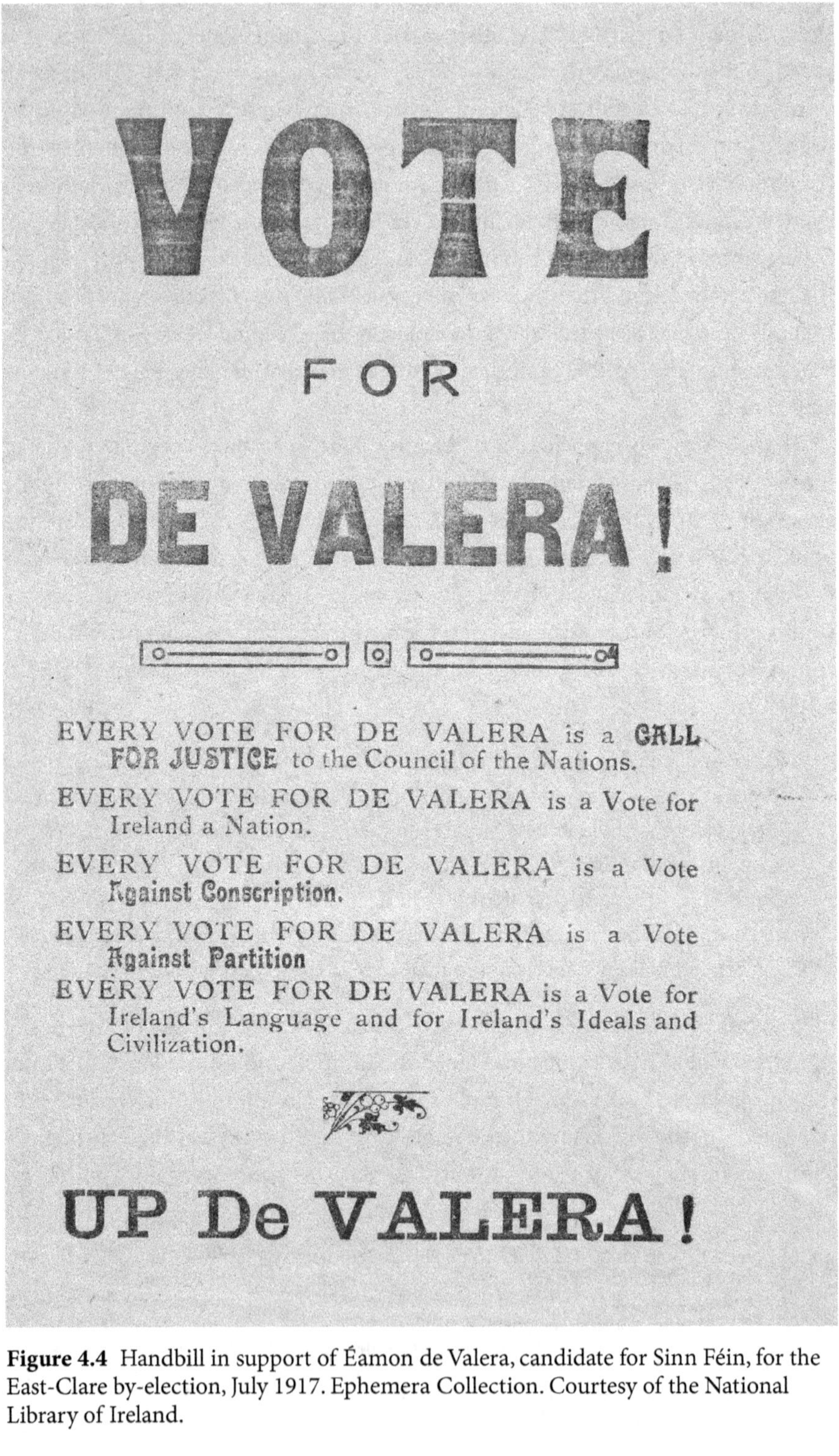

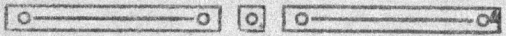

Figure 4.4 Handbill in support of Éamon de Valera, candidate for Sinn Féin, for the East-Clare by-election, July 1917. Ephemera Collection. Courtesy of the National Library of Ireland.

Figure 4.5 Election handbill for the East-Clare by-election calling on people to vote for Éamon de Valera, July 1917. Ephemera Collection. Courtesy of the National Library of Ireland.

Among the variety of posters, drawings, poems and printed speeches, one testified to the need to counter Sinn Féin propaganda. 'Nothing but the strenuous opposition of the Irish Party has STOPPED conscription in Ireland',[77] read the poster. Clearly, the Irish Party had been relentlessly portrayed as the advocate of conscription. It therefore had to react in order to refute such an accusation.

That the activists campaigning for de Valera 'abandoned the guarded language'[78] was clearly noticeable. The candidate alarmed some supporters by the tenor of his speeches.[79] De Valera was not solely a former 1916 leader, and staunch anti-British separatist, he was also a vehement opponent to the participation of Irishmen in the conflict. One particularity of the East-Clare by-election was the relatively pro-German stance adopted by speakers. For instance, on 1 July 1917, one activist addressed a crowd at Lisdoonvarna, claiming that England had one hand on Ireland's throat and the other in her pocket: 'Germany

---

[77] UCDA, Éamon de Valera Papers (1882–1985), P150/550, electoral poster in support of Lynch, 'Conscription!', July 1917.
[78] Laffan, *The Resurrection of Ireland*, 110.
[79] David Fitzpatrick, 'De Valera in 1917: the Undoing of the Easter Rising', in *De Valera and His Times*, ed. John O'Carroll and John Murphy (Cork: Cork University Press, 1983), 101–102.

is trying to compel her to release her grasp. We have no grudge against Germany',[80] he stated. Whereas earlier meetings in favour of Sinn Féin candidates had primarily attacked the overtly conciliatory policy of Redmond towards the British Government, the East-Clare by-election introduced a rhetoric of treason that had been virtually absent from previous electoral campaigns. This was all the more surprising given that US intervention had seemingly stifled any pro-German rhetoric in Ireland (this, at least, was what was believed by France's representatives). During the meeting, Thomas McDonagh called anyone who joined the English Army a traitor.[81] This invites us to qualify the findings of previous scholarly research which has asserted that while recruits did come in for some insults and mockery from the beginning of the conflict, following the destruction of the 10th (Irish) Division Irish soldiers tended to be pitied and mourned.[82] What transpires from the East-Clare contest is an unprecedented and violent depiction of Irish soldiers as traitors, a qualification that had never been publicly ventured before. De Valera introduced a more aggressive tone, evidence of the changing mood within Sinn Féin, of its becoming a more resolute and more vehement movement. Contrary to what the representatives of France had believed, US involvement did not in fact put a damper on the anti-British tone of all Sinn Féin candidates. On 5 July 1917, at Carran, de Valera proclaimed: 'We will have the ruins of the British Empire. It is my wish that the British Empire will be blown into ruins.'[83] For de Valera, a German victory thus became an explicitly endorsed catalyst contributing to the achievement of the goal of complete independence for Ireland. England's defeat would lead to Ireland's recognition as an independent state at the Peace Conference. At Crusheen, on 8 July 1917, Alderman Cole rejoiced at the difficulties confronting the British Empire: 'England is sinking fast, thank God. We will get to the Peace Conference.'[84] France's representatives were mistaken, having wrongly believed that US involvement in the war was a source of embarrassment for Sinn Féin.

During the East-Clare by-election, members of the Irish Party violently countered Sinn Féin, taking the fight to Sinn Féin during the latter's meetings. At a meeting at Broadford in support of Lynch (candidate of the Irish Party), David Sheehy (MP) denounced the 'Conscription Bogey', and directly targeted Sinn

[80] TNA, CO 904/23/3, Sinn Féin meetings, Report 'The Sinn Féin Movement', 1917, p. 41.
[81] Ibid.
[82] Ben Novick, *Conceiving Revolution: Irish Nationalist Propaganda during the First World War* (Dublin: Four Courts Press, 2001), 51.
[83] TNA, CO 904/23/3, Sinn Féin meetings, Report 'The Sinn Féin Movement', 1917, p. 42.
[84] Ibid., p. 43.

Féin: 'their opponents knew in their hearts, that eight months before the Dublin rebellion conscription for this country had been killed by Redmond and Dillon in the House of Commons. That was an irrefutable fact, and cant or calumny could not overcome it (loud cheers).'[85] Conscription 'was wholly unacceptable and would be resisted to the utmost, by all sections of nationalists, both pro- and anti-war'[86] but it appears that portraying the Irish Party as an advocate of compulsory military service (a completely normal political rhetoric during election times) sufficed to convince rural populations that they were actually being manipulated. If it remains tricky to guess the motivations of civilian communities in casting a vote for Sinn Féin, the RIC and France's consular services firmly maintained that conscription was the main source in radicalizing farmers, labourers and other agricultural sections of rural Ireland. Partition and conscription similarly infuriated the Catholic Church and Sinn Féin; but when it comes to the electorate, farmers, shopkeepers, labourers and other rural communities were (perhaps in all likelihood) more likely to cast a vote for Sinn Féin to avoid conscription. During the electoral contest, Sinn Féin needed to call on the help of the Irish Volunteers, who acted as a shield to protect speakers at their meetings. Volunteers 'were obliged to use the ash plant in order to protect Sinn Féin supporters from being mauled by these infuriated females'.[87] John Flanagan, who belonged to the Knockerra Company, travelled to Ennis to help the Sinn Féin candidate, Éamon de Valera, in the organization of meetings. They helped 'in keeping the anti-Sinn Féin element in that town under control. That element was mainly composed of the wives and families of British soldiers then fighting for England in the First World War.'[88]

At the East-Clare by-election, on 10 July 1917, de Valera won 5,010 votes against 2,035 for his rival. East-Clare had been represented in the British Parliament for twenty years by Major William Redmond, recently killed on the Western Front, at Messines. The constituency was therefore regarded as an electoral stronghold for the Irish Parliamentary Party. The RIC Inspector reported that the parliamentary election provided 'an enormous impetus to the disloyal movement'[89] and such a sweeping victory led to demonstrations all over

---

[85] *Freeman's Journal*, 2 July 1917.
[86] Timothy Bowman, William Butler and Michael Wheatley, *The Disparity of Sacrifice. Irish Recruitment to the British Armed Forces, 1914–1918* (Liverpool: Liverpool University Press, 2020), 58.
[87] MIA, BMH, WS1316, witness statement from John Flanagan, former Commandant, Second Battalion, West Clare Brigade, 15 December 1955, p. 4.
[88] Ibid.
[89] TNA, CO 904/157/1, Reports of the State of the Country, 1916–1918, Report from Captain Dickie, Intelligence Officer, Headquarters, Southern District, 31 July 1917.

the Southern District. Young men carried Sinn Féin flags, others delivered violent and seditious speeches. In County Sligo, celebrations for Sinn Féin were sometimes 'interrupted by protests from serving soldiers' wives – separation women – and by soldiers invalided home'.[90]

The RIC Inspector alerted London that among the many motives causing the move towards Sinn Féin 'the fear of conscription which prevail[ed] over the South of Ireland, [was] probably the strongest, especially among farmers' sons and the shop assistant class'.[91] Conscription acted as an immediate and tangible threat. In this report, no mention was made of Sinn Féin's newly endorsed aspirations. Electoral leaflets and hand-outs drew on both the urgent need to resist conscription and on the representation of Ireland's right to self-government at the future Peace Conference. In the mind of Paul Cambon, the East-Clare electoral victory settled undeniably the ascendancy of that party in Ireland.[92]

Figure 4.6 Éamon de Valera addressing supporters from Ennis Court House, 11 July 1917. Keogh Photographic Collection. Courtesy of the National Library of Ireland.

---

[90] Michael Farry, *Sligo. The Irish Revolution, 1912–1923* (Dublin: Four Courts Press, 2012), p. 34.
[91] TNA, CO 904/157/1, Reports of the State of the Country, 1916–1918, Report from Captain Dickie, Intelligence Officer, Headquarters, Southern District, 31 July 1917.
[92] AD, Political and Commercial Correspondence, Great War, 1914–1918, Ireland, 1CPCOM/546, telegram from Paul Cambon to the President of the Council, 12 July 1917.

Figure 4.7 Clare by-election, July 1917. Victory parade led by pipers with Countess Markievicz. Keogh Photographic Collection. Courtesy of the National Library of Ireland.

The Kilkenny by-election

A few weeks later, another by-election provided further evidence of the shift in nationalist opinion towards republicanism. On 10 August 1917, William Cosgrave, a former 1916 rebel,[93] won the Kilkenny by-election by 772 votes against 392 for his nationalist party opponent.[94] During the contest, campaigners urged the Irish to cast a vote for Sinn Féin, promising that it would protect them from compulsory service. On 29 July 1917, at Castlecomer, Alderman Cole urged people to 'resist unto death'[95] if any attempt was made to enforce conscription. Stephan O'Meara publicly asked a meeting in Kilkenny on that very same day: 'Where are the men today that went to fight for England? Search the plains of Flanders and Gallipoli or the bottom of the Mediterranean and you may find

---

[93] UCDA, W. T. Cosgrave Papers (1917–1993), P285/298, Proceedings against W. T. Cosgrave in relation to his activities in the Easter Rising, 4 May 1916.
[94] TNA, CO 904/157/1, Reports on the State of the Country, 1916–1918, Item 128, Southern District, August 1917.
[95] TNA, CO 904/23/3, Sinn Féin meetings, Report 'The Sinn Féin Movement', 1917, p. 44.

them.'⁹⁶ 'Were it not for Sinn Féin, some of your bones would be whitening today in France or the Dardanelles,'⁹⁷ explained Father O'Donoghue at a meeting in Upperchurch (County Tipperary). He attacked the Irish Party, accusing them of 'succeeding in getting young Irishmen to join the British Army to have their bones bleached in France, the Dardanelles, Mesopotamia, or wherever British incompetence led them.'⁹⁸ All these examples referred to Easter Week 1916 as a political insurrection aimed at preventing conscription in Ireland. 'When recently in England I saw a number of young men on crutches and if it were not for Easter Week the Irish young men would be in the same condition,'⁹⁹ lamented another speaker, at a meeting at Ballylanders (County Limerick) on 22 July 1917. De Valera went so far as to call for a further act of martyrdom in the eventuality of a military service act. On 30 July 1917, he urged Irishmen and Irishwomen to resort to physical violence in order to prevent conscription: 'They talk of enforcing conscription in Ireland. If they try to enforce conscription, it is our dead bodies they will have to conscript, and they will have to take the dead bodies of some of their own too. It is better to die fighting in an Irish trench than to die in a trench in Flanders fighting for our only enemy.'¹⁰⁰

Éamon de Valera had no compunctions about voicing his support for bloodshed and his animosity to Ireland's only enemy. At a meeting at Callan (County Kilkenny) on 5 August, he urged Irish citizens to resist conscription come what may: 'Let it be your dead bodies they will conscript.'¹⁰¹ As during the East-Clare by-election, support for Germany was clearly expressed. 'I am not ashamed to call for three cheers for the Germans and that God may bless their arms,'¹⁰² Austin Stack shouted on 31 July 1917, during a meeting at Abbeydorney (County Kerry).

However, it was still essential that a clear demarcation be established between Sinn Féin and the Parliamentary Party. Opposition to recruitment and the lugubrious insistence on the fate of Irish soldiers lying in Belgium, France and in the Dardanelles did not suffice to provide a manifesto or an agenda. Only Sinn Féin could open the path leading to a complete independence for Ireland. 'Ireland is going to be represented at the Peace Conference and will claim her independence at it,'¹⁰³ de Valera promised, at a meeting in Tullamore (Queen's County) on 31 July

---

96 Ibid.
97 Ibid., p. 56.
98 Ibid., p. 49.
99 Ibid., p. 57.
100 Ibid., p. 48.
101 Ibid., p. 45.
102 Ibid., p. 48.
103 Ibid., p. 49.

1917. At Miker (County Limerick), Ernest Blythe made a pledge to the audience that an Irish Republic would be obtained by having Ireland represented at the Peace Conference.[104] At a meeting in Newtowncashel (County Longford), on 2 August 1917, P. J. McCrain categorically excluded any possibility of accepting Home Rule.[105] Henry Boland poured scorn on what he called 'Colonial Home Rule or any other kind of Home Rule' during his address in Lanesboro, County Longford, on 5 August 1917.[106] Sinn Féin needed to discredit devolution, Home Rule and the Irish Party.

All advocates of Sinn Féin adopted the same narrative during meetings. They all reiterated their conviction that Easter Week 1916 had saved the Irish from being drafted into the British Army. At Ballaghadereen (County Roscommon), on 24 July 1917, Countess Markievicz drew a link between conscription and Easter Week 1916, in the process devising a narrative according to which the 1916 rebels knew of a plan to conscript the Irish and had thus decided to rise against the Empire: 'We knew, too, that a Bill to conscript Ireland was already printed. We stopped all that by going out. Where would you boys be if conscription had passed? You would be manuring the soil in Flanders, Gallipoli, and elsewhere.'[107]

At Clonakilty (County Cork), on 12 August 1917, she declared that 'it was Easter Week they had to thank for having their young men at home to work their farms and walk the streets instead of dying in the Dardanelles or in the fields of Flanders'.[108] A few days later, at Fahy (County Leitrim), the same argument was given by Ginnell before a large crowd: 'Conscription was knocked on the head owing to the events of Easter Week. Redmond came over to Ireland to get young men to join the British Army to become cannon fodder, to become manure for the fields of Flanders and food for the fishers in Suvla Bay.'[109]

At Frankford (King's County), on 19 August 1917, J. Dalton publicly thanked 'the men of Easter Week who prevented conscription in Ireland',[110] urging Irish people not to forget the primary goal of the 1916 rebellion. Descriptions of disabled soldiers in England nourished fears among local populations, thus giving them another reason to listen to Sinn Féin. At a meeting at Skibbereen (County Cork), on 26 August 1917, John O'Hurley spoke of his recent journey to England and of certain encounters:

---

[104] Ibid., p. 52.
[105] Ibid., p. 53.
[106] Ibid., p. 54.
[107] Ibid., p. 93.
[108] Ibid., p. 59.
[109] Ibid., p. 61.
[110] Ibid., p. 62.

> I have recently travelled a bit in England and saw there a lot of young men. They were in uniform – blue hospital uniform. They were on crutches. I am glad to see such a number of young men present here, sound in limb and body. Owing to the sacrifices of the men of Easter 1916, they have not been conscripted.[111]

In deliberately giving accounts of the suffering endured by soldiers on the front, the Sinn Féin activist was ensuring that young Irishmen were in a position to measure what they could plausibly face in the near future.

Catholic churchmen relayed this Sinn Féin narrative, illustrating a shift in the attitude of the clergy. At Cootehill (County Cavan), on 2 September 1917, Reverend Father O'Connell claimed:

> only for Sinn Féin, the bones of the young men now listening to me would be whitening on the plains of Flanders to-day. De Valera said I am a firm believer in physical force. The Irish Party's last constitutional act was to agree to a measure of conscription for Ireland. Had it passed, your body to-day would be manuring their plains of Flanders and Gallipoli.[112]

John Redmond was described as the traitor who was ready to sacrifice the youth of Ireland to remain in power. Calumnious attacks were recurrent throughout 1917 against the Irish Parliamentary Party, who had to be made to appear the advocates of conscription, if Sinn Féin were to be allowed to capture and channel Irish fears. That very same day, at Castletownroche (County Cork), another Sinn Féiner reminded his audience that 'were it not for the rising of Easter Week, there would be conscription to-day in Ireland and the young men here to-day would be slaughtered in France for our worst enemy. We don't want another rebellion but if they try to put conscription in force we will have another rising.'[113] Physical resistance was a legitimate option in the eyes of Sinn Féin. The party nonetheless unequivocally pledged they would do their utmost to avoid armed violence while strenuously resisting conscription. Countess Markievicz addressed a crowd of 1,500 at Trim (County Meath), on 10 September and linked the action of the 1916 leaders to their commitment to protecting their people from forced service in the British Army:

> I say we were justified, because if we had not gone out Easter Week, conscription would have been passed for Ireland and instead of you all being here to-day, you

---

[111] Ibid., p. 64.
[112] Ibid., p. 65.
[113] Ibid., p. 67.

would most of you young men be out in Flanders or elsewhere, shedding your blood for England.[114]

Such rhetoric proved to be an essential component of the Sinn Féin message, as all those who espoused the Sinn Féin argument insisted on the alleged correlation between the 1916 insurrection and the effective opposition to the introduction of conscription in Ireland.

A few days later, at Newcastle West (County Limerick), she reiterated the same arguments: 'Only for the fighting in Easter Week, conscription within a fortnight would be enforced in Ireland.'[115] By deliberately pretending to reveal sensitive information about a conspiracy to conscript the Irish in 1916, the Countess ensured the rebels would be looked upon with more clemency. At a meeting held in St Mary's Hall, in Belfast, on 8 October 1917, Ginnell claimed that the martyrs of Easter Week were the men who had prevented the British Government from putting the conscription act in force in this country, and who had therefore saved the Irish 'from manuring Belgium or making fodder for the cannons of the nations of Europe in this war'.[116] On 2 November 1917, the Countess delivered a lecture at the Theatre Royal, County Waterford, to a large crowd. Cheers resonated in the audience, when she confessed in a dramatic tone: 'We knew conscription was coming, and we knew the only way to block conscription was to fight (cheers).'[117] Compared to de Valera, who repudiated the right of any Irishman to enrol in the British Army and called them traitors, Countess Markievicz never condemned Irishmen fighting in the British Army. She simply adopted an attitude of commiseration. This was particularly obvious when, on 7 October 1914, at Castlewellan (County Down), she told the audience: 'The Home Rule Bill on the Statute Book was a carrot for the Irish donkey to follow. I sigh when I think of the many poor Irish boys deluded foolish lads who have died fighting for England in the Dardanelles and Flanders.'[118]

A series of collateral episodes during the period fortified Sinn Féin, while testifying to the increasingly violent line towards which the Irish Volunteers were moving. When Thomas Ashe, a political prisoner, died as a result of a forced-feeding gone wrong on 25 September 1917, his funeral gave rise to an unprecedented display of paramilitary demonstration in Dublin that 'had not

---

[114] Ibid., p. 68.
[115] Ibid., p. 100.
[116] Ibid., p. 76.
[117] *Evening News*, 3 November 1917.
[118] TNA, CO 904/23/3, Sinn Féin meetings, Report 'The Sinn Féin Movement', 1917, p. 103.

been seen since the death of Parnell'.[119] 'Almost all Dublin was in mourning, and a procession estimated to be 30,000 to 40,000 people followed the coffin through the crowded streets.'[120] Immediately behind the coffin came about 150 clergymen, 8,000 members of the Irish Transport Workers' Union, 10,000 members of various trade bodies, and 9,000 Irish Volunteers. A series of errors by the British authorities fanned the revolutionary support for Sinn Féin. Nevertheless, these factors remained secondary compared to the main reason for the movement's popularity: its association with the opposition to conscription and with the securing of the country's sovereign independence. When Thomas Ashe died on 25 September 1917, the way the British handled the affair appalled General de la Panouse: 'What is saddening is to see that the authorities gave to the party more influence and authority by stupidly letting die Thomas Ashe when he was in jail for a political motive.'[121] Popular agitation, revived by his death, gave another opportunity to the French observers to voice their criticism of British rule in Ireland: 'The English have understood nothing of the Irish mind-set.'[122]

Árd Fheis: the Sinn Féin Convention in October 1917

Before the October 1917 Convention, local newspapers reminded the Irish that the electoral victory in four parliamentary seats could not deter the British from imposing compulsory service. A nationwide political revolution had to be carried out in order to protect the Irish from conscription. On 17 October 1917, a daily newspaper issued the following statement:

> The dark shadow of conscription – of forced military service in foreign countries, the blighting curse of militarism in its most hateful form – looms threateningly before us like an angry cloud that clots out God's sunlight and makes even the fairest land dreary and desolate. English statesmen had an opportunity at the outbreak of the war and when the Act was placed on the statute book to demonstrate their good faith by immediately calling an Irish Parliament into being. They did not do that, and everything they have done since, so far as

---

[119] AD, Political and Commercial Correspondence, Great War, 1914–1918, Ireland, Home Affairs (1918–1922), 95CPCOM/1, report on the situation of Ireland, 25 April 1918.
[120] Kee, *The Green Flag*, 608.
[121] SHD, Third Republic (1870–1940), Army Staff, 7N1254, telegram from General de la Panouse to the Minister for War, 15 October 1917.
[122] SHD, Third Republic (1870–1940), Army Staff, 7N1261, telegram from General de la Panouse to the Minister for War, 29 October 1917; SHD, Third Republic (1870–1940), Army Staff, 7N679, Section des Renseignements Généraux, 2ème Bureau, 15 October 1917.

Ireland is concerned, only helps to pile up the proof that they are deliberately and knavishly deceiving Ireland. Whatever sacrifices the struggle against it involves, there must be no conscription for Ireland.[123]

A few days later, this ominous prediction was reiterated:

Conscription in Ireland is coming to a head, and there are good grounds for believing that on the re-assembling of Parliament a determined effort will be made to bring Ireland within the scope of the Compulsory Military Service Act. We have been warning the country for some weeks that as soon as the supply of men began to flag in Great Britain the Government would be compelled to turn its attention to the Irish anomaly. The thing has come about as predicted. We learned yesterday on the inspired authority of the whole London Press, that the Government is now contemplating the application of conscription to Ireland. It is plain, therefore that the menace of conscription is a very real one.[124]

By September 1917, Sergeant Burke, Intelligence Officer for the Midlands and Connaught, acknowledged that fears of conscription were driving shop-keepers and farmers towards Sinn Féin. He reported that local populations were shifting from constitutional nationalism to a more extreme stance of republicanism: 'Sinn Féin will only keep its hold on the people as long as they believe it will keep them from conscription.'[125] That same month, the RIC Inspector of the Southern District wrote that open and flagrant sedition was aired by Sinn Féin speakers.[126]

By October 1917, the state of the country was becoming more and more prone to agitation, as British soldiers began measuring the repercussions of seditious anti-British speeches. That month, the RIC Inspector called to the attention of the British Cabinet the fact that an increasing number of arrests of armed Volunteers had been made (in Cork alone, about 700 men turned out on 21 October and thirteen of their leaders were arrested). Drilling was proceeding quite openly in most counties. For the first time, an investigation into the relations between local populations and soldiers was ordered.[127] Men openly tried to induce soldiers to desert the army, and offered them £1 a week. When prisoners were marched down streets to be removed to railway stations, some

---

[123] *The Kilkenny People*, 17 October 1917.
[124] *The Kilkenny People*, 23 September 1916.
[125] TNA, CO 904/157/1, Reports on the State of the Country 1916–1918, Report from Sergeant Burke, Intelligence Officer, Midlands and Connaught District, 30 September 1917.
[126] TNA, CO 904/157/1, Reports on the State of the Country, 1916–1918, Items 120–122, Southern District, September 1917.
[127] TNA, CO 904/157/1, Reports on the State of the Country, 1916–1918, Item 103, Southern District, October 1917.

soldiers showed sympathy for them.[128] Such incidents remained rare, and did not correspond to the mood of all battalions. They nevertheless remained problematic insofar as they could pose a serious threat to the already-crumbling authority of the British in Ireland. Accordingly, as conscription became a more and more likely scenario, British soldiers were either induced to desert, to betray their uniform, or were being looked upon with suspicion.

When Sinn Féin summoned a convention in Dublin on 25 and 26 October 1917, 1,700 representatives of the 1,200 clubs from all over Ireland attended.[129] As far as France's Consul to Dublin was concerned, their gathering in the Mansion House was a sufficient proof of the powerlessness of the British Government.[130] The Sinn Féin Convention operated as another watershed, and 'consolidated the new united party which had developed during the previous six months'.[131] Internal quarrels no longer impeded the movement, as all separatist factions had by now sided unconditionally with Sinn Féin. During that Convention, de Valera was unanimously elected president.

All the representatives of Sinn Féin pledged their unconditional allegiance to an Irish Republic and vowed to secure Ireland's claim to self-government.[132] In order to do so, and in the name of the Irish people, the Irish needed to deny the right and oppose the will of the British Parliament and British Crown, making use of any and every means available to weaken the power of England.[133] De Valera played a leading part in drafting the new Sinn Féin Constitution, insisting that the primary goal of Sinn Féin was 'to get international recognition for our Irish Republic'.[134] Leaders were confident they could work towards full recognition of Ireland's entitlement to have its cause heard by the conference. Dwelling on the inefficient policy of John Redmond, who had stood up in the House of Commons and joyfully acquiesced 'in pledging the blood of Ireland to the only country that Ireland had ever fought',[135] the Convention identified the Peace Conference as its first primary means through which to secure an Irish Republic. In order to advance the cause of complete independence, Sinn Féin

---

[128] Ibid.
[129] Laffan, *The Resurrection of Ireland*, 118.
[130] AD, Political and Commercial Correspondence, Great War, 1914–1918, Ireland, 1CPCOM/546, telegram from the Consul of France in Dublin to the Minister for Foreign Affairs, 29 October 1917.
[131] Laffan, *The Resurrection of Ireland*, 121.
[132] UCDA, W. T. Cosgrave Papers (1917–1993), P285/300, Sinn Féin Constitution, 25 October 1917, p. 3.
[133] Ibid.
[134] UCDA, de Valera Papers (1882–1985), P150/568, extract from de Valera's address at the Sinn Féin Convention, 25 October 1917.
[135] TNA, CO 904/23/5, Report of the Proceedings of the Sinn Féin Convention held in the Round Room, Mansion House, Dublin, 25–26 October 1917, p. 7.

resorted to constitutionalism, the only weapon through which to channel Wilsonian ideals. Above anything else, a constituent assembly chosen by the people of Ireland had to be elected in order to guarantee the legitimacy of Ireland's claim.

A secret report from one of France's representatives was presented to the French Minister for Foreign Affairs. It maintained that the October 1917 Sinn Féin Convention had completed the transformation of Sinn Féin into a clear and effective force opposed to the Irish Parliamentary Party. Equipped with an executive governing body, the party espoused a clear political line in the service of the goal of full independence. 'In nine months', one daily newspaper claimed, 'the country ha[d] been won and organised by Sinn Féin.'[136] Griffith and de Valera expected to detach the Irish people from the parliamentarians and sought to convince the Irish that the essential claim of Ireland ought to be the complete independence of an Irish Republic, a claim motivated by the goals of war of the Allies.[137] In other words, the Sinn Féin Convention was a bitter humiliation of the Irish Parliamentary Party. The claim that England ought now to allow Ireland to determine its own form of government was an astute rhetorical ploy, one ideally compatible with the language of Wilsonian principles. From now on, wrote France's representative, 'the Irish question [was] continuously broached from an international point of view'.[138] When Sinn Féin gathered in Dublin, 'they pronounced a new constitutional project, in short a direct proclamation of war to the Government and the existing regime'.[139]

As is evident from various sources, October 1917 reconfigured the course of Irish history and brought about a shift in the strategy of Sinn Féin. Even though the Irish Parliamentary Party made it publicly clear they would not support conscription, all over Ireland 'Sinn Féin triumph[ed] and the Catholic Clergy now support[ed] them'.[140] A year before the 1918 general elections, General de la Panouse had the conviction that Sinn Féin now represented the overwhelming majority of Irish public opinion.[141] Sinn Féin's rhetoric of international recognition inflicted a heavy blow not only to the Irish Parliamentary Party but also to the

---

[136] *Nationality*, 3 November 1917.
[137] AD, Political and Commercial Correspondence, Great War, 1914–1918, Ireland, Home Affairs (1918–1922), 95CPCOM/1, report on the situation of Ireland, 25 April 1918.
[138] Ibid.
[139] SHD, Third Republic (1870–1940), Army Staff, 7N1254, letter from General de la Panouse to the Minister for War, 22 October 1917.
[140] SHD, Third Republic (1870–1940), Army Staff, 7N679, Section des Renseignements Généraux, 2ème Bureau, 15 October 1917.
[141] SHD, Third Republic (1870–1940), Army Staff, 7N1254, letter from General de la Panouse to the Minister for War, 22 October 1917.

Irish Volunteers. The evidence for this is that a few weeks after the Sinn Féin Convention and for the first time since the beginning of the Great War, the number of men drilling in the Southern District was reported to be 1,750 as opposed to the 3,841 Irish Volunteers drilling in November 1917.[142] Even though RIC Inspectors failed to comment on the decreasing number of those who were drilling, it can be argued that de Valera's rhetoric conditioned a transfer of allegiance from the Irish Volunteers to Sinn Féin. When independence for Ireland appeared to be achievable through an international process of recognition, the idea that an election could (more effectively, and at lesser cost) achieve the same objective as a military revolution began to spread in the minds of the Irish Volunteers. The declining number of Volunteers drilling did not necessarily mean they had deserted the organization. However, the coincidence does reflect the fact that Sinn Féin now offered sufficient guarantees both against conscription and for the international recognition of Ireland as an independent nation.

The argument according to which the Peace Conference was of strategic importance for Ireland's future temporarily attenuated the gradual militarization of the Volunteers. In November 1917, France's military attaché wrote a bold comment: 'the easiest thing now would be to let the Irish govern themselves'.[143] We can legitimately wonder if General de la Panouse had not, at this stage, come to a realization of the influence of the Sinn Féin rhetoric on Irish nationalist opinion. For the first time, whereas he had *always* hitherto advocated conscription and Home Rule, he seemed to be suggesting that the best way to solve the Irish question was to grant Ireland self-government.

The shifting position of the Roman Catholic clergy

All over the country, followers of the Irish Party continued to organize meetings, reiterating the constitutional nationalist argument, and countering the rhetoric of Sinn Féin. On 7 October, at a meeting in Teconnaught (County Down), John J. Donovan, MP, criticized the ingratitude of Sinn Féin and spoke of the good work done by the Irish Party. In front of 2,000 people, he denounced their far-fetched ideal of complete independence, reminding his audience that Home Rule had been placed on the statute book in 1914. Insisting on John Redmond's dedication

---

[142] TNA, CO 904/157/1, Reports on the State of the Country, 1916–1918, Item 72, Southern District, January 1918.
[143] SHD, Third Republic (1870–1940), Army Staff, 7N1261, telegram from General de la Panouse to the Minister for War, 29 October 1917.

to the Irish cause, he emphasized that the Irish Parliamentary Party were unanimously against conscription.[144] In November 1917, J. P. Farrell, MP, and T. J. Conway warned the 1,500 people in attendance at a meeting in Lisdrumchere and Carrickmacross (County Monaghan), that Sinn Féin would only lead to disaster. They pointed out what the constitutional movement had achieved for the country during the past forty years.[145] On 16 December, in Legga (County Longford), Farrell again criticized Sinn Féin and tried to counter its rhetoric: 'it was the Irish Party that saved [you] from conscription',[146] he said. But such speeches did not succeed in putting a brake on the march of Sinn Féin. It appeared that the tide of Sinn Féin popularity was difficult to turn back.

Further evidence of the crucial importance of the period between February and October 1917 is to be found in the changing position of the Roman Catholic clergy. Support from the Church gave the party the aura it needed to ensure its ultimate political legitimation. Whether out of pragmatic interest and opportunism or from fear of losing their grasp on their congregations, 'the majority of the younger RC clergy, and some of the older priests, gave active assistance to the Sinn Féin party'.[147] A shift (coupled with a degree of hierarchical divide) took place. While the bishops remained faithful to the Irish Party and did not transfer (yet) their allegiance to Sinn Féin, local curates now embraced its ideology.[148] The Inspector of the Midlands and Connaught reported that the 'majority of the younger RC clergy and some of the older priests [were] giving active assistance to the Sinn Féin party and some of the religious orders [were] also in sympathy with this party'.[149] Younger clergymen tended to give their support, more or less officially and openly, to Sinn Féin. Bishops and senior clergy still pledged an unconditional allegiance to the Irish Parliamentary Party.

Generally speaking, the lower clergy had always more or less followed popular opinion in order to maintain both control of and proximity to their flocks. Priests 'were often drawn into Sinn Féin at the urging of uninfluential enthusiasts

---

[144] TNA, CO 904/21/3, Ireland: Dublin Castle Record, National Organizations, 11 October 1917.
[145] TNA, CO 904/21/3, Ireland: Dublin Castle Record, National Organizations, 22 November 1917.
[146] TNA, CO 904/21/3, Ireland: Dublin Castle Record, National Organizations, 9 January 1918.
[147] TNA, CO 904/157/1, Reports on the State of the Country, 1916–1918, Report from Sergeant Burke, Intelligence Officer, Midlands and Connaught District, 31 May 1917.
[148] TNA, CO 904/157/1, Reports on the State of the Country, 1916–1918, Report from Captain Dickie, Intelligence Officer, Headquarters, Southern District, 31 May 1917.
[149] TNA, CO 904/157/1, Reports on the State of the Country, 1916–1918, Report from Sergeant Burke, Intelligence Officer, Midlands and Connaught District, 31 May 1917.

rather than rushing into the vanguard to assume command'.¹⁵⁰ In order to retain their moral and spiritual influence, local priests and clergymen needed to lend their unreserved backing to revolutionary movements, for fear of being deprived of their charismatic authority in the community. From Dublin, Alfred Blanche reported:

> Bishops began to worry about the progress being made by Sinn Féin, especially since Sinn Féin took on an air of republicanism. They started to rail against it, warning their flocks against the dangers of such a movement. [...] unfortunately for them, priests under the authority of anti-Sinn Féin bishops tended to give their unstinting support to the demonstrations organized by the party, going as far as to come out in favour of a Republic. Priests have realized that the stream carrying rural populations towards Sinn Féin cannot be curbed and if they want to survive, both morally and materially, they have no choice but to agree to swim with the tide.¹⁵¹

In July 1917, Paul Cambon wrote that the clergy publicly associated themselves with the separatist cause. He reported that the bishops had issued instructions asking priests to abstain from participating in any activity that was related to politics.¹⁵² But insofar as the terms of the circulars were rather vague, they did not prevent priests from lending their whole-hearted support to the party.

Although a clear distinction existed as a rule between the bishops and the priests, Cardinal Logue, who had vehemently condemned Sinn Féin and had been discredited in the minds of young seminarians in Maynooth, gave his open backing to the party for the first time, in February 1918. The shift in the position of the Irish clergy has often been associated with the anti-conscription pledge of April 1918 and the direct intervention of the Catholic bishops against conscription in Ireland. However, even before the vote on conscription in the House of Commons, the representative of the Catholic Church in Ireland publicly endorsed the idea of the complete and unconditional independence of the country. As has been noted by Alfred Blanche, while Cardinal Logue refrained from using the word 'independence', his words were sufficiently clear to get across to the Irish Catholic community that the Church had reached a position where it endorsed the manifesto of Sinn Féin. Whereas a few months

---

[150] David Fitzpatrick, *Politics and Irish Life 1913–1921: Provincial Experiences of War and Revolution* (Cork: Cork University Press, 1998), 117.
[151] AD, Political and Commercial Correspondence, Great War, 1914–1918, Ireland, 1CPCOM/547, telegram from Alfred Blanche to M. Pichon, Minister for Foreign Affairs, 19 February 1918.
[152] AD, Political and Commercial Correspondence, Great War, 1914–1918, Ireland, 1CPCOM/546, telegram from Paul Cambon to the Minister for Foreign Affairs, 7 July 1917.

earlier, in October 1917, Cardinal Logue had temporized, suggesting that 'it [was] madness to think about an Irish Republic, madness to think to be represented during the Peace Conference, madness to resort to armed rebellion to fight against England',[153] he now ambiguously supported 'a full autonomy for Ireland'.[154]

The growing number of Sinn Féin sympathizers

That a significant development was under way in Ireland was not only evidenced by the correspondence of France's consular representatives but also by the reports of the RIC. As is borne out in police reports of the time, young men in rural districts, out of 'dislike to military service and fear of conscription',[155] were applying for membership and pouring into the ranks of Sinn Féin. Popular unrest was mostly due to 'the vast bulk consisting of hot-heated and irrational young fellows who [were] opposed to conscription and who [saw] in it a source of excitement'.[156] When representatives of France visited Ireland during the summer of 1917, asking farmers and labourers how they felt about the war, some 'answered their benefit was at least five times higher than in peace time'.[157] While local rural populations benefited from the conflict, all those who were questioned categorically asserted that they '[would] not go to the army unless they [were] forced to do so'.[158] 'Never had agricultural goods been sold at such prices. And surprisingly enough, those who benefit from that look[ed] towards Sinn Féin, considered as a guarantee against being sent to the front.'[159] All over the island, men who benefited from the war economy began to dread being conscripted and sent to the front. Studies dealing with conscription and the Irish revolution usually tend to focus on April 1918, the month when the House of Commons

---

[153] AD, Political and Commercial Correspondence, Great War, 1914–1918, Ireland, 1CPCOM/546, Report of the Mission Flynn to Ireland, August-September-October 1917.
[154] AD, Political and Commercial Correspondence, Great War, 1914–1918, Ireland, 1CPCOM/547, letter from Alfred Blanche to the Minister for Foreign Affairs, 11 February 1918.
[155] TNA, CO 904/157/1, Reports on the State of the Country, 1916–1918, Report from Sergeant Burke, Intelligence Officer, Midlands and Connaught District, 31 May 1917.
[156] TNA, CO 904/157/1, Reports on the State of the Country, 1916–1918, Report from Sergeant Burke, Intelligence Officer, Midland and Connaught District, 31 December 1917.
[157] AD, Political and Commercial Correspondence, Great War, 1914–1918, Ireland, 1CPCOM/546, Report of the Mission Flynnn to Ireland, August-September-October 1917.
[158] SHD, Third Republic (1870–1940), Army Staff, 7N1254, letter from Colonel de la Panouse to the Minister for War, 15 December 1916.
[159] AD, Political and Commercial Correspondence, Great War, 1914–1918, Ireland, 1CPCOM/545, mission of the French bishops to Ireland, 7–14 October 1916.

voted in favour of the introduction of conscription in Ireland.¹⁶⁰ Nonetheless the pervasive and ominous sense that conscription could be resorted to in order to quieten discontent in Ireland had emerged as early as August 1914 and had grown steadily during the year 1917. Once Redmond had publicly denounced British intentions to conscript the Irish, Sinn Féin alighted on a way of attracting popular support. After all, if the Irish Party, the ally of the Liberal Party, was apprehensive about the imposition of conscription on the Irish, the danger was clearly a real one. Sinn Féin was in a position where it could astutely reap some domestic benefits, increasing its support on the part of those social classes most likely to suffer from a military service bill.

In May 1917, for the first time in many months, the RIC Inspector of the Southern District alerted the British Cabinet that the 'Sinn Féin movement [was] progressing rapidly in this district by the formation of Sinn Féin clubs'.¹⁶¹ In the Midlands and Connaught, Sergeant Burke realized that 'Sinn Féin clubs continue[d] to be formed throughout the district, and now number[ed] close to 100. No county in the district [was] without them. Sinn Féin appear[ed] to attract itself more adherents, for reasons already stated, and especially among the farming class and shop boys as the only safeguard against conscription. The idea that the Redmondite party favoured conscription [was] one of the causes of its political decline.'¹⁶² Paul Cambon reported in July 1917 that 'all over Ireland, clubs and societies of Sinn Féin [were] being founded, with an increasing number of members'.¹⁶³ On 22 July 1917, when the recently released Sinn Féin leaders held meetings in the district of Longford, about 5,000 people attended. They did so not to listen to the promise of armed rebellion, but out of fear of being drafted into the British Army.¹⁶⁴

At the end of 1917, the RIC Inspector of the Midlands and Connaught listed 'between 230 and 240 clubs'¹⁶⁵ in the district alone. At that time, all over Ireland, the Colonial Office numbered 1,039 clubs (66,279 Sinn Féiners).¹⁶⁶ A year later,

---

160 Adrian Gregory, '"You might as well recruit Germans": British public opinion and the decision to conscript the Irish in 1918', in *Ireland and the Great War: 'A War to Unite Us All?'*, ed. Adrian Gregory and Senia Pašeta (Manchester: Manchester University Press, 2002), 113–132.
161 TNA, CO 904/157/1, Reports on the State of the Country, 1916–1918, Report from Captain Dickie, Intelligence Officer, Southern District, 31 May 1917.
162 TNA, CO 904/157/1, Reports on the State of the Country, 1916–1918, Report from Sergeant Burke, Intelligence Officer, Midlands and Connaught District, 31 July 1917.
163 AD, Political and Commercial Correspondence, Great War, 1914–1918, Ireland, 1CPCOM/546, telegram from Paul Cambon to the Minister for Foreign Affairs, 7 July 1917.
164 TNA, CO 904/157/1, Reports on the State of the Country, 1916–1918, Report from Sergeant Burke, Intelligence Officer, Midlands and Connaught District, 31 July 1917.
165 TNA, CO 904/157/1, Reports on the State of the Country, 1916–1918, Report from Sergeant Burke, Intelligence Officer, Midlands and Connaught District, 31 December 1917.
166 TNA, CO 903/19, Chief Secretary's Office, Judicial Division, Intelligence Notes, 1918, p. 48.

there were now 112,080 members in the island (1,354 clubs).[167] A close analysis of the membership of Sinn Féin clubs reveals that the party did not significantly increase its support in the immediate aftermath of the 1916 uprising. One year after the rebellion, in April 1917, there were only 166 Sinn Féin clubs (which represented no more than 11,000 men) in existence throughout the country. Six months later, by December 1917, membership was 66,270,[168] which means that between April 1917 and December 1917 membership was multiplied by six. That significant increase of Sinn Féin membership throughout 1917 is borne out by the reports of RIC Inspectors. There were only two Sinn Féin clubs in Sligo at the end of March 1917, by the end of July, a total of fifteen clubs, with a membership of 773, had been established in the county.[169]

At the end of 1917, each RIC Inspector was required to evaluate the number of Sinn Féin clubs in his county. County Fermanagh numbered twenty-two clubs (1,665 members).[170] County Tyrone, where Sinn Féin made substantial progress during the latter part of the year, had thirty-six clubs, with a membership of 2,135.[171] In County Carlow, Sinn Féin made considerable headway, especially amongst the younger generation, and had a total of nine clubs (542 members). In County Dublin, the movement also made considerable strides during the latter half of the year, with a membership of 422. After the victory of the Sinn Féin candidate at the South Longford election, Sinn Féin began to spread in County Kildare and three clubs were formed in June 1917, with fifteen clubs totalling a membership of 851 by December.[172] The same trend was in evidence in County Kilkenny. In June 1917 there were only six clubs. Six months later, there were twenty-one clubs, with a membership of 1,869.[173] Twenty-four clubs were formed in 1917 in County Westmeath whereas none had been in existence in 1916.[174] In autumn 1917, the RIC Inspector for County Wexford reported that the 'Sinn Féin movement had made great progress, and at the end of the year there were 41 clubs in the county with a membership of 1,892'. In County Wicklow, there was no club in 1916, but after the Longford election in May 1917, the RIC noticed that the movement was beginning to spread and at the end of June, four clubs had been formed, with a membership of 125. By December 1917,

---

[167] Ibid.
[168] Ibid.
[169] Farry, *Sligo. The Irish Revolution, 1912–1923*, 33.
[170] TNA, CO 903/19, Chief Secretary's Office, Judicial Division, Intelligence Notes, 1917, p. 2.
[171] Ibid., p. 3.
[172] Ibid., p. 4.
[173] Ibid., p. 5.
[174] Ibid., p. 6.

fourteen clubs were in existence, with a membership of 561.[175] In County Kerry, the first half of 1917 was generally peaceful and free from any agrarian trouble, boycotting or intimidation. Easter Week passed off quietly. However, the Longford election and the release of Sinn Féin rebel prisoners in June 1917 caused much excitement throughout the county and contributed to the multiplication of Sinn Féin clubs, the number of which, by the end of 1917, had risen to forty-six, with 2,456 members.[176] The Longford election seems to have given a new impetus to Sinn Féin in County Limerick too. In May 1917, Sinn Féin started to form clubs, and at the end of the month, seven had been established. By December, fifty-six clubs had already been established, with a membership of 3,828.[177] Even though he did not give the number of Sinn Féin clubs in existence in his county before June 1917, the Inspector of County Tipperary N.R. admitted that the Longford election, coupled with the release of former 1916 rebels, fortified Sinn Féin strength in the county, which had thirty-seven clubs and 2,230 members by January 1918.[178] In County Tipperary S.R., thirty-eight clubs had been created in 1917 alone.

Connaught was also concerned by the growing popularity of Sinn Féin. With thirteen and twenty-one clubs respectively, County Galway E.R. and W.R. experienced demonstrations and serious outrages, all of them supported indirectly by the younger clergy. County Leitrim, described in January 1917 as a 'peaceable and orderly county, free from boycotting, intimidation, and agrarian trouble', had also been won over to support for Sinn Féin, with forty-three clubs in December and a total membership of 2,268.[179] Without giving the exact number of clubs at the beginning of 1917, the Inspector for County Mayo underlined that at the close of the year there was a total of fifty-nine clubs in the county. Changes began to emerge in County Sligo in June 1917. By December, Sinn Féin had established forty-three clubs with a membership of 2,762.[180] In October 1917, the Intelligence Officer estimated the number of Sinn Féin clubs to be 315 in the Midlands and Connaught alone.[181] There could be no room for doubt as to the motivations and expectations of these new Sinn Féiners: 'The great mass of the people who have joined Sinn Féin have done so to join a new

---

[175] Ibid., p. 7.
[176] Ibid., p. 9.
[177] Ibid., p. 10.
[178] Ibid., p. 11.
[179] Ibid., p. 13.
[180] Ibid., p. 13.
[181] TNA, CO 904/157/1, Reports on the State of the Country, 1916–1918, Report from Sergeant Burke, Intelligence Officer, Midlands and Connaught District, 31 October 1917.

political body, to avoid conscription and to be on the popular side.'[182] It appears obvious that if there had not been a significant rise in support for Sinn Féin in 1917, the activities of the party would not have been the object of such careful attention on the part of the RIC in their secret reports.

Conclusion

Fears of being conscripted overnight represented a tangible and immediate threat that embittered local populations. They played a determining role in radicalizing civilian populations during the four by-elections. It was indeed (according to police inspectors and France's representatives to Dublin and London) this tangible concern that triggered the change over time, the gradual – and far from immediate – shift of allegiances in nationalist Ireland. Electoral material for the four by-elections addressed a wide range of concerns among the local populations. But all of them consistently warned the Irish that they could be drafted one day. In portraying the Irish Party as a strong advocate of compulsion, Sinn Féin significantly weakened the constitutional movement and did sow doubts in the minds of the nationalist electorate. Anti-conscription rhetoric merged with narratives of self-determination in 1917, and when the US entered the war in April of the same year, claims for self-determination increased the legitimacy of Sinn Féin. US intervention gave credibility and resonance to this claim as Sinn Féin now offered the Irish a viable political alternative. This included independence, a seat at the Peace Conference, and resistance to conscription. With the entry of the US, Sinn Féin could easily devise a plausible rhetoric of complete independence, compatible with the Wilsonian vision of the post-war order.

---

[182] TNA, CO 904/157/1, Reports on the State of the Country, 1916–1918, Report from Sergeant Burke, Intelligence Officer, Midlands and Connaught District, 30 November 1917.

5

The Wartime Internationalization of the Irish Question (April 1917–March 1918)

As soon as the United States entered the war in April 1917, it became a matter of urgency to find a solution to the Irish question. General de la Panouse claimed that the Irish question, from being a purely domestic British concern had become an international wartime concern, one which had to be dealt with without delay.[1] By May 1917, France's representatives had concluded that the Irish question was now 'a matter of war'.[2] Since the outbreak of the First World War, the Irish situation had been envisaged from an exclusively domestic point of view. With the US demanding that the Irish question be dealt with, there was now evidence of a sudden internationalization of it.[3] France's military attaché stated that the Irish problem 'ha[d] a ricochet effect on the relations between Great Britain and the United States and on their possible cooperation with the Allies'.[4] France urgently needed to have the guarantee that the Irish question would not prevent the US from supporting the Allies.

US intervention: a blow to the separatist movement?

By the time the US entered the war, George Plunkett had been elected in February 1917, and Sinn Féin was being entirely reorganized. An analysis of the correspondence of Alfred Blanche leads to the conclusion that the entry of the

---

[1] Service Historique de la Défense, Vincennes (hereafter SHD), Third Republic (1870–1940), Military Headquarters (1914–1918), 16N3007, telegram from General de la Panouse to the General Commander-in-Chief of the French Armies in the North and North East of France, 14 May 1917.
[2] SHD, Third Republic (1870–1940), Army Staff, 7N1254, telegram from General de la Panouse to the Minister for War, 1 May 1917.
[3] Stephen Hartley, *The Irish Question as a Problem in British Foreign Policy, 1914–1918* (New York: St Martin's Press, 1987), 113.
[4] SHD, Third Republic (1870–1940), Military Headquarters (1914–1918), 16N3223, telegram from General de la Panouse to the Minister for War, 27 March 1917.

US in the conflict 'struck a blow to the rebellious party'.⁵ Careful attention needs to be given to the issue in order to understand what exactly the Consul for France to Dublin meant by this contention. In December 1917, Alfred Blanche claimed that US intervention had modified relations between Sinn Féin and Irish-Americans. He went on:

> In the recent period, the money received from the other side of the Atlantic has decreased and the moral support of the United States has been gradually lost. Unfortunately, the clumsiness of police interventions and the deplorable Thomas Ashe affair have momentarily revived Sinn Féin. Since then, Sinn Féin leaders have been shouting till they are hoarse in an attempt to find issues they can protest about. Conscription would therefore be welcomed by them insofar as it would help stir up another crusade and justify new martyrs. As the months go by, US public opinion is coming down more and more strongly on the side for war, with the result that Irishmen in the US are increasingly abandoning their German sympathies and turning away from Sinn Féin. The money which until last year was given to Sinn Féin for its fight against England is now being transferred to the [Irish Parliamentary] Party, to help them in wartime. The biggest Irish Club in Chicago published a manifesto in which they stated that any Irishman who would take sides against the Allies would be an enemy to the US. Members of the United Irish League in America sent a message to the Irish underlining that any Irishman who adopted an attitude that was contrary to the interests of the United States would considerably damage the cause of Ireland and would dishonour the Irish race. If it was the case that the Irish hoped to obtain a seat at the Peace Conference, they could not possibly envisage such an option without the support of the US. By alienating American public opinion they would compromise their efforts; their only chance is therefore lay in the modification of their position towards the Allies and, consequently, to England itself.⁶

By 1914, foreign-born Americans made up over a seventh of the total of the US population. In 1900 alone, nearly five million Americans were first or second generation Irish.⁷ Irish-Americans, the second largest immigrant group after German-Americans, represented an extremely influential element in American

---

[5] Archives Diplomatiques du Ministère des Affaires Étrangères, La Courneuve (hereafter AD), 'Political and Commercial Correspondence, Great War, 1914–1918, Ireland', 1CPCOM/546, telegram from M. Alfred Blanche to the Minister for Foreign Affairs, 21 December 1917.

[6] AD, Political and Commercial Correspondence, Great War, 1914–1918, Ireland, 1CPCOM/546, telegram from M. Alfred Blanche to the Minister for Foreign Affairs, 21 December 1917.

[7] Francis M. Carroll, *American Opinion and the Irish Question, 1910–1923. A Study in Opinion and Policy* (Dublin: Gill & Macmillan, 1978), 3; Francis M. Carroll, *America and the Making of an Independent Ireland. A History* (New York: New York University Press, 2021), 2.

public opinion.⁸ By August 1914, the Irish Parliamentary Party attracted great numbers of Irish-Americans through the United Irish League of America,⁹ an Irish-American association dedicated to land reform in Ireland.¹⁰ Other Irish-American organizations (Clan na Gael, Ancient Order of Hibernians, to mention only two) were among the diverse groups to spearhead an isolationist policy when the war broke out in August 1914 in Europe.¹¹ At the outset of the war, activities of Irish-American circles included 'a variety of local activities to thwart the growing spirit of militarism [...], including boycotts of preparedness parades, a compelling crusade against the introduction of military training in the schools, and a campaign attacking the local press for its unfair coverage of the war',¹² all in the intention of increasing resistance to American interventionism.¹³ While heralding the need for American isolationism, American neutrality had permitted supporters of the Irish separatist project to fund seditious movements in Ireland and establish contact with the German embassy in Washington at the outset of the war in the hope of capturing the support of the Reich. Financial assistance from Irish-American associations (such as Clan na Gael) proved vital in arming the 1916 rebels.¹⁴ US neutrality remained a condition *sine quo non* for Irish-American activists ready to envisage the military defeat of Great Britain and France as the alternative capable of ensuring the complete independence of Ireland. French and British concerns that Irish-Americans and German-American activities would thwart any possible intervention into the war were dispelled by America's declaration of war in April 1917.¹⁵

Wilson's address to the American Congress brought about a significant shift among Irish-Americans. In a country that looked on 'hyphenated Americans' with suspicion and resentment,¹⁶ those who had voiced anti-British feelings and hoped for a German victory were exposed to the wrath of the Wilson

---

[8] Alan J. Ward, *Ireland and Anglo-American Relations, 1899–1921* (Toronto: University of Toronto Press, 1969), 30–69.
[9] Carroll, *America and the Making of an Independent Ireland*, 2.
[10] Philip Bull, 'The United Irish League, 1898–1900: The Dynamics of Irish Agrarian Agitation', *Irish Historical Studies* 33, no. 132 (2003): 404–423.
[11] On the role of Irish-American communities in fostering and advocating an isolationist approach see Joseph Cuddy, *Irish-America and National Isolationism* (New York: Arno Press, 1976).
[12] Elizabeth McKillen, 'Ethnicity, Class and Wilsonian Internationalism Reconsidered: The Mexican-American Immigrant Left and U.S. Foreign Relations, 1914–1922', *Diplomatic History* 25, no. 4 (2001): 574.
[13] Julia Irwin, *Making the World Safe: The American Red Cross and a Nation's Humanitarian Awakening* (Oxford: Oxford University Press, 2013). Irwin challenges the idea that the period 1914–1917 was a time of neutrality for the US. Focusing on the humanitarian efforts of groups such as the Red Cross and the Commission for Relief in Belgium, Irwin amply demonstrates that millions of Americans sought to define an active humanitarian role for their country.
[14] Carroll, *America and the Making of an Independent Ireland*, 8–9.
[15] Hartley, *The Irish Question*.
[16] Carroll, *America and the Making of an Independent Ireland*, 23.

administration.[17] Little tolerance was shown for disloyal elements in American society. Wilson expected to quieten discontent among Irish-Americans only insofar as it would improve diplomatic relations with Britain,[18] but he knew that a solution to the Irish question would help him capture the political support of the Irish diaspora for his vision of a post-war international world order.[19]

The Irish Party subsequently began to receive funds originally raised for seditious groups in Ireland, while Irish-American associations, such as the Friends of the Irish Freedom,[20] now refrained from spreading anti-British and anti-Allied propaganda. At the end of December 1917, France's Consul to Dublin rejoiced at what he called 'the embarrassment of Sinn Féin'.[21] It remains unclear why Alfred Blanche chose to speak of the declining influence of Sinn Féin at a time when figures for membership of Sinn Féin were rising. Was Blanche suggesting that there was a confusion in the Sinn Féin message when he portrayed the party as being embarrassed? Was the Consul unaware of the multiplication of Sinn Féin clubs? As previously seen in Chapter 4, de Valera had adopted a resolutely anti-British and pro-German stance when he delivered speeches during the 1917 East-Clare and Kilkenny by-elections. This invites us to qualify the idea that Wilson's intervention had put an end to disloyal seditious speeches by Sinn Féin or by its supporters. France's Consul was however solely drawing on published archival material. He could not draw on all the transcripts of speeches delivered by Sinn Féin activists during electoral contests. This can account for what can be seen as a somewhat sweeping generalization on his part, one which does not bear up when additional evidence is examined concerning Sinn Féin's post-April 1917 position.

Blanche's reports nonetheless offer us a significant contrast with the conclusions drawn by historians of the Irish Revolution.[22] This needs to be noted,

---

[17] Michael Doorley, *Justice Daniel Cohalan, 1946–1965. American Patriot and Irish-American Nationalist* (Cork: Cork University Press, 2019), 71–73.
[18] Carroll, *American Opinion and the Irish Question*, 19.
[19] Bernadette Whelan, *United States Foreign Policy and Ireland: From Empire to Independence, 1913–1929* (Dublin: Four Courts Press, 2006), 29.
[20] Following the Irish Race Convention in New York City on 4 and 5 March 1916, 2,000 Irish-Americans attended and founded the Friends of Irish Freedom (FOIF). The Friends of Irish Freedom sought to raise awareness as to the Irish question, to support and fund any nationalist paramilitary and political force/movement within Ireland. When the US entered the war, membership within the organization significantly dropped. For a complete history of this Irish-American association see Michael Doorley, *Irish-American Diaspora Nationalism. The Friends of Irish Freedom, 1916–1935* (Dublin: Four Courts Press, 2005).
[21] AD, Political and Commercial Correspondence, Great War, 1914–1918, Ireland, 1CPCOM/546, telegram from M. Alfred Blanche to the Minister for Foreign Affairs, 3 January 1918.
[22] Michael Laffan, Joseph Lee, Roy Foster, F. S. L. Lyons, David Fitzpatrick and Diarmaid Ferriter (to mention but a few) did not report any evidence of embarrassment or inconsistency in Sinn Féin at the end of 1917, following the intervention of the US.

as it is indisputable that in December 1917, in spite of four by-elections secured by Sinn Féin, and of the October 1917 Mansion House Convention, Alfred Blanche, in his capacity as Consul-General to Dublin, was confidently writing: 'Things could possibly lead to the rapid death or paralysis of the Sinn Féin party.'[23] In his considered opinion, the British ought to take advantage of what represented an unexpected opportunity to solve the Irish question once and for all. In December 1917, despite the re-organization of Sinn Féin that had turned it into a united separatist front, and despite the four by-election victories and the widening gap between popular opinion and the Irish Party, there was nothing, in his mind, to indicate that the situation could not in fact be reversed.

According to France's representative to Dublin, in December 1917, the fall of the Irish Parliamentary Party was not inevitable but conscription still needed to be avoided at all cost: 'the emotion such a measure would cause in Ireland would give them a new reason to agitate about. The entry of the US struck a blow to the rebel party in Ireland. One must now be careful not to offer them a new electoral plank with which to foster rebellion and help the party to regain its popularity',[24] he wrote to the French Ministry for Foreign Affairs. Blanche insisted that the implementation of conscription would undeniably 'resurrect the Sinn Féiners [...] whose prestige ha[d] been declining for several months'.[25] France's political and military authorities consistently argued that conscription could resurrect the party. It was therefore seen as the crux of the matter, something to be avoided at all costs, if further agitation on the island was to be prevented. Henry Duke's memorandum based on postal censorship mirrored Blanche's observations:[26] on the whole the situation in Ireland was improving and 'Sinn Féin was losing ground'.[27] In January 1918, Duke pointed out that the present situation was less threatening than it had been twelve or even six months earlier. He attributed these changes to the disillusionment of many with regard to German intentions, to the changed attitude of the United States, and to the clear evidence that the military might of England would be enough to quell any signs of rebellion.[28] However, he admitted that in some parts of the country, dissident sections were

---

[23] AD, Political and Commercial Correspondence, Great War, 1914–1918, Ireland, 1CPCOM/546, telegram from M. Alfred Blanche to the Minister for Foreign Affairs, 21 December 1917.
[24] Ibid.
[25] Ibid.
[26] The National Archives (hereafter TNA), Cabinet Papers (hereafter CAB), 24/38/33, memorandum from H. E. Duke, The Situation in Ireland, 5 January 1918.
[27] Adrian Gregory, '"You might as well recruit Germans": British public opinion and the decision to conscript the Irish in 1918', in *Ireland and the Great War: 'A War to Unite Us All?'*, ed. Adrian Gregory and Senia Pašeta (Manchester: Manchester University Press, 2002), 118.
[28] TNA, CAB 24/38/33, memorandum from H. E. Duke, The Situation in Ireland, 5 January 1918.

continuing to drill and that the theft of arms both from barracks and from soldiers on leave had increased.

By December 1917, Alfred Blanche and Henry Duke were reporting a shift in public opinion. While the recent by-elections had offered Sinn Féin a number of spectacular victories, the internationalization of the Irish question could still permit, in Blanche's mind, the Irish Parliamentary Party to reclaim their position as a defender of the Irish nation. Even though (as seen in Chapter 4) Sinn Féin was said to have won over the overwhelming majority of Irish public opinion, Blanche was in disagreement with General de la Panouse. The two were in disagreement on their assessment of the strength of the Sinn Féin party. Blanche thought a solution aimed at consolidating the Irish Party was still possible but General de la Panouse, from the vantage-point of his office in London, maintained that Sinn Féin was now the official opposition to the British and nothing could be done to avoid that.

Colonel House and Ireland

By the time the US entered into the war,[29] Colonel House (July 1858–March 1938) had already stated to the British Foreign Secretary, Sir Edward Grey, that the American people would 'go to limits unthinkable to bring about a just solution'[30] to the European conflict. On 11 January 1916, Colonel House had met Ambassador Walter Page and Lloyd George and conveyed to them that 'the United States would like Great Britain to do those things which would enable the United States to help Great Britain win the war'.[31] The House–Grey Agreement was eventually signed on 22 February 1916, though Wilson did not succeed in convincing Congress to enter the war. A few months later, when the US did finally enter the war, the Irish question shifted from the theatre of British politics to the larger stage of international wartime diplomacy.

---

[29] Ross Kennedy, *The Will to Believe: Woodrow Wilson, World War I, and America's Strategy for Peace and Security* (Kent (Ohio): Kent University State Press, 2009); John Milton Cooper, *Woodrow Wilson: a Biography* (New York: Knopf, 2009). Kennedy contends that Wilson saw a German victory as a threat to America's security and national interests. According to him, Wilson hoped to rebuild the international political system to protect the US from the repercussions of European power struggles. In his major biography of Woodrow Wilson, Cooper instead argues that by 1917 Wilson believed that the US needed to take an active part in the fighting to earn a leading role at the peace table.

[30] Yale University Library (hereafter YUL), Manuscript Section, Private Papers of Colonel Edward House (1885–1938), Edward Grey to Colonel House, 22 September 1915.

[31] Charles Seymour, ed., *The Intimate Papers of Colonel House, Volume II. From Neutrality to War, 1915–1917* (London: Ernest Benn Limited, 1926), 124.

As soon as the US entered the war, representatives from the Senate, Congress and other political spheres indicated their categorical support for the implementation of Home Rule in Ireland.[32] US intervention provided a greater visibility for Irish-Americans who were in favour of Home Rule. Shane Leslie, editor for the periodical *Ireland*, wrote a column in the newspaper *America* a few days after the US declaration of war against Germany. On 28 April 1917, he published an article entitled 'What does Ireland Want?',[33] in which he insisted that Home Rule remained the most practical and legitimate form of government for the Irish, thus dismissing the scenario of an Irish Republic.

In April 1917, France's military attaché to London insisted that President Wilson was now facing opposition from Congress: 'the treatment of the Irish by England is in flagrant contradiction with her pretentions for the oppressed small nations'.[34] If Britain welcomed US intervention in the war effort, it was now under the obligation, if it were to be consistent, to modify its policy towards Ireland. Sir Cecil Spring Rice, British Ambassador to Washington, summed up Wilson's position in April 1917, emphasizing how the Irish question afforded Irish-Americans a means of putting pressure on the US President: 'The President is by descent an Orangeman and by education a Presbyterian. But he is the leader of the Democratic Party in which the Irish play a prominent part, and he is bound in every way to give consideration to their demands.'[35]

Local newspapers throughout Ireland reported that the British Government would now have to demonstrate to Wilson that they were serious in their resolve to hammer out a solution for Ireland. In its editorial, the *Freeman's Journal* quoted Asquith in order to highlight once again how important the Irish factor was for the Allies, more precisely for the United States. It pointed out that 'the Government at last realise[d] the importance of an Irish settlement as a war measure'.[36] From April 1917 onwards, public opinion in both America and Australia, favourable to Irish independence, became 'a great source of anxiety to the British'.[37] On 28 and 29 April 1917, 200 American Congressmen sent a telegram to Lloyd George demanding an early settlement of the Irish problem in

---

[32] Charles Callan Tansill, *America and the Fight for Irish Freedom, 1866–1922* (New York: The Devin-Adair Co., 1957), 227.
[33] *America*, 28 April 1917.
[34] AD, Political and Commercial Correspondence, Great War, 1914–1918, Ireland, 1CPCOM/546, telegram from General de la Panouse to the Minister for Foreign Affairs, 24 April 1917.
[35] *Letters and Friendships of Sir Cecil Spring Rice, II*, letter to Lord Robert Cecil, 13 April 1917, p. 393.
[36] *Freeman's Journal*, 23 March 1917.
[37] Military Archives of Ireland (hereafter MAI), Bureau of Military History, 1913–1921 (hereafter BMH), WS687, witness statement from Rev. Monsignor M. Curran, former Secretary to Archbishop Walsh, 17 June 1952, p. 201.

accordance with the principles announced by Wilson in his address to the Congress.[38] France's representatives scrutinized Anglo-American encounters and reported on how the Irish question was complicating negotiations. To grant Home Rule would immediately assuage American worries. It would endorse Wilson's vision of a new international order and silence Sinn Féin. Even more importantly it would save the Irish Parliamentary Party.

The April 1917 Irish Convention: a 'flat failure'[39] or a 'political camouflage'[40]?

Five days after the US entry into the war, on 10 April 1917, Wilson wrote to Robert Lansing, State Secretary, that he should instruct Walter Hines Page, his ambassador to London, to urge the British Prime Minister to find a satisfactory method of self-government for Ireland. Wilson's move 'was a remarkably forceful warning of the British that full American participation in the war effort would be in part dependent on a solution to the ongoing domestic Irish problem'.[41] On his behalf, Walter Page invited the British Prime Minister to discuss immediate Home Rule for Ireland on 17 April 1917.[42] It must be borne in mind that Wilson dreaded the possibility of an Irish Republic. Home Rule, 'upon conditions prescribed by the British Government, was as far was he was inclined to go'.[43] Lloyd George suggested to Page that Wilson should directly contact Arthur J. Balfour, Foreign Secretary, who was to visit the US to negotiate American support for the war effort. When Balfour landed in the US on 22 April, he was introduced to Wilson by Lansing the following day. On 30 April, he was invited to the White House for dinner.[44] According to Balfour, 'neither the President nor any Member of the Government [..] said a word [...] about Ireland'.[45] On 5 May, Lansing informed Balfour that the US government 'found it difficult to cope' with anti-British elements in the country and informally requested Balfour to tell Lloyd George to 'do something to remove this hostility of persons of Irish

---

[38] Ibid.
[39] Tansill, *America and the Fight for Irish Freedom*, 243.
[40] *Irish World*, 23 February 1918.
[41] Carroll, *America and the Making of an Independent Ireland*, 24.
[42] National Archives of Ireland (hereafter NAI), Manuscript Section (hereafter MS), 841D.00/106, letter from President Wilson to Secretary Lansing, 18 April 1917.
[43] Tansill, *America and the Fight for Irish Freedom*, 251.
[44] Carroll, *America and the Making of an Independent Ireland*, 25.
[45] House of Lords Library, David Lloyd George Papers (1882–1945), F60/2/13, Balfour to War Cabinet, 1 May 1917.

blood and of their American sympathizers'.[46] While Balfour was in the US, 'Congress introduced numerous resolutions asking the British government to take steps to provide some form of self-government'[47] in Ireland.

After several weeks of procrastinations, on 16 May 1917, Lloyd George issued a letter to the representatives of the political parties in Ireland in which he announced that the Government wished 'to put an end to a state of affairs which [was] productive of immense evil not only to Ireland but to Great Britain and the Empire'.[48] His intention was either to immediately implement Home Rule, with a five-year exclusion of the six counties of Ulster, or to summon a convention that was to define the terms of an agreement between the parties. The following day, on 17 May, John Redmond, as leader of the Irish Parliamentary Party, came out in favour of a convention, categorically repudiating any proposal to exclude the six counties of Ulster.[49] On 19 May 1917, in the House of Commons, Laurence Ginnell asked the undersecretary of state for foreign affairs if he would inform the House of any communication and discussions that had been entered into between the American and British Governments with reference to Ireland. Lord Robert Cecil declined to answer. Ginnell then asked the Prime Minister if 'equal independence for small nations as for large, and especially for Ireland'[50] would be envisaged. Russia's declaration in relation to the independence of Poland was referred to, in order to ramp up the pressure on the British Cabinet. On 21 May, Sinn Féin declared they would not attend a convention whose representatives had not been directly elected by the Irish people. That position led General de la Panouse to conclude that the convention was doomed. The following day, in the House of Commons, Lord Curzon opposed temporary exclusion and backed the idea of a convention. The Irish Unionist Alliance (1 June), the Ulster Unionist Council (8 June), the Catholic Clergy of Maynooth (19 June), and the workers' unions (22 July) all announced that they would participate in a convention and rejected the plan for the implementation of Home Rule with a five-year temporary exclusion of the six north-east counties of Ulster.

The month of de Valera's electoral victory coincided with the opening of the Irish Convention.[51] Lloyd George hoped 'to placate American opinion and to

---

[46] Robert Lansing, *War Memoirs of Robert Lansing* (Indianapolis: Bobbs-Merrill, 1935), 276–277.
[47] Carroll, *America and the Making of an Independent Ireland*, 28.
[48] *Report of the Proceedings of the Irish Convention*, (Dublin: HMSO, 1918), p. 50, Appendix 1, letter from Lloyd George to John Redmond, 16 May 1917.
[49] Denis Gwynn, *The Life of John Redmond* (London: Harrap, 1932), 550.
[50] Hansard, House of Commons Debates, series 5, vol. 92, cc1798, Ginnell to House of Commons, 19 April 1917.
[51] Robert Kee, *The Green Flag. A History of Irish Nationalism* (London: Weidenfeld & Nicolson, 1972), 604–617.

weaken the impact of the anti-war Irish lobby in the United States'.[52] In order to secure full cooperation from the US and reassure Wilson as to their determination to find a definitive solution to the Irish question, Lloyd George appointed a committee that was to oversee further talks between the Irish Party and the Ulster Unionists. Contemporary commentators in Washington responded favourably to the move. It has been argued that it was the July 1917 Sinn Féin Convention that finally brought about the metamorphosis of Sinn Féin, as John Redmond found himself trapped in the Irish Convention whereas Éamon de Valera, a former 1916 rebel, emerged victorious from the East-Clare by-election on 17 July.[53] However (as seen in Chapter 4), the demand for total independence had already been voiced before the audience present at the Sinn Féin Convention in the Dublin Mansion House. In June 1917 Arthur Griffith had furthermore delivered a speech at a Westmeath convention in which he made clear that the independence of Ireland was now the main objective of the party.[54] In light of this, any resolution adopted by the Irish Convention would inevitably fail to meet the political expectations of Sinn Féin.

Sinn Féin envisaged participating in discussions with the British (at a future Irish convention), but only on condition that the following points were agreed on previously: (1) complete independence of Ireland, (2) an Irish Republic, and (3) that a pledge be given to the US and Europe by the British Government that it would ratify the majority decision of the participants in the convention.[55] As Sinn Féin secured its second by-election victory, Wilsonian rhetoric was taking hold. The demand for complete independence was shaping the new direction of the party. In short, resentment, popular unrest and fear of conscription did not in themselves suffice to distance itself from the constitutional party. After all, Redmond had been steadfast in his opposition to both conscription and to partition. In the interests of Sinn Féin, there had to be a 'clear water' difference of aims between Sinn Féin and the Irish Party. Such a distinction could not merely be a question of the methods to be adopted (revolutionary insurrection against constitutional nationalism); it also had to neutralize the

---

[52] Michael Laffan, *The Resurrection of Ireland. The Sinn Féin Party, 1916–1923* (Cambridge: Cambridge University Press, 1999), 106. Francis M. Carroll disregards the idea that the Irish Convention was merely a diversion thought up by Lloyd George to mollify the United States. He agrees with R. B. McDowell that the British had been preoccupied since the Rising with the issue of how to implement some form of Irish self-government. See Francis M. Carroll, *America and the Making of an Independent Ireland*, 30, and R. B. McDowell, *The Irish Convention, 1917–1918* (London: Routledge & Kegan Paul, 1970), 76.
[53] Kee, *The Green Flag*, 591–604.
[54] *Irish Independent*, 25 June 1917.
[55] Kee, *The Green Flag*, 591–604.

similarity in aims that Sinn Féin and the Irish Party appeared to have, when from March 1917 onwards Redmond left no stone unturned in his opposition to conscription and his public disparagement of the British Government. Sinn Féin needed to rethink its ideology. And as the party had always advocated the goal of an independent nation and a republic, it could now construct, with the international situation considered to be favourable to small stateless nations, a new version of its fundamental narrative, one formulated in the language of Wilsonian principles. An independent Ireland had always been the aspiration of Sinn Féin and of all paramilitary and underground societies that had existed in Ireland. Now, it appeared that the goal of Irish independence could be a plausible constitutional demand. The Irish Parliamentary Party supported Home Rule, as a limited form of autonomy, but, as the Ambassador for France to London stated, 'they never really wanted an independent Ireland'.[56] Furthermore, when Sinn Féin started to advocate total independence, the Home Rule supporters appeared jaded and somewhat stale, but more importantly, as being less committed to the cause of Ireland. On 9 July 1917, Sinn Féin issued a manifesto in which it stated its opposition to the Irish Convention, an initiative which implied that the Irish Parliamentary Party had entered into talks with Ulster Unionists at Westminster. Constitutional nationalists could now easily be portrayed as having been tricked into taking part in discussions that would ultimately offer nothing to Ireland. Any sign of a rapprochement with the Irish Party would have obscured the distinction between the clear lines of Sinn Féin's uncompromising position and the contours of the Irish Parliamentary Party policy.

Alfred Blanche knew that Carson and Redmond would never succeed in reaching an agreement: 'A letter from the Prime Minister summoning a delegation for a Convention? This is all that was offered to an impatient and irritated public opinion whose scepticism grows, as procrastination continues.'[57] Of greater interest is the fact that in his letter to the Quai d'Orsay he urged that immediate action be taken. And compared to what General de la Panouse suggested, for Blanche the only possible answer was a political resolution of the crisis. Blanche categorically opposed conscription as a solution for the country. He discounted the idea that the response had to be military. Blanche considered that 'the Government must agree to the risk in order to reach a solution, however imperfect or defective, but an immediate and clear solution is

---

[56] AD, Political and Commercial Correspondence, Great War, 1914–1918, Ireland, 1CPCOM/545, telegram from Paul Cambon to the Minister for Foreign Affairs, 3 May 1916.
[57] AD, Political and Commercial Correspondence, Great War, 1914–1918, Ireland, 1CPCOM/546, telegram from Alfred Blanche to the Minister for Foreign Affairs, 26 January 1918.

better than endless uncertainty that encourages all kinds of discontent and agitation'.[58]

In order to create a favourable and more serene atmosphere for the convention the Irish Parliamentary Party had pressed the British to grant amnesty to the remaining Easter Week prisoners. On 17 June, the Government accepted and released the men. On 1 July, the Bishop of Cork called for the union of all the Irish to ensure the convention's success. The first meeting was held on 25 July 1917, in the Regent House, Trinity College Dublin. The Convention then proceeded to elect Sir Horace Plunkett as Chairman, and Sir Francis Hopwood as Secretary.[59] On 26 July, 8 and 9 August, the following three meetings adopted a framework for the organization and the work of the Convention. Three meetings then took place in Belfast followed by three others in Cork. At that time, the Friends of Irish Freedom had prepared a petition calling for Irish independence which had been circulated throughout the United States, securing several hundred thousand signatures.[60] On 24 January 1918, the British Prime Minister issued a letter to George N. Plunkett requesting that a delegation present the work of the Convention in London. In February, meetings started again at a time when unrest was slowly taking hold of the west of the country.

Procrastinations were endangering the stability of the Irish Parliamentary Party, as well as affording Sinn Féin another opportunity to challenge the British and establish itself as the main opponent to conscription. More than anything else, what the Irish Convention managed to achieve, according to General de la Panouse, was to paralyse the British, leaving them prey both to the intransigence of the Unionists and to the suspicions of the Nationalists:

> Since the very first moment the Convention was established, it was clear the participants would never hammer out an agreement and that the Government would have to find a solution itself. For the last six months, the Government has had plenty of time to prepare for this. However, it did nothing, even appearing to be taken aback by the failure of the Convention to come up with anything. The Government promised not to implement conscription without presenting a Home Rule project to the Parliament. Nevertheless, US pressure persuaded M. Lloyd George and his colleagues to make the promise of a new Home Rule bill.[61]

---

[58] Ibid.
[59] *Report of the Proceedings of the Irish Convention*, (Dublin: HMSO, 1918), p. 9.
[60] Tansill, *America and the Fight for Irish Freedom*, 233.
[61] SHD, Third Republic (1870–1940), Army Staff, 7N1254, telegram from General de la Panouse to the Minister for War, 22 April 1918.

In retrospect, we can wonder if Lloyd George had in turn opted for what the historian Alvin Jackson has called 'Asquith's delaying tactics'.[62] Did the British sincerely hope to reach an agreement? In the minds of France's representatives, the Irish Convention was merely another ploy to win time. But for what purpose? General de la Panouse immediately anticipated the sterile role of the Convention, suggesting that even if a solution were to emerge from the negotiations, Sinn Féin would deliberately paralyse and block the establishment of a government.[63] The Convention, in his eyes, was merely yet another delaying tactic through which to defer momentarily any consideration of or solution to the Irish question, while offering a political pledge to Britain's US ally.[64] The idea that the Irish Convention was ultimately a move designed to reassure Washington and to postpone any radical decision for the future administration of Ireland, further weakening the Irish Parliamentary Party in the process, was gaining credence in the corridors of Westminster. It was also being voiced in the dispatches of the representatives of the French Republic to Dublin, London and Washington.

In the United States, voices were heard expressing the widespread suspicion that following the US entry into the conflict, a repressive policy in Ireland was now unthinkable, with the result that the British Cabinet had therefore to contemplate some path to conciliation. However, whatever the enthusiasm it might arouse, it was pointed out that the Irish Convention looked like yet another episode intended only to delay matters further and 'to placate American public opinion'.[65] Irish-Americans indeed expressed grave doubts, claiming that the Irish Convention would end in deadlock due to the intransigent position of Ulster Unionists.[66] From New York, on 12 March 1918, André Tardieu (High Commissioner for France in the US) sent a report to the Minister for Foreign Affairs in which he explained that partition was unanimously condemned among Irish-Americans: 'the separatist claims of Ulster seem to the overwhelming majority of Americans to be as unjustifiable as the secession of South Carolina'.[67] Tardieu highlighted that American public opinion backed the Irish Convention and urged England to accept that the majority of Irish-Americans disagreed

---

[62] Alvin Jackson, *Home Rule: An Irish History, 1800–2000* (London: Weidenfeld & Nicolson, 2003), 140.
[63] SHD, Third Republic (1870–1940), Army Staff, 7N1254, letter from General de la Panouse to the Minister for War, 22 October 1917.
[64] Ibid.
[65] *New York Evening Post*, 25 May 1917.
[66] *Irish World*, 23 February 1918.
[67] AD, Political and Commercial Correspondence, Great War, 1914–1918, Ireland, 1CPCOM/547, letter from André Tardieu to the Minister for Foreign Affairs, 12 March 1918.

with partition. The day Tardieu sent his telegraph to Paris, on 12 March 1918, the Marquess of Salisbury lectured the Government in the House of Lords, warning that the present situation in Ireland had become a danger to the Empire and a menace to the successful prosecution of the war, and insisting that it was 'incumbent on His Majesty's Government to enforce the law in that country'.[68] On 21 March 1918, during a debate in the House of Commons, Arthur Lynch took the opposite direction and pointed out that 'the remedy for the present state of unrest in Ireland [could] not [be] the brutal application of military force but the resolute removing from the path of the people of all the evils from which they unjustly suffer'.[69] Condemning the recourse to martial law in Ireland and the inflexibility of the British Cabinet, Lynch broached the question of the Irish Convention, pointing out that 'the Convention ha[d] been in existence now for many months, and, if it were a real, valid, and honest institution, that Convention would be ready with its Report'.[70] His speech echoed concerns in Ireland, France and the United States, as diplomats had clearly expected to be given word of a timetable for the committee to issue its conclusions. Widespread suspicion arose at the beginning of 1918 and was spread by the press in Ireland, with most daily newspapers accusing the British Government of deliberately seeking to make the Irish Convention fail.[71] Lynch warned the Prime Minister that all over Ireland the British were being said to 'keep it alive by a sort of artificial respiration, knowing that as long as the mere name of Convention [was] kept alive the Government [could] avoid what for months ha[d] been their plain duty, namely, to look the Irish problem straight in the face'.[72] That the Irish Convention sprang from the need to placate possible discontent among Irish-Americans, and to reassure Wilson, was something that was acknowledged by foreign diplomats.[73] However, while in confidence they reported that it was merely a move to mollify American public opinion, within political circles there was the growing conviction that it was too late to find a political compromise, as the goal of Home Rule was being met with increasing skepticism in nationalist Ireland.[74]

---

[68] Hansard, House of Lords Debates, series 5, vol. 29, cc367, Marques of Salisbury to the House of Lords, 12 March 1918.
[69] Hansard, House of Commons Debates, series 5, vol. 104, cc1296, Lynch to House of Commons, 21 March 1918.
[70] Ibid.
[71] *Nationality*, 2 March 1918.
[72] Hansard, House of Commons Debates, series 5, vol. 104, cc1295, Lynch to House of Commons, 21 March 1918.
[73] Laffan, *The Resurrection of Ireland*, 106.
[74] Hansard, House of Commons Debates, series 5, vol. 104, cc1295, Lynch to House of Commons, 21 March 1918.

When the Irish Convention sat on 4 and 5 April 1918 in order to wrap up its conclusions, their final report was drafted. Nonetheless it would not be published until 13 April, when all the attention was directed to the Military Service Bill. But what did this final report advocate? According to the draft, there was a provisional approval of the establishment of a senate consisting of 40 or 60 members. In addition, instead of the original elected Irish members sitting at Westminster, it was considered that the Lower House of the Dublin parliament would consist of 100 or 120 members.[75] Regarding the figures for the Unionist population in Ireland, it was agreed that the Unionists should be offered a forty per cent share of representation in the Lower House, to be guaranteed by a set of effective procedures.[76] This Convention succeeded in bringing together Nationalists and Unionists from the south and west of the country. Ulster Unionist delegates objected to the implementation of Home Rule for the whole of Ireland, as it 'would intensify existing divisions in Ireland and prove a constant menace to the Empire'.[77] Ulster Unionists, unsurprisingly, blocked any solution for a united Ireland. The Irish Convention 'had really been a flat failure'[78] that 'finally disposed of the myth that any settlement was possible',[79] accentuating the fragility of the Irish Party, to the benefit of Sinn Féin.

The *Irish World* pointed out at the time that the Irish Convention was merely 'political camouflage'.[80] Quoting one Irish MP who had expressed the viewpoint that Ulster, and not England, denied Home Rule for Ireland, the editorial concluded that the Irish Convention was a masquerade to conceal the fact that the British Cabinet had always been submitted to the 'Carsonite dictation'. Reminding its readers of the defiance of Ulster after successive House of Commons votes in favour of Home Rule before the outbreak of the Great War, followed by the raising of the Ulster Volunteer Force, the newspaper pointed out that 'the majority of the Irish people ha[d] made their will known on the question of Home Rule', adding that Asquith and Lloyd George had never effectively been able to silence 'a very significant minority'. The accusation was as follows:

> the Prime Minister of England summoned a Convention to try and coax the Orange faction to be law abiding but in fact, since this numerically insignificant faction is still bent on having its own way despite the British Government, the

---

[75] *Report of the Proceedings of the Irish Convention*, (Dublin, HMSO, 1918), p. 13.
[76] Ibid.
[77] *Report of the Proceedings of the Irish Convention*, (Dublin, HMSO, 1918), p. 33, Report of Ulster Unionist Delegates to Irish Convention, 5 April 1918.
[78] Tansill, *America and the Fight for Irish Freedom*, 243.
[79] F. S. L. Lyons, *Ireland since the Famine* (Dublin: Fontana Press, 1973), 386.
[80] *Irish World*, 23 February 1918.

world will be told that the failure of the Irish to agree stands in the way of that Government carrying out its benevolent intentions towards Ireland. Are there not sufficient grounds for suspecting that Lloyd George's Convention from the outset was nothing more than political camouflage?

All in all, it appears that the Irish Convention was an exercise which only served to mask the powerlessness of the British Cabinet, as France's diplomatic representatives indicated. But there was more to it than that; while the *Irish World* regarded the Convention as a sign of weakness intended to cover a political defeat, France's emissaries suspected that the Irish Convention had been summoned to act as a dilatory strategy, while maintaining a *status quo*.

British procrastination

The position of the French authorities regarding the Irish question appeared simple: the British ought either to repress the agitation in the country or implement Home Rule, but under no circumstances could they leave Ireland in such a state of turmoil. Alfred Blanche opposed conscription as soon as the British began to talk about it. General de la Panouse considered, on the contrary, that conscription could help raise 100,000 more recruits, but that in compensation Home Rule had first to be granted to the Irish. Blanche insisted that agitation did not stem from the 1916 insurrection or the following executions, but sprang from the incapacity of the British Government to take action. In his capacity as Consul-General to Dublin, Blanche had explicitly stated that the answer to the Irish question had to be political, not military. Months of procrastination, conflicting visions, and embittered and antagonistic political visions had weakened both the British Government and the Irish Parliamentary Party. This political vacuum enabled Sinn Féin to strengthen its standpoint and to offer the Irish people the alluring proposition that an independent and sovereign nation might emerge by the end of the war. Initially, the British did not wish to take any drastic measures for fear of undermining the Irish Convention.[81] But there was another reason which explained why the possibility of repressing agitation in Ireland was downplayed.

As the war went on and talks of a peace conference began, both the French and American authorities agreed on the need to act in order to break the

---

[81] SHD, Third Republic (1870–1940), Army Staff, 7N1261, telegram from General de la Panouse to the Minister for War, 18 February 1918.

stalemate in Ireland. US entry in the conflict was a source both of French hopes and French anxieties.[82] All representatives to Washington unequivocally reported that the solution to the Irish question conditioned the full support of the US for the Allies. According to General de la Panouse, this explained why Sir Edward Carson resigned from the Government as he clearly knew that the answer to Ireland's unrest no longer lay in either London or Dublin, but in Washington. In other words, US entry into the war made it impossible for Britain to take drastic military action in Ireland. In the aftermath of the 1916 uprising, repression had been an option, and General Maxwell's unwavering decision to execute the leaders of the rebellion, in spite of the British Cabinet's desires at the time to quieten brewing popular discontent in the country, were evidence that repression had once been possible. Such a repression had generated discontent throughout Ireland and in the US. However, the British authorities in Ireland could still shape a narrative enabling them to announce and justify the executions, without there being any widespread questioning of their entitlement to take such action.

When the US entered the war in April 1917 the decision threw British policy off balance, leaving few alternatives available to the British Government. From then on, repression was *no longer* an option. While Redmond found himself caught up in the ineffectual and time-consuming exercise of the Irish Convention, the only possible manoeuvre for the British, as Blanche noted, was to grant Home Rule immediately, even with the exclusion of the six northern counties, and establish a new administrative system for the country.[83] A direct implementation of Home Rule would, politically speaking, have been the most pragmatic solution. However, by the beginning of 1918, the British Cabinet appeared totally paralysed. In short, if repressive measures needed to be taken, they had to be adopted before the US entered the war. Following the involvement of Washington in the war, the only way out was a political settlement.

From Washington, Tardieu warned the Minister for Foreign Affairs that should the Convention fail, the US Congress 'could vote, at a large majority, all or some of the resolutions in favour of Irish autonomy'.[84] Tardieu was worried that the financial and material support of the US for the war effort was conditional on success in dealing with the Irish question. Another of his dispatches, received the following day, warned that a successful Convention (where an agreement would

---

[82] SHD, Third Republic (1870–1940), Private Papers, 6N155, telegram from General de la Panouse to the Minister for War, 28 January 1918.
[83] SHD, Third Republic (1870–1940), Military Headquarters (1914–1918), 16N3009, telegram from General de la Panouse to the Minister for War, 4 March 1918.
[84] AD, Political and Commercial Correspondence, Great War, 1914–1918, Ireland, 1CPCOM/547, letter from André Tardieu to the Minister for Foreign Affairs, 12 March 1918.

be hammered out between Nationalists and Unionists) would unquestionably have dramatic implications for England. Economic independence, he argued, would allow the Irish to trade with foreign powers, such as France, and Tardieu even envisaged the possibility of re-opening the sea-routes between Cork and France, 'that England, for the last 50 years, had blocked'.[85] With the US demanding that a solution be found to the Irish question, putting more and more pressure on the British Government, the French authorities imagined a series of propaganda initiatives aimed at increasing the number of volunteers in Ireland, and thus preventing the British from imposing conscription. In January 1918 (and since the outbreak of the conflict), recruitment in Ireland had become a concern for the French, not so much from a military angle (as they knew the British needed to replace the heavy losses suffered by their armies), but from a political perspective: to ensure the unrestricted participation of the US in the conflict.

From fear of another black '47 to fear of conscription (January–March 1918)

When, on 5 January 1918, Sir Auckland Geddes, Minister for Recruitment, reiterated that the Government did not envisage conscription for Ireland, the British hoped that his declaration would put an end to unrest. But there were other factors which infuriated local populations, suggesting that revolutionary agitation was no longer conditioned solely by the threat of conscription.

By December 1917, the RIC Inspector for the Midlands and Connaught was unambiguous: 'the general growth of Sinn Féin is due to a belief that it is Ireland's bulwark against conscription'.[86] On the whole, the 'hot-heated and irrational young fellows [...] are opposed to conscription and [...] see in it a source of excitement', he explained.[87] General de la Panouse confessed his bewilderment at the situation in Ireland: 'What a curious Irish situation, where there is no military conscription and no Government that would dare to implement it. Ireland is not suffering as much as the two other kingdoms. Its population lives in affluence that the English and Scottish populations have not experienced for a long time.'[88]

---

[85] Ibid.
[86] TNA, CO 904/157/1, Reports on the State of the Country, 1916–1918, Item 87, Midlands and Connaught District, December 1917.
[87] Ibid.
[88] SHD, Third Republic (1870–1940), Army Staff, 7N1261, telegram from General de la Panouse to the Minister for War, 18 February 1918.

Popular unrest intensified in January 1918, when armed raids began on the houses of soldiers and civilians alike, especially in the Southern District.[89] On 2, 3, 10 and 25 January, individuals broke into houses to steal rifles and ammunition.[90] There was evidence of a bitter and aggressive anti-British public feeling, the brunt of which was borne by the police. On 1 March, individuals threw bombs into the Westport barracks. On 3 March, at Clifden (County Galway), Sinn Féiners interrupted a nationalist meeting in the town hall and stoned the policemen who were on duty. One constable reported that young men would do anything rather than join the army, which could partly explain the ongoing agitation in the area.[91] In prosperous districts, where locals were 'so slightly affected by the war as compared with Great Britain, there [was] no real reason for discontent, but the number of young men, whom the Government [would] neither conscript nor permit to emigrate, as many of them would have done in normal times, [was] the cause of continual unrest'.[92] In the Midlands and Connaught, local populations had initially joined the movement 'because it was looked on as the bulwark against conscription'.[93] Fear of being conscripted merged with greed and material motivations.

Another factor contributed to the radicalization of rural communities. Agricultural populations now hoped that Sinn Féin would help them to acquire land and properties, with individuals now demanding they be allocated plots of lands. This triggered a large-scale spate of land disturbances, forcible dispossessions and intimidations. In the House of Commons, on 17 January 1918, one unionist MP warned the Government that by deliberately doing nothing, farmers were 'being rapidly hauled into their net'.[94]

> Of the older farmers in Ireland who bought their farms under the Land Act, who were all settling down quietly, nearly 90 per cent were against Sinn Féin and against these agitators at the beginning. What is happening now? They are being led away by the bribes the Sinn Féiners are offering, for the Sinn Féiners say, "If you join us, the Government are afraid of us, and we will have a republic shortly, and then no man in Ireland will pay taxes." These older farmers are led away by

---

[89] TNA, CO 904/157/1, Reports on the State of the Country, 1916–1918, Item 72, Southern District, January 1918.
[90] Ibid.
[91] TNA, CO 904/157/1, Reports on the State of the Country, 1916–1918, Item 54, Midlands and Connaught District, March 1918.
[92] Ibid.
[93] TNA, CO 904/157/1, Reports on the State of the Country, 1916–1918, Item 65, Midlands and Connaught District, February 1918.
[94] Hansard, House of Commons Debates, series 5, vol. 101, cc559, Archdale to House of Commons, 17 January 1918.

the idea that they will get their lands free, without any taxation at all, as soon as the Sinn Féiners upset the Government and have an Irish Republic. That seems rather ridiculous, but every Sinn Féin paper is repeating that in its leading articles day after day.'[95]

As the RIC Inspector of that district confessed, the 'great bulk of the poorest classes [were] eagerly joining this movement from cupidity; originally it was popular purely and simply because it was looked on as the bulwark against conscription'.[96] Sinn Féin followers hoped that the political victory of the party would guarantee them land. Agrarian expectations in part conditioned the support for Sinn Féin in Connaught and Midland counties, where a wave of lawlessness and disorder in February 1918 surprised the British authorities.[97] Sinn Féin began a policy of cattle driving and land seizure on behalf of the Irish Republic. Sligo and Roscommon, described as the counties most seriously affected, registered the consequences of the ineffectiveness of the police, as cattle driving went on in daylight. In Sligo, 100 farms were visited by Sinn Féiners, 'who gave notice to their holders of what they were about to do, and asked them to be present in order that an agreement might be come to'.[98] Whereas conscription had initially triggered a strong anti-British feeling in Ireland, farmers and labourers now 'hope[d] to get land on their own terms, and believe[d] Sinn Féin [would] do it for them'.[99] It would thus appear that the original attraction towards Sinn Féin mutated into an agrarian demand for land.

Several other factors played into the renewed inclination of nationalist populations to support Sinn Féin, leading to an upsurge in agitation throughout the country. When agents from Great Britain came to buy goods in Ireland, at premium prices, local populations expressed their resentment at what they labelled an act of arbitrary British seizure of their goods. With exports from Ireland to Britain virtually uncontrolled, the capital was then subjected to the same controls on imports as any British city, prices rose faster than wages, and communal kitchens multiplied.[100] Alfred Blanche reported (as early as December 1917), the first signs of incipient famine seemed to be threatening Dublin. People were now queuing at shops.[101] For anyone with a minimum of knowledge of

[95] Ibid.
[96] TNA, CO 904/157/1, Reports on the State of the Country, 1916–1918, Item 65, Midlands and Connaught District, February 1918.
[97] Ibid.
[98] Ibid.
[99] Ibid.
[100] Padraig Yeates, *A City in Wartime, Dublin 1914–1918* (Dublin: Gill & Macmillan, 2012), 444–451.
[101] AD, Political and Commercial Correspondence, Great War, 1914–1918, Ireland, 1CPCOM/546, telegram from Alfred Blanche to the Minister for Foreign Affairs, 28 January 1918.

Irish history, such an ominous development was enough to revive the strongest of anti-British feelings. That factor helps better understand the agitation that spread in southern Ireland. Blanche was convinced that the prevailing misery and the extreme difficulty of obtaining food were the factors behind the wave of unrest. While acknowledging the growing popularity of Sinn Féin, he insisted that the primary cause of the disturbances was the fear of impending famine: 'raids for arms are increasing in the West of the country where populations suffer from a sort of famine and where it would appear that infantile mortality has taken on dramatic proportions'. It was at this same period that the Controller for Food deprived Ireland of bacon, as all pigs available for slaughter had been shipped to England. A group of Sinn Féin activists requisitioned thirty-six pigs being driven in the street, doing so in the name of the republic. The animals were about to be sent to England, and the separatists took them to the town slaughterhouse, where they were immediately killed and delivered to a butcher in Dublin, so that the entire city had the assurance of getting enough bacon for the following days.[102] In wartime, the rise in the prices of everyday goods left local populations extremely vulnerable to conditions of hardship. In a district where 'the Potato Famine remained a living memory that cast a shadow over Irish public life',[103] unsettling food shortages and wartime accounts of starvation in other European countries accounted for famine anxiety in the civilian populations, reviving painful memories. Even though the incidence of death and illness remained stable, 'Fear of hunger, rather than hunger itself, lay at the centre of this agitation.'[104] Such fear was enough to accentuate the bitterness and mistrust of local populations.

Confidential reports forwarded to Paris highlighted the economic hardship encountered by civilian populations in the west of Ireland.[105] Prices of food had increased considerably, with the result that the cost of 'feeding the inferior two-legged cattle – men – ha[d] risen by 114 per cent'[106] according to a local newspaper. Arthur Griffith addressed the question of food shortage and reassured his readers that it was being 'promptly handled'.[107] In Ennis (County Clare), the local Sinn Féin Club supplied 150 families with potatoes. In order to

---

[102] Ibid.
[103] John Borgonovo, *The Dynamics of War and Revolution: Cork City, 1916–1918* (Cork: Cork University Press, 2013), 169.
[104] Ibid., p. 173.
[105] AD, Political and Commercial Correspondence, Great War, 1914–1918, Ireland, Home Affairs (1918–1922), 95CPCOM/1, report on the situation of Ireland, 25 April 1918.
[106] *Irish Opinion*, 30 March 1918.
[107] *Nationality*, 5 January 1918.

protect agrarian population from destitution and starvation, Sinn Féin created a Food Committee on 9 March 1918, making sure that every county would benefit from Ireland's production of food.[108] Members of the Food Committee purchased food directly from farmers and distributed it to workmen at cost price.[109] Even the *Freeman's Journal*, unreservedly a supporter of Home Rule and of the constitutional party, underlined that agitation had legitimate grounds, as 'since 1914, exportations had increased by 82%'.[110] That clearly meant that the effect of increased volume of exports to Great Britain was to deprive local populations of a larger share in Irish food production. That threat of hunger explained the agrarian policy adopted by Sinn Féin.

The beginning of 1918 gave further impetus to Sinn Féin in a context where the evolution of the social and economic situation of the country was largely dependent on the outcome of the war. Food emerged as a new cause of anxiety, drawing on the perennial mistrust of English intentions. Wartime economic prosperity had previously often been highlighted in the reports on the situation of the island. However, three and a half years into the war there could now be no hiding the fact that food shortages were infuriating populations, especially in western counties, or that local populations were demanding that food produced in Ireland be reserved to the Irish people.[111] Lawlessness and agrarian agitation modified the everyday life of the southern districts. Raids for arms, cattle driving, and evictions increased. In the city of Cork, where famine anxiety grew as a result of food rationing, local community leaders set up the short-lived Cork People's Food Committee in January 1918 in order to counter the designs of separatist actors who were intent on engaging in violent protest against the British authorities.[112] Delegates of the Food Committee were determined to compel butchers and cattle exporters not to export fresh meat but to negotiate instead with the Committee, thus raising considerable opposition to their action from those in the cattle trade. Such initiatives did not prevent sporadic violence throughout the country.

Cattle driving and raids, together with a generalized climate of fear resulting from a series of fanatical acts of violence, all testified to the rapid evolution of the situation in Ireland. In February 1918, Sir Bryan Mahon, Commander-in-Chief of the British Forces in Ireland, introduced martial law in County Clare.[113] That

[108] *Young Ireland*, 9 March 1918.
[109] *Nationality*, 5 January 1918.
[110] *Freeman's Journal*, 1 March 1918.
[111] *Irishman*, 2 March 1918.
[112] Borgonovo, *The Dynamics of War and Revolution*, 175–179.
[113] Tansill, *America and the Fight for Irish Freedom*, 255.

same month, agitation over food broke out across the country, most commonly in the form of republican-sanctioned land seizures.[114] Anarchical violence spread, proving 'an embarrassment to Sinn Féin and a liability to its attempts to woo moderate but disgruntled Home Rulers'.[115] Martial law provoked the intervention of American representatives, who immediately 'demanded a solution in accordance with the principles of Lloyd George and President Wilson'.[116] On 2 March 1918, Lord French visited Ennis in order to measure the extent of agrarian unrest. When John Redmond died on 6 March 1918, the French Intelligence Services informed the Minister for War that his death coincided with the escalation of violence in the country.[117] In western counties, raids on isolated houses, attacks on civilians, cattle-driving and requisitions of land by Sinn Féiners punctuated the ongoing and sterile debates in the House of Commons. Counties Clare and Mayo were the most exposed, followed by Sligo, Roscommon and Galway.[118] American and British soldiers reported being openly insulted by Sinn Féiners. Armed raids became increasingly common and Sinn Féin began to control all exportations of meat to Great Britain to make sure local populations were not deprived of what their country produced in wartime.

In this atmosphere, Sinn Féin operated as an umbrella under which armed revolutionaries, former 1916 rebels and Irish Volunteers alike could shelter while observing and adapting to changes in the Irish wartime climate. It has been argued that the four successive electoral contests in 1917 'provided both a need and an opportunity for co-operation among the various elements of the heterogeneous Sinn Féin movement'.[119] However, Sinn Féin did not control all underground paramilitary organizations. While the nationalist press reiterated their unreserved support for John Redmond and blamed Sinn Féin for the agitation,[120] the more radical newspapers immediately claimed that all the unrest was the responsibility of isolated actors and was in no sense the concerted action of Sinn Féin.[121] Reports from RIC Constables mentioned cattle driving, attacks on properties, and other outrages. All were attributed to

---

[114] Borgonovo, *The Dynamics of War and Revolution*, 182.
[115] Kee, *The Green Flag*, 614.
[116] SHD, Third Republic (1870–1940), Army Staff, 7N679, Section des Renseignements Généraux, 2ème Bureau, 15 February 1918.
[117] Ibid.
[118] AD, Political and Commercial Correspondence, Great War, 1914–1918, Ireland, Home Affairs (1918–1922), 95CPCOM/1, report on the situation of Ireland, 25 April 1918.
[119] Laffan, *The Resurrection of Ireland*, 115.
[120] *Freeman's Journal*, 22 March 1918.
[121] *New Ireland*, 2 March 1918.

Sinn Féin or to the Irish Volunteers. For his part Blanche categorically rejected these claims.[122]

Unholy alliances, survival and despair

In March 1918, noting a climate of sporadic but increasing unrest in southern counties, the Consul-General for France in Dublin reiterated his conviction that the regime and not the people was the problem. 'As long as a system taking into account the expectations of the majority is not adopted, nothing that the Vice-Chancellors and Secretaries for State will do will be able to change anything',[123] wrote Alfred Blanche. Yet the British Cabinet did not intervene.

What the British Government refrained from at the political level of its administration of Ireland was carried out on the more local scale. Constitutional nationalist communities and unionist populations entered into a pact to unite against Sinn Féin. While the Irish Convention crippled any chance of revival for the Irish Parliamentary Party, at the local level, nationalist and unionist populations were finding a common cause in their opposition to Sinn Féin. Political strategies and shared concerns convinced the Unionists to back the Irish Party during the Waterford by-election on 22 March 1918. Following the death of John Redmond, his son, William Archer Redmond, ran for election. Interestingly, the *Gaelic American* admitted that John Redmond had left a vacuum in the leadership of the Irish Party, 'but as the Party [was] now a spent force, sure of defeat at the next election, it [did] not matter much who [was] elected in his place, except if there be a change of policy'.[124] Yet out of 2,006 ballots cast, Captain William Redmond secured 1,242 votes against 764 for M. White (candidate for Sinn Féin).[125] During the campaign, women supporting the Irish Party attacked Sinn Féiners, and even though Sinn Féin was defeated, the RIC commented that in what had formerly been a stronghold of the Irish Party, the separatist republican party had managed to capture 35 per cent of the electorate.[126] In order to be able to run for election in Waterford, William Redmond had resigned the seat he had occupied in East Tyrone since 1910. This

---

[122] AD, Political and Commercial Correspondence, Great War, 1914–1918, Ireland, 1CPCOM/546, telegram from Alfred Blanche to the Minister for Foreign Affairs, 28 January 1918.
[123] AD, Political and Commercial Correspondence, Great War, 1914–1918, Ireland, 1CPCOM/547, telegram from Alfred Blanche to the Minister for Foreign Affairs, 5 March 1918.
[124] *Gaelic American*, 9 March 1918.
[125] *Freeman's Journal*, 25 March 1918; *Irish Independent*, 25 March 1918.
[126] TNA, CO 904/105, County Inspector's report, Waterford, March 1918.

created another vacancy. On 27 March, the East Tyrone Unionist Association issued a circular in which they demanded all Unionists vote for the Irish Party candidate, Thomas Harbison. During the previous general elections in 1910, the unionist candidate had secured 2,968 votes against 3,108 for the Irish Parliamentary Party but, in March 1918, the unionist community decided not to present a candidate, in order to counter Sinn Féin. On 5 April 1918, Séan Milroy, the official Sinn Féin candidate, lost by 1,802 votes to 1,222. Sinn Féin had previously been defeated by the Irish Party candidate during the South Armagh by-election, in February 1918, without the withdrawal of the Unionist candidate (T. W. Richardson).[127] (When analysing the outcome of these three contests, it seems, after all, that Blanche was, to a certain extent, right to think that the Irish Party could still survive.)

Even though, Sinn Féin lost the contest, the *Gaelic American* published an editorial entitled 'The End of Redmondism', in which it was clearly indicated that the Irish Party could not hide the ongoing surge for republicanism throughout the country by invoking its success in the South Armagh election.[128] *Nationality* offered reassurance to its readers, insisting that 'the two pro-English factions'[129] had agreed to stand together but would no longer be able to lure the Irish into submission. Arthur Griffith prophetically added: 'They wave for the better duping of the country and they prey upon different flags. They are in one heart and intention against the Freedom of the Irish Nation.'[130] The unnatural alliance between the Irish Party and the unionist candidates was an indication of how dangerous Sinn Féin had become, of how popular it was. This particular election was the recurrent anti-conscription narrative that the Sinn Féin candidate drew upon. One poster for the by-election in South Armagh read: 'Vote for McCartan and No Conscription'.[131] Another handbill in support of the Sinn Féin candidate read 'Is Conscription Coming?'[132] The handbill reminded the electorate that Easter Week 1916 had been effective in postponing conscription, warning that 'England [was] now crying aloud that Conscription in Ireland [was] necessary'.

---

[127] Laffan, *The Resurrection of Ireland*, 124.
[128] *Gaelic American*, 9 March 1918.
[129] *Nationality*, 2 March 1918.
[130] Ibid.
[131] National Library of Ireland (hereafter NLI), EPH C473, election handbill issued to encourage people to vote for Patrick McCartan, 1918.
[132] NLI, Irish Large Books, ILB 300, Item 92, by-election handbill for Patrick McCartan, 1918.

Figure 5.1 Election handbill issued to encourage people to vote for the Sinn Féin candidate for South Armagh, Patrick McCartan, in February 1918. Ephemera Collection. Courtesy of the National Library of Ireland.

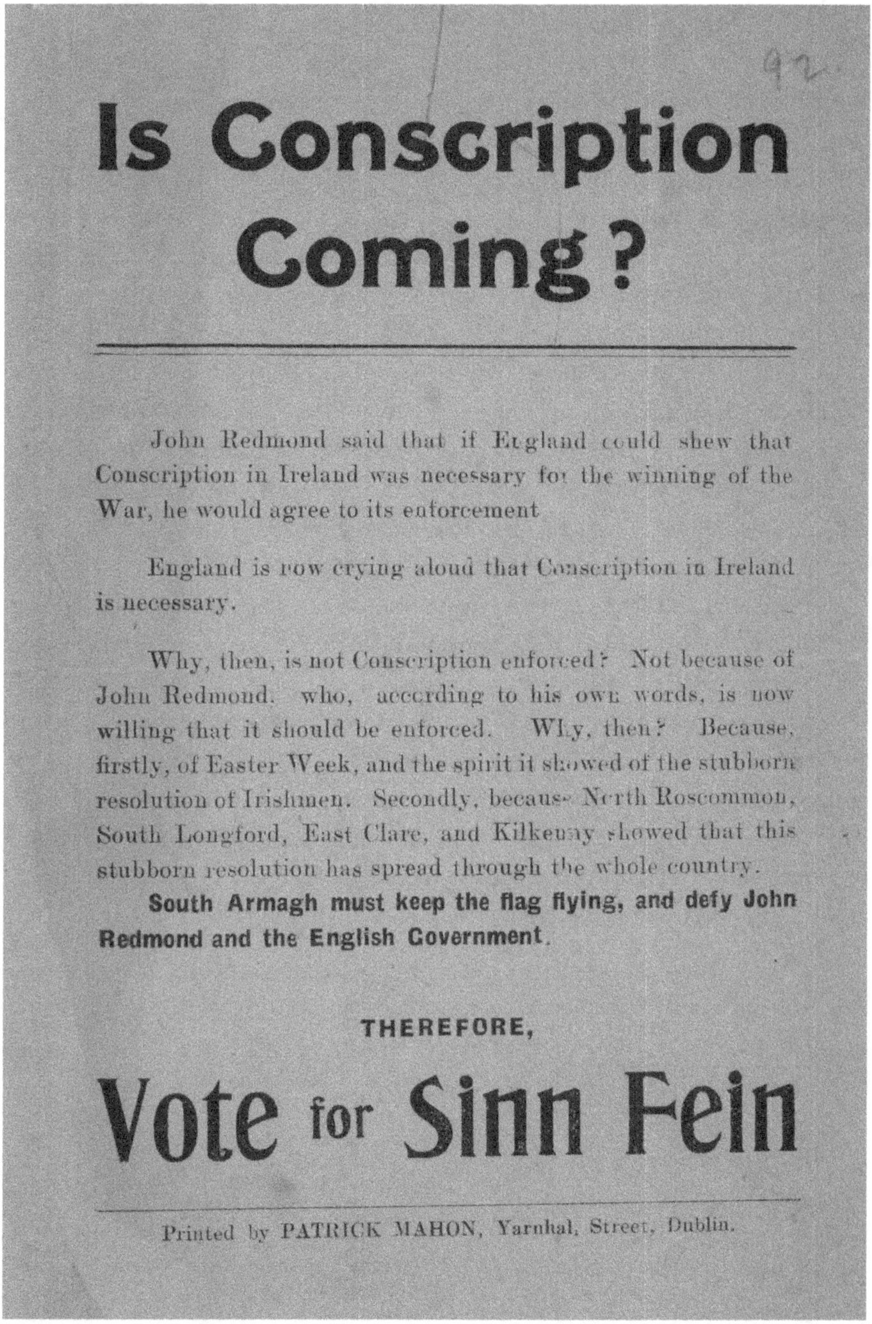

Is Conscription Coming?

John Redmond said that if England could shew that Conscription in Ireland was necessary for the winning of the War, he would agree to its enforcement

England is now crying aloud that Conscription in Ireland is necessary.

Why, then, is not Conscription enforced? Not because of John Redmond, who, according to his own words, is now willing that it should be enforced. Why, then? Because, firstly, of Easter Week, and the spirit it showed of the stubborn resolution of Irishmen. Secondly, because North Roscommon, South Longford, East Clare, and Kilkenny showed that this stubborn resolution has spread through the whole country.

South Armagh must keep the flag flying, and defy John Redmond and the English Government.

THEREFORE,

Vote for Sinn Fein

Printed by PATRICK MAHON, Yarnhal, Street, Dublin.

Figure 5.2 By-election handbill for Patrick McCartan, Sinn Féin candidate for the South Armagh constituency, February 1918. Ephemera Collection. Courtesy of the National Library of Ireland.

The goal of the Peace Conference takes hold

Weeks before the conscription crisis of April 1918, Sinn Féin had only one goal; that of securing a seat for Ireland at the Peace Conference. On 8 January 1918, Wilson's address to Congress introduced his vision of post-war order through his Fourteen Points.[133] On 18 January 1918, in the Mansion House, Dublin, Éamon de Valera dragged Woodrow Wilson into the Irish question when he provocatively asserted that the US President would be 'as big a hypocrite as Lloyd George' if he did not back Ireland's claim for full independence.[134] In March 1918, André Tardieu confessed from New York that the appropriation of Wilsonian ideals by Sinn Féin was the real cause of the death of the Irish Parliamentary Party: 'Sinn Féin spent so much time advocating an independent republic that they greatly complicated the task of the Nationalists and made it difficult to accept anything less than the status of an independent republic, such as the imperial status of self-government dominion.'[135]

Tardieu attributed the success of the seditious party to its political agenda. The party looked westwards, to both American and to its President for the redefinition of its rhetoric, drawing from this new source an improved capacity to fight legislatively against the Irish Parliamentary Party. The threat of conscription was, along with the demands for total independence, decisive in the shift within nationalist Ireland towards republicanism. *New Ireland* published an editorial in which self-determination for Ireland was announced unambiguously as the goal of Sinn Féin.[136] Narratives of complete independence were bolstered by a more generalized post-war vision of international security and justice:

> The small nation, the weak nation, the poor nation, must have the same access to the international tribunal and the same protection from the international authority as the big, the strong, or the wealthy nation. The cause of international civilization is Ireland's cause, and it must be Ireland's duty and privilege to champion it, and to take it up in such a manner as will command the world's attention and respect.[137]

---

[133] Trygve Throntveit, 'The Fable of the Fourteen Points: Woodrow Wilson and National Self-Determination', *Diplomatic History* 35, no. 3 (2011): 445–481. Throntveit argues that 'such national self-determination – the principle that groups bound by common language or lines of descent have a right to political and territorial independence – was not one of Wilson's Fourteen Points and was never central to his peace program'.
[134] *Freeman's Journal*, 19 January 1918.
[135] AD, Political and Commercial Correspondence, Great War, 1914–1918, Ireland, 1CPCOM/547, telegram from André Tardieu to the Minister for Foreign Affairs, 11 March 1918.
[136] *New Ireland*, 2 March 1918.
[137] Ibid.

In March, numerous demonstrations took place, during which slogans were based upon Ireland's right to determine its own political destiny.[138] 'How close we are to our total independence!',[139] wrote a journalist of the *Irishman*. Recalling Ireland's legitimate right to independence, he asserted that self-government was not a domestic, but an international issue. The newspaper quoted the words of Reverend O'Connell at an East Cavan Sinn Féin meeting: 'Now the opportunity for Ireland has come to have her cause heard and judged by the nations. Now or never is her chance of self-determination!'[140] In their opposition to any modification to the UK's existing constitutional arrangements, the Ulster Unionists had, ironically, ultimately brought about the coalescence of the overwhelming majority of nationalist Ireland. Even if Home Rule for the whole of Ireland were to be granted, the nationalist population that had previously supported the Irish Party would not accept it. Their main preoccupation was now the Peace Conference and the need for Sinn Féin to have as many representatives as possible elected. When the Ambassador for France to Rome consulted with Mgr. O'Riordan, he was told that the Irish clearly now disregarded the original Home Rule Bill, and would now no longer accept its provisions.[141]

Another element enabling to assess the growing disinterest in the goal of Home Rule is to be found in responses to the death of John Redmond. Reactions in local newspapers offer a significant insight into how nationalist public opinion had shifted. On consulting daily newspapers of all political hues, the reader is prompted to reflect on the generally ungrateful tone of the comments. The *Irishman* pointed out that flags were flown at half-mast over English institutions in both England and Ireland to 'pay tribute to the deceased's services to the British Empire',[142] yet other opinions are surprising in their contemptuousness. One daily newspaper praised Mgr. Hallinan for refusing to celebrate a solemn requiem for him in Limerick.[143] 'He was an Imperialist who evidently sincerely believed in the efficacy of the British Empire.'[144] The editor added: 'In face of such manifestation from Imperial England that he served so well, Nationalist Ireland can afford him the charity of its silence.'[145] In its obituary, *The Times* reminded its

---

[138] *Young Ireland*, 2 March 1918.
[139] *Irishman*, 30 March 1918.
[140] Ibid.
[141] AD, Political and Commercial Correspondence, Great War, 1914–1918, Ireland, 1CPCOM/547, letter from the Ambassador for France in Rome to the Minister for Foreign Affairs, 6 May 1918.
[142] *Irishman*, 16 March 1918.
[143] *Young Ireland*, 30 March 1918.
[144] Ibid.
[145] Ibid.

readers that 'the real Mr Redmond was a man whose ingrained respect for British civilization was never really shaken by a rhetorical devotion to the Irish, or rather, the Anglo-Irish tradition of Nationalism'.[146] Interestingly *Irish Opinion*, in its issue just after Redmond's death, gave the following explanation for such spectacular disregard for his legacy: 'He staked everything on the chance of Home Rule then, and he lost.'[147] According to the journalist, the incapacity of the Irish Parliamentary Party to develop a rhetoric matching the expectations of the Irish led to its decline. Such a claim mirrored the opinions voiced by Irish-Americans.[148] Sinn Féin aspired to the complete independence of their nation, not to a settlement of the Irish question within the British imperial order, something the American Consul at Queenstown had understood:

> The strong feeling excited by the conscription proposals has tended to strengthen the radical elements, and such a measure of Home Rule as might have been accepted in 1914, would probably completely fail of acceptance now. The Sinn Féin group desires no Home Rule but desires absolute severance from the British Empire and independence of it. The Constitutional Nationalists represented by the very able "report of twenty-two Nationalist members of the Irish convention" are willing to remain a nation in the empire, related to the parliament at Westminster as Canada or Australia are related. They do not wish to remain in the United Kingdom but only in the British Empire.[149]

The representation of Ireland at the Peace Conference was now a goal that was enshrined in the minds of all the Irish-Americans who had been won over by Wilson's grand vision and who now regarded Home Rule as being out of tune with the new political climate of the time. In January 1918, André Tardieu, High Commissioner for France in the US, wrote that the Home Rule doctrine had lost all its appeal in the United States.[150] Tardieu had been appointed in April 1917 and from his position in Washington, he had monitored the shifts in US public opinion to the Irish question. His reports clearly suggested that the aspiration to Home Rule no longer captured the hearts and minds of Irish-Americans. What also illustrated the transformation of Irish-American popular opinion was the need for André Tardieu to report directly to his Minister for Foreign Affairs. In

---

[146] *The Times*, 7 March 1918.
[147] *Irish Opinion*, 16 March 1918.
[148] *Gaelic American*, 9 March 1918.
[149] University of California, Santa Barbara Library (hereafter UCSBL), Charles Montgomery Hathaway Papers (1895–1939), 1/45, Official correspondences, report on the political situation in the South of Ireland, 5 May1918, p. 3.
[150] AD, Political and Commercial Correspondence, Great War, 1914–1918, Ireland, 1CPCOM/546, telegram from André Tardieu to the Minister for Foreign Affairs, 25 January 1918.

his capacity as High Commissioner, Tardieu drew up regular reports dealing with the meetings, interviews and achievements of his mission to the US. On rare occasions, he felt the need to provide a broader picture, ominously suggesting how the Irish question risked threatening the forthright and unqualified contribution of the US to the war effort. In a report, the Minister for Foreign Affairs understood that among Irish-Americans, the right of Ireland to determine itself was implicitly part of the Allies' agenda of establishing a new international order after the war. While being careful not to comment on the post-war tensions that such a commitment would give rise to in Britain (and with Britain), the report indicated that in Boston, during a march celebrating the anniversary of the 1803 execution of Robert Emmett, the demand for the independence of Ireland had been loudly voiced by those present.[151] At the anniversary commemoration of Emmett's death, at Faneuil Hall, Boston, speakers urged the Congress to back the principle of self-determination for small nations and to grant 'complete freedom and autonomy of Ireland from English rule or domination in any form'.[152] During a meeting of the Irish Progressive League at the Central Opera House, on 20 February 1918, hundreds of people were unable to find even standing room. The goal of the meeting was to raise funds for the establishment of an Irish embassy in Washington. A sum of about $2,000 was collected.[153] Legislative steps were also being taken to press for the recognition of Ireland as an independent nation. On 3 March, a sizeable meeting took place in Boston, at Faneuil Hall, 'to demand that Ireland be given her Independence, and that the Irish people of the United States be given the assurance that Ireland is included in the small countries for WHOM the war is being waged'.[154] On 13 March, the State of Massachusetts voted a resolution to back the participation of Ireland in the future Peace Conference. Meanwhile, the Gallagher resolution, requesting that the Irish be allowed to vote for their future administration, had been presented to the US Congress. In Congress, William Borah, Senator from Idaho, had prepared a resolution according to which 'all nationalities, constituting as they [did] the individuals of international law, ha[d] an inalienable right to the free disposition of themselves and to the international recognition of their separate political entities'.[155] The situation was

---

[151] AD, Political and Commercial Correspondence, Great War, 1914–1918, Ireland, Home Affairs (1918–1922), 95CPCOM/1, report on the situation of Ireland, 25 April 1918.
[152] *Gaelic American*, 9 March 1918; *Boston Globe*, 4 March 1918.
[153] *Gaelic American*, 2 March 1918.
[154] Ibid.
[155] *Irish World*, 16 February 1918.

serious enough to compel Carson to sail to the United States to warn the Americans against the lobbying of Irish-American circles.[156]

When Finland declared its independence in January 1918, Sinn Féin welcomed the event, which added substance to the comparable Irish claims.[157] Irish-Americans had gone so far as to approach foreign powers, asking for their support of Irish independence. At the time, M. Thiebeaut, France's representative in Stockholm, reported that foreign delegations in Sweden had received documents and leaflets concerning Ireland's claim for total independence.[158] One of the signatories of the documents, Thomas St John Gaffney, had been Consul for the United States in Dresden and Munich, before being dismissed at the behest of the British Government. Sinn Féin had no knowledge of the existence of such pamphlets in Sweden, and it appears that the propaganda being distributed was the initiative of the Friends of Irish Freedom in association with a German-Irish Society presided by M. de Schorleber, former Minister for Agriculture.[159] American support thus operated largely independently of Sinn Féin and its representatives. This example of uncoordinated propaganda was evidence that, by 1918, 'Irish-Americans firmly believe Irish independence [was] implicitly recognized in the war goals of the Allies'.[160]

In Australia, Archbishop Mannix was also active in promoting the case of Irish independence. Born in Ireland, where he was ordained as a priest in 1890, he notably delivered one speech at a large meeting in Melbourne at which resolutions were endorsed by over 100,000 people.[161] Mannix called upon the American Government to invite duly accredited Irish representatives to the International Peace Conference.[162] German newspapers similarly expressed their sympathies for the gallant country which sought to obtain its freedom at the Peace Conference.[163] In their statement of demands, they coupled freedom of the seas and an access for the German Navy to the call for the complete independence of Ireland.[164]

---

[156] Ibid.
[157] AD, Political and Commercial Correspondence, Great War, 1914–1918, Ireland, 1CPCOM/546, telegram from Alfred Blanche to the Minister for Foreign Affairs, 10 January 1918.
[158] AD, Political and Commercial Correspondence, Great War, 1914–1918, Ireland, 1CPCOM/546, telegram from Thiebeaut, Minister for the Republic in Stockholm, to the Minister for Foreign Affairs, 21 January 1918.
[159] AD, Political and Commercial Correspondence, Great War, 1914–1918, Ireland, 1CPCOM/547, letter from Alfred Blanche to the Minister for Foreign Affairs, 15 March 1918.
[160] AD, 161CPCOM4, telegram from Rome to the Minister for Foreign Affairs, March 1918.
[161] *Catholic Bulletin*, March 1918.
[162] *Gaelic American*, 9 March 1918.
[163] *Abendzseitung*, 26 March 1918.
[164] *Vossische Zeitung*, 11 May 1918.

Conclusion

As far as France's representatives were concerned, the Irish Convention cynically illustrated that Lloyd George had in turn opted for 'Asquith's delaying tactics'.[165] Faced with the impossibility of repressing separatist activists, the British measured the direct consequences of the US entry into the war. The Irish Convention reassured the American ally, complicated the task of the Irish Parliamentary Party now trapped in sterile negotiations with the unionist leaders, and gave carte blanche to Sinn Féin to rise publicly as the new challenger in Irish domestic politics. By the time the Irish Convention submitted its conclusions, conscription, the Wilsonian discourse of self-determination, and then, later on, the exploitation of fears of food shortage, actual famine and land disputes had further embittered local communities.

Wilson's post-war vision of the new international order spoke loud and clear to the changing aspirations of Irish public opinion. Whereas Home Rule remained intrinsically linked to the political order that could enforce conscription, it now appeared to the Irish that, thanks to the resolution adopted by the US Congress, they were in a position to gain more than devolution, without even being conscripted. US involvement triggered not only the internationalization of the Irish question, but also paradoxically swept away the conditions within which support for Home Rule had previously seemed self-evident. Home Rule, the century-long project of nationalist Ireland, suddenly appeared less attractive. Meanwhile the Irish Parliamentary Party remained chained to the British in the hope of achieving their original goal; devolution of power within the constitutional order of the United Kingdom and the Empire.

---

[165] Jackson, *Home Rule. An Irish History*, 140.

6

Conscription, Betrayal and the Agony of the Irish Parliamentary Party (April 1918)

When conscription was introduced in January 1916 for unmarried men, followed in May 1916 by the Military Service Act,[1] it applied to Great Britain only, not to Ireland. British politicians prudently wished to avoid unnecessary unrest in Ireland. As the war continued, civilian populations in Great Britain resented being conscripted while the Irish people (still part of the United Kingdom) were spared from military service. British workers expressed their discontent all over Great Britain and publicly 'objected to further sacrifices on its part without corresponding sacrifices from Ireland'.[2] But according to some, there is very little indication that Irish conscription was required to sell the Military Service Act to the British people: 'Conscripting Ireland was punishment; a vindictive act to ease the pain.'[3] Before the 1918 conscription crisis, RIC Constables, the military authorities in Ireland, representatives of the Irish Party and French diplomats all warned against the introduction of a military service bill in Ireland. All pointed out that it would be materially and physically impossible to enforce conscription. If France's representatives supported the contention that the British were indeed motivated by the desire to appease discontent within Great Britain, they nonetheless considered that other motivations were at play.

From the Ulster 'conscription cry' to the German offensive

Following the successive by-election victories for Sinn Féin, the prospect of conscription was again mentioned when Ulster Unionists called for the British

---

[1] Dittmar Dahlmann, 'Parliaments', in *The Cambridge History of the First World War, Volume II, The State*, ed. Jay Winter (Cambridge: Cambridge University Press, 2014), 57.
[2] Alan J. Ward, 'Lloyd George and the 1918 Irish Conscription Crisis', *Historical Journal* 17, no. 1 (1974): 111.
[3] Adrian Gregory, '"You might as well recruit Germans": British public opinion and the decision to conscript the Irish in 1918', in *Ireland and the Great War: 'A War to Unite Us All?'*, ed. Adrian Gregory and Senia Pašeta (Manchester: Manchester University Press, 2002), 127.

Government to coerce Ireland, repress political unrest, and if need be, impose conscription in the name of the brotherhood between the four kingdoms. In the House of Commons, it was gradually becoming clear that 'no further demands [could] be made upon the man-power of Great Britain without an assurance from the Government of its intention to bring forward a concurrent measure for compulsory military service in Ireland'.[4]

At a debate in the House of Commons, on 14 January 1918, Auckland Geddes, Minister for National Service, explained that the Government had 'decided for the present not to ask this House for powers to introduce compulsory service in Ireland'.[5] A few days later, during a meeting he had with General de la Panouse, Geddes clearly explained to the French that the British Government would not extend military conscription to Ireland.[6] Three days later, on 17 January 1918, Ulster Unionists demanded in the House of Commons that no other responsibilities and sacrifices be made by the people of Great Britain without having first extended military service to Ireland. Sir Edward Archdale was probably the most passionate speaker in the House. He tried to convince the honorable members that conscription could no longer be accepted for the three kingdoms of Great Britain without its implementation in Ireland.[7] Another MP pointed out that the three kingdoms of Great Britain had been conscripted at the beginning of 1916, and therefore disagreed with Ireland's not participating in the security – even survival – of the whole British Empire.

> We feel we have no right to be left out from the other portions of the United Kingdom in doing our duty by the Empire. We want to bear the Empire's burdens and enjoy the Empire's blessings and privileges, whatever they are, and we want to identify ourselves with, and to take our part if necessary in, the defence of the Empire, as much as in the blessings of peace, which she has given us before the War and we hope will give us after the War.[8]

Geddes eventually intervened to stress that introducing conscription would be nothing short of a political blunder:

---

[4] Hansard, House of Commons Debates, series 5, vol. 101, cc526, Archdale to House of Commons, 17 January 1918.
[5] Hansard, House of Commons Debates, series 5, vol. 101, cc68, Geddes to House of Commons, 14 January 1918.
[6] Service Historique de la Défense, Vincennes (hereafter SHD), Third Republic (1870–1940), Private Papers, 6N155, telegram from General de la Panouse to the Minister for War, 15 January 1918.
[7] Hansard, House of Commons Debates, series 5, vol. 101, cc557, Archdale to House of Commons, 17 January 1918.
[8] Hansard, House of Commons Debates, series 5, vol. 101, cc561, Coote to House of Commons, 17 January 1918.

It is not expedient at the present moment from the point of view of the prosecution of the War, to launch out into the consideration of a scheme, whatever it may be, in connection with the application of compulsory service to Ireland. I beg the House to accept my assurance for what it is worth, absolutely honest, that I approach this question without any political bias. I have looked at it, so far as I can, with absolutely honest and un-biased eyes. I can assure Hon. Members that in my judgment it would be folly, from the point of view of the War at the present moment, to suggest the application of compulsory service to Ireland, and I would beg of the House to allow the consideration of the Main Question now to be resumed.[9]

Conscription for Ireland thus came in for the sole public support of Ulster Unionists. The more they insisted on sending the Irish to the battlefields of Europe, the more conscription appeared to be a punitive undertaking. Edward Carson purposely resigned from his position in the British Government, in a move which gave him complete freedom of action. In February 1918, he toured the counties of Ulster and delivered passionate and scathing speeches against Home Rule. His speeches were met with open demonstrations and an impromptu referendum was organized. *The Times* echoed the position of Ulster Unionists that 'it would be impossible and unjust to bring out men of 40 to 50 in England, Scotland, and Wales, while men of 20 to 30 [were] left by the hundred thousand to loaf and enjoy their souls in Ireland'.[10] 'What possible objection could there be to placing Ireland on the same footing as the rest of the United Kingdom in the matter of service in the war for civilization?', asked the journalist. However, most of the liberal press in Great Britain was reluctant at the idea of seeing conscription implemented in Ireland and warned that 'it would be needlessly provocative (in view of the past slackness and past mistakes in Ireland) to insist suddenly on conscription in that country without paying regard to such solid political facts as the Home Rule Act and the Convention'.[11] No more than 60,000 men would be obtained through the measure whereas an immediate Home Rule would permit the authorities to send to the front tens of thousands of soldiers who were now stationed in Ireland.[12] It would also bring at least 50,000 voluntary recruits under the British flag once Home Rule had been enacted. On the whole, as noted in a report forwarded to the French Minister for Foreign Affairs, the supporters of

---

[9] Hansard, House of Commons Debates, series 5, vol. 101, cc580, Geddes to House of Commons, 17 January 1918.
[10] *The Times*, 3 April 1918.
[11] Ibid.
[12] *Manchester Guardian*, 2 April 1918.

conscription for Ireland were to be found in British public opinion rather than in the political spheres of Westminster. 'But Unionist newspapers were more and more pressing for it',[13] and the more they pressed for it, the more the Government thought of implementing it.

Public opinion before the April 1918 conscription crisis was voiced in the nationalist daily newspapers that reflected the various shades of green. By the end of March 1918, the *Freeman's Journal* was stating with influence that

> Any attempt to pass a Conscription Act or to enforce it would produce such a temper in Ireland as would divert from the front of this most critical hour far more troops than the most drastic application of the Military Service Act could secure. Not merely is the policy impracticable; it is the most disastrous that any of the Allied cause could embark on in Ireland.[14]

Once again, Irish local newspapers drew a correlation between Easter Week 1916 and the cry to resist conscription, thus legitimating further the uprising in the light of its effect in opposing compulsory service.

War concerns and domestic issues became even more interwoven in March 1918, when the Germans launched Operation Michael (also dubbed the *Kaiserschlacht*) on the Somme. Following the signing of the Brest-Litovsk Treaty on 3 March 1918, one million German soldiers were moved from Russia to the Western Front.[15] An Armistice had taken place on 17 December 1917 between the new Soviet Government and the Germans, but peace negotiations did not begin until February 1918. At that time, General Eric Ludendorff was able to marshal approximately one million German soldiers on the western borderlands of the Russian Empire.[16] The Bolsheviks resigned themselves to the inevitable, finally signing peace terms with Germany on 3 March 1918 after several weeks of peace negotiations.[17] When Russia signed the peace with Germany, it 'materially improved Germany's strategic position and raised her army's flagging morale'.[18] And beyond this, 'cessation of hostilities in the east reopened the

---

[13] Archives Diplomatiques du Ministère des Affaires Étrangères, La Courneuve (hereafter AD), Political and Commercial Correspondence, Great War, 1914–1918, Ireland, Home Affairs (1918–1922), 95CPCOM/1, report on the situation of Ireland, 15 June 1918.
[14] *Freeman's Journal*, 28 March 1918.
[15] Christoph Mick, '1918: Endgame', in *The Cambridge History of the First World War, Volume I, Global War*, ed. Jay Winter (Cambridge: Cambridge University Press, 2014), 134.
[16] Ibid.
[17] Borislav Chernev, *Twilight of Empire. The Brest-Litovsk Conference and the Remaking of East-Central Europe, 1917–1918* (Toronto: University of Toronto Press, 2017), 210.
[18] Alexander Watson, *Enduring the Great War. Combat, Morale and the Collapse in the German and British Armies, 1914–1918* (Cambridge: Cambridge University Press, 2008), 185.

possibility of a decisive German victory on the Western Front'.[19] At that time, the French Army was still recovering from mutinies,[20] and with only 300,000 men by March 1918, the Americans did not represent sufficient support for the British Expeditionary Corps. On 21 March 1918, the Germans attacked on the Western Front, with the clear objective of breaking through the British front. On that day alone, they captured 21,000 British soldiers and inflicted a total of 38,512 casualties on the British. On 31 March, the Operation Michael offensive had cost the British 177,739 casualties, the French 77,000 and the Germans 239,800.[21]

It was following Operation Michael on 21 March 1918 that the British Cabinet took their contentious decision to introduce conscription in Ireland. In doing so, 'they guaranteed the failure of any attempt to settle the Irish question on the basis of Home Rule as recommended by the Irish Convention, wrecked the credibility of the Irish Parliamentary Party and permanently alienated a wide swathe of Irish opinion'.[22] Nonetheless, as evidenced by diplomatic archives, and through information relative to Sinn Féin's position in regards to the Irish Convention, the Convention was merely a delaying strategy, aimed at winning time. It had not been envisaged as a solution to the Irish question.

Emergency measures taken by the British Cabinet during a meeting on 23 March 1918 spoke for the urgency to release additional manpower. All in all, the British drafted 5,000 officer cadets and recalled 88,000 men on leave from France. In addition, 18-year-olds, so far spared from active service in France, could now be sent immediately in the event of an emergency.[23] On 25 March, Geddes' proposals were discussed by the War Cabinet. Raising the age limit to 45 or 50 (in order to recruit 50,000 or 60,000 more men) was a possibility alongside the eventuality of cancelling all exemptions. Finally, Geddes' proposals envisaged conscription for Ireland.[24] At the time, the equivalent of a division, approximately 13,000 strong, and ten reserve battalions, were stationed in Ireland. The Minister for National Service estimated that 150,000 men of military age could be recruited. By raising the age to 45, a further 25,000 could be obtained. On 26 March, the Head of the RIC, General Byrne, ominously declared to the Prime Minister that conscription of the Irish would be a blunder: 'by passing and enforcing such a measure, both the whole of the Catholics and

---

[19] Ibid., 172.
[20] Ibid., 184.
[21] Mick, '1918: Endgame', 149.
[22] Gregory, 'You might as well recruit Germans', 113.
[23] TNA, CAB 23/5/63, War Cabinet Minutes, 23 March 1918.
[24] TNA, CAB 23/5/64, War Cabinet Minutes, 25 March 1918.

nationalists in Ireland would be united against the British Empire'.[25] General Byrne had no doubt it would be a mistake, that there would be a great difficulty in enlisting men and that in towns there would be actual riots. Henri Duke, in his capacity as Chief Secretary for Ireland, expressed his opposition to conscription, even after the German offensive. He confidentially reported that the introduction of conscription 'would consolidate into one mass of antagonism all the nationalist elements in Ireland, politicians, priests, men and women'.[26] That was on 27 March 1918. At a time when men were desperately needed in France, General Sir Bryan Mahon reported that at least 100,000 soldiers could be drafted into the army, but he knew that extra troops would simultaneously have to be shipped to Ireland to enforce conscription. Mahon appeared to be the only advocate of conscripting the Irish and had always been in favour of conscription for Ireland, while among members of the Government, a strong feeling existed that England, Scotland and Wales could not reasonably be required to send more men to the army as long as Ireland was spared military service.[27]

Heated debates and some revelations

On 4 April 1918, Chief Secretary for Ireland, Henri Duke, had anticipated that parliament was not likely to 'consent to place further burdens of service on the British population without requiring service from Ireland'.[28] However, he reminded the British Cabinet that Irish opinion was solidly against conscription and that the efforts of Sinn Féin were directed solely toward the prevention of conscription. He suggested granting a measure of self-government (as the majority of the Irish Convention had agreed to propose). On 6 April 1918, the Prime Minister summoned all his ministers:

> I do not know any grounds of justice or equity on which conscription could not be applied to Ireland. We have now decided that we cannot apply these drastic, far-reaching, and devastating proposals to England, Scotland, and Wales without applying conscription to Ireland, where there is not even a rationing system. We cannot go to the House of Commons and ask our people to make sacrifices, sacrifices which the Irish in America are making, and leave the Irish at home

---

[25] TNA, CAB 23/5/66, War Cabinet Minutes, 27 March 1918.
[26] TNA, CAB 24/26, memorandum from Henri Duke, 27 March 1918.
[27] TNA, CAB 24/9/98, Sir Bryan Mahon to Sir William Robertson, 5 April 1917.
[28] TNA, CAB 24/47/33, Memorandum by Chief Secretary, Compulsory Service in Ireland, 4 April 1918.

out. We propose to bring in a Conscription Bill, which will include Ireland, but which will provide for the application of conscription to Ireland by Order of Council.[29]

While Lloyd George knew that conscription would create trouble in Ireland and would take time to implement, 'he spoke at length of equity of sacrifice'.[30] Only Herbert Fisher (President of the Board of Education) asked the Prime Minister to clarify the actual military advantage of applying conscription to Ireland. He was absolutely convinced, along with the Cabinet, that it was above all a matter of justice in wartime for the three other kingdoms. Nevertheless, he urged that the proposal be looked at strictly as a matter of cold military necessity.[31]

As early as 5 April 1918, a dramatic and unexpected piece of news spread all over Ireland: the British Government had decided to ask for conscription in Ireland.[32] At first, the correspondent in London of the *Irish Independent* thought it amounted merely to a tactic to induce the Irish to enrol, after which 'if they [did] not do so, conscription [would] be signed off with the stroke of a pen'. The comment sounded plausible, to begin with, given that public opinion had already stated that the country would never allow conscription to take place, and secondly because the representatives of the British Government in Ireland had begged the British Cabinet to abandon their policy. As to the assessment that conscription would never been enacted, the correspondent of the *Irish Independent* was certainly right; April 1918 represented another political move to quieten Ulster Unionists, as well as British public opinion, and obtain as many recruits as possible.

On 9 April 1918, the issue was debated in the House of Commons, where it gave rise to heated debates. In reality, manpower had always been a persistent issue for the War Cabinet, even before the March 1918 German offensive. Conscription for Ireland was presented to the public as the question of taking on a fair share of the burden shared by the United Kingdom, and also as a security issue. Carson reminded the House of Commons that he had always felt, and had publicly expressed the conviction that 'no distinction ought to be drawn between any part of the United Kingdom'.[33] He professed he had absolutely no right to ask 'that [his] own part of the United Kingdom should be spared'.[34] This intervention

---

[29] TNA, CAB 23/6/7, War Cabinet Minutes, 6 April 1918.
[30] Gregory, 'You might as well recruit Germans', 123.
[31] TNA, CAB 23/6/7, War Cabinet Minutes, 6 April 1918.
[32] *Freeman's Journal*, 6 April 1918.
[33] Hansard, House of Commons Debates, series 5, vol. 104, cc1444, Carson to House of Commons, 9 April 1918.
[34] Ibid.

testified to the position which Ulster Unionists had consistently adopted since the outbreak of the conflict. However, the Irish Party objected to any involuntary sacrifice on the part of the Irish. One MP warned Lloyd George: 'You can force your measure through by weight of numbers, just as the Germans forced you back on the Western Front, but you will not touch the hearts or the minds of Irishmen by such a policy.'[35] Another MP intervened: 'I prophesy that your military Conscription in Ireland will be a complete failure, an abject failure. Look at the moral effect it will have. I am not talking about Ireland at the moment.'[36] The issue of conscription had always been more or less conditional on the settlement of the question of Home Rule. One MP reminded the Prime Minister:

> But I say now, even at this hour, that if the Government set up an Irish Parliament I would on the following day – and thousands of other young Irishmen would follow my example – rally to the Colours, because then we would know that we would be fighting not on behalf of the plutocrats and tyrants of this country, but on behalf of the liberties of our own land.[37]

It also became clear that members of the Irish Party in the House of Commons had lost faith in the British Government. Joseph Devlin sarcastically asked the Prime Minister:

> How do I know, and what guarantee have we that when the War is over, and when the fields of Europe and France are red with Irish blood, that your declaration of devotion to small nationalities is anything more but a scrap of paper, like that which has caused this War.[38]

That day, as the House of Commons was meeting for the first time to debate the Military Service Bill, the Episcopal Standing Committee, under the leadership of Cardinal Logue, met in Maynooth and described conscription as 'a fatal mistake, surpassing the worst blunders of the past four years'.[39] The evidence that Wilsonian ideals were well-entrenched within public opinion was to be found in the arguments echoed in Irish newspapers, national and local. The *Irish*

---

[35] Hansard, House of Commons Debates, series 5, vol. 104, cc1386, Farrell to House of Commons, 9 April 1918.
[36] Hansard, House of Commons Debates, series 5, vol. 104, cc1415, Keating to House of Commons, 9 April 1918.
[37] Hansard, House of Commons Debates, series 5, vol. 104, cc1423, Lundon to House of Commons, 9 April 1918.
[38] Hansard, House of Commons Debates, series 5, vol. 104, cc1372, Devlin to House of Commons, 9 April 1918.
[39] *Irish Independent*, 10 April 1918.

Independent explained that compulsory service could not 'be enforced in Ireland and the attempt to impose it expose[d] the Home Rule scheme to the state of fiasco'.[40] It went further: 'the action which the Government propose to take is a denial of the doctrines which have been expounded by President Wilson and adopted by the statesmen of the Allied Powers'.[41] The *Freeman's Journal* also pointed out that conscription would be in total opposition to the war goals of the Allies.[42] When the Irish Parliamentary Party, under the leadership of John Dillon, issued a declaration stating they would oppose conscription at any cost,[43] this could easily be associated with a revolutionary rhetoric, but it was clearly not in the habits of the Irish Party to use such a violent language. While rumours were spreading all over the country, it remained the case, as reported by the *Freeman's Journal*, that nothing had happened yet.[44]

Irish-Americans reacted with terror when they heard of Lloyd George's potential move.[45] From San Francisco, T. P. O'Connor cabled John Dillon and alerted him that such an 'insane blunder [would] paralyze friends and encourage bitterest enemies in America. It [would be] an insane blunder which would again render hostile the best efforts of the Irish leaders everywhere.'[46] If the Irish question had become an international issue, conscription was now a British domestic concern. And this was precisely the argument highlighted, on 9 April, in the House of Commons. It was only fair to ask Ireland to contribute to the war effort, at a time when 50-year-old men in England, Scotland, and Wales were being called up to serve under the flag. The argument developed by Lloyd George, on 9 April, was the suggestion that 'no Home Rule bill had ever integrated the denial/relinquishment of the imperial government from the military questions'.[47] This point directly focused on the responsibility of the Irish Parliamentary Party.

Another argument aimed at countering Lloyd George was to be found in the final report of the Irish Convention.[48] Its sub-commission (composed of three Unionists and two Nationalists) had clearly explained that it would be impossible to impose the Military Service Bill without the cooperation and the consent of the

---

[40] *Irish Independent*, 9 April 1918.
[41] Ibid.
[42] *Freeman's Journal*, 8 April 1918.
[43] *Freeman's Journal*, 9 April 1918.
[44] *Freeman's Journal*, 6 April 1918.
[45] *Chicago Citizen*, 19 April 1918.
[46] *Freeman's Journal*, 11 April 1918.
[47] AD, Political and Commercial Correspondence, Great War, 1914–1918, Ireland, Home Affairs (1918–1922), 95CPCOM/1, report on the situation of Ireland, 15 June 1918.
[48] *Report of the Proceedings of the Irish Convention*, (Dublin: HMSO, 1918), p. 9

Irish Parliament.[49] Devlin remarked that the Sub-Committee of the Irish Convention had clearly positioned itself in terms of its opposition against compulsory service for Ireland, and quoted their conclusions.[50] Devlin insisted that the committee was not entirely composed of Home Rule followers, that it contained three strongly anti-Home Rule loyalists. In the final report of the Irish Convention, all five members reiterated the conclusions forwarded to the Grand Committee in November 1917, in which the conclusion reached was the practical impossibility of enforcing conscription.[51] In their final report, the sub-committee highlighted that 'any measure of this character [had to] be submitted to the Irish Parliament before it could be forced on Ireland'.[52] Devlin portrayed conscription not only as an anti-Home Rule measure, but as an anti-Irish policy that would compromise the support of loyal populations to the Crown. Captain Sheehan took up this same argument and reminded the Prime Minister that 'it would take him three Army Corps in Ireland to get one Army Corps out of it'.[53] Substantial information gathered from RIC Constables and from the military in Ireland reinforced the belief that additional troops would have to be shipped to Ireland in the event of conscription. For all these reasons, Devlin begged Lloyd George to act with wisdom.[54]

Other Irish MPs publicly accused the Government of endangering constitutional nationalism. Sir Richard Cooper took the floor and publicly blamed the Prime Minister for deliberately ringing the death knell of the Irish Party: 'I cannot conceive that any Minister could present a case in a manner that was more calculated to create the resentment of the Irish Nationalists.'[55] In his view, the policy was a deliberate attempt to undermine the authority of the Irish Party. But for what purpose?

The following day, on 10 April 1918, Thomas Harbison admitted that even in unionist constituencies, it would be delicate to implement conscription and no one could predict what the outcome would be.[56] Even though Carson and the

---

[49] SHD, Third Republic (1870–1940), Army Staff, 7N1261, telegram from General de la Panouse to the Minister for War, 10 April 1918.
[50] Hansard, House of Commons Debates, series 5, vol. 104, cc1371, Devlin to House of Commons, 9 April 1918.
[51] *Report of the Proceedings of the Irish Convention* (Dublin, HMSO, 1918), Report of the Sub-Committee of Defence and Police to the Grand Committee, 29 November 1917, p. 118.
[52] Ibid.
[53] Hansard, House of Commons Debates, series 5, vol. 104, cc1406, Sheehan to House of Commons, 9 April 1918.
[54] Hansard, House of Commons Debates, series 5, vol. 104, cc1373, Devlin to House of Commons, 9 April 1918.
[55] Hansard, House of Commons Debates, series 5, vol. 104, cc1408, Cooper to House of Commons, 9 April 1918.
[56] Hansard, House of Commons Debates, series 5, vol. 104, cc1542, Harbison to House of Commons, 10 April 1918.

Unionist Party had pledged their unconditional allegiance to conscription, civilian protestant populations condemned the recourse to conscription.[57] *New Ireland* reprinted a pledge made by protestants all over Ireland in which they protested against conscription.[58] The *Irish Independent* reprinted protestant views that described conscription as an act of 'military despotism',[59] while the *Freeman's Journal* informed its readers that a large number of protestant Irishmen and Irishwomen had signed a pledged against conscription.[60] On 12 April, during another debate in the Commons, the Chief Secretary argued in favour of the prior establishment of a parliament in Dublin, before imposing conscription. His suggestion comforted Devlin, who begged the Cabinet not to worsen the situation. Gradually, Irish MPs such as Devlin came to concede that if conscription could be envisaged, it could only be so after the establishment of an Irish parliament.[61]

A stab in the back of the dead man: a second execution of dead heroes

On the front, the refusal of the Irish people to contribute to the war effort led to the singling out of some front-line Irish battalions, causing them to come in for vicious criticism.[62] Second-Lieutenant Parr of the 2nd Royal Scots Fusiliers wrote to his parents that he would 'sooner shoot an Irishman than a Hun!'[63] G. Mortimer, a gunner with the 69th Brigade, Royal Garrison Artillery, regretted that Ireland was 'a constant source of trouble' and deplored it could not 'be submerged for about five minutes'.[64] Another English gunner thought that '90 per cent of the country [were] traitors and the other 10 per cent [were] neutral and [were] not on [their] side.'[65] Many British soldiers condemned the selfishness

---

[57] Military Archives of Ireland (hereafter MAI), Bureau of Military History, 1913–1921 (hereafter BMH), WS721, Nicholas Smyth, member of the Irish Volunteers, County Tyrone, p. 3.
[58] *New Ireland*, 27 April 1918.
[59] *Irish Independent*, 22 April 1918.
[60] *Freeman's Journal*, 22 April 1918.
[61] Hansard, House of Commons Debates, series 5, vol. 104, cc1931, Devlin to House of Commons, 12 April 1918.
[62] Emmanuel Destenay, 'La captivité des combattants irlandais de la Première Guerre mondiale: propagande de guerre, transferts de loyauté et résistances', *Revue historique* 678 (2016): 328–329.
[63] University of Leeds Library (hereafter ULL), Liddle Collection (First World War) (1914–1918), General Aspects (1914–1918), GS 1227, Second Lieutenant Parr to his parents, 23 May 1918.
[64] ULL, Liddle Collection (First World War) (1914–1918), Egypt and Palestine (1914–1918) GS 1136, G. Mortimer to his father, 26 May 1918.
[65] ULL, Liddle Collection (First World War) (1914–1918), Royal Navy and Merchant Navy General Aspects (1914–1918), EP 094, Charles Winterbourne to a relative, 21 July 1918.

of the Irish, 'the spoilt child of the family who kick[ed] at England as a kid in a temper kick[ed] his nurse',[66] repeatedly stating their conviction that Irish citizens were duty bound to help in the war effort.

Mobilization against conscription in Ireland modified the views of the Irish that were held by many British soldiers, and regular Irish troops attached to British divisions experienced frequent and direct provocations. Harry Loughlin and his fellow countrymen of the 2nd Royal Dublin Fusiliers expressed their disappointment at being the subject of remarks 'by other regiments who up to the affair would not say anything to us'.[67] Father Gill acknowledged that 'the affairs in Ireland [did] not make things easier for [Irish troops].[68] Though he did not elaborate any further on the difficulties experienced by the 2nd Royal Irish Rifles, anti-conscription agitation in Ireland profoundly affected front-line soldiers. One English officer, Major Nightingale, with the 1st Royal Munster Fusiliers, took exception to some British soldiers' negative comments and to their continual harassment of his men. In April 1918, he confessed: 'That's the hardest part of the whole show, to feel we've been through a rotten battle and wherever we go it's always – "There go the Sinn Féiners".'[69] Major Nightingale defended his units and did not hesitate to reprimand other British soldiers. His intention was to support Irish combatants and to counter the climate of abuse and mistrust to which they were exposed. His evidence indicates that numerous British soldiers implicitly questioned their loyalty and sarcasm was sometimes combined with vicious, albeit groundless accusations. When the 1st Royal Munster Fusiliers joined an English division, it was rumoured that all the officers and soldiers of the 16th (Irish) Division had 'put down their arms and walked over to the Bosch'.[70] It can be justifiably argued here that the episode of the Easter Rising 1916 was dismissed as a military operation conceived by a handful of republicans, with little support from the population. However, the anti-conscription movement was giving voice to a defiance of British rule on the part of the whole of nationalist Ireland.[71] Like the vast majority of British public

---

[66] ULL, Liddle Collection (First World War) (1914–1918), Royal Navy and Merchant Navy General Aspects (1914–1918), RNMN/WALLIS, S. J. Wallis to a relative, 8 October 1918.
[67] Dublin City Library and Archives (hereafter DCLA), Monica Roberts Collection, vol. i, RDFA/001/02, Harry Loughlin to Monica Roberts, 17 June 1917.
[68] Irish Jesuit Archives, Dublin (hereafter IJA), CHP 1/25, Father Henry Gill to Irish Fr Provincial Thomas V. Nolan SJ, 29 May 1918.
[69] TNA, Domestic Records of the Public Record Office, Nightingale Papers (1910–1926), PRO 30/71/3, Major Nightingale to his mother, 24 April. 1918.
[70] Ibid.
[71] Jérôme aan de Wiel, *The Catholic Church in Ireland, 1914–1918: War and Politics* (Dublin: Irish Academic Press, 2003), 211.

opinion, British officers and men strongly resented Ireland's refusal to consent to the war effort.

General de la Panouse maintained that public opinion in Great Britain played a decisive role in the decision of the British to impose conscription on Ireland: 'There is certainly in England a strong public demand to ask for young Irishmen to be obliged to serve, as do young men from the other kingdoms, and unanimously it is believed that 40 to 50-year-old English men cannot properly be compelled to enrol while 20, 30 and 40-year-old Irishmen peacefully stay home.'[72] That public opinion in Great Britain objected to the Irish not being drafted to the army was indeed right. However, without disregarding the role played by popular discontent in Great Britain, it was clearly the case that as the war went on and casualties multiplied, strategic concerns called for more men on the Somme. General de la Panouse believed that discontent of English, Scottish and Welsh populations coupled with the German offensive in March 1918 made it possible for the British Cabinet to impose conscription in Ireland, which then 'brought together Home Rule and the military service bill'.[73] France's military attaché had always supported conscription for Ireland. What he objected to was the idea of enforcing conscription without implementing Home Rule.[74] The vote for conscription emanated partly, as he reported, from the need to end an unpleasant debate in Great Britain, to preserve morale, and placate domestic public opinion. However, as previously highlighted, if indeed there were some 500,000 men of military age (547,827 to be precise), it was necessary to deduct from this figure the number of men who had already enlisted in the Army (from 1914 onwards 33,221), the overall number of people who did not match the medical and physical criteria (107,492), and those men whose work was deemed indispensable and could therefore not be drafted (247,875).[75] So, the British Government was left with a total of 161,239 men who could be drafted. Why then persist in envisaging conscription? What was the purpose?

On 9 April 1918, in the House of Commons, the Prime Minister phrased his speech in such a way as to carry the unconditional implication that the Irish Party consented to conscription:

---

[72] SHD, Third Republic (1870–1940), Army Staff, 7N1261, telegram from General de la Panouse to the Minister for War, 8 April 1918.
[73] SHD, Third Republic (1870–1940), Army Staff, 7N1254, letter from General de la Panouse to the Minister for War, 24 June 1918.
[74] SHD, Third Republic (1870–1940), Army Staff, 7N1261, telegram from General de la Panouse to the Minister for War, 8 April 1918.
[75] SHD, Third Republic (1870–1940), Army Staff, 7N1254, letter from Colonel de la Panouse to the Minister for War, 17 November 1916.

Ireland, through its representatives, assented to the War, voted for the War, supported the War. The Irish representatives, and Ireland, through its representatives, without a dissentient voice, committed the Empire to this War. They are fully as responsible for it as any part of the United Kingdom.[76]

Lloyd George trapped the Irish Parliamentary Party by his suggestion of a continuity between their support for the British in September 1914 and the need to enforce conscription now, in 1918. Lloyd George's statement was the final contribution to the utter discrediting of the Irish Party in the eyes of Irish popular opinion. France's Consul-General to Dublin vehemently deplored what he saw as the appalling behaviour of the British Prime Minister:

> The Prime Minister's suggestion to conscript Ireland has been beyond anything that public opinion, even the most pessimistic, could have imagined. His speech has given the most striking and decisive justification to the arguments employed for the last two years by Sinn Féin against the Nationalists. It has shown that the Irish Parliamentary Party, under the leadership of John Redmond, had always done its utmost to support the English Government, in the most humiliating situations. It is too soon to know what this disaster will lead to. [...] Conscription is thus purely a military issue: it is no longer a constitutional or political issue. [...] Irish public opinion will be united against conscription.[77]

Whereas the French insisted on the idea that conscription and Home Rule represented the two faces of the same coin, when Lloyd George publicly argued the case that the Irish Party had given its consent for the war and, indirectly, its support for conscription, he was accelerating the discrediting of the Irish Parliamentary Party. France's representatives to London and Dublin knew that the three electoral victories of the Irish Party had been secured thanks to the support of local unionist populations, which meant that common interests between unionist and nationalist populations could still forge strong political alliances during by-elections. Even though, the official Irish Parliamentary Party 'no longer disposed of a solid and stable grass roots',[78] electoral alliances between long-standing enemies underlined the will to avoid at all costs the consolidation of support for a republican party that would threaten the legacy of both the Irish Party and the Ulster Unionists.

---

[76] Hansard, House of Commons Debates, series 5, vol. 104, cc1358, Lloyd George to House of Commons, 9 April 1918.
[77] AD, Political and Commercial Correspondence, Great War, 1914–1918, Ireland, 1CPCOM/547, telegram from Alfred Blanche to the Minister for Foreign Affairs, 10 April 1918.
[78] AD, Political and Commercial Correspondence, Great War, 1914–1918, Ireland, 1CPCOM/547, telegram from Alfred Blanche to the Minister for Foreign Affairs, 20 April 1918.

On 16 April 1918, when the Bill was passed through Parliament by 276 to 134, the MPs of the Irish Parliamentary Party stormed out of the House of Commons.[79] The bill united the whole of nationalist Ireland, propelled Sinn Féin to the forefront of opposition, and finally decapitated the Irish Parliamentary Party. When the British Parliament gave its consent for the extension of conscription to Ireland, 'it [gave] the impulsion which was needed, and the last barrier [was] hauled down. The spirit of Sinn Féin, resolutely nationalist, that was brewing deafeningly, spread at the surface and penetrated all which was not unionist in Ireland.'[80] Alfred Blanche had long foreseen the drastic consequences of conscription. But no one would have thought that Lloyd George would have weakened even more the Irish Parliamentary Party, which, after the death of its leader, was now hanging by a thread. Lloyd George's rhetoric showed that he did consider the two questions (Home Rule and military service) as being intrinsically linked.[81] For the interests of the Irish Party, such a scenario was the worst imaginable.

The French had long since implored the British to grant Home Rule to the Irish, as 'the only way to reach a solution'.[82] When the French heard of the vote at Westminster, de la Panouse esteemed that the British Cabinet had made a terrible blunder in pushing for a vote on conscription, without granting Ireland a significant amount of autonomy.[83] In the aftermath of the vote, as de la Panouse noticed, protest against conscription gripped all parts of Ireland.[84] When the French offered to send another delegation to Ireland in order to plead the cause of the Allies, the British Minister for Foreign Affairs objected. After close consultation with his counterpart, the French Minister for Foreign Affairs explained that 'the British Government, which habitually welcomes [their] actions with fervour, would prefer that [they] abstain from any initiative'.[85] The British had permitted the French, less for disinterested motives and much more probably out of political need, to send a series of delegations to the island during

---

[79] Michael Laffan, *The Resurrection of Ireland. The Sinn Féin Party, 1916–1923* (Cambridge: Cambridge University Press, 1999), 134.
[80] AD, Political and Commercial Correspondence, Great War, 1914–1918, Ireland, 1CPCOM/547, telegram from Alfred Blanche to the Minister for Foreign Affairs, 20 April 1918.
[81] SHD, Third Republic (1870–1940), Army Staff, 7N1261, telegram from General de la Panouse to the Minister for War, 10 April 1918.
[82] SHD, Third Republic (1870–1940), Army Staff, 7N1254, letter from General de la Panouse to the Minister for War, 8 April 1918.
[83] SHD, Third Republic (1870–1940), Army Staff, 7N1254, letter from General de la Panouse to the Minister for War, 15 April 1918.
[84] Ibid.
[85] AD, Political and Commercial Correspondence, Great War, 1914–1918, Ireland, 1CPCOM/547, letter from the Minister for Foreign Affairs to M. Lefas (deputy), 10 May 1918.

the conflict.[86] If the question of the unsuccessful or relatively limited impact of the delegations is left aside, the French representatives nonetheless provided precious and minutely-detailed information as to what was happening in the country. London's stern and categorical refusal to consent to a French delegation being sent to Ireland was evidence that the British had come to terms with the idea that no political or foreign solution to the Irish question was likely to emerge.

'The miracle has been performed'[87]

In villages and towns, in the meetings of county councils and in homes alike, the decision of the British Parliament sparked off the most passionate and inflamed expression of hatred of the British ever seen in Ireland. On 18 April, all sections of nationalist Ireland gathered in the Mansion House in Dublin and pledged to oppose conscription at all costs. Devlin and Dillon, the most prominent leaders of the Irish Parliamentary Party, joined forces with de Valera, Griffith, and other more marginal elements of the Irish political spectrum, in their opposition to conscription. 'The miracle has been performed', rejoiced *New Ireland*, 'Irishmen in their anxiety as to their common future are united as they have never been before.'[88] The unnatural alliance between Unionists and Nationalists spoke of a common vision of Ireland, that reminded the editor of *New Ireland* that 'the most extraordinary unity of opinion hostile to conscription prevail[ed], showing that at long last ALL IRELAND realize[d] the absolute oneness of interests amongst all its people. Conscription ha[d] wrought the miracle, and never again [could] politicians frighten one section of Irishmen with the hypothetical antagonism of another section.'[89] *The Leader* reported: 'Under its stimulus Ireland thinks and resolves as one man.'[90]

On 18 April, in Maynooth, Cardinal Logue and the bishops pledged to resist conscription and to assist the Irish in their opposition to military service. The bishops described conscription as 'an oppressive and inhuman law which the Irish people ha[d] a right to resist by every means that [were] consonant with

---

[86] Aan de Wiel, *The Catholic Church in Ireland*, 128–152.
[87] *New Ireland*, 20 April 1918.
[88] Ibid.
[89] Ibid.
[90] *The Leader*, 27 April 1918.

the law of God'.[91] The Archbishop of Dublin, the Bishops of Cork and Limerick (to mention only a few), began to organize the fight. In Cork, churches advised their flocks to remain calm and resist any attempt to conscript the young men of Ireland.[92] On 20 April 1918, the Labour Party held a meeting in the Mansion House and swore to resist conscription by all means. Mass mobilization of workers against conscription took place around the country and over 100,000 workers signed the anti-conscription pledge at meetings and trade union offices.[93] On 21 April, in parishes the length and breadth of Ireland, priests speaking to their parishioners announced that people were to come at 3pm with a signed paper, in order to write up an accurate list of people taking the oath against conscription. With the official stand taken by the clergy, Sinn Féin could now claim to have a confessional endorsement, and any opposing voices were rapidly silenced. Father Maguire, of Flagmount (County Clare), denounced the signing of the anti-conscription covenant on 21 April, and an attempt was made to burn his church down only a few days later.[94] With the exception of some of the younger members, the Roman Catholic clergy had always been generally anti-Sinn Féin. However, on 21 April, 'at a man, they declared against conscription'[95] and sided with their former enemy, Sinn Féin. 'At present a sort of Holy War against the British Army is being preached and priests use very forcible language in denouncing conscription, stating they will themselves lead their people to death sooner than accept it',[96] stated an RIC Constable. Public resentment was generally stoked up by the dread of conscription. It now took a decidedly anti-British turn under the joint leadership of Sinn Féin leaders and the Roman Catholic Church.[97] By doing so, the bishops were adding to the growing reservations in the country regarding the projects for a future Home Rule. When Pope Benedict XV refused to excommunicate Cardinal Logue and other bishops, his decision offered Sinn Féin a degree of papal impunity while plunging the Irish Parliamentary Party into the abyss.[98]

[91] *Irish Independent*, 19 April 1919.
[92] University of California, Santa Barbara Library (hereafter UCSBL), Charles Montgomery Hathaway Papers (1895–1939), 1/43, Official correspondences, report on the situation of Ireland, 25 April 1918, p. 4.
[93] Padraig Yeates, *A City in Wartime, Dublin 1914–1918* (Dublin: Gill & Macmillan, 2012), 462.
[94] TNA, CO 904/157/1, Reports of the State of the Country, 1916–1918, Item 41, Southern District, April 1918.
[95] TNA, CO 904/157/1, Reports of the State of the Country, 1916–1918, Item 37, Midlands and Connaught District, April 1918.
[96] Ibid.
[97] TNA, CO 904/157/1, Reports of the State of the Country, 1916–1918, Item 28, Midlands and Connaught District, May 1918.
[98] AD, Political and Commercial Correspondence, Great War, 1914–1918, Ireland, 1CPCOM/547, letter from the Ambassador for France in Rome to the Minister for Foreign Affairs, 6 May 1918.

Whereas the clergy had previously remained hostile to the separatist republican movement in the aftermath of the rebellion,[99] the Catholic Church now took a very strong attitude against conscription and threatened to excommunicate Roman Catholic members of the RIC and the Dublin Metropolitan Police, should they attempt to enforce conscription.[100] Open attempts to lure the police away from their professional allegiance was made, with one local priest in East Galway warning RIC Inspectors that should they help enforce conscription they would be traitors to their country.[101] At a concert at Maryborough (Queen's County), Reverend Father Walsh advised the police to throw off their jackets and not go against their countrymen.[102] From his headquarters, Major General Doran, Intelligence Officer for the Southern District, witnessed the merging of the various streams of discontent.[103] His counterpart in the Northern District, Captain Whitfield, talked about 'the fusion of the R.C. Church, the Parliamentary Nationalists, and the Sinn Féin party',[104] all of whom had pledged to resist conscription at all costs and had signed a pledge. A meeting for women was held in Central Hall, Exchequer Street, Dublin. The hall was packed, with many women able to find only standing room. Women of all classes and religious denominations attended, under the presidency of Miss Louise Bennett, who delivered a passionate speech in which she urged her countrywomen to support the men in their terrible ordeal. She believed that the means of resistance commended to them would be of a passive nature, and the Irishwomen's International League also advocated passive resistance against conscription, carrying out a comprehensive distribution of leaflets.[105]

Overnight, the Military Service Act of April 1918 further precipitated the turn of events at a critical juncture in Irish history. In North Tipperary, the County Inspector described how the bill had conjured up 'hostility, indignation,

---

[99] Paul Bew, *Ideology and the Ulster Question: Ulster Unionism and Irish Nationalism, 1912–1916* (Oxford: Clarendon Press, 1994), 389.
[100] TNA, CAB 24/49/2, memorandum from H. E. Duke, Irish Opinion as to Conscription in Ireland, 21 April 1918.
[101] TNA, CO 904/157/1, Reports of the State of the Country, 1916–1918, Item 28, Midlands and Connaught District, May 1918.
[102] TNA, CO 904/157/1, Reports of the State of the Country, 1916–1918, Item 8, Midlands and Connaught District, July 1918.
[103] TNA, CO 904/157/1, Reports of the State of the Country, 1916–1918, Report from Major General Doran, Intelligence Officer, Headquarters, Southern District, 30 April 1918.
[104] TNA, CO 904/157/1, Reports of the State of the Country, 1916–1918, Report from Captain Whitfield, Intelligence Officer, Northern District, Irish Command, 29 April 1918.
[105] *New Ireland*, 27 April 1918. For the participation of women associations during the anti-conscription crisis see Senia Pašeta, 'New Issues and Old: Women and Politics in Ireland, 1914–1918', in *Irish Women in the First World War Era. Irish Women's Lives, 1914–1918*, ed. Jennifer Redmond and Elaine Farrell (London: Routledge, 2019), 116–118.

and fury'.[106] In East Cork, the whole of the nationalist population sided with Sinn Féin and 'enlisted under its banner'.[107] In various parts of the country railway men employed by Irish companies pledged to discontinue working as soon as trains would be used for the conveyance of conscripted men.[108] In Clonmel, the Railway Locomotive Staff were notified that they would be ordered to strike if conscription became law. In Drogheda and Dundalk, railway and transport workers were warned to expect orders to cease work, while in Omagh, the police heard rumours that RIC barracks would be attacked if conscription was implemented.[109] On 23 April, a twenty-four-hour strike was voted in all the cities of Ireland (except Dublin) in protest against the bill. Shops and pubs remained closed, no trains ran, and no post was delivered.[110] From Cork, it was reported that a general stoppage of work had also taken place.[111]

The following day, a National Defence Fund was discreetly launched. On 21 May, it had raised £160,000 and by 3 June the amount had already reached £215,000.[112] By then, sixteen counties were already represented in the list of contributions to the National Defence Fund.[113] 'Since the passing of the Military Service Act there is only one subject which occupies the minds of the people of South of Ireland', noted one inspector of the RIC, 'namely how to resist, or anyhow to avoid the conscription.'[114] Previously, the Sinn Féin organization comprised all those elements hostile to British rule but the fear of conscription now brought together all classes of people. 'Those who were not previously unionists in sympathy but who were with England in this war have made a common cause with Sinn Féin to resist it',[115] stated one RIC Inspector. Observers within the RIC were unanimous in noting the unquestionable signs pointing to the emergence of a united front against compulsory service.

---

[106] TNA, CO 904/105, County Inspector's report, North Tipperary, April 1918.
[107] TNA, CO 904/106, County Inspector's report, East Cork, April 1918.
[108] TNA, CAB 24/49/2, memorandum from H. E. Duke, Irish Opinion as to Conscription in Ireland, 21 April 1918.
[109] TNA, CAB 24/48/73, memorandum from H. E. Duke, Chief Secretary, Organization of Irish Resistance to Conscription, 18 April 1918.
[110] Laffan, *The Resurrection of Ireland*, 135.
[111] UCSBL, Charles Montgomery Hathaway Papers (1895–1939), 1/43, Official correspondences, report on the situation of Ireland, 25 April 1918, p. 6.
[112] AD, Political and Commercial Correspondence, Great War, 1914–1918, Ireland, Home Affairs (1918–1922), 95CPCOM/1, report on the situation of Ireland, 15 August 1918.
[113] *Freeman's Journal*, 25 May 1918.
[114] TNA, CO 904/157/1, Reports of the State of the Country, 1916–1918, Item 41, Southern District, April 1918.
[115] TNA, CO 904/157/1, Reports of the State of the Country, 1916–1918, Item 37, Midlands and Connaught District, April 1918.

After the vote, the British authorities reported that all over the country, 'innumerable resolutions were passed by all sorts of bodies to impress on the authorities that it [was] quite impossible to carry out the Act'.[116] While city and county councils were supportive of efforts at voluntary recruitment, they heartily condemned any attempts to introduce conscription. In County Cork, magistrates passed resolutions against the act.[117] Limerick County Council and Limerick City Council passed a similar measure, while Waterford County Council issued a similar circular.[118] From his prison cell in England, Desmond Fitzgerald, Sinn Féin candidate for the Pembroke Division of Dublin, proclaimed that 'Ireland [was] now solely governed by an alien soldering and a secret police which sought to help that government to secure the whole of Ireland's young manhood for military uses'.[119]

In the eyes of nationalist Ireland, John Redmond (who had died in March 1918) remained responsible for Britain's attempt to conscript Ireland. It is vital to remember what the promises of the British Government were before August 1914 and what could be logically expected after the end of the conflict. Asquith had passed the Home Rule Bill but postponed its implementation to the end of the conflict. The bill would be enacted at the end of the war, but there was still no solution to opposition from Ulster Unionists and Sinn Féin had won a number of by-elections in 1917.[120] While raids and a variety of other disturbances and violations of public order had been registered throughout the country from January 1918 onwards, it was the passing of the act in the House of Commons in April 1918 which 'gave an impetus to the raids for arms and thefts of gelignite and other explosives'.[121]

The military stationed in Ireland naturally noticed this unprecedented shift. Captain MacLeod (Cameron Highlanders) was stationed at Limerick barracks with his unit in April 1918, and thus had direct experience of the effects of conscription in the revival of an undercurrent of anti-British feeling among local populations:

---

[116] TNA, CO 904/157/1, Reports of the State of the Country, 1916–1918, Item 41, Southern District, April 1918.

[117] UCSBL, Charles Montgomery Hathaway Papers (1895–1939), 1/43, Official correspondences, report on the situation of Ireland, 25 April 1918, p. 4.

[118] Waterford City and County Archives (hereafter WCCA), Lismore Castle Estate Papers (1731–1969), Waterford County Council Minutes, 28 April 1918.

[119] University College Dublin Archives (hereafter UCDA), Desmond Fitzgerald Papers (1894–1959), P80/12, letter or speech from Desmond Fitzgerald delivered to the press for the election of the Pembroke Division of Dublin, December 1918.

[120] Stephen Gwynn, *John Redmond's Last Years* (London: E. Arnold, 1919), 105–3.

[121] TNA, CO 904/157/1, Reports of the State of the Country, 1916–1918, Item 41, Southern District, April 1918.

On the march to the barracks from the station, we passed through crowded streets. There was some hissing and booing and cries of 'Sinn Fein!' and 'Hoch der Kaiser'. Today has been a holiday throughout the town, as all the civilians have been singing a pledge against conscription. They paraded in the afternoon about 6,000 strong and marched through the streets with bands and banners.[122]

From the outbreak of the conflict, 'farmers had [had] no interest at all in the war'.[123] Passivity and indifference for the war could sum up their attitude.[124] When the farmers, shopkeepers and workers who had turned a blind eye while enjoying the economic benefits of the war gradually realized they could be required overnight to leave their country and their family for the war, their silent support for Britain turned into a vociferous protest. Men were already planning how to escape the measure. In Galway and remote parts of Connemara 'people [were] leaving their work to live in the hills, so terrified [were] they'.[125] The RIC Inspector, on a visit to Achill Island (County Mayo), even heard of trenches being dug, together with tunnels, in the mountains near Dugort in order to facilitate concealment of arms and the evacuation of the locals. Many young men in the south, '[were] sleeping out at night'.[126] With these groups of young men leaving their homes to create a nucleus of resistance outside their usual place of abode, the result was a further consolidation of the armed movement and a strengthening of the bonds between these men. (At the local level, paramilitary organizations were emerging and would later on play a major part in the War of Independence against the British authorities.)

One direct consequence of the act was the immediate resignation of a number of RIC Constables.[127] Weekly and monthly reports of the Royal Irish Constabulary highlighted that the unanimous stand against conscription motivated some

---

[122] ULL, Peter Liddle Collection, (First World War) (1914–1918), General Aspects (1914–1918), GS 1027 MACLEOD, letter from Jock Dunning (Captain 2nd Cameron Highlanders) to his mother, 23 April 1918.

[123] Aan de Wiel, *The Catholic Church in Ireland*, 117.

[124] Against these views, Niamh Gallagher and Catriona Pennell contend that farmers and labourers strongly supported the war effort. Gallagher argues that the Great War was 'an all-Irish war effort' and maintains that 'the efforts of rural Ireland to cultivate more tillage in early 1917 were an important means by which those who lived in agricultural areas responded to the demands of war'. Niamh Gallagher, *Ireland and the Great War. A Social and Political History* (London: Bloomsbury, 2019), 81. Similarly, Catriona Pennell maintains that British farmers and labourers expressed their loyalty to Britain in wartime through increased agricultural output rather than military enlistment. Catriona Pennell, *A Kingdom United: Popular Responses to the Outbreak of the First World War in Britain and Ireland* (Oxford: Oxford University Press, 2012), 192.

[125] TNA, CO 904/157/1, Reports of the State of the Country, 1916–1918, Item 28, Midlands and Connaught District, May 1918.

[126] Ibid.

[127] TNA, CO 904/157/1, Reports of the State of the Country, 1916–1918, Item 37, Midlands and Connaught District, April 1918.

constables to step down, as they refused to force their fellow citizens to enrol, and knew they could be exposed to violent attacks. Others unambiguously stated to their superiors that they would be unable to implement conscription. Relations between local populations and the Royal Irish Constabulary were entering a new phase. Constables would now have to turn against their friends, relatives and countrymen in order to enforce the policies of the British authorities. Even though the number of resignations appears to have been modest, the phenomenon was nonetheless evidence of a redefinition of the allegiance of some constables, involving a shift away from the established British authorities to the (as yet putative) authority of the Irish Republic. 'They themselves say that they are asked to do the dirty work of enforcing it', wrote one RIC Inspector, 'and are then to be handed over under the Home Rule bill, having made themselves unpopular with their friends and their church. Thus their attitude is one of great uncertainty.'[128] Such a gloomy assessment was bound to raise concerns in London. In the eventuality of conscription being implemented, officers-in-command did not even know where the allegiance of their constables would lie. In addition, any resignation could expose the RIC to considerable dangers, in these troubled times. Sensitive and personal information, confidential details concerning the precise quantities of weapons and ammunition conserved in police stations; all intelligence data could potentially be compromised.

Preparing the fight here and abroad

On examining the interaction between the April 1918 conscription crisis and the social climate in the country, the evidence suggests that the Irish Volunteers, the paramilitary organization which had refused to pledge allegiance to John Redmond in September 1914, suffered from the direct consequences of the conscription crisis. Their commanding officers were suddenly faced with a sharp increase in enrolments, as conscription became a more and more plausible eventuality.

With the country in the grip of the fear of conscription, the Volunteers' ranks were thrown open to anyone who wished to join. The result 'was a big influx of men into the Volunteers'.[129] In April 1918, the threat of conscription 'brought a

---

[128] Ibid.
[129] MAI, BMH, WS1498, Witness statement from Michael Murray, former Captain, Ballynarcargy Company, Westmeath Brigade, 21 September 1956, p. 2.

great influx of men into the Volunteer movement',[130] reported a former activist. Second-Lieutenant Flynn, Ballinadee Company, similarly noticed that the threat to enforce conscription in Ireland in the spring of 1918 'led to an increase in the membership of the Ballinadee Company'.[131] Depending on localities, increases varied greatly. In the neighbourhood of Bandon (County Cork), around forty individuals joined the Irish Volunteers as a result of conscription[132] while the membership of the Galbally Company rose to over 100 men (compared to twenty-five combatants previously in the unit).[133] In the locality of Ardmore (County Waterford), a significant growth in membership took place with the enrolment of 500 men.[134] Tralee battalions and companies adjacent to the town (County Kerry) also registered a surge, by about 400, up to a figure of 900 men.[135] While recruitment operated all over the country, membership did not mean an unconditional willingness to back the ideology of armed revolutionary organization. Indeed, officers of the Irish Volunteers highlighted the pragmatic expectations of these new recruits, who hoped above all to receive protection in the event of their being drafted into the British Army. Civilians joined the paramilitary organization largely to avoid being conscripted, not to foment another insurrection.

Yet as the threat of conscription receded, companies registered comparable losses in their membership.[136] All over the island, the anticipation of conscription had resulted in an increase of membership for the Irish Volunteers, a dynamic which was subsequently attenuated or reversed following the decision to defer implementation. In Donegal, the local paramilitary leaders confessed that men 'ceased to attend parades and club meetings, leaving [the unit] as before, with only the stalwarts who were determined to fight for freedom remaining in the ranks'.[137] Departures of newly-enrolled activists occurred in all the units: 'the danger of

---

[130] MAI, BMH, WS0838, Witness statement from Sean Moyland, former Officer-in-Command, 2nd Battalion, Cork II Brigade, and later Officer-in-Command of Cork IV Brigade, 6 May 1953, pp. 59–60.
[131] MAI, BMH, WS1621, Witness statement from Con Flynn, former Second-Lieutenant, Ballinadee Company, Bandon Battalion, Cork III Brigade, 24 May 1957, p. 5.
[132] Ibid.
[133] MAI, BMH, WS1021, Witness statement from Amos Reidy, member of the West Limerick Irish Volunteers, 12 October 1954, p. 1.
[134] MAI, BMH, WS1229, witness statement from James Mansfield, former member of the IRA West Waterford Brigade, 14 June 1955, p. 2.
[135] MAI, WS1011, Witness statement from Patrick Garvey, Brigade Adjutant of Tralee, 15 September 1954, pp. 7–8.
[136] MAI, BMH, WS1498, Witness statement from Michael Murray, former Captain, Ballynarcargy Company, Westmeath Brigade, 21 September 1956, p. 2.
[137] MAI, BMH, WS1448, Witness statement from Patrick Breslin, former Adjutant, I Donegal Brigade, 27 June 1956, pp. 5–6.

conscription was past and many of those who rushed into the Volunteers in the spring of 1918 had departed, almost disrupting the organization'.[138] Commanding officers unanimously asserted that 'when the conscription crisis died down all, or practically all, of [their] influx of members took their departure again'.[139]

There was a significant difference between enrolling in the Irish Volunteers and joining Sinn Féin. Membership of Sinn Féin was merely a political stance, but once a civilian transferred to the paramilitary organization he was required to attend training, learn how to use a rifle, and engage in military action against British troops, if required. Witness statements from former commanding officers pointed out that the year 1918 represented a significant turning point when it came to a hike in the number of Volunteers. However, they also acknowledged that the conscription scare did more real service to Sinn Féin than to the Volunteers.[140] Opposition to conscription manifested itself in the increase in Sinn Féin memberships and then to some civilians joining the paramilitary organization during the 1918 conscription crisis. But it was Sinn Féin that caught the attention of populations that were liable to be affected by the introduction of conscription. The *Irishman* claimed that membership of the Sinn Féin club in Letterkenny increased by 75 per cent,[141] while in Sligo alone it noted that 'no fewer than 103 new clubs ha[d] been affiliated within the past few weeks'.[142] In the city of Cork, membership rose 'from about 1,500 members [...] to between 4,000 and 5,000 in a single week'.[143] In the north of Ireland, Sinn Féin clubs swelled significantly with 'about 300 in the Northern District, with Cavan and Drogheda having the largest number'.[144]

When conscription was voted in the House of Commons on 18 April 1918, Sinn Féin immediately sent the Lord Mayor of Dublin to Washington in order to gather support from the US Congress and the Irish-American communities.[145] Jean Jusserand, Ambassador to France in Washington, had rarely written to the Minister for Foreign Affairs in relation to Irish matters during the whole course

---

[138] MAI, BMH, WS0838, Witness statement from Sean Moyland, former Officer in command, 2nd Battalion, Cork II Brigade, and later Officer in Command of Cork IV Brigade, 6 May 1953, p. 60.
[139] MAI, BMH, WS1399, Witness statement from Thomas Peppard, former officer of Fingal Brigade 1955, p. 8.
[140] MAI, BMH, WS0492, Witness statement from John McCoy, 16 March 1951, p. 36.
[141] *Irishman*, 11 May 1918.
[142] *Sligo Champion*, 11 May 1918.
[143] TNA, CO 904/157/1, Reports of the State of the Country, 1916–1918, Item 41, Southern District, April 1918.
[144] TNA, CO 904/157/1, Reports of the State of the Country, 1916–1918, Item 10, Northern District, July 1918.
[145] AD, Political and Commercial Correspondence, Great War, 1914–1918, Ireland, 1CPCOM/547, letter from Alfred Blanche to the Minister for Foreign Affairs, 20 April 1918.

of the conflict. By April 1918, he was reporting to his hierarchy in Paris twice in less than two days. Wilson could 'no longer turn a deaf ear to the claims of the Irish',[146] wrote the ambassador. In order to counter the efforts of the Lord Mayor of Dublin, the British had dispatched Lord Reading, who promised Wilson everything would be done to bring England and the US together and to quieten discontent among Irish-Americans. From Washington's vantage point it seemed that the British Ambassador had managed to reach an agreement with Wilson: on 28 April, he sent a cable to London in which he strongly recommended the immediate application of Home Rule before the full implementation of conscription. In a private meeting with Jusserand, the British envoy underlined that everything would be done to prevent riots and bloodshed.

An unpopular move among the British authorities in Ireland

As early as June 1916, Jean des Longchamps had warned the French Minister for Foreign Affairs that 'its application in Ireland would certainly lead to a general uprising'.[147] In October 1916, a secret report underlining the dangers following the persistent evocation of conscription in Ireland was sent to the Cabinet of the British Prime Minister.[148] It warned that conscription would create considerable difficulties throughout the country. As long as recruitment operated on a voluntary basis, the Irish people never felt compelled to join the ranks of an army to which they felt no affiliation. Although anti-recruitment campaigns had taken place all over the island, this had not deterred the 132,202 men from volunteering for the war.[149] RIC inspectors feared however that conscription would both undermine the Irish Parliamentary Party and resurrect Sinn Féin. So, why did the British vote conscription?

Based on the evidence of the secret police reports and the minutes of Cabinet meetings, all the representatives of British rule in Ireland had strong reservations concerning the implementation of conscription. Lord Wimborne, then Lord Lieutenant for Ireland; H. E. Duke, acting as Chief Secretary, General Byrne, Head of the RIC, and General Mahon, Commander-in-Chief, opposed the idea

---

[146] AD, Political and Commercial Correspondence, Great War, 1914–1918, Ireland, 1CPCOM/547, letter from Jean Jusserand to the Minister for Foreign Affairs, 26 April 1918.
[147] AD, Political and Commercial Correspondence, Great War, 1914–1918, Ireland, 1CPCOM/545, telegram from Jean des Longchamps to the Minister for Foreign Affairs, 2 June 1916.
[148] TNA, CAB 37/157/15, Recruiting in Ireland, 7 October 1916.
[149] *Statistics of Military Effort of the British Empire during the Great War* (London: HMSO, 1922), 363.

to a man. Beyond the obvious effect of the measure, that of consolidating a united and determined opposition and a climate of unrest in the country, there were four points which caused concern: (1) many of the 161,000 eligible men were working in British factories on war production or were farming, providing essential food supplies,[150] (2) the necessary increase in the number of soldiers garrisoned in Ireland, following the introduction of the measure, would partially offset the number of men enlisting, (3) the issue was one with a potential for 'serious disaffection in Canada, Australia, and South Africa [not to mention] a possible rupture with America';[151] and (4) conscription would have jeopardized the Irish Convention which had been searching for a solution to the Irish problem since July 1917.[152] Furthermore, already by October 1916, British military authorities were well aware that 'young men would probably take to the hills and would have to be rounded up by the police assisted by soldiers'.[153]

France's representatives also knew that conscription was not a realistic option. What steps were to be taken in the event of conscripts refusing to present themselves to the barracks? Riots and social unrest in other parts of the British Empire against conscription had highlighted how a minority could oppose a federal law.[154] So how would Britain enforce conscription if the whole of Ireland were to rise up against the authorities? General de la Panouse had grasped from the beginning that the imposition of conscription, without the agreement of the Irish MPs and without a settlement of the question of the constitutional status of Ireland, could only lead to the most grotesque situation: 'every single conscript would stay home waiting to be fetched. An operation that could be repeated 50,000, 100,000 or even 200,000 times would take up a lot of time and would be a severe strain on police numbers. It would make the Government look ridiculous.'[155] British military authorities also anticipated the troubles resulting from the implementation of conscription, as local populations would side with the dissidents, hide the conscripts, and even attack the RIC. With the moral support of the clergy on the side of those hostile to the measure, any serious attempt to implement conscription was a recipe for local insurrections.

---

[150] Ward, 'Lloyd George and the 1918 Irish Conscription Crisis', 108.
[151] George A. Riddell, *Lord Riddell's War Diary, 1914–1918* (London: Nicholson and Watson, 1933), 239.
[152] Ward, 'Lloyd George and the 1918 Irish Conscription Crisis', 109.
[153] TNA, CAB 37/157/15, Recruiting in Ireland, 7 October 1916.
[154] Margaret Levi, 'The Institution of Conscription', *Social Science History* 20, no. 1 (1996): 133–167.
[155] SHD, Third Republic (1870–1940), Army Staff, 7N1254, telegram from General de la Panouse to the Minister for War, 22 April 1918.

Of greater cause for worry, warned the RIC inspector, any form of conscription 'would play into the hands of Sinn Féin and would enable Sinn Féiners to denounce another gross mismanagement of Irish affairs by the British government'.[156] In October 1916, another RIC Inspector noted that the 'introduction of this measure would kill the Constitutional Party'.[157] Whereas it is often argued that Sinn Féin benefited from Easter Week 1916 in the gradual strengthening of its appeal in the country, the evidence from reports and from the private correspondence of the British and the French authorities is that in the aftermath of the uprising, Sinn Féin did not succeed in reaching out to nationalist populations. The general prosperity of Irish farmers, coupled with a disinclination for any further episode of rebellion, were all factors that were consistent with the position publicly taken by individual Roman Catholic bishops and parish priests, who stated their opposition to seditious 'nonsense'. The release from prison of rebels was gradually losing its freshness and novelty, while the leaders of the rebellion and those most intransigent in their opposition to the Crown were and would remain as fanatical as ever. In short, 'the movement was losing the support given by the general public for lack of any really material grievance to agitate about'.[158] The consensus among French political representatives in Ireland, British military authorities in Ireland, and shared by at least some members of the Cabinet in London, was that Irish affairs above all needed to be left aside and as far as possible undisturbed for the duration of the war. Private correspondence between France's representatives to Ireland and the Minister of Foreign Affairs revealed how, in the minds of the French authorities, questions that were specific to the play of British politics were directly threatening the legitimacy and credibility of the Irish Parliamentary Party. At the time, one secret report to the British Prime Minister in October 1916 warned that 'any attempt at implementing conscription would lead to disastrous consequences'.[159] A year later, in December 1917, Alfred Blanche concluded that any attempt at conscripting the Irish 'would only be welcomed to justify another crusade and create new martyrs'.[160] Conscription could 'resurrect the Sinn Féiners [...] whose prestige ha[d] been declining for

---

[156] TNA, CAB 37/157/15, Recruiting in Ireland, 7 October 1916.
[157] Ibid.
[158] TNA, CO 904/157/1, Reports of the State of the Country, 1916–1918, Item 83, Southern District, December 1917.
[159] SHD, Third Republic (1870–1940), Army Staff, 7N1253, telegram from Colonel de la Panouse to the Minister for War, 30 October 1916.
[160] AD, Political and Commercial Correspondence, Great War, 1914-N1918, Ireland, 1CPCOM/546, telegram from Alfred Blanche to the Minister for Foreign Affairs, 21 December 1917.

several months'.¹⁶¹ French political and military authorities were all of the opinion that conscription could resurrect the party.

In his report to the Prime Minister dated 2 April 1918, James O'Connor, Attorney General of Ireland, called conscription a 'blunder', warning the British Cabinet that their stubbornness would 'inevitably lead to a rebellion'. As a Catholic Nationalist in close touch with popular opinion in Ireland and who had lost both his sons to service, he considered that conscription for Ireland would not only create animosity and dissidence throughout the country, its practical effects, in terms of the additional number of military recruits, would be negligible. First of all, in military terms, enforcement of the measure would be slow and painstaking, requiring a considerable presence of British troops to supervise the process. Conscripts could possibly disobey and display their reluctance to be incorporated. There was the probability that priests would be shot while defending their congregations. O'Connor pointed out that the Roman Catholic Church, at the national and at the local level, would leave no stone unturned when defending its flocks. From an international point of view, to impose conscription on Ireland would have direct implications for soldiers of Irish origin who were serving in American, Australian, Canadian and New Zealand regiments stationed in France: 'its introduction would draw them away from their commitment to the war effort', he warned. Out of loyalty and honesty to the British Cabinet, the Attorney General for Ireland argued that the Government had to (1) pass Home Rule, with powers of full fiscal autonomy, (2) organize a comprehensive recruitment campaign, and (3), in the event of men failing to volunteer for service, re-consider the question of Irish conscription three months later.¹⁶² The day Lloyd George received O'Connor's report, Balfour telegraphed Colonel House asking for Wilson's opinion regarding conscription in Ireland. He strongly warned the British not to risk it.¹⁶³ The fundamental conviction of General de la Panouse was that the British knew conscription would not be feasible for the Irish and had only voted it in the knowledge that it could not be implemented.

Conscription: a counter-Wilsonian move?

Was conscription a diplomatic move on the part of the British to regain control over Irish affairs? This, at any case, was what France's military attaché seemed

---

[161] Ibid.
[162] TNA, CAB 24/47/29, James O'Connor, Attorney General for Ireland, to the Prime Minister, 2 April 1918.
[163] Francis M. Carroll, *America and the Making of an Independent Ireland. A History* (New York: New York University Press, 2021), 34.

to think. In this respect, the fact that the British presented the Military Service Bill in April 1918, after the death of John Redmond, was not merely a coincidence.

On 3 June, the Lord Lieutenant to Ireland announced that conscription had now been postponed until 1 October.[164] Before then, the country had to either raise 50,000 volunteers for the war effort, followed by the supply of two to three thousand recruits per month, or conscription would immediately apply.[165] This clearly supports the claim that the British never really intended to conscript the Irish. So what was the point of the bill, considering that the British Government then chose not to implement conscription, adopting an approach that was regarded as clear proof that 'they had given up on Home Rule and on conscription in Ireland'?[166] With the death of Redmond, it seemed that conscription had been abandoned only as a way to abandon Home Rule.[167] On 20 June, during a debate in the House of Lords, the Marquess of Londonderry spoke in favour of conscripting the Irish as early as possible, arguing that 'the difficulties of the Government would have been minimized to a very large extent had they not put off Conscription until they had tried a system which was doomed to failure.'[168] He blamed Lloyd George and his predecessor for not measuring the gravity of the situation at the outbreak of the conflict.[169] Lord Curzon declared that for the time being conscription was to be abandoned, arguing that 'If [Ireland] could not have Home Rule [Ireland] could not also have Conscription.'[170] Five days later, on 25 June 1918, in the House of Commons, Lloyd George gave the same impression, while also expressing his wish to see a resolution to the Irish question before the end of the war.[171] Lloyd George pointed out that by not enforcing conscription, the British Cabinet was seeking to protect the British authorities in Ireland who had spoken out against conscription. In order to preserve trust between Dublin Castle and Westminster, he certified that he could not ignore

---

[164] Gallagher, *Ireland and the Great War*, 152–153.
[165] AD, Political and Commercial Correspondence, Great War, 1914–1918, Ireland, Home Affairs (1918–1922), 95CPCOM/1, report on the situation of Ireland, 15 August 1918.
[166] SHD, Third Republic (1870–1940), Army Staff, 7N1254, letter from General de la Panouse to the Minister for War, 24 June 1918.
[167] SHD, Third Republic (1870–1940), Army Staff, 7N679, Section des Renseignements Généraux, 4ème Bureau, 15 June 1918.
[168] Hansard, House of Lords, series 5, vol. 30, cc295, The Marquess of Londonderry to the House of Lords, 20 June 1918.
[169] Ibid.
[170] Hansard, House of Lords, series 5, vol. 30, cc330, Lord Curzon to the House of Lords, 20 June 1918.
[171] Hansard, House of Commons, series 5, vol. 30, cc956, Lloyd George to the House of Commons, 25 June 1918.

the concerns expressed by the governing authorities in Ireland, and could not enforce conscription against their will.[172] It is indeed likely that, as has been argued, conscription for Ireland was a measure that was introduced by the British government, albeit not with the intention that it be implemented. What lay behind the conscription crisis was the need to enforce a new conscription policy in Britain: 'a policy which could not work in Ireland and which may not even have been intended to work, was introduced in order to force through a workable conscription policy in Britain'.[173] In other words, it was needed to placate British public opinion by making the civilian populations of England, Scotland and Wales think that the Irish would now be required to do their share. In May 1918, once the bill had been passed, 'it was no longer needed to mollify public opinion: the British public simply had to think that the government intended to conscript Ireland, the government did not have go to the trouble of doing so'.[174] France's representatives also concluded that there was a need to appease British public opinion. This was not however, according to General de la Panouse, the main reason of that move. Indeed, a new administration could not be discredited and disregarded so abruptly, when it was just taking command.

According to General de la Panouse, the British never really wanted Home Rule for the Irish. And even though British political designs for Ireland were entering a new phase in May 1918, with Lloyd George now drawing up a bill which excluded six counties in the north,[175] the French military attaché had the firm belief that the British were promising Home Rule precisely *because* they knew Sinn Féin would never accept it. On 28 May, 4 and 10 June, Bonar Law announced to the House of Commons that a Home Rule Bill was being prepared. This was met with dismay and expressions of sarcasm. The *Irish Independent* commented on the 'will-o'-the-wisp Home Rule'[176] with much irony. The Ambassador of France to the Vatican had learnt from Mgr. O'Riordan that the Irish now clearly disregarded the original Home Rule Bill and would no longer

---

[172] Hansard, House of Commons, series 5, vol. 30, cc959, Lloyd George to the House of Commons, 25 June 1918.
[173] Gregory, 'You might as well recruit Germans', 128.
[174] Ibid.
[175] On 1 May 1918, Lloyd George revealed his project for the island to the Irish MPs. In the hope of contenting both Unionists and Nationalists, the Prime Minister devised a scenario which consisted in the implementation of Home Rule in Ireland, with the exception of six counties in Ulster (Antrim, Armagh, Down, Fermanagh, Londonderry and Tyrone), coupled with the establishment of a national parliament in Dublin, where Nationalist and Unionist representatives would sit in equal numbers.
[176] *Irish Independent*, 11 June 1919.

accept it.[177] On 9 April 1918, in the House of Commons, Lloyd George had in effect administered a *coup de grâce* to the Irish Parliamentary Party and had trampled on the grave of John Redmond.[178] Having thus thrown Irish public opinion even more fully into the arms of Sinn Féin, he could now elaborate a new project in the full knowledge that Sinn Féin would reject it. General de la Panouse knew that Sinn Féin, since the establishment of the Irish Convention in July 1917, had consistently refused to participate in the negotiations. Lloyd George was well aware that whatever the Government could offer at this stage would never receive the agreement of Sinn Féin. Firstly, because the party was now totally devoted to the goal of an independent republic, in the light of its espousal of Wilsonian ideals, and secondly because they no longer wanted to deal directly with London and knew the general elections were nearing. In May 1918, General de la Panouse wrote that the revised Home Rule project would have implications for the entire United Kingdom and would redefine the relation between Westminster and the three kingdoms.[179] Ulster would then have been obliged to give up, an eventuality which was a cause for serious concern in the House of Lords, because the establishment of a federal government would have undermined its authority and privileges. 'A federal Home Rule', concluded one secret report, 'would have led to the dislocation of the United-Kingdom.'[180] This idea reflected the gradual spread of the rather toxic effects of the Irish question into the general bloodstream of British politics. As the negotiations continued, the idea of Home Rule mutated into a federal system where the Parliament of Westminster would retain imperial powers, whereas England, Wales and Scotland, as well as Ireland, would all have their respective national parliament. What had started as a domestic issue for the British and had obliged London to rethink its ambiguous relationship with Ireland was now directly threatening the unity of the United Kingdom.

Conclusion

In April 1918, the British position was based on the assessment that conscription could not apply to England, Scotland and Wales without also applying to

---

[177] AD, Political and Commercial Correspondence, Great War, 1914–1918, Ireland, 1CPCOM/547, letter from the Ambassador for France in Rome to the Minister for Foreign Affairs, 6 May 1918.
[178] Hansard, House of Commons Debates, series 5, vol. 104, cc1358, Lloyd George to House of Commons, 9 April 1918.
[179] SHD, Third Republic (1870–1940), Army Staff, 7N1254, telegram from General de la Panouse to the Minister for War, 6 May 1918.
[180] AD, Political and Commercial Correspondence, Great War, 1914–1918, Ireland, Home Affairs (1918–1922), 95CPCOM/1, report on the situation of Ireland, 15 August 1918.

Ireland.[181] When the tenor of the debates in the House of Commons are examined, it appears obvious that the British included Ireland in the Military Service Bill based on what they regarded as considerations of equity. All the kingdoms of Great Britain were now to contribute equally to the war effort. What had been granted to Ireland in January 1916, namely its exclusion from compulsory service, could no longer be sustained or justified in the eyes of the British Government. For this reason, Irish conscription was called 'a cold-blooded piece of cynicism'.[182] Following the introduction of the Military Service Act in April 1918 'Home Rule was permanently discredited [...] and it was linked in the popular mind with conscription'.[183] However, France's representatives seemed to disagree with the logic that the inclusion of Ireland was *only* aimed at contenting local populations in Great Britain. As seen in Chapter 5, following the US entry into the conflict, the British were no longer in a position where they could repress seditious activists. The Irish Convention appeared to represent little more than a 'political camouflage', along the lines of 'Asquith's delaying tactics'[184] prior to the outbreak of the war. What was to be hoped for, in the mind of General de la Panouse, was the resumption by the British authorities of their control of the island.

---

[181] TNA, CAB 23/6/7, War Cabinet Minutes, 6 April 1918.
[182] Gregory, 'You might as well recruit Germans', 128.
[183] Ibid., p. 128.
[184] Alvin Jackson, *Home Rule: An Irish History, 1800–2000* (London: Weidenfeld & Nicolson, 2003), 140.

7

Endgame (May 1918–December 1918)

The exclusion of Ireland from the 1916 Military Service Act was clear evidence that the country was to be treated differently from the three other constituent national territories which together made up the United Kingdom. By the end of 1916, conscription had already become an ongoing preoccupation for the Irish, a question that was slowly but surely leading to the radicalization of nationalist Ireland. By the beginning of 1917, Sinn Féin was in a position to gain the support of an increasingly worried population that wished to resist the enforcement of a military service bill. Moreover, the US entry into the war led to a further partial loss of control of the situation in Ireland by the British Government. Woodrow Wilson, through Colonel House, demanded that a settlement be reached for the ongoing and unresolved Irish question and the American position was that repression was no longer an option. In this enlarged, more international context, the demand for self-determination took over from the original demand for Home Rule. In order to pre-empt any further sedition in Ireland, the British now needed to elaborate a new narrative taking into account the fact that Ireland could represent a direct danger to the strategic goals of the Allies. In such circumstances, it was nevertheless essential that any plotting or collusion with the enemy be stamped out. What would be known as the German plot could thus rightly be regarded as a further instance of an ongoing counter-Wilsonian policy on the part of the British authorities in the context of the war effort.

The German plot

On 12 May 1918, the British nominated a new Viceroy, Lord French, and a new Chief Secretary, Edward Shortt. General Sir Frederik Shaw was appointed Commander-in-Chief of Ireland, while on 4 June, James Campbell became Lord Chancellor. Convinced that the replacement of General Maxwell by General Mahon illustrated the willingness of the British Government to reach an agreement with the Nationalists in order to levy the 160,000 remaining men who could serve in the army, the French were nonetheless somewhat intrigued by the steps subsequently taken by the British. Several civil servants were replaced. The Lord Lieutenant, the Principal Secretary, the Lord Chancellor, the Lord Chief Justice, and the Commander-in-Chief, in effect all those who appeared to be sympathetic to the Irish cause, were asked to step down. 'That change was so complete and theatrical', wrote General de la Panouse 'that one could ask what the intention of the British Government is.'[1] He went on: 'If all of this has not been done with a deliberate intention (which is doubtful) the government clearly made a mistake.'[2]

The arrest of the Sinn Féin leaders had been under discussion long before Operation Michael.[3] No action had however been taken. In the immediate aftermath of the passing of the Military Service Act for Ireland, Great Britain was faced with a widespread and almost unanimous opposition in Ireland. While the arrest of prominent Sinn Féin activists was intended as 'a sudden and crippling blow at the separatist movement',[4] it actually embittered nationalist populations even more.

On the night of 17 May 1918, leaders of the Sinn Féin party were arrested in Dublin, and the following day, arrest took place all over Ireland.[5] Around one hundred Sinn Féiners were captured by the British authorities. (When he was arrested by the British, de Valera had almost completed the writing of a booklet entitled *Ireland's Case against Conscription*,[6] which would subsequently be published.) Most of those arrested were then deported to Great Britain. On 19 May 1918, General French reported to His Majesty George V that the affair 'met with quite unexpected success'.[7] On 20 May, Dublin Castle issued a declaration stating that the activists had been found guilty of high treason. As he read through the report sent from Dublin, the French Minister for Foreign Affairs grasped that the British sought to neutralize Sinn Féin.[8] That very same

---

[1] Service Historique de la Défense, Vincennes (hereafter SHD), Third Republic (1870–1940), Army Staff, 7N1254, letter from General de la Panouse to the Minister for War, 24 June 1918.
[2] Ibid.
[3] Michael Laffan, *The Resurrection of Ireland. The Sinn Féin Party, 1916–1923* (Cambridge: Cambridge University Press, 1999), 142.
[4] Ibid., p. 143.
[5] Paul Bew, *Ireland: The Politics of Enmity, 1789–2006* (Oxford: Oxford University Press, 2007), 388.
[6] Éamon de Valera, *Ireland's Case against Conscription* (Dublin: Maunsel & Company Ltd., 1918).
[7] Parliamentary Archives London, F48/6/12, General French to King George V, 19 May 1918.
[8] Archives Diplomatiques du Ministère des Affaires Étrangères, La Courneuve (hereafter AD), Political and Commercial Correspondence, Great War, 1914–1918, Ireland, Home Affairs (1918–1922), 95CPCOM/1, report on the situation of Ireland, 15 August 1918.

day, *The Times* reported that 'the Irish Government had discovered a German plot'.⁹ The following day, the British divulged a large number of documents.¹⁰ When the Government eventually released confidential information, it was discovered that the carefully assembled evidence related to relations between the German Government and some leaders of the 1916 uprising, without however providing any actual evidence as to the alleged German conspiracy. Reactions to this so-called evidence provided were marked by widespread skepticism, even embarrassment, and it was *The Times* that led the fight against what appeared to be a plot against the Irish. On 25 May, the newspaper underlined that there was 'no evidence of the guilty complicity in a German plot of any individual'.¹¹ Quoting several English dailies, the Irish press pointed out that the liberal English press had demanded the disclosure of substantive evidence and were clearly not convinced by Lloyd George's accusations. The *Daily News* urged the Government to issue more specific evidence of German and German-American machinations.¹² The *Daily Chronicle* pressed the Government to give full disclosure of the evidence that 'de Valera and his comrades were plotting with the enemies of Britain and America for a treacherous blow against [Britain] to synchronise with the German offensive in the West'.¹³ In Ireland, the arrests of Sinn Féiners amused local newspapers.¹⁴ *Nationality* denounced the 'English plot against Sinn Féin' in its editorial:

> England dreads the ordeal and, still more the outcome, of Ireland's appeal to the Peace Conference – the Conference, and the only Conference, that will have authority in the re-shaping of Europe after the world war has come to an end. Sinn Féin has lifted Ireland out of the wretched condition to which her politicians, weakened and corrupted by Parliamentarianism, had lowered her.¹⁵

Similarly, the *Freeman's Journal* issued extensive coverage of the alleged plot:

> Mr Lloyd George has launched his thunderbolt in the form of part of the evidence of the alleged pro-German plot in Ireland. We give the statement in full below, and many people will be surprised to learn from a perusal of it that what is presumably an important discovery covers a period during which the leading

---

⁹ *The Times*, 20 May 1918.
¹⁰ *The Times*, 21 May 1918.
¹¹ *The Times*, 25 May 1918.
¹² *Daily News*, 25 May 1918.
¹³ *Daily Chronicle*, 25 May 1918.
¹⁴ SHD, Third Republic (1870–1940), Army Staff, 7N679, Section des Renseignements Généraux, 4ème Bureau, 15 June 1918.
¹⁵ *Nationality*, 1 June 1918.

Sinn Féiners who have been deported were under lock and key. We are told that a second rising in Ireland was planned for last year, but that it broke down only because Germany was unable to send troops.[16]

On 18 May 1918, the Second Irish Race Convention met in the Central Opera House, in New York City. At the time Sinn Féiners were being deported to England, the Convention called for 'the application to Ireland of President Wilson's noble declaration of the right of every people to self-rule and self-determination'.[17] A few days later, on 24 May, a delegation from the Irish Race Convention called at the White House to request an audience with Wilson.[18] The American Consul at Queenstown, C. M. Hathaway, wrote to Ambassador Walter Page, explicitly referring to a conspiracy against Sinn Féin: 'The Government's charge of a German plot and its arrests of Sinn Féin leaders in that connection is presumably a conspiracy to vilify Ireland and discredit the Irish cause abroad so as to relieve the British Government of the handicap of foreign sympathy (and particularly American sympathy) with Ireland's lack of freedom of self-determination.'[19] The American Embassy in London reported to the Secretary of State, pointing out that the press in Britain and in Ireland were generally of the opinion that 'the whole affair ha[d] been based upon the weakest sort of evidence in order to injure the cause of Ireland and interfere with the opposition to conscription'.[20] John Dillon, who succeeded Redmond after the latter's death on 6 March 1918, and whose fate was to be the last leader of the Irish Parliamentary Party, published a declaration in the *Irish Independent* in which he condemned the villainy of the British. According to him, there could remain no doubt that the British had deliberately engineered the demise of the Irish Party, acting 'with a stupidity amounting to malignity'.[21]

The British were taking steps consistent with the implementation of coercive measures to counter separatism in Ireland. On 31 May, Dublin Castle announced the decision to prohibit all military demonstrations in the counties of Limerick and Tipperary. Figures for arrests and requisitions increased at the beginning of June. In the House of Lords, the Marquess of Londonderry congratulated Lord

---

[16] *Freeman's Journal*, 25 May 1918.
[17] *Gaelic American*, 20 May 1918.
[18] Library of Congress (hereafter LC), Manuscript Division, Woodrow Wilson Papers (1786–1957), letter from Joseph P. Tumulty to President Wilson, 24 May 1918.
[19] National Archives of Ireland (hereafter NAI), Manuscript Section, CSO/RP/1917/2869, letter from C. M. Hathaway to Walter Page, 23 May 1917.
[20] NAI, MS, 800 I/143a, letter from the American Embassy in London to the Secretary of State, 28 May 1918.
[21] *Irish Independent*, 23 May 1918.

French 'on the step he ha[d] taken in placing under restraint those traitors, men of alien origin, and disloyal men who ha[d] brought Ireland to the condition in which she [was] at the present moment'.[22] On 3 July, Sinn Féin, the Gaelic League and the Irish Volunteers were all declared to be seditious organizations and were outlawed.[23] The following day, General Shaw, Commander-in-Chief in Ireland, forbade all unauthorized public meetings, assemblies and sports or athletic events.[24] One intelligence officer reported that 'the cutting off of the heads of the conspiracy which ha[d] weighed on the country for the past two years ha[d] been an enormous relief to all decent citizens'.[25] Nonetheless, such relief gave rise to unprecedented unrest in the country. The Irish Southern Command warned that the 4 July 1918 proclamation banning meetings and assemblies without a permit 'ha[d] done away with the means of disseminating sedition in the open and public manner'.[26] Demonstrations and gatherings might well have been prohibited, but that did not deter the Unionists from their annual 12 July celebration of the Battle of the Boyne. When large demonstrations took place in Belfast, it seemed that nothing had really changed since 1913. While the British declared Sinn Féin to be a dangerous association, and all over the country public meetings were forbidden and arms seized, the orders issued by Dublin Castle appeared to apply solely to nationalist assemblies.

On the road to victory: summer 1918

When on 5 May 1918, Devlin and de Valera spoke shoulder to shoulder at a meeting against conscription at Ballaghaderreen (County Roscommon), this reinforced the idea that the constitutional party was seeking to imply that they had always been opposed to conscription. Possible consensus between the Irish Party and Sinn Féin on the issue did not however lead to any political agreement or electoral pact. In May 1918, for the by-election in East Cavan, the Sinn Féin and constitutional candidates were set one against the other before the voters of

---

[22] Hansard, House of Lords, series 5, vol. 30, cc297, the Marquess of Londonderry to the House of Lords, 20 June 1918.
[23] Robert Kee, *The Green Flag. A History of Irish Nationalism* (London: Weidenfeld & Nicolson, 1972), 622.
[24] David Fitzpatrick, *Politics and Irish Life 1913–1921; Provincial Experiences of War and Revolution* (Cork: Cork University Press, 1998), 130.
[25] The National Archives (TNA), Colonial Office (hereafter CO), CO 904/107, Southern District Intelligence Report, May 1918.
[26] TNA, CO 904/157/1, Reports of the State of the Country, 1916–1918, Item 4, Report of Headquarters, Irish Command Southern District, July 1918.

the constituency. After all, how could the Irish Party entertain any reasonable hope of a political alliance with Sinn Féin, when several previous by-elections had been won thanks to the support of southern Unionists? On 18 April 1918, two days after the conscription bill was passed, Samuel Young, the 96-year-old MP of East Cavan passed away. A new by-election followed and Mr O'Hanlon was nominated as the candidate on 26 April. In order to avoid a campaign that would once again damage the Irish Party, O'Hanlon offered Griffith, the Sinn Féin candidate in East Cavan, a deal: both candidates would step down and a 'neutral' candidate would then be chosen, in concertation between Sinn Féin and the Irish Parliamentary Party. Presented as a guarantee aimed at protecting the holy alliance against conscription, the move was indeed a tactic aimed at dissimulating the deliquescence of the constitutional party. However, based on the precedent of the March 1918 by-election, which had been won by the Irish Party thanks to the support of unionist populations, it appeared unacceptable from the point of view of Sinn Féin to accept such an alliance, given the fact that, in the defence of the Union, the Irish Party had contributed to the defeat of its candidates only a few weeks earlier. Sinn Féin thus ignored calls for a pact in East Cavan. Cooperation between advanced and constitutional nationalists had clearly reached its limits.

Apart from their shared opposition to conscription, Sinn Féin and the Irish Parliamentary Party clearly disagreed on the future administration of Ireland. *The Leader* indicated that beyond the sense of being united in their opposition to conscription, 'there [were] several important matters upon which the parties who [were] united against Conscription [were] of different minds'.[27] Ideological rivalries between those demanding complete independence and others calling for Home Rule further widened the gap between constitutionalism and republicanism. Some newspapers described the vanishing of the holy union as 'regrettable',[28] while others backed Griffith's decision to run for election in the name of Sinn Féin:

> Mr Griffith stands for a clear and well-defined policy – the sovereign independence of Ireland. What does his opponent stand for? Does he follow Mr Devlin and claim Colonial Home Rule, or does he follow Capt. Gwynn, Mr John Clancy, Mr John O'Dowd and Mr John Fitzgibbon, the members of the Irish Party who signed the Convention majority report which would give to Ireland a status less than that proposed for the East African blacks?[29]

[27] *The Leader*, 4 May 1918.
[28] *New Ireland*, 27 April 1918.
[29] *The Kilkenny People*, 25 May 1918.

United in their fight against the Military Service Act, Sinn Féin advocated the complete independence of Ireland, whereas members of the Irish Parliamentary Party remained staunch advocates of the devolution of legislative powers within the framework of the Union. The dissenting visions of what Ireland ought to be did not either disappear, in spite of a climate of shared apprehension created by the issue of conscription. A vote for Griffith would ensure that Ireland 'would be nailing the anti-conscription flag to the mast, and assert her right to a full measure of National freedom'.[30] Griffith himself, in his newspaper *Nationality*, insisted that the future of what Ireland ought to become was a matter of profound disagreement between Sinn Féin and the Home Rule party. He stated:

> The proposal of Mr Dillon is that we should mutually agree to ignore the right of the people of East Cavan to choose their own representative and instead force upon their acceptance some person whose essential virtue is that he is neutral in this great issue of Irish affairs. That proposal we cannot accept [...] We shall not, in the case of Cavan nor of any of the part of Ireland, permit the old system of political bosses and packed Conventions, which prevailed in Ireland for nearly 20 years past and effectually choked the authentic voice of the nation, to be resuscitated. [...] There can be a Unity of Co-operation between Sinn Féin and its opponents on the matter of conscription. There can be no Unity of Amalgamation. Unity on the question of conscription need not be impaired, and could not be impaired, by difference of convictions on other questions.[31]

Devlin had hesitated as to whether or not it was sensible to nominate a candidate for the electoral contest. However, as the *Freeman's Journal* highlighted, presenting someone to guide the nation 'in these days of unparalleled danger and difficulty'[32] was an absolute necessity. The Irish Party had decided not to put forward a candidate for the King's County by-election on 19 April 1918. Patrick McCartan, who had been deported to England in February 1917, and had travelled to America after his release in order to make Ireland's case before the US Congress, was running for election as the Sinn Féin candidate.[33] It was largely out of pride, that the Irish Party proposed a candidate in East Cavan, and that candidate consequently came in for violent accusations. 'Every vote cast for

---

[30] Ibid.
[31] *Nationality*, 11 May 1918.
[32] *Freeman's Journal*, 25 May 1918.
[33] University College Dublin Archives (hereafter UCDA), W. T. Cosgrave Papers (1917–1993), P285/344, postcard for the King's County by-election, 1918.

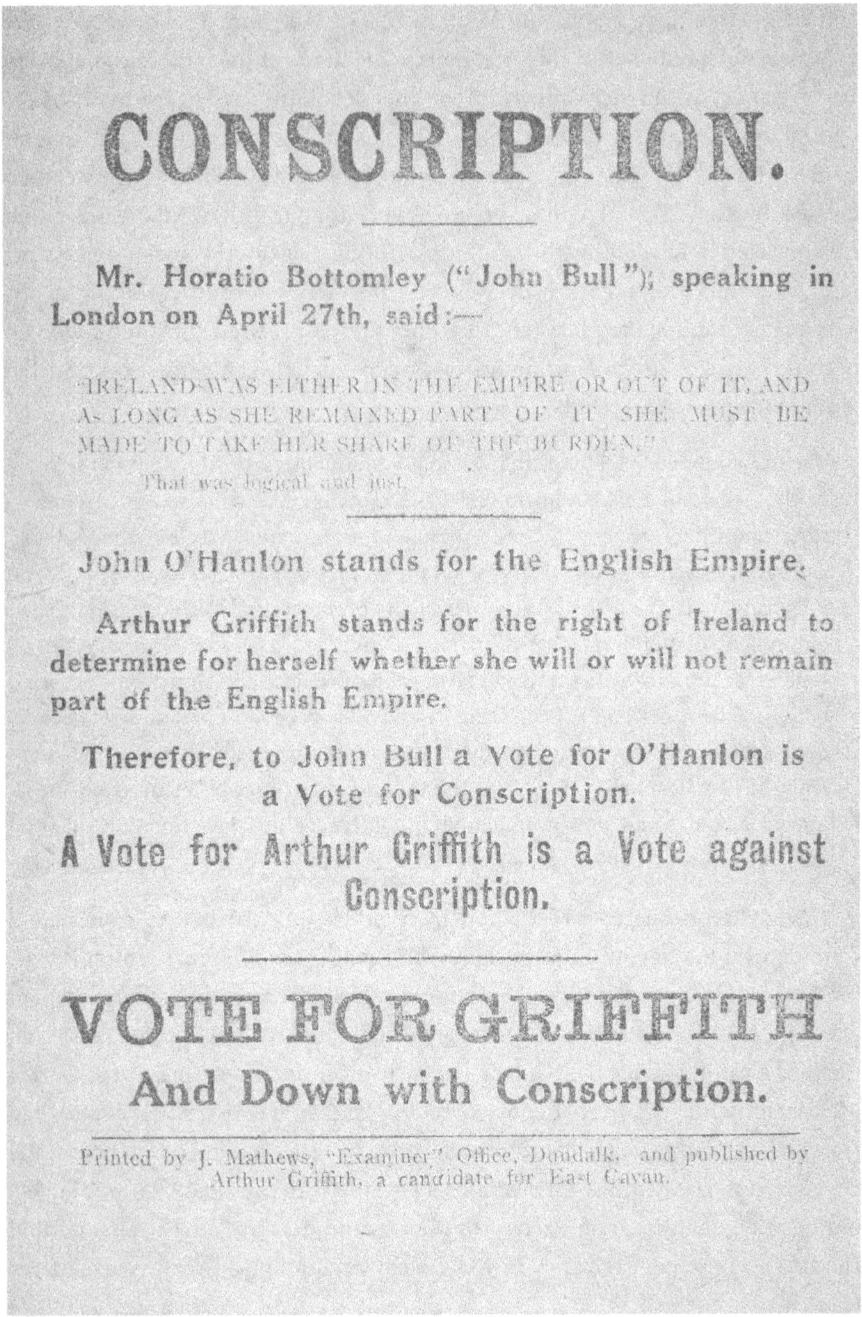

CONSCRIPTION.

Mr. Horatio Bottomley ("John Bull"), speaking in London on April 27th, said:—

"IRELAND WAS EITHER IN THE EMPIRE OR OUT OF IT, AND AS LONG AS SHE REMAINED PART OF IT SHE MUST BE MADE TO TAKE HER SHARE OF THE BURDEN."

That was logical and just.

John O'Hanlon stands for the English Empire.

Arthur Griffith stands for the right of Ireland to determine for herself whether she will or will not remain part of the English Empire.

Therefore, to John Bull a Vote for O'Hanlon is a Vote for Conscription.

A Vote for Arthur Griffith is a Vote against Conscription.

VOTE FOR GRIFFITH
And Down with Conscription.

Printed by J. Mathews, "Examiner" Office, Dundalk, and published by Arthur Griffith, a candidate for East Cavan.

Figure 7.1 Election and anti-conscription leaflet seeking support for Arthur Griffith, the Sinn Féin candidate in the East-Cavan by-election (held on 20 June 1918). Ephemera Collection. Courtesy of the National Library of Ireland.

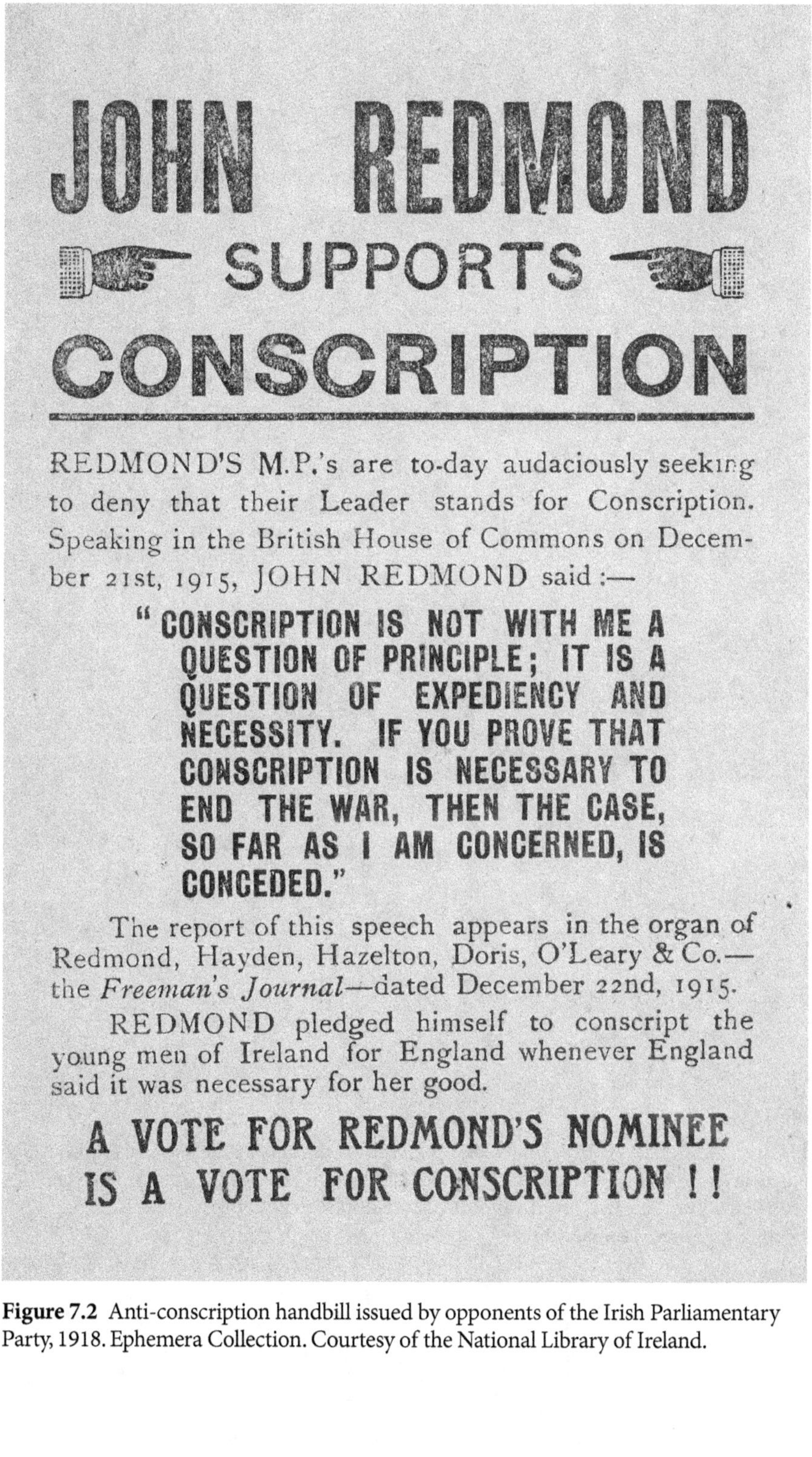

JOHN REDMOND
👉 SUPPORTS 👈
CONSCRIPTION

REDMOND'S M.P.'s are to-day audaciously seeking to deny that their Leader stands for Conscription. Speaking in the British House of Commons on December 21st, 1915, JOHN REDMOND said :—

> "CONSCRIPTION IS NOT WITH ME A QUESTION OF PRINCIPLE; IT IS A QUESTION OF EXPEDIENCY AND NECESSITY. IF YOU PROVE THAT CONSCRIPTION IS NECESSARY TO END THE WAR, THEN THE CASE, SO FAR AS I AM CONCERNED, IS CONCEDED."

The report of this speech appears in the organ of Redmond, Hayden, Hazelton, Doris, O'Leary & Co.— the *Freeman's Journal*—dated December 22nd, 1915.

REDMOND pledged himself to conscript the young men of Ireland for England whenever England said it was necessary for her good.

A VOTE FOR REDMOND'S NOMINEE IS A VOTE FOR CONSCRIPTION !!

Figure 7.2 Anti-conscription handbill issued by opponents of the Irish Parliamentary Party, 1918. Ephemera Collection. Courtesy of the National Library of Ireland.

CONSCRIPTION.

CAPTAIN REDMOND, M.P.

Elected for Waterford March 23rd.

Conscription Bill Introduced April 9th.

Appointment to Lord French's "Intelligence Department" announced May 2nd.

Capt. Redmond is still a Member of the Irish Party.

EAST CAVAN!
VOTE FOR GRIFFITH
And Kill Conscription.

Printed by J. Mathews, "Examiner" Office, Dundalk, and published by Arthur Griffith, a candidate for East Cavan.

Figure 7.3 Election campaign leaflet for Arthur Griffith for the East-Cavan by-election in June 1918 criticizing the stance of Captain William Redmond and the Irish Party for their perceived support of conscription. Ephemera Collection. Courtesy of the National Library of Ireland.

Griffith is a vote for Ireland's right to be free; every vote cast for O'Hanlon is a vote cast for slavery',[34] shouted speakers on electoral platforms.

On 19 June 1918, Griffith won, by 3,785 to 2,581 votes.[35] The campaign had publicly exposed the weakness of the Government: 'there is still the feeling that the present Government is weak',[36] wrote General de la Panouse. Indeed the Irish question was entirely clouding domestic politics in the country, as 'throughout Old Ireland, Sinn Féin triumph[ed], while the government remain[ed] powerless and ridiculous and nationalist deputies [did] not dare to sit at Westminster'.[37] 'In principle', as has been argued, 'the government had simply postponed implementing the Military Service Act, and it warned that conscription would be enforced if a renewed voluntary recruiting scheme failed to result in a sufficient number of troops'.[38] Nonetheless, the postponement of compulsory service in no sense assuaged fears.

Paris heard from its emissaries that the representation of Ireland at the Peace Conference remained a goal pursued by Sinn Féin. On 4 July, for the anniversary of Independence Day, a 37-page manifesto was submitted to Wilson, only a few days after the extension of conscription to Ireland.[39] On 11 June 1918, some members of Sinn Féin had drawn up an address to be forwarded to Wilson. One week later, the Lord Mayor of Dublin, Laurence O'Neill, who had been dispatched to Washington with the job of communicating the address to the President of the United States, had written to the American Ambassador, informing him that the text would not be published before 4 July. When it was finally released on 4 July 1918 – the symbolic and politically charged date of America's declaration of (republican) independence – the desperation felt by Ireland's representatives was brought home to Irish-Americans. The address to the American President highlighted the fact that Wilson's 'exhortations ha[d] inspired the Small Nations of the world with fortitude to defend to the last their liberties against oppressions'.[40] Dwelling on the memory of the support offered by the Irish

---

[34] *Nationality*, 15 June 1918.
[35] Laffan, *The Resurrection of Ireland*, 149.
[36] SHD, Third Republic (1870–1940), Army Staff, 7N1254, telegram from General de la Panouse to the Minister for War, 6 May 1918.
[37] SHD, Third Republic (1870–1940), Army Staff, 7N1254, telegram from General de la Panouse to the Minister for War, 1 July 1918.
[38] Laffan, *The Resurrection of Ireland*, 150.
[39] UCDA, de Valera's Papers (1882–1985), P150/604, documents relating to the anti-conscription campaign, booklet entitled *The Case for Ireland Re-Stated to the President of the United States of America on Independence Day 1918* (Wilson Hartnell & Co., Dublin, 4 July 1918).
[40] UCDA, de Valera's Papers (1882–1985), P150/606, manifesto 'To the President of the United States of America', 11 June 1918, p. 12.

during the American Revolution, it drew strong parallels between the aspiration of the thirteen colonies to free themselves and the case now being put by the Irish, before America and before the world, in its demand for self-government and international recognition.

The document went on to state that, in spite of the opposition it had come in for, 'Sinn Féin remain[ed] the most powerful political organization in Ireland'.[41] And even though the threat of conscription had forged an alliance between all the traditional political parties in Ireland, it was Sinn Féin which had successfully established itself as the authoritative voice of opposition to the decision of the British authorities.

In September 1918, local newspapers were still lingering on the possible introduction of conscription. In an editorial entitled 'Conscription Menace', the *Irish Independent* warned its readers that 'there appear[ed] to be no indication that the policy of "disaster and danger" ha[d] been abandoned by the Government'.[42]

> On the contrary, it is officially announced today that the period for voluntary recruiting has been extended to October 15, and that, should voluntary recruiting fail, the preliminary steps to enforce conscription can only be taken when Parliament is sitting.[43]

Writing from Queenstown, Cork, the American Consul underlined that the Irish were no longer reconcilable within the existing constitutional framework of the United Kingdom:

> The naked skeleton of the Irish situation (stripped of innumerable considerations of varying importance) seems to be that the native Irish race, comprising three-quarters of the population of the island, are held against their will in subjection by an alien race. While this condition continues, no settlement appears to be possible. The situation is complicated by the presence in Ireland of a minority, the descendants of British colonialists and conquerors who originally came to Ireland to hold Ireland down in the English interest and who, different in race mental habits, and religion, object vigorously to being subjected to the native Irish majority.[44]

---

[41] SHD, Third Republic (1870–1940), Army Staff, 7N1254, telegram from General de la Panouse to the Minister for War, 8 July 1918.
[42] *Irish Independent*, 21 September 1918.
[43] *Irishman*, 28 September 1918.
[44] University of California, Santa Barbara Library (hereafter UCSBL), Charles Montgomery Hathaway Papers (1895–1939), 1/50, Official correspondences, report on the political situation in the South of Ireland, 12 September 1918, p. 3.

In an international climate now propitious to demands for national independence, aspirations to complete separation from Great Britain, along with the continuing threat of conscription, contributed to creating a climate favourable to Sinn Féin.

> The presumed imminence of peace negotiations on the basis of the principles enunciated by President Wilson occupies an increasing space in the Irish press. Letters and addresses by prominent citizens are appearing from day to day, and editorial articles in all the papers reflect the universal interest in the application of President Wilson's principles to Ireland, and indicate in accord with the respective views of the authors that self-determination is or is not applicable. A further move toward unity is the action of the Irish Labour Party which has decided to withdraw its candidates for the next general election. This action is thought to mean the throwing of the entire labour vote to the Sinn Féin candidates.[45]

On 15 November 1918, the first words of the issue of *An tÓglách* returned to the thorny subject of conscription for Ireland: 'Although the war is now unmistakingly nearing its close, the English Government has not yet definitely renounced its threat to conscript Irishmen for the English Army.' The violent political rhetoric adopted in the article hinted at the existence of an agenda intended to 'initiate a campaign of extermination against the Irish people'.[46] By the time urban and rural communities whole-heartedly celebrated the end of the conflict,[47] conscription was still described as the final tool, the ultimate political measure for the British to enforce in order to prevent Ireland's appearance at the table of the Peace Conference. The political narrative in *An tÓglách* was careful not to go into the details as to how conscription could be enforced (or needed to be enforced) in the eventuality of a cease-fire, or of an armistice. Nonetheless, the argument put forward was that the English Government would not hesitate to latch on to any pretext enabling it to sabotage years of constitutional accomplishments. Prior to the December 1918 general elections, the *Roscommon Journal* called to the attention of its readers the fact that 'the Conscription Act [was] still on the Statute Book, and Mr Lloyd George's silence on the subject of conscription in his election address [was] too significant to ignore'.[48] The local

---

[45] UCSBL, Charles Montgomery Hathaway Papers (1895–1939), 1/55, Official correspondences, report on the political situation in the South of Ireland, 4 November 1918, pp. 3–4.
[46] *An tÓglách*, 15 November 1918.
[47] Niamh Gallagher, *Ireland and the Great War. A Social and Political History* (London: Bloomsbury, 2019), 167–169.
[48] *Roscommon Journal*, 7 December 1918.

newspaper then decided to publish 'An Election Song' taking up the issue, with one stanza explicitly linking Sinn Féin resistance to conscription. Without the rebel party, the lyrics claimed, conscription might have well been enforced to Ireland:

> When Conscription hovered o'er the land
> Sinn Féin was all we had.
> The Party could not raise a hand
> To save one stalwart lad.
> God bless Sinn Féin! Then cry aloud
> And shout it o'er an o'er,
> We don't forget our votes they'll get
> For Ireland free once more.[49]

In November 1918, RIC Constables reported that 'sons [were] frightening their fathers as to what [would] happen if the fathers [didn't] vote Sinn Féin'.[50] During the contest, armed Volunteers 'were engaged in checking the register of voters, organizing transport to take the voters to the polls [...] and escorting the ballot boxes and such duties'.[51] They met 'with considerable hostility, particularly in Longford town. This opposition was generally from the wives of Irishmen who were serving in the British Army and from the camp followers of the British Army'.[52]

At that time, the British Government had properly apprehended the strength of the movement directed against its authority. It thus embarked on a counter-propaganda campaign in the United States, aimed explicitly at discrediting Sinn Féin.[53] On 2 November 1918, Senator Phelan presented President Wilson with a petition from Roman Catholic priests in San Francisco in support of self-determination for the Irish. On 13 November 1918, the Sinn Féin headquarters in Harcourt Street, Liberty Hall and the Mansion House were all attacked by hostile crowds, many of them Irish soldiers. The rooms in Harcourt Street were totally wrecked, after which troops were temporarily confined to barracks.[54]

---

[49] Ibid.
[50] TNA, CO 904/107, County Inspector's report, Mayo, November 1918.
[51] Military Archives of Ireland (hereafter MAI), Bureau of Military History (1913–1921) (hereafter BMH), WS479, witness statement from Michael Murphy, former member of Longford Brigade Irish Volunteers, 23 February 1951, p. 3.
[52] Ibid.
[53] Charles Callan Tansill, *America and the Fight for Irish Freedom, 1866–1922* (New York: The Devin-Adair Co., 1957), 275–283.
[54] *Irish Independent*, 14 November 1918.

December 1918: the triumph of the Internationalists

When he received news of the outcome of the election, General de la Panouse concluded that 'the official Party ha[d] virtually ceased to exist'.[55] Retaining only

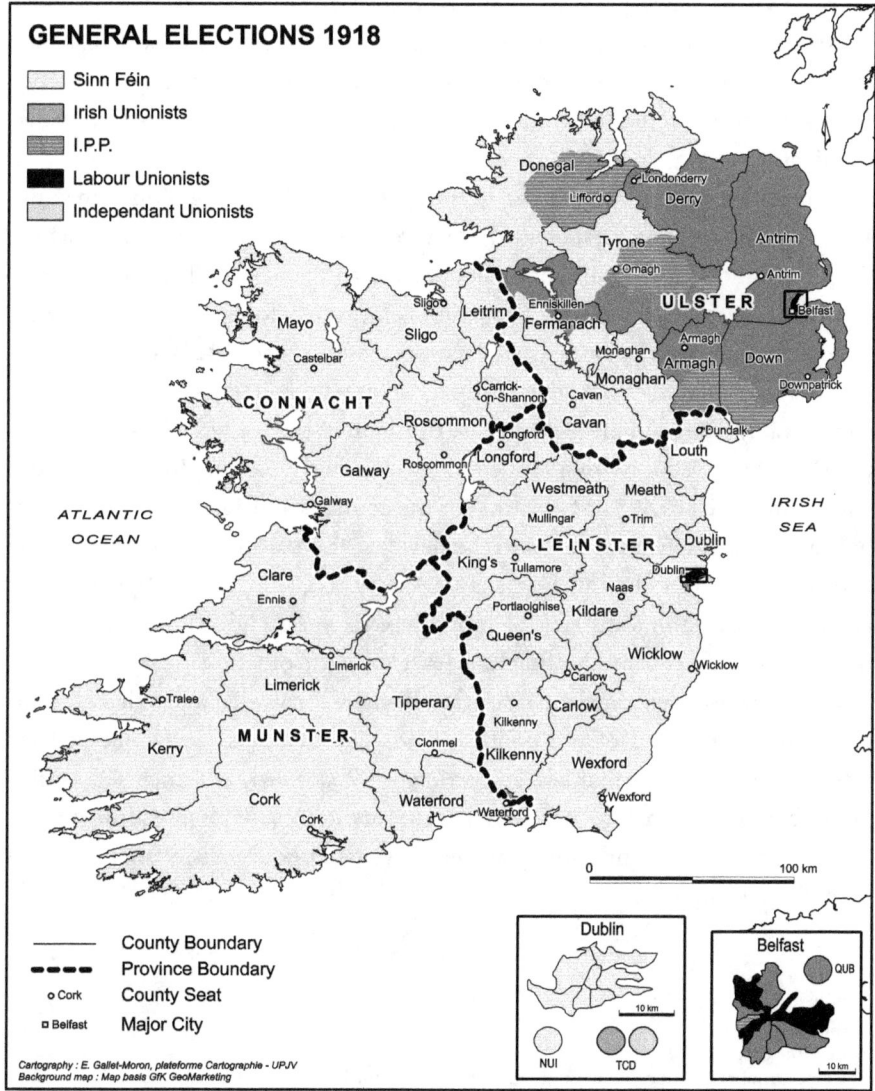

Map 7.1 Ireland and the 1918 general elections. Courtesy of Emilie Gallet-Moron.

---

[55] SHD, Third Republic (1870–1940), Inter-Allied Cooperation, 4N31, telegram from General de la Panouse to the Minister for War, 1919.

six seats, the Irish Parliamentary Party was now plunged into limbo of vestigial constitutional nationalism. After a 37-year-political career, Dillon was defeated in East Mayo. Out of the 13,000 votes cast, 9,000 were in support of de Valera. 'One might have thought', commented France's military attaché, 'that Louth, South Wexford and East Tipperary were safe seats; they too have been overthrown.'[56] Contrary to what could be read elsewhere, General de la Panouse insisted on the resounding victory secured by Sinn Féin. In Cork City for instance, the two Sinn Féin candidates notched up 41,000 votes compared to 19,000 votes scattered between the two unionist and the two nationalist candidates.[57]

Three other factors contributed to the spectacular victory of Sinn Féin at the 1918 general elections. First of all, there were twenty-six constituencies in which the constitutional party did not in fact present any candidate. This meant that a quarter of the votes 'had thus gone to Sinn Féin, even before polling day'.[58] (What would have happened had the Irish Party presented a candidate is hard to know.) Secondly, in March 1918, the British Parliament had passed a law which considerably extended the right to vote throughout the United Kingdom. At the parliamentary elections in 1910, 697,337 men had voted in Ireland, a figure which amounted to 575,011 electors for the counties and 122,326 for the urban borough constituencies. Thanks to the new law, the 1918 Representation of the People Act, the overall number was increased by 600,000. The law stipulated that (1) all men living in a district for more than six years and (2) all women over thirty who paid a rent amounting to at least £5 a year, or whose husband had the right to vote, were enfranchised.[59] Alfred Blanche forwarded a detailed account of the transformation of the political landscape that such a law entailed for Ireland. He mentioned that 'a large portion of [those newly enfranchised would] be in favour of Sinn Féin precisely because its ideas [were] spreading among civilian populations and among women; even the bourgeoisie [was] offering them fervent support'.[60]

---

[56] Ibid.
[57] Ibid.
[58] Kee, *The Green Flag*, 624.
[59] Diane Urquhart, 'Unionism, Orangeism and War', in *Irish Women and the Vote: Becoming Citizens*, ed. Louise Ryan and Margaret Ward (London: Routledge, 2019), 138–154; Margaret Ward, '"Rolling up the Map of Suffrage": Irish Suffrage and the First World War', in *Irish Women and the Vote*, 260–287; Fionnuala Walsh, *Irish Women and the Great War* (Cambridge: Cambridge University Press, 2020), 164–193.
[60] Diplomatic Archives of the French Ministry for Foreign Affairs (hereafter AD), Political and Commercial Correspondence, Great War, 1914–1918, Ireland, 1CPCOM/547, letter from Alfred Blanche to the Minister for Foreign Affairs, 15 March 1918.

What would also play into the hands of Sinn Féin was the number of young men and women[61] who, back in 1910, had not been able to vote and who had taken careful note of the reneging on the promise of Home Rule following the rise of popular opposition in Ulster, the 1914 Curragh incident, the Janus-faced rhetoric of Asquith, and later, Lloyd George's obsession with the implementation of conscription in Ireland. These citizens, now provided with the opportunity to vote in the first UK election following the end of the Great War, were now looking both to Sinn Féin and the US to make good on the achievement of full independence for Ireland. Despite the fact that, in accordance with an amendment introduced by Lord Harcourt, the £150 deposit traditionally paid to be able to run for office would only be reimbursed when the candidate had sworn allegiance,[62] this did not in the least deter Sinn Féin and its representatives from either standing in the elections or from losing a considerable amount of money. The third factor that came into play was emigration, which had been deliberately curtailed by the British during the war in order to stave off any shortages of labour during the conflict.[63] General de la Panouse invited the Minister for Foreign Affairs not to underestimate the weight of young male and female voters who had not be able to emigrate:

> These spectacular majorities are not the direct consequences of a complete turnaround in public opinion on the part of the old electors; they are due rather to the votes cast by women and young men who were participating for the first time. For the last four years, there has been no emigration from Ireland.[64]

---

[61] Patrick Maume, *The Long Gestation. Irish Nationalist Life, 1891–1918* (Dublin: Gill & Macmillan, 1999), 193; Senia Pašeta, *Irish Nationalist Women, 1900–1918* (Cambridge: Cambridge University Press, 2013), 250; Brian Farrell, *The Founding of Dáil Éireann* (Dublin: Gill & Macmillan, 1971), 45–50. Brian Farrell contends that the Irish Party could not have been beaten without the changes introduced by the Representation of the People Act. In response, James McConnel has pointed out that the Irish Party lost much support among the older generation and those who already had the vote. McConnel argues that the franchise reform did not transform the course of Irish history and maintains that support for Sinn Féin was not sectional but cross-generational. James McConnel, 'The Franchise Factor in the Defeat of the Irish Parliamentary Party, 1885–1918', *Historical Journal* 27, no. 2 (2004): 355–377; James McConnel, *The Irish Parliamentary Party and the Third Home Rule Crisis* (Dublin: Four Courts Press, 2013).
[62] AD, Political and Commercial Correspondence, Great War, 1914–1918, Ireland, 1CPCOM/547, letter from Alfred Blanche to the Minister for Foreign Affairs, 15 March 1918.
[63] David Fitzpatrick, 'Home front and everyday life', in *Our War: Ireland and the Great War*, ed. John Horne (Dublin: Royal Irish Academy, 2008), 136. Fitzpatrick supports the contention of France's representatives. He argues that '[w]ithout the war, it may well be argued that, most of the manpower driving the revolutionary movement would have been absent'.
[64] SHD, Third Republic (1870–1940), Inter-Allied Cooperation, 4N31, telegram from General de la Panouse to the Minister for War, 1919. Here, clearly General de la Panouse supported the argument that the success of Sinn Féin had been consolidated by young voters.

Because of the war 'and the abrupt drop in emigration, there was a far higher proportion of that youth in Ireland than there had been for generations'.[65]

Conclusion

Even after conscription was officially postponed, but before being entirely abandoned by the British authorities, the issue remained a simmering threat lurking between May and December 1918. The German plot, as has been amply demonstrated, was merely a pretext seized upon to crush the republican movement and to regain control over the Irish situation. Portrayed as a wartime threat both to the security of Great Britain and to the cause of the Allies, the plot, even though its credibility was discounted by the American and French Consuls, was used to justify repression. It enabled the British to regain control over the country, which had been partly lost since the US intervention in April 1917. Months before the conscription crisis of April 1918, the goal of Home Rule had already been completely discredited. Conscription acted as an ominous threat that was sufficiently tangible to detach local communities from their habitual support for the Irish Parliamentary Party. When the British Parliament passed the Military Service Act for Ireland, the decision showed to nationalist populations that Sinn Féin had indeed been right, and that conscription had all this time been a part of the scenario envisaged by the British. It was, moreover, a scenario which the Irish Party, now deprived of its charismatic leader, had failed to dissuade the British from incorporating into its legislative provisions for Ireland.

---

[65] Kee, *The Green Flag*, 609.

Epilogue

How the Great War transformed Ireland

When war broke out in August 1914, the Irish situation had reached a stalemate. The threat to resort to paramilitary force had been 're-introduced into Ireland by the Ulster Covenanters after well towards fifty years of relatively peaceful agitation by parliamentary methods'.[1] Parliamentary methods had brought Home Rule to the statute book and constitutional opposition to Home Rule had been defeated in the Parliament of the United Kingdom. Through popular volunteer enrolment (via the Ulster Volunteer Force), die-hard unionists stroke a potentially irreversible and mortal blow to the confidence in the parliamentary methods which had become predominant over time throughout nationalist Ireland, by way of the political hegemony of the Irish Parliamentary Party. While Asquith's dilatory policy proved to be vital in preserving peace in Ireland, it came at a price, that of keeping alive the expectation of a consensual settlement of terms, to be worked out between Nationalists and Unionists. The decision to go to war with Germany brought about a dramatic reconfiguration of the situation in Ireland. Edward Carson immediately vowed to defend the British Empire in its hour of need. John Redmond declared his hope and expectation that battalions would be raised in order to protect the coasts of the island. He quickly found himself compelled to express his full support for the war effort and for the recruitment of Irishmen in the British Army. Such evidence tends to mitigate the claim, frequently made, according to which 'nationalist Ireland did enter the war in 1914'.[2] Initially, the Irish Party needed only to call for volunteers

---

[1] University of California, Santa Barbara Library (hereafter UCSBL), Charles Montgomery Hathaway Papers (1895–1939), 1/50, Official correspondences, report on the political situation in the South of Ireland, 12 September 1918, p. 15.

[2] Catriona Pennell, 'More than a "Curious Footnote": Irish Voluntary Participation in the First World War and British Popular Memory', in *Towards Commemoration. Ireland in War and Revolution, 1912–1923*, ed. John Horne and Edward Madigan (Dublin: Royal Irish Academy Press, 2013), 42.

who were to protect the island, not to fight abroad. Yet the split within the Irish Volunteers, coupled with the initial, extremely prudent inclination to stand back from the conflict in evidence among shopkeepers, merchants, farmers and workers, who were to side gradually, cautiously and tentatively with Sinn Féin when the threat of conscription flared up, offers significant evidence that nationalist Ireland never fully backed the war effort.

When in January 1916 the British Government approved the implementation of compulsory service, the measure applied to Great Britain only, Ireland being exempted. Irish recruits did however continue to enrol voluntarily. When a rebellion broke out in April 1916, it lasted less than a week, but inflicted considerable losses on both sides. Families of soldiers who had lost their lives in Belgium, France or in Gallipoli were certainly not inclined to applaud an uprising that, indirectly, amounted to a further snub for their loved ones. There followed an implementation of repressive measures by the authorities, and it is indisputable that the executions of the leaders of the Rising embittered and divided local communities. However, the assumption that Sinn Féin captured the support of nationalist populations in the immediate aftermath of the 1916 uprising, or that the party successfully imposed itself as the main voice of opposition to the British Government, supplanting the Irish Parliamentary Party following the repression, does not bear scrutiny when the documented evidence from that period, regarding the climate of public opinion in nationalist Ireland, is examined carefully. There were several attempts to bring about a political compromise between May and October 1916. All of them failed. France's representations to Dublin and London advocated immediate implementation of Home Rule (albeit in an imperfect form). However, the problem remained the outright refusal, within Ulster unionist opinion, of any form of devolution, as provided by the Government of Ireland Act. Meanwhile, the Irish Party refused any partition of the island. Neither side yielded, staunchly maintaining the positions they had formerly espoused. The issue of conscription re-emerged, in October 1916, in an atmosphere of heated debates in the House of Commons. It was to remain a time-bomb that was to tick for the duration of the conflict, providing further impetus to the consolidation of support for Sinn Féin. Indeed, the transfer of nationalist allegiances from the constitutional movement of the Irish Party to Sinn Féin is a shift which began with the issue of conscription. By December 1916, observers were pointing out that the fears of conscription were precipitating the shift to Sinn Féin on the part of young men who could be potentially affected. The overriding concern in nationalist Ireland was the tangible, immediate threat of conscription.

Sinn Féin played what was a subtle game: that of drawing on the fears of conscription, while nurturing a narrative focused on the goal of self-determination. The issues of conscription and international recognition were complementary, and mutually sustaining. Even those who endorsed the goal of Home Rule could look towards Sinn Féin if they became convinced that the Irish Party was colluding with the British Government to bring about the implementation of conscription in Ireland. Sinn Féin activists thus portrayed the Irish Party as the covert supporter of conscription, perfidiously implicated in the British imperial orchestration of the destinies of young Irishmen. During the four by-election campaigns in Ireland in 1917, the draft resonated as a recurrent threat hanging over a largely rural nationalist Ireland, a society already traumatized by emigration and population decline. In political leaflets, speeches on electoral platforms and newspaper editorials, there was a widespread emphasis on the threat of conscription, widely acknowledged as the deciding issue in electoral support. An immediate risk coupled with a future aspiration: these were the two key planks in the policy devised by Sinn Féin. The real question, when the period between October 1916 and December 1918 is surveyed, is whether Sinn Féin would have managed to attract and win over the support of nationalist Ireland had the question of conscription not emerged. Would the demand for self-determination, in itself, have been sufficient to deal a death blow to the Irish Party? I believe not.

Just as the period of American neutrality brought to an end by the US entry into the war in April 1917 had allowed Irish-American communities to openly voice their support for Germany and to engage with the German authorities in New York, the proclamation of war on Germany triggered a political shift within these same, influential communities, which found themselves compelled to pledge their allegiance to the Allied cause. While the entry of the US on the side of the British and the French was potentially unsettling for Irish revolutionary republicanism, it was to offer Sinn Féin an effective and useable ideological weapon with which to fight in elections against the Irish Parliamentary Party. US entry into the conflict thus acted as a double-edged sword: to a certain extent, it silenced or attenuated pro-German propaganda and it underpinned Sinn Féin in its quest for national sovereignty. April 1917 thus offered Sinn Féin the opportunity to present to the opinion of nationalist Ireland a viable political alternative to Home Rule, while forcing the British to envisage a comprehensive political settlement for Ireland. This decisive shift would prove to be a trap for Redmond insofar as the prospect of a devolution of powers within the United Kingdom's constitutional order now appeared a timid option, in comparison with the Wilsonian goal of national self-determination. In addition, the Irish Convention reinforced the conviction that the Irish Party was caught up in a web of sterile ongoing debates, and that it was in no position to achieve a settlement. It could thus be arraigned as nothing more than the latest or the last in a line of manoeuvres aimed at gaining time, a continuation of 'Asquith's delaying tactics'.[3] Having been called upon by their US ally to take action to pacify Ireland, the British had summoned a convention. France's representatives knew full well that nothing would come out of the talks. The situation had changed little since the fruitless, drawn-out discussions of 1913–1914. Meanwhile, with the Irish Party caught up in the palavers of the convention, there was now a vacuum waiting to be filled with a new agenda: fresh demands and aspirations, now part (and parcel) of a profoundly reshaped order of political imagining. The atmosphere of bitterness and mistrust that for so long had complicated relations between Great Britain and Ireland (and which the project of Home Rule had sought to overcome) now grew stronger. The fall-out from the war and from the failure to resolve the constitutional stalemate over Home Rule was, by the end of 1917, casting a cloud over the political climate in both Ireland and in the House of Commons. Things did not change utterly in Ireland, at least not overnight. They changed gradually, over time.

It has come to be argued (and to a large extent accepted) that by April 1918 the British had incorporated Ireland in the provisions of the Military Service Bill, out of a need to 'appease the British public'[4] which resented the latitude left to the Irish in playing their part in the provisions for compulsory service. While not entirely discounting such claims, France's representatives in Britain and Ireland pointed to other factors that were at play. In their view, it was a policy adopted by the British authorities as a means through which to regain control over Irish affairs, which they had in part forfeited when the US entered the war in April 1917.

Diverging destinies

My original intention in this study was to offer a comprehensive account of what conscription achieved, what it changed, and what part it played in the transformation of Ireland in the years between 1914 and 1918. Drawing on the diplomatic archives for the period, I eventually came to the conclusion that there

---

[3] Alvin Jackson, *Home Rule: An Irish History, 1800–2000* (London: Weidenfeld & Nicolson, 2003), 140.
[4] Ibid., 129.

was a need to enlarge the scope of the project, with a view to offering new perspectives for the study of American international relations during the era, while furthering investigations into the field of wartime diplomacy. By throwing light on one, often-neglected, aspect of the history of Ireland at the start of the twentieth century, through where the concerns of social history connect to issues of international relations and diplomatic history, my aim here has been to offer an assessment of the influence of American and British positions, in either thwarting or stoking up, directly or indirectly, the dynamic of Irish revolution.

Asquith's delaying strategy did however mirror what were the actual realities of the climate within Ireland. By the outbreak of the war in the summer of 1914, the British had reached an impasse. Ulster Unionists would never agree to Home Rule. The onward march of constitutional nationalism (channelling the nationalist demands for Home Rule) had been halted by the threat of paramilitary rebellion against an act of the British Parliament, a rebellion which furthermore invoked principles of loyalty and allegiance. The Great War momentarily put a damper on the bitter divisions within Ireland. For a time, there seemed to be a holly alliance between nationalist and unionist leaders in Ireland. This enabled the British authorities to enlist an unprecedented number of Irish voluntary recruits into the British Army. Whether in October 1916 or during the Irish Convention in 1917, or even in 1918, the same sterile negotiations that had failed during the summer of 1914 were repeated. One of the two sides would have to give up, if the constitutional stalemate was to be resolved and if the parties were to move on and to return to a re-established form of constitutional politics in the aftermath of the suspension brought about by the Great War. When the US entered the war, among their demands was the settlement of the Irish question. The internationalization of the Irish question further eroded the position of the British Government. The exclusion of Ireland from the Military Service Bill in January 1916 had already exposed the fact that the island was treated differently from the rest of the United Kingdom. Acknowledgement of this egregious difference strengthened the position of the American Government in its demand for a settlement for Ireland. The consequent internationalization of the question in turn weakened the position of the British, who had little option but to agree to the summoning of the Irish Convention. The Convention in effect trapped Redmond, while leaving the way clear for Sinn Féin.

Following US entry into the war, a policy of coercion could only be envisaged if wartime security concerns explicitly justified it. Through the Irish Convention and, subsequently, the conscription crisis in April 1918, the British authorities twice countered Wilsonian rhetoric. They first delayed any settlement of the

Irish constitutional question, trapping the Irish Party within the ongoing discussions of the Convention. Through the inclusion of the island within the provisions of the April 1918 Military Service Act, Britain appeared to be reaffirming its total control over affairs in Ireland. When Sinn Féin finally established itself as the dominant political force within nationalist Ireland, the British conjured up the German plot and used it as a pretext to reassert undisputed control over affairs in Ireland.

Was the fall of the Irish Party inevitable? French diplomatic observers had the conviction that the loss in electoral support for the Irish Parliamentary Party merely threw into harsh light the underlying and intractable problem that had long faced Redmond. Paul Cambon was convinced that there had always been a gap between the expectations of the Irish Party and the aspirations nourished by their electoral base. In his view, the Irish Parliamentary Party had never wanted to break entirely with Great Britain. It had anticipated a situation in which it would achieve a political settlement enabling it to be the dominant political force for the government of Ireland, in accordance with the institutions laid out in the provisions of the 1914 Government of Ireland Act, while also retaining constitutional entitlement to parliamentary representation at Westminster. Conversely, the Catholic élites, which had been the support base of the Irish Parliamentary Party since the 1880s and the transformational achievement of Parnell, regarded the Home Rule as a first step towards the goal of sovereign independence for Ireland.[5] Ambassador Paul Cambon argued that there had always been a gap between what Redmond had expected to achieve and what his electoral basis hoped for Ireland. And the accelerated tempo of wartime politics had further widened the gap. He wrote:

> Redmond had advanced the administrative machinery of Home Rule so that [the Irish] could preserve in Westminster a situation [the Irish Party] intended to benefit from. They hoped to remain the sole beneficiaries of the favours of the metropolis. Home Rule had only been accepted by the Irish insofar as it was a first step towards the complete emancipation of their nation. Links with Great Britain (so strongly advocated by Irish MPs) had, in the minds of their electorate, to be broken as quickly as possible.[6]

---

[5] On this point, Senia Pašeta has argued that the Catholic élite expected Home Rule to be the first step towards the complete taking over of the administration of the country. Senia Pašeta, *Before the Revolution: Nationalism, Social Change and Ireland's Catholic Elite, 1879–1922* (Cork: Cork University Press, 1999).

[6] Archives Diplomatiques du Ministère des Affaires Étrangères, La Courneuve (hereafter AD), Political and Commercial Correspondence, Great War, 1914–1918, Ireland, 1CPCOM/545, telegram from Paul Cambon to the Minister for Foreign Affairs, 3 May 1916.

It was Cambon's view that conscription precipitated the now inevitable divorce between nationalist Ireland and the Irish Party. The French diplomatic representative reported that the Irish Parliamentary Party had always been willing to maintain Ireland within the United Kingdom, even while advocating greater autonomy. Their agenda clearly did not include self-determination and a complete separation from Great Britain.

National minorities, post-war order and disillusions

Even before the convening of the Peace Conference in Paris, when war was still raging throughout Europe, France's representatives had warned their government that Wilson's declaration had spurred separatist aspirations in Ireland. On 29 April 1918, in a letter to the Minister for War, General de la Panouse conceded that the vision of a post-war international order gravitating around the principles of self-determination and self-government for small nations had attracted support in Ireland, notably that of the Irish Catholic clergy and hierarchy.[7] For this reason, when it comes to the analysis of the transformation of Ireland and the revival of Sinn Féin, Easter Week 1916 cannot be regarded as the crucial factor accounting for the change in aspirations and allegiances in Ireland. The complexity and the contingency of the factors interwoven in the period 1916–1918 have to be acknowledged, despite the fact that the Declaration of Independence promulgated by the First Dáil on 21 January 1919 did clearly underline that the Irish Republic had been proclaimed during Easter Week 1916, thus highlighting the significance (or perhaps the need to create a foundational myth) of the failed rebellion, and establishing a continuity between April 1916 and January 1919. The contention that Easter Week 1916 had transformed the course of Irish history, or that it triggered a gradual shift towards republicanism, testifies to the need to legitimize the uprising (initially regarded as a stab in the back by local populations, nationalist and unionist) and thus to ensure a degree of credibility for the separatist nationalist cause in the aftermath of what was a military fiasco. The effectiveness of the continuity thus postulated, as it could retrospectively be pointed to from the standpoint of January 1919, was the effect of a gradualist, and by no means linear or necessary, change over time. Even the country's 'advanced' separatists, in the context of the by-election campaigns in

---

[7] Service Historique de la Défense, Vincennes (hereafter SHD), Third Republic (1870–1940), Army Staff, 7N1254, letter from General de la Panouse to the Minister for War, 29 April 1918.

1917, had felt the need to shape a narrative according to which the 1916 rebellion had been aimed at opposing conscription in Ireland (as seen in Chapters 3 and 4). In seeking the support of the electorate in 1917, they were fully aware that fears of being drafted overnight were enough to stoke anxieties of local communities. This was primarily what could enable them to activate an underlying sense of mistrust. France's representatives to Dublin and London, along with American diplomats and the reports of RIC Constables, all unequivocally stressed that the ongoing threat of conscription was an ever-ticking time-bomb, constantly able to trigger a shift in allegiances from the Irish Party to Sinn Féin. In the conclusions drawn by France's consular representatives, conscription alone is foregrounded as the issue that played a determining role in the metamorphosis of political allegiances within nationalist Ireland. The ominous force of conscription coalesced with the attractions of the goal of self-determination. Together they were to prove decisive in redirecting the course of Irish history in the context of the Great War.

As the world converged in Paris in 1919, the collapse and fragmentation of the Austro-Hungarian, German and Ottoman Empires was well under way. The Irish had already brandished their claim for self-government and had secured an initial political victory. Compared to other stateless nations or colonized peoples, the constitutional and legislative mechanisms already in place had legitimized and substantiated the reiterated aspirations of nationalist Ireland. Wilson's professed ideals galvanized nationalist movements. Across Europe, Czechs, Slovaks, Poles and many other small European nations expected Wilson to look into their 'respective territorial and sovereign problems'.[8] Stateless peoples sent representatives to Paris to plead their cause with Wilson. Following the convening of Dáil Éireann at the Mansion House in Dublin in January 1919, a delegation was sent to Paris to appeal to Wilson. However the President never consented to receive it.[9] It appears Wilson had no desire to complicate diplomatic relations with Great Britain by intervening in favour of Irish independence.[10] When they realized that the Paris Peace Conference had substantially disregarded the American President's blueprint for a post-war order, many delegations travelled

[8] Bernadette Whelan, *United States Foreign Policy and Ireland: From Empire to Independence, 1913-1929* (Dublin: Four Courts Press, 2006), 178.
[9] Alan J. Ward, *Ireland and Anglo-American Relations, 1899-1921* (Toronto: University of Toronto Press, 1969), 166-188; Gerard Keown, *First of the Small Nations. The Beginning of the Irish Foreign Policy in the Inter-War Years, 1919-1921* (Oxford: Oxford University Press, 2016), 36-67; Emmanuel Destenay, '"L'Irlande est à Paris et elle frappe à la porte!" Les revendications indépendantistes irlandaises et la Conférence de la Paix (janvier–juin 1919)', *20 & 21 Revue d'Histoire* 147, no. 3 (2020): 17–29.
[10] Whelan, *United States Foreign Policy and Ireland*, 184.

to the United States in the hope of appealing to the Senate. Éamon de Valera reached the United States in summer 1919 and toured the country to drum up support for Irish aspirations to independence.[11]

In the US, the Labour Bureau of the American Commission on Irish Independence identified the imperialist roots of the war, arguing that 'the real motive and actual effect of the tremendous holocaust was imperialist expansion, England's commercial supremacy, exploitation of the common people (the workers)',[12] and denouncing Wilson's signing of the Treaty of Versailles. Imperialism was openly challenged as the direct trigger of the four-year cataclysm. Meanwhile the American labour movement dreamt of a working-class internationalism that would defeat international capital. As far as Irish-Americans were concerned, they regarded 'the Irish revolution as a key battle in the international class struggle whose outcome would critically influence the well-being of workers in the United States'.[13] Wilson's vision of self-determination was accused of being a further consolidation of the grasp of international finance and colonial domination, at the expense of oppressed nations and working classes, in both developing and industrialized countries. Irish-American labour organizations echoed Lenin's definition of the Great War as the crystallization of inter-imperial rivalries.

Neither Sinn Féin leaders nor Dáil Éireann ever contemplated a socialist alternative to Wilsonianism. Other anti-colonial radicals in the post-war British and French Empires did so, with Lenin, leader of the Russian revolution which had taken Russia out of the war in 1917 and which had comprehensively erased the Tsarist imperial order, offering the most important and cataclysmic model for a transfigured post-war world. Lenin's concept of 'national self-determination' 'implied the dismantling of colonial empires'.[14] This he defined as the 'right of peoples to secede from oppressive regimes',[15] a right that would ultimately undermine the capitalist-imperialist world order and shape a post-war anti-imperialist communism.[16] Another, less well-known, attempt to devise an

---

[11] Francis M. Carroll, *America and the Making of an Independent Ireland. A History* (New York: New York University Press, 2021), 66–74.

[12] *New Majority*, 15 January 1921.

[13] Elizabeth McKillen, 'Ethnicity, Class and Wilsonian Internationalism Reconsidered: The Mexican-American Immigrant Left and U.S. Foreign Relations, 1914–1922', *Diplomatic History* 25, no. 4 (2001): 554.

[14] Erez Manela, *The Wilsonian Moment: Self-Determination and the International Origins of Anticolonial Nationalism* (Oxford: Oxford University Press, 2007), 37. Manela investigates how intellectuals in countries such as China, Egypt or India harnessed the Wilsonian principle of 'self-determination' to create the basis for anti-colonial movements.

[15] Ibid.

[16] V. I. Lenin, *Imperialism, the Highest Stage of Capitalism* (Moscow: Foreign Languages Publishing House, 1917).

alternative post-war order originated with Frank Walsh, a labour lawyer who served on the American Commission on Irish Independence. Walsh undertook to 'create a League of Oppressed Nationalities that would include such diverse groups as Lithuanians, Liberians, Filipinos, and Puerto Ricans and become a powerful anti-imperialist force in world politics'.[17]

Like many other embittered non-imperial peoples, the Irish resorted to more radical and revolutionary methods to loosen their ties with the British Empire. The Irish War of Independence (1919–1921), following the assassination of two RIC constables and the convening of the first national assembly in the Mansion House in Dublin, ran parallel to de Valera's American-wide campaign to gain the support of US public opinion. But as hopes of reaching a constitutional settlement with Britain dwindled, the Irish came to the bitter realization that Wilson would not, and could not, challenge the post-war order that had emerged from the ruins of the Great War.

---

[17] McKillen, 'Ethnicity, Class and Wilsonian Internationalism Reconsidered', 576.

Bibliography

Primary Sources

France

Service Historique de la Défense (Vincennes)

Armée de Terre, Troisième République (1870–1940)
  Organisme interalliés, section française
    Série 4N31. Conseil supérieur de guerre. Front franco-britannique (1917–1919)
  Fonds privés
    Série 6N155. Fonds Clémenceau. Rapports des attachés militaires à Londres (1917–1922)
  État-major de l'Armée
    Série 7N700. Période des hostilités. Section anglaise. Correspondance et renseignements reçus de l'attaché militaire à Londres (1914–1915)
    Série 7N679. Période des hostilités. 2ème Bureau. Bulletins d'informations (1917–1919)
    Série 7N1253. Attaché militaire. Grande-Bretagne. Situation politique en Grande-Bretagne (1914–1917)
    Série 7N1254. Attaché militaire. Grande-Bretagne. Situation politique en Grande-Bretagne (1917–1918)
    Série 7N1255. Attaché militaire. Grande-Bretagne. Situation politique en Grande-Bretagne (1918–1920)
    Série 7N1261. État-major de l'Armée. Attaché militaire. Grande-Bretagne. Doubles des rapports de l'attaché militaire (1915–1918)
  Grand Quartier Général (1914–1918)
    Série 16N2968. 2ème Bureau E. Angleterre. Rapport des attachés militaires à Londres (1914–1917)
    Série 16N3007. Bureau Correspondant des TOE. Angleterre. Rapport es attachés militaires et du ministère des affaires étrangères (1917–1918)
    Série 16N3009. Bureau Correspondant des TOE. Angleterre. Rapport es attachés militaires et du ministère des affaires étrangères (1917–1918)
    Série 16N3223. 3ème Bureau TOE. Angleterre. Correspondance échangée entre le gouvernement et les représentants diplomatiques et attachés militaires (1915–1919)

Archives Diplomatiques du Ministère des Affaires étrangères (La Courneuve)

Correspondance politique et commerciale (1897–1940)
  Guerre 1914–1918
    1CPCOM86. Première Guerre mondiale. États-Unis
    1CPCOM499-514. Première Guerre mondiale, 1915–1918. États-Unis
    1CPCOM545-547. Première Guerre mondiale, 1914–1918. Irlande
Correspondance politique et commerciale (1918–1940). Série Z Europe
  95CPCOM1-9. Irlande
Correspondance politique et commerciale. Nouvelle série (1897–1914)
  161CPCOM4. Grande-Bretagne
Papiers d'agents. Archives privées
  93PAAP13. Jean-Jules Jusserand. Correspondance politique (1915–1916)
  166PAAP174. André Tardieu. Mission aux États-Unis. Question irlandaise (1918–1919)

Great Britain

Imperial War Museum

War diary of David Starrett (1914–1918)

Parliamentary Archives, Houses of Parliament

David Lloyd George Papers (1882–1945)

University of Leeds Library

Peter Liddle Collection (First World War) (1914–1918)

The Nation Archives London

Cabinet Papers
  CAB 23, War Cabinet and Cabinet Minutes (1916–1939)
  CAB 24, War Cabinet and Cabinet Memoranda (1915–1939)
  CAB 37, Cabinet Office: Photographic Copies of Cabinet Papers (1880–1916)
Colonial Office Papers
  CO 903, Colonial Office: Ireland (1885–1919)
  CO 904, Ireland: Dublin Castle Records (1795–1926)

Domestic Records of the Public Record Office
  PRON 30/71, Guy Nightingale Papers (1919–1926)
Parliamentary Archives
  Cd. 8279, *Royal Commission on the Rebellion in Ireland. Report of the Commission.* London, HMSO, 1916.
  Cd. 8311, *Royal Commission on the Rebellion in Ireland. Minutes of Evidence.* London, HMSO, 1916.
War Office Papers
  WO 32, War Office and Successors: Registered Files (General Series) (1845–1999)
  WO 95, Royal Army Medical Corps, World War One and Army of Occupation War Diaries (1914–1923)

Republic of Ireland

Irish Jesuit Archives

Irish Jesuit Chaplains in the First World War (1895–2020)
  CHP 1/25, Letters to the Irish Fr Provincial Thomas V. Nolan SJ from Fr Henry Gill SJ during his time as a chaplain (1914–1918)
  CHP 1/63, Letters to Thomas V. Nolan SJ from Fr Joseph Wrafter SJ written while serving as chaplain (1915–1918)

Military Archives of Ireland

Bureau of Military History (1913–1921)

National Archives of Ireland

Manuscripts section
  CSO/RP/1917/2869, letter from C. M. Hathaway to Walter Page, 23 May 1917

National Library of Ireland

Ephemera Collection
Irish Large Books
Keogh Photographic Collection (1915–1930)
Manuscript Section
  Sinn Féin Provincial Correspondance (1916–1917)

RTÉ Ireland

Cashman Collection (1905–1966)
Murtagh Collection (1911–1932)

University College Dublin Archives

Desmond Fitzgerald Papers (1894–1959)
Éamon de Valera Papers (1882–1985)
William Cosgrave Papers (1917–1993)

Waterford City and County Archives

Lismore Castle Estate Papers (1731–1969)

United States

Library of Congress

Woodrow Wilson Papers (1786–1957)

University of California, Santa Barbara Library

Charles Montgomery Hathaway Papers (1895–1939)

Yale University Library

Colonel House Papers (1885–1938)

Selected newspapers

Abendzseitung
America
An tÓglách
Belfast Evening Telegraph
Catholic Bulletin
Clare Champion
Chicago Citizen

Cork Celt
Daily Chronicle
Daily News
Evening News
Freeman's Journal
Gaelic American
Irish Independent
Irishman
Irish Opinion
Irish Volunteer
Irish World
Longford Leader
Manchester Guardian
Morning Post
Nationality
New Ireland
New York Evening Post
Roscommon Journal
Sinn Féin
Sligo Champion
Sunday Times
The Kilkenny People
The Dundalk Examiner and Louth Advertiser
The Leader
The Nation
The New York Times
The Times
The Irish Times
Vossische Zeitung
Washington Star
Worker's Republic
Young Ireland

Published manuscripts and memoirs

Barry, Tom. *Guerrilla Days in Ireland*. Dublin: Irish Academic Press, 1949.
Cooper, Bryan. *The 10th (Irish) Division at Gallipoli*. Dublin: Irish Academic Press, 1918.
De Montmorency, Henry. *Sword and Stirrup: Memories of an Adventurous Life*. London: G. Bell and Sons, 1936.

Falls, Cyril. *The History of the 36th (Ulster) Division*. London: Constable, 1922.
Gwynn, Denis, ed. *The Letters and Friendships of Sir Cecil Spring-Rice: A Record*. Boston: Houghton Mifflin Co., 1929.
Gwynn, Denis. *The Life of John Redmond*. London: Harrap, 1932.
Lansing, Robert. *War Memoirs of Robert Lansing*. Indianapolis: Bobbs-Merrill, 1935.
Moynihan, Maurice, ed. *Speeches and Statements by Éamon de Valera 1917–1973*. Dublin: Gill & Macmillan, 1980.
Riddell, George. *Lord Riddell's War Diary, 1914–1918*. London: Nicholson and Watson, 1933.
Tynan, Katharine. *The Years of Shadow*. London: Constable, 1919.

Secondary Sources

Ireland at the beginning of the twentieth-century

Augusteijn, Joost. *Mayo. The Irish Revolution, 1912–1923*. Dublin: Four Courts Press, 2022.
Bartlett, Thomas. *The Cambridge History of Ireland, 1880 to the Present*. Cambridge: Cambridge University Press, 2018.
Bartlett, Thomas, and Keith Jeffery, ed. *A Military History of Ireland*. Cambridge: Cambridge University Press, 1996.
Beckett, Ian, ed. *The Army and the Curragh Incident, 1914*. London: Bodley Head for the Army Records Society, 1986.
Bew, Paul. *Ideology and the Ulster Question: Ulster Unionism and Irish Nationalism, 1912–1916*. Oxford: Clarendon Press, 1994.
Bew, Paul. *Ireland: The Politics of Enmity, 1789–2006*. Oxford: Oxford University Press, 2007.
Bull, Philip. 'The United Irish League, 1898–1900: The Dynamics of Irish Agrarian Agitation', *Irish Historical Studies* 33, no. 132 (2003): 404–423.
Burke, John. *Roscommon. The Irish Revolution, 1912–1923*. Dublin: Four Courts Press, 2022.
Coleman, Marie. *County Longford and the Irish Revolution*. Dublin: Irish Academic Press, 2003.
Correlli, Barnett. *Britain and Her Army, 1509–1970: a military, political and social survey*. London: Allen Lane, 1970.
Cronin, Seán. *Irish Nationalism: A History of Its Roots and Ideology*. Dublin: Irish Academic Press, 1980.
Cullen, Seamus. *Kildare. The Irish Revolution, 1912–1923*. Dublin: Four Courts Press, 2021.
Denman, Terence. *A Lonely Grave: The Life and Death of William Redmond*. Dublin: Irish Academic Press, 1995.

Destenay, Emmanuel. *Shadows from the Trenches. Veterans of the Great War and the Irish Revolution (1918-1923)*. Dublin: University College Dublin Press, 2021.

Dooley, Terence. *'The Land for the People'. The Land Question in Independent Ireland*. Dublin: University College Dublin Press, 2004.

Dooley, Terence. *Monaghan. The Irish Revolution, 1912-1923*. Dublin: Four Courts Press, 2017.

Fanning, Ronan. *Fatal Path: British Government and Irish Revolution (1910-1922)*. London: Faber & Faber, 2013.

Farrell, Brian. *The Founding of Dáil Éireann*. Dublin: Gill & Macmillan, 1971.

Farry, Michael. *Sligo. The Irish Revolution, 1912-1923*. Dublin: Four Courts Press, 2012.

Feeney, Brian. *Antrim. The Irish Revolution, 1912-1923*. Dublin: Four Courts Press, 2021.

Ferriter, Diarmaid. *The Transformation of Ireland, 1900-2000*. London: Profile Books, 2004.

Fitzpatrick, David. *Politics and Irish Life 1913-1921: Provincial Experiences of War and Revolution*. Cork: Cork University Press, 1998.

Fitzpatrick, David, ed. *Revolution? Ireland 1917-1923*. Dublin: Trinity History Workshop, 1990.

Fitzpatrick, David, ed. *Terror in Ireland, 1916-1923*. Dublin: Lilliput Press, 2012.

Foster, Roy. *Modern Ireland, 1600-1972*. London: Allen Lane, 1988.

Grant, Adrian. *Derry. The Irish Revolution, 1912-1923*. Dublin: Four Courts Press, 2018.

Hall, Donald. *Louth. The Irish Revolution, 1912-1923*. Dublin: Four Courts Press, 2019.

Hall, Donald, and Martin Maguire. *County Louth and the Irish Revolution, 1912-1923*. Dublin: Irish Academic Press, 2019.

Hepburn, Anthony. *Catholic Belfast and Nationalist Ireland in the Era of Joe Devlin, 1871-1934*. Oxford: Oxford University Press, 2008.

Hill, Jacqueline, ed. *A New History of Ireland, VII, Ireland, 1921-1984*. Oxford: Oxford University Press, 2003.

Jackson, Alvin. *Home Rule: An Irish History, 1800-2000*. London: Wiedenfeld & Nicolson, 2003.

Jackson, Alvin. *Ireland 1798-1998: Politics and War*. Oxford: Oxford University Press, 1999.

Joannon, Pierre. *Histoire de l'Irlande et des Irlandais*. Paris: Perrin, 2005.

Kee, Robert. *The Green Flag. A History of Irish Nationalism*. London: Weidenfeld & Nicolson, 1972.

Laffan, Michael. *The resurrection of Ireland. The Sinn Féin Party, 1916-1923*. Cambridge: Cambridge University Press, 1999.

Lee, Joseph. *Ireland 1912-1985: Politics and Society*. Cambridge: Cambridge University Press, 1989.

Lee, Joseph. *The Modernization of Irish Society, 1848-1918*. Dublin: Gill & Macmillan, 1973.

Leerssen, Joep, ed. *Parnell and his Times*. Cambridge: Cambridge University Press, 2020.

Lyons, F. S. L. *Charles Stewart Parnell*. London: Gill & Macmillan, 1977.
Lyons, F. S. L. *Culture and Anarchy in Ireland, 1890–1939*. Oxford: Oxford University Press, 1979.
Lyons, F. S. L. *Ireland since the Famine*. Dublin: Fontana Press, 1973.
Lyons, F. S. L. *John Dillon: A Biography*. London: Routledge & Kegan Paul, 1968.
Lyons, F. S. L. *The Fall of Parnell*. London: Routledge & Kegan Paul, 1960.
Lyons, F. S. L. *The Irish Parliamentary Party, 1890–1910*. London: Faber, 1951.
Maume, Patrick. *The Long Gestation. Irish Nationalist Life, 1891–1918*. Dublin: Gill & Macmillan, 1999.
McCarthy, Patrick. *Waterford. The Irish Revolution, 1912–1923*. Dublin: Four Courts Press, 2015.
McCluskey, Fergal. *Tyrone. The Irish Revolution, 1912–1923*. Dublin: Four Courts Press, 2014.
McConnel, James, 'The Franchise Factor in the Defeat of the Irish Parliamentary Party, 1885–1918', *Historical Journal* 27, no. 2 (2004): 355–377.
McConnel, James. *The Irish Parliamentary Party and the Third Home Rule Crisis*. Dublin: Four Courts Press, 2013.
McGarty, Patrick. *Leitrim. The Irish Revolution, 1912–1923*. Dublin: Four Courts Press, 2020.
Miller, David. *Church, State and Nation in Ireland, 1898–1921*. Dublin: Gill & Macmillan, 1973.
Mulvagh, Conor. *The Irish Parliamentary Party at Westminster, 1900–1918*. Dublin: University College Dublin Press, 2016.
Ó Broin, León. *Revolutionary Underground: The Story of the Irish Republican Brotherhood, 1858–1924*. London: Gill & Macmillan, 1976.
O'Callaghan, John. *Limerick. The Irish Revolution, 1912–1923*. Dublin: Four Courts Press, 2018.
O'Carroll, John, and John Murphy, ed. *De Valera and His Times*. Cork: Cork University Press, 1983.
Paget, George. *A History of the British Cavalry, 1816–1919, vol. 7, The Curragh Incident and the Western Front, 1914–18*. London: Leon Cooper, 1996.
Pašeta, Senia. *Before the Revolution: Nationalism, Social Change and Ireland's Catholic Elite, 1879–1922*. Cork: Cork University Press, 1999.
Phoenix, Éamon. *Northern Nationalism: Nationalist Politics, Partition and the Catholic Minority in Northern Ireland, 1890–1940*. Belfast: Ulster Historical Foundation, 1994.
Purcell, Daniel. *Fermanagh. The Irish Revolution, 1912–1923*. Dublin: Four Courts Press, 2022.
Travers, Pauric. *Donegal. The Irish Revolution, 1912–1923*. Dublin: Four Courts Press, 2022.
Vaughan, W. E., ed. *A New History of Ireland, VI, Ireland Under the Union, II, 1870–1921*. Oxford: Oxford University Press, 1996.

Ward, Alan J. 'Models of Government and Anglo-Irish Relations'. *Albion: A Quarterly Journal Concerned with British Studies* 20, no. 1 (1988): 19–42.

Ward, Margaret, *Unmanageable Revolutionaries. Women and Irish Nationalism*. London: Pluto Press, 1995.

Wheatley, Michael. *Nationalism and the Irish Party: Provincial Ireland 1910–1916*. Oxford: Oxford University Press, 2005.

Williams, Desmond, ed. *The Irish Struggle*. London: Routledge & Kegan Paul, 1966.

Ireland and the First World War

Aan de Wiel, Jérôme. *The Catholic Church in Ireland, 1914–1918: War and Politics*. Dublin: Irish Academic Press, 2003.

Aan de Wiel, Jérôme. *The Irish Factor, 1899–1919: Ireland's Strategic and Diplomatic Importance for Foreign Powers*. Dublin: Irish Academic Press, 2008.

Borgonovo, John. *The Dynamics of War and Revolution: Cork City, 1916–1918*. Cork: Cork University Press, 2013.

Bowman, Timothy, William Butler, and Michael Wheatley. *The Disparity of Sacrifice. Irish Recruitment to the British Armed Forces, 1914–1918*. Liverpool: Liverpool University Press, 2020.

Callan, Patrick. 'Ambivalence towards the Saxon shilling: the attitudes of the Catholic Church in Ireland towards enlistment during the First World War', *Archivium Hibernicum* 41, no. 10 (1986): 99–111.

Callan, Patrick. 'British recruitment in Ireland, 1914–1918', *Revue Internationale d'Histoire Militaire* 63 (1985): 41–50.

Callan, Patrick. 'Recruiting for the British Army in Ireland during the First World War', *Irish Sword* 17, no. 66 (1987): 42–56.

Callan, Patrick. 'The Irish Soldier: A Propaganda Paper for Ireland September–December 1918', *Irish Sword* 15 (1983): 67–75.

Cousin, Collin. *Armagh and the Great War*. Dublin: The History Press, 2011.

Dennehy, John. *In a Time of War: Tipperary, 1914–1918*. Dublin: Merrion Press, 2013.

Dockrill, Michael, and David French, ed. *Strategy and Intelligence: British Policy during the First World War*. London: Bloomsbury Academic, 1996.

Fitzpatrick, David, ed. *Ireland and the First World War*. Dublin: Trinity History Workshop, 1986.

Fitzpatrick, David. 'The Logic of Collective Sacrifice: Ireland and the British Army, 1914–1918', *The Historical Journal* 38, no. 4 (1995): 1017–1030.

Gallagher, Niamh. *Ireland and the Great War. A Social and Political History*. London: Bloomsbury, 2019.

Gregory, Adrian, and Senia Pašeta, ed. *Ireland and the Great War: 'A War to Unite Us All?'*. Manchester: Manchester University Press, 2002.

Hennessy, Thomas. *Dividing Ireland. World War I and Partition*. London: Routledge, 1998.
Horne, John, ed. *Our War: Ireland and the Great War*. Dublin: Royal Irish Academy, 2008.
Jeffery, Keith. *Ireland and the Great War*. Cambridge: Cambridge University Press, 2000.
Johnstone, Kevin. *Home or Away: The Great War and the Irish Revolution*. Dublin: Gill & Macmillan, 2010.
McConnel, James. 'Recruiting Sergeants for John Bull? Irish Nationalist MPs and Enlistment during the Early Months of the Great War', *War in History* 14, no. 4 (2007): 408–428.
McDowell, R. B. *The Irish Convention, 1917–18*. London: Routledge & Kegan Paul, 1970.
Morrissey, Conor. 'Protestant nationalists and the Irish conscription crisis 1918'. In *Small Nations and Colonial Peripheries in World War I*, edited by Gearoid Barry, Roisin Healy and Eurico Del Lago, 55–72. Leiden: Brill, 2016.
Novick, Ben. *Conceiving Revolution: Irish Nationalist Propaganda during the First World War*. Dublin: Four Courts Press, 2001.
Pašeta, Senia. *Irish Nationalist Women, 1900–1918*. Cambridge: Cambridge University Press, 2013.
Pennell, Catriona. *A Kingdom United: Popular Responses to the Outbreak of the First World War in Britain and Ireland*. Oxford: Oxford University Press, 2012.
Redmond, Jennifer, and Elaine Farrell, ed. *Irish Women in the First World War Era. Irish Women's Lives, 1914–1918*. London: Routledge, 2019.
Ryan, Louise, and Margaret Ward, ed. *Irish Women and the Vote: Becoming Citizens*. Dublin: Irish Academic Press, 2007.
Stubbs, John. 'The Unionists and Ireland, 1914–18', *Historical Journal* 33, no. 4 (1990): 875–876.
Walsh, Fionnuala. *Irish Women and the Great War*. Cambridge: Cambridge University Press, 2020.
Ward, Alan J. 'Lloyd George and the 1918 Irish Conscription Crisis', *The Historical Journal* 17, no. 1 (1974): 107–129.
Yeates, Padraig. *A City in Wartime, Dublin 1914–1918*. Dublin: Gill & Macmillan, 2012.

Ireland's troops in the First World War

Bowman, Timothy. *The Irish Regiments in the Great War. Discipline and Morale*. Manchester: Manchester University Press, 2003.
Denman, Terence. *Ireland's Unknown Soldiers: the 16th Division in the Great War*. Dublin: Irish Academic Press, 1992.
Destenay, Emmanuel. 'The Impact of Political Unrest in Ireland on Irish soldiers in the British army, 1919–1918: a re-evaluation', *Irish Historical Studies* 161, no. 2 (2018): 50–63.

Dooley, Thomas. *Irishmen or English soldiers, The Times and World of a Southern Catholic Irish Man (1876-1916) Enlisting in the British Army*. Liverpool: Liverpool University Press, 1995.

Duffy, Christopher. *Through German Eyes: The British and The Somme 1916*. Dublin: Phoenix Press, 2007.

Dungan, Myles. *Irish Voices from the Great War*. Dublin: Irish Academic Press, 1995.

Fox, F. *The Royal Inniskilling Fusiliers in the World War*. London: Constable, 1928.

Grayson, Richard. *Dublin's Great Wars. The First World War, the Easter Rising and the Irish Revolution*. Cambridge: Cambridge University Press, 2018.

Harris, Henry. *The Irish Regiments in the First World War*. Cork: Mercier Press, 1968.

Harris, Henry. *The Royal Irish Fusiliers*. London: Leo Cooper Ltd., 1972.

Johnstone, Tom. *Orange, Green and Khaki. The Story of the Irish Regiments in the Great War, 1914-18*. Dublin: Gill & Macmillan, 1992.

Lemisko, Lynn. 'Morale in the 16th (Irish) Division, 1916-1918', *Irish Sword* 81, no. 1 (1997): 207-233.

Leonard, Jane. 'The reaction of Irish officers in the British army to the Easter Rising of 1916'. In *Facing Armageddon: The First World War Experienced*, edited by Cecil Hugh and Peter Liddle, 256-269. London: L. Cooper, 1996.

Macdonagh, Michael. *The Irish at the Front*. London: Hodder and Stoughton, 1916.

Orr, Philip. *The Road to the Somme: Men of the Ulster Division tell their Story*. Belfast, Blackstaff Press, 1987.

Simkins, Peter. *Kitchener's Army: The Raising of the New Armies, 1914-1916*. Barnsley: South Yorkshire, Pen & Sword Military, 2007.

Snape, Michael. *God and the British Soldier: Religion and the British Army in the First and Second World Wars*. London: Routledge, 2005.

Stanley, Jeremy. *Ireland's Forgotten 10th Division*. Ballycastle: Impact Printing Ltd., 2003.

Ireland and the 1916 Rising

Caulfield, Max. *The Easter Rebellion*. Dublin: Gill & Macmillan, 1995.

Coogan, Tim Pat. *1916: The Easter Rising*. London: Phoenix, 2005.

Edwards, O. Dudley, and Fergus Pyle, ed. *1916: The Easter Rising*. London: MacGibbon and Kee, 1968.

Martin, Francis Xavier, '1916 – Myth, Fact and Mystery', *Studia Hibernica*, 7 (1967): 7-128.

McGarry, Fearghal. *The Rising Ireland: Easter 1916*. Oxford: Oxford University Press, 2010.

Purdon, Edward. *1916 Rising*. Cork: Mercier Press Ltd., 1999.

Ryan, Desmond. *The Rising*. Dublin: Golden Eagle Books Limited, 1949.

Townshend, Charles. *Easter 1916, the Irish Rebellion*. London: Penguin Books, 2005.

Essays on the impact of the 1916 Rising and appreciations of the historiography of the Irish Revolution

Beiner, Guy. 'Between Trauma and Triumphalism: The Easter Rising, the Somme and the Crux of Deep Memory in Modern Ireland', *Journal of British Studies* 46, no. 2 (2007): 366–389.

Crowley, Cornelius. 'How to Do Things with Words, and Deeds, and Blood', *Textes et contextes* 9, no. 1 (2014). Available online: https://preo.u-bourgogne.fr/textesetcontextes/index.php?id=1131 (accessed 15 August 2021).

Curtin, Nancy J. '"Varieties of Irishness": Historical revisionism, Irish style', *Journal of British Studies* 35, no. 2 (1996): 195–219.

Destenay, Emmanuel. 'La légende noire de l'IRA: entre historiographie "révisionniste" et mythologie unioniste', *Revue historique* 690, no. 1 (2019): 405–425.

Longley, Edna. 'The Rising, the Somme and Irish memory'. In *Revising the Rising*, edited by Ni Dhonnchadha Marin and Dorgan Theo, 69–95. Derry: Field Day, 1991.

Moody, T. W. 'Irish history and Irish mythology', *Hermathena* 124, no 1. (1978): 6–24.

Ireland and Irish-American Relations

Brundage, David. *Irish Nationalists in America: The Politics of Exile, 1798–1998*. Oxford: Oxford University Press, 2016.

Carroll, Francis M. *America and the Making of an Independent Ireland. A History*. New York: New York University Press, 2021.

Carroll, Francis M. *American Opinion and the Irish Question, 1910–1923. A Study in Opinion and Policy*. Dublin: Gill & Macmillan, 1978.

Cronin, Seán. *Washington's Irish Policy, 1916–1986. Independence, Partition, Neutrality*. Dublin: Irish Books and Media, 1987.

Cuddy, Joseph. *Irish-America and National Isolationism*. New York: Arno Press, 1976.

Doorley, Michael. *Irish-American Diaspora Nationalism. The Friends of Irish Freedom, 1916–1935*. Dublin: Four Courts Press, 2005.

Doorley, Michael. *Justice Daniel Cohalan, 1946–1965. American Patriot and Irish-American Nationalist*. Cork: Cork University Press, 2019.

Hartley, Stephen. *The Irish Question as a Problem in British Foreign Policy, 1914–1918*. New York: St Martin's Press, 1987.

Schmuhl, Robert. *Ireland's Exiled Children. America and the Easter Rising*. Oxford: Oxford University Press, 2016.

Tansill, Charles Callan. *America and the Fight for Irish Freedom, 1866–1922*. New York: The Devin-Adair Co., 1957.

Ward, Alan J. *Ireland and Anglo-American Relations, 1899–1921*. Toronto: University of Toronto Press, 1969.

Whelan, Bernadette. 'American Propaganda and Ireland during the World War One. The Work of the Committee on Public Information', *Irish Studies Review* 25, no. 2 (2017): 141–169.

Whelan, Bernadette. 'Recognition of the Irish Free State, 1924. The Diplomatic Context of the Appointment of Timothy Smiddy as the First Irish Minister to the US', *Irish Studies in International Affairs* 26, no. 1 (2015): 121–125.

Whelan, Bernadette. *United States Foreign Policy and Ireland: From Empire to Independence, 1913–1929*. Dublin: Four Courts Press, 2006.

Selected academic works on the Paris Peace Conference

Knock, Thomas. *To End All Wars: Woodrow Wilson and the Quest of a New World Order*. Oxford: Oxford University Press, 1992.

MacMillan, Margaret. *Peacemakers: The Paris Conference of 1919 and Its Attempt to End War*. London: John Murray, 2001.

Manela, Erez. *The Wilsonian Moment: Self-Determination and the International Origins of Anticolonial Nationalism*. Oxford: Oxford University Press, 2007.

McKillen, Elizabeth. 'Ethnicity, Class and Wilsonian Internationalism Reconsidered: The Mexican-American Immigrant Left and U.S. Foreign Relations, 1914–1922', *Diplomatic History* 25, no. 4 (2001): 553–587.

McKillen, Elizabeth. 'The Corporatist Model, World War I, and the Public Debate over the League of Nations', *Diplomatic History* 15, no. 2 (1991): 171–197.

Throntveit, Trygve. 'The Fable of the Fourteen Points: Woodrow Wilson and National Self-Determination', *Diplomatic History* 35, no. 3 (2011): 445–481.

Selected academic works on revolutionary France and Europe

Blanning, T. C. W. *The French Revolutionary Wars, 1787–1802*. London: Hodder, 1996.

Come, Donald R. 'French Threat to British Shores, 1793–1798', *Military Affairs* 16, no. 4 (1952): 174–188.

Grab, Alexander. *Napoleon and the Transformation of Europe*. New York: Palgrave Macmillan, 2003.

Kolla, Edward James. *Sovereignty, International Law and the French Revolution*. Cambridge: Cambridge University Press, 2017.

Kubben, Raymond. *Regeneration and Hegemony. Franco-Batavian Relations in the Revolutionary Era, 1795–1803*. Leiden, Boston: Martinus Nijhoff, 2011.

Murphy, John A. *The Expedition to Bantry Bay, 1796*. Cork: Mercier Press, 1997.

Pakenham, Thomas. *The Year of Liberty: The Story of the Great Irish Rebellion of 1798*. London: Abacus, 2000.

Owen, Connelly. *The Wars of the French Revolution and Napoleon, 1792–1815*. London: Routledge, 2006.

Selected academic works on international relations before the First World War

Andrew, Christopher. 'France and the Making of the Entente Cordiale', *Historical Journal* 10, no. 1 (1967): 89–105.

Barlow, Ima Christina. *The Agadir Crisis*. Chapel Hill: University of North Carolina Press, 1940.

Barraclough, Geoffrey. *From Agadir to Armageddon: Anatomy of a Crisis*. New York: Holmes and Mier, 1982.

Hayne, M. B. *The French Foreign Office and the Origins of the First World War (1898–1914)*. Oxford: Oxford University Press, 1993.

Wilson, Keith. 'The Agadir Crisis, the Mansion House Speech, and the Double-Edgedness of Agreements', *Historical Journal* 15, no. 3 (1972): 513–532.

Selected academic works on the First World War

Chernev, Borislav. *Twilight of Empire. The Brest-Litovsk Conference and the Remaking of East-Central Europe, 1917–1918*. Toronto: University of Toronto Press, 2017.

Clark, Christopher. *Sleepwalkers: How Europe Went to War in 1914*. London: Allen Lane, 2012.

Cooper, John Milton. *Woodrow Wilson: a Biography*. New York: Knopf, 2009.

Irwin, Julia. *Making the World Safe: The American Red Cross and a Nation's Humanitarian Awakening*. Oxford: Oxford University Press, 2013.

Kennedy, Ross. *The Will to Believe: Woodrow Wilson, World War I, and America's Strategy for Peace and Security*. Kent (Ohio): Kent University State Press, 2009.

Levi, Margaret. 'The Institution of Conscription', *Social Science History* 20, no. 1 (1996): 133–167.

Strachan, Hew. *Financing the First World War*. Oxford: Oxford University Press, 2004.

Strachan, Hew. *The First World War*. London: Penguin Books, 2005.

Strachan, Hew. *The First World War, Volume I, To Arms*. Oxford: Oxford University Press, 2003.

Strachan, Hew. *The Outbreak of the First World War*. Oxford: Oxford University Press, 2004.

Watson, Alexander. *Enduring the Great War. Combat, Morale and the Collapse in the German and British Armies, 1914–1918*. Cambridge: Cambridge University Press, 2008.

Winter, Jay, ed. *The Cambridge History of the First World War, Volume I, Global War*. Cambridge: Cambridge University Press, 2014.

Winter, Jay, ed. *The Cambridge History of the First World War, Volume II, The State*. Cambridge: Cambridge University Press, 2014.

Winter, Jay, ed. *The Cambridge History of the First World War, Volume III, Civil Society*. Cambridge: Cambridge University Press, 2014.

Selected academic works on Ireland's first Dáil

Carroll, Francis M., ed. *The Irish Commission on Irish Independence, 1919: The Diary, Correspondence and Report*. Dublin: Irish Manuscript Commission, 1985.

Carroll, Francis M. *Money for Ireland: Finance, Diplomacy, Politics and the First Dáil Éireann Loans, 1919–1936*. Santa Barbara: Greenwood Press, 2002.

Destenay, Emmanuel. "'L'Irlande est à Paris et elle frappe à la porte!" Les revendications indépendantistes irlandaises et la Conférence de la Paix (janvier–juin 1919)', *20 & 21 Revue d'Histoire* 147, no. 3 (2020): 17–29.

Farrell, Brian. *The Founding of Dáil Éireann*. Dublin: Gill & Macmillan, 1971.

Keown, Gerard. *First of the Small Nations. The Beginning of the Irish Foreign Policy in the Inter-War Years, 1919–1921*. Oxford: Oxford University Press, 2016.

Index

Act of Union, 1801, 4
Agadir Crisis, 2
agricultural exports, 72–3
agricultural production, 42, 72
Amending Bill, 28
American Truth Society, 67–8
ammunition factories, 73
An tÓglách, 209
Anglo-American relations, 10
Anglo-French relations, 1–3
Anglo-Irish relations, 8–9, 43–4
anti-British sentiment, 41, 74, 184–5
anti-colonial radicals, 223–4
anti-conscription movement, 12
    first opposition, 74
    press, 75
    South Longford by-election, 98–103
    strength of feeling, 75
    support for Redmond, 76–80
    whiff of pro-German propaganda, 76
anti-conscription myth, Easter Rising, 84–5, 89, 98–9, 106–7, 113–14, 115–17
anti-government violence, 6, 48
anti-recruitment unrest, 40–7, 48, 49
Archdale, Sir Edward, 166
archival material, 13–16
armed republicanism, displays of, 45–7
arms importation, 27–8
Ashe, Thomas, funeral, 117–18
Asquith, Herbert, 3–4, 30, 94, 137, 218, 219
    compromise policy, 64–6
    and the Curragh incident, 23
    de la Panouse on, 26, 28
    First World War strategy, 29
    general elections, 1910, 20
    Home Rule Bill, 20–2
    on Home Rule crisis, 27
    laissez-faire policy, 28
    Parliament Act, 20–1
    weakening of authority, 69
Australia, 162

Balfour, Arthur, 20, 138–9
Ballymote, 42
Benedict XV, Pope, 181
Birrell, Augustine, 43, 45
Bismarck, Otto von, 1
Blanche, Alfred, xvii, xx, 15
    and British procrastination, 146
    on British regime, 154
    on Catholic clergy support for Sinn Féin, 124
    on conscription, 179, 191–2
    on famine treat, 150–1
    on First World War intervention, 132
    on the Irish Convention, 141–2
    opposition to conscription, 146
    on Sinn Féin, 134–6, 151
    on suffrage, 212
Blythe, Ernest, 115
Boland, Henry, 115
Borah, William, 161
Boyne, Battle of the, 4
Brest-Litovsk Treaty, 168
British Army
    casualties, 80
    Home Rule crisis, 22–9
    Irish casualties, 36–7
    Irish divisions, 34
    recruitment decline, 80–3
    volunteer enlistment, 32–4, 39, 48, 80, 81, 216, 219
British procrastination, 68-70, 142, 143, 146–8, 163
Buckingham Palace Conference, 28
by-elections, 1917, 90
Byrne, General, 189–90

Cambon, Paul, xvii–xviii, 1, 5, 15, 39, 61, 95
    on Catholic clergy support for Sinn Féin, 124
    on conscription, 221
    on East-Clare by-election, 106
    on Easter Rising, 58, 63

on First World War, 35, 36
on Home Rule Bill, 21
on Home Rule crisis, 27
on the IPP, 220–1
political correspondence, xviii
on Redmond, 220
on Sinn Féin clubs, 126
Campbell, James, 197–8
Carson, Sir Edward, 21, 24, 28, 29–34, 46, 50, 147
   entry into government, 38–9
   and equity of sacrifice, 171–2
   and partition, 64, 68
   resignation, 167
   support for the war effort, 215–16
Casement, Roger, 50, 67
Catholic clergy, 6, 76–7, 79–80, 102, 116, 121, 123–5, 180–2, 191, 221
Chambers, James, 43
Chicago Tribune, 59
civil war threat, 1914, 3–4
compromise attempt, 64
Connaught Rangers, 56
Connolly, James, 59
conscription
   An tÓglách narrative, 209
   British reservations, 189–92
   and consent, 72
   debates, 170–5, 196
   as diplomatic move, 192–5
   dread of, 78
   and English public opinion, 177
   fear of, 71–2n1, 107, 111, 118–19, 129, 148–54, 183, 209–10
   first opposition, 74
   in Great Britain, 81
   and the Home Rule Act, 79
   House of Commons debate, 166–7
   introduction, 6–7, 43, 125–6, 165–71
   military advantage, 171
   mobilization against, 181
   opposition, 76–80, 91, 172–5, 180–6, 209–10, 222
   opposition to compulsion, 43–4
   parliamentary consent given, 179
   postponed, 193–4, 207, 214
   press attitudes, 75, 118–19
   public opinion on, 168
   Sinn Féin opposition, 88, 91, 96–8
   South Longford by-election and, 98–103
   threat, 1916, 71–6
   threat of, 214, 216–17, 222
   Ulster Unionists conscription cry, 165–70
conscription crisis, 7–8, 158, 168
conscription scares, 8, 10, 30, 41–2, 77–8
consent, and conscription, 72
constitutional nationalism, 4, 19, 22, 26–7, 91, 122–3, 219
conventional narratives, 5–10
Conway, T. J., 123
Cooper, Sir Richard, 174
Corcoran, Canon, 100
Cosgrave, William, 113
counties, 18(map)
Curragh incident, the, 22–6, 69, 213
Curran, Reverend, 103
Curzon, Lord, 139, 193

Dáil Éireann, convening of, 222
Daily Chronicle, 199
Daily News, 24, 199
Dalton, J., 115
Dardanelles offensive, 34, 85
de la Panouse, Louis, xviii–xix, 5, 12–13, 15, 66, 198
   on anti-conscription movement, 76
   on Asquith, 26, 28
   on conscription, 146, 148, 166, 177, 179, 190, 192
   on the Curragh incident, 25
   on death of Ashe, 118
   on East Cavan by-election, 207
   on East-Clare by-election, 140
   and the Easter Rising, xviii–xix, 51–2, 54–5
   on English public opinion, 177
   on general elections, 1918, 211, 213
   on Home Rule, 194–5
   and Home Rule controversy, 94
   on Home Rule crisis, 22, 23–4, 26, 70
   on the Irish Convention, 139, 142
   on Irish Volunteers, 40
   and partition, 68
   on recruitment decline, 80
   on Sinn Féin, 62, 97, 121–2

on socioeconomic situation, 72–3
on South Longford by-election, 102
on Ulster revolt, 21–2
and US First World War intervention, 147
de Valera, Éamon
   anti-conscription myth, 106–7
   anti-conscription rhetoric, 106
   arrest, 198
   East-Clare by-election, 103, 105–7, 108, 109–12, 114, 134
   elected Sinn Féin president, 120
   general elections, 1918, 212
   Ireland's Case against Conscription, 198
   Kilkenny by-election, 114–15, 134
   Proclamation of the Irish Republic, 105
   pro-German rhetoric, 109–10, 134
   release, 103
   support for bloodshed, 114
   and Wilson, 158
de Wiel, A., 8n25
Declaration of Independence, 221
des Longchamps, Jean, xix–xx, 15, 35, 39, 48, 62
   on conscription, 80, 189
   on Easter Rising, 55–6
   and partition, 66–7
   on Sinn Féin, 45, 46, 47, 67
   on UVF and Irish Volunteer responsibility, 68–9
Devine, T. J., 86
Devlin, John, 32
Devlin, Joseph, 64, 172, 174, 175, 203
devolution, 19, 20, 28, 56, 88, 217–18
Dillon, John, 58, 59, 86, 101, 173, 212
diplomatic archives, 14–16
diversionary 'Irish' conflict, 5
dominion status, 96
Donegal Independent, 77–8
Donovan, John J., 122–3
Drumkeeran, 80
Dublin
   anti-recruitment unrest, 41
   Ashe funeral, 117–18
   Mansion House meeting, 49
   Sinn Féin Convention, 1917, 96–8, 119–20
   St Patrick's Day parades 1916, 45

Dublin Metropolitan Police, 41, 51
Duke, Henry, 135–6, 170–1, 189–90

East Cavan by-election, 201–3, 204, 205, 207
East-Clare by-election, 103–7, 108, 109–12, 113, 114, 134, 140
Easter Rising, 51–2, 53, 54–5, 216
   aftermath, 57–63
   American reaction, 59–62
   anti-conscription myth, 84–5, 89, 98–9, 106–7, 113–14, 115–17
   British troops, 54
   casualties, 54
   conventional narratives, 5–10
   deportations, 61
   executions, *see* executions
   fighting, 52, 54
   as foundational myth, 221
   general amnesty, 103–5, 142
   Irish troops reaction to, 56–7
   lack of popular support, 55–6
   local populations and, 54
   prisoners released, 69, 78–9
   rebel numbers, 52
   rebel surrender, 55
   responses to, 55–7
   sentences, 57
   Sinn Féin legitimizes, 83
   UVF and Irish Volunteer responsibility, 68–9
economic divide, 19
economic hardship, 151–2
economic independence, 148
economic prosperity, 72
emigration, 74, 213–14, 217
Emmett, Robert, execution, 161
Entente Cordiale, the, 1–3
Episcopal Standing Committee, 172
executions, xviii, 58, 67, 71, 81, 147
   American reaction, 59–62
   conventional narratives, 5–6
   importance, 57
   Irish troops reaction to, 57
   political reactions, 58–9

family divisions, First World War, 37–8
famine, 150–2

farmers
  opposition to conscription, 185
  radicalization, 149–50
  socioeconomic situation, 72–4
Farrell, J. P., 123
Finland, 162
First World War
  accounts of the suffering, 115–16
  Armistice, 7
  Battle of the Somme, xix, 84–5
  Brest-Litovsk Treaty, 168
  casualties, 80, 107
  centenary, 9
  conventional narratives, 7–8
  Dardanelles offensive, 34, 85
  declaration of war, 3–4, 29
  diversionary 'Irish' conflict, 5
  dynamics of, 7–8
  family divisions, 37–8
  French anxieties, 14–15
  Gallipoli landings, 36–7
  German unrestricted submarine warfare, 82–3
  impact, 215–18
  indifference, 9
  Irish casualties, 36–7
  Irish support, 8–9
  Irish troops reaction to the rising, 56–7
  Operation Michael offensive, 168–9
  outbreak, 5, 29–34, 219
  propaganda, 34–8
  service percentages, 82
  social repercussions, 73–4
  support for the war effort, 215–16
  support for war effort, 72
  US intervention, 11, 12, 16, 129, 131–2, 133, 136–7, 146–7, 217, 219
  volunteer enlistment, 31–3, 34–5, 148
  war economy, 39–40, 152
  wounded demobilized men, 82
Fisher, Herbert, 171
Fitzgerald, Desmond, 184
Fitzpatrick, David, 6n16, 213n63
food prices, 151
food shortage, 83, 150–2, 163
foundational myth, 221–2
France
  concerns, 41
  concerns about Sinn Féin, 45–6, 47
  diplomatic archives, 14–16
  and the Easter Rising, 51–2, 62
  failure, 47
  First World War anxieties, 14–15
  Military Service Bill concerns, 44–5
  outbreak of war predictions, 5
  relations with Ireland, 2
  strategy, 15
Franco-Prussian War, 1
Franz Ferdinand, Archduke, assassination of, 3–4
Freeman's Journal, 30, 42, 44, 137, 152, 168, 172–3, 175, 199–200, 203
French bishops delegation, 62, 75–6
Friends of Irish Freedom, 134, 142

Gaelic American, 51, 154, 155
Gaelic League, 201
Gallagher, Rev. A., 79
Gallagher, Niamh, 185n124
Galway City Volunteers, 31
Geddes, Sir Auckland, 148, 166–7, 169
general amnesty, 103–5, 142
general elections, 1910, 19–20
general elections, 1918, 6, 7, 211–14
German Navy, xix, xx, 51
German plot, the, 197–201, 214, 220
German-Irish Society, 162
Germany
  approaches to, 49–51
  and the Easter Rising, 51–2
  financial support pact, 50
  Ireland turns to, 2–3
  propaganda, 41
Ginnell, Laurence, 58, 83–9, 117, 139
Government of Ireland Act, 220
Grey, Edward, 1, 61, 136
Griffith, Arthur, 105, 140, 151–2, 155, 202–3, 204, 206, 207

Harbison, Thomas, 155, 174
Harcourt, Lord, 213
Home Rule, xvii, xix, 19–29, 4, 35, 56, 70, 147, 179, 194–5, 216, 218
Home Rule Act, 63, 79
Home Rule Bill, xix, 20–9, 30–1, 38–9, 66
Home Rule controversy, 91–4
Home Rule crisis, 20–9
Hopwood, Sir Francis, 142

House, Colonel Edward, 136, 197
House–Grey Agreement, 136

imperialism, 223
Independent, The, 29–30, 42
international security, 158
internationalization, 131–63, 219
    and British procrastination, 146–8
    the Irish Convention, 138–46
    Peace Conference goal, 158–62
    US intervention, 131–40, 153, 160–1,
        163, 217, 218, 219, 222–3
Ireland, 18 (map)
    and Anglo-French relations, 2–3
    relations with France, 2
    transformation of, 57–63
    turn to Germany, 2–3
Irish Convention, xix, 91, 138–46, 147, 163,
    173–4, 196, 218, 219–20
Irish Independent, 65–6, 100, 171, 172–3,
    175, 194–5, 208
Irish National Aid Association, 61
Irish nationalism, 4
Irish Opinion, 160
Irish Parliamentary Party (Irish Party), 11,
    31, 38, 56, 83–9, 95–6, 129
    achievements, 97
    aims, 141
    consensus with Sinn Féin, 201–3
    credibility wrecked, 169
    critiques, 69
    denounced, 84–5
    East Cavan by-election, 202–3, 205
    East-Clare by-election, 107, 109, 110–11
    and the Easter Rising, 63
    eclipse of, 12, 16
    electoral victories, 178
    and equity of sacrifice, 172
    and executions, 58
    fall of, 5, 135, 220–1
    general elections, 1918, 212
    Home Rule controversy, 93–4
    hostility towards, 47, 49
    humiliation, 121
    the Irish Convention, 142, 143, 163,
        218, 220
    Irish-American support, 133, 134
    legitimacy, 215
    mistrust, 72

North-Roscommon by-election, 89
    opposition to conscription, 44, 88,
        122–3, 126, 173
    political strategy, 19
    popular legitimacy, 82–3
    procrastinations, 142
    rivalry with Sinn Féin, 94
    Sinn Féin defeats, 1917, 6
    Sinn Féin narrative, 217
    South Longford by-election, 98, 100–1,
        102, 103
    support, 46, 76–7, 79, 80
    support for the war effort, 215–16
    trapped, 177–8
    Waterford by-election, 154–5
    West Cork election, 1916, 78
Irish Progressive League, 161
Irish radical nationalism, 66
Irish Republic
    Proclamation of, 105–6, 221
    Sinn Féin unconditional allegiance to,
        120
Irish Times, The, 23, 25, 34, 65
Irish Volunteers, 27–8, 29, 31–2, 33, 38–9,
    41, 68–9, 117, 152–3, 216
    American financial support, 51
    decline, 122
    East-Clare by-election involvement,
        111
    general amnesty procession, 104
    increase in membership, 186–8
    numbers, 122
    outlawed, 201
    St Patrick's Day parades 1916, 45
    seditious attitude, 40
Irish War of Independence, 224
Irish World, 145–6
Irish-American diaspora, 13, 15
Irish-Americans, 50–1, 60, 132–4, 143–4,
    160–2, 173, 223
Irishman, 159, 188

Jackson, Alvin, 143
June negotiations collapse, 69, 70
Jusserand, Jean Jules, xx, 51, 61, 188–9

Kenna, Mark, 37–8
Kilkenny by-election, 113–18, 134
Kilkenny People, The, 107

King's County by-election, 203
King's Own Scottish Borderers, 27–8

labour exchange system, 40
Laffan, M., 6n18, 71–2n1
laissez-faire policy, 28, 68
language, 4
Lansing, Robert, 138
Leader, The, 180
legal rights, 27
Lenin, V. I., 223
Leslie, Shane, 60, 136–7
Liberal Party, 20, 26
Lincolnshire Regiment, 54
Lloyd George, David, 136, 137–8
    becomes Prime Minister, 78–9
    Home Rule controversy, 92–3, 94
    the Irish Convention, 139–40
    Page visits, 138
    and partition, 64–5
    postponement of conscription, 193–4
    procrastinations, 143, 163
    proposes introduction of conscription in Ireland, 170–1, 172
    traps IPP, 177–8
local authorities, opposition to conscription, 44
Logue, Cardinal, 124–5, 172, 180–1
Londonderry, Marquess of, 193, 200–1
Longford Leader, 75, 99–100
Lonsdale, Sir John, 58
Loughlin, Harry, 57
Lusitania, RMS, sinking of, 35
Lynch, Arthur, 144

McCartan, Patrick, 203
McCrain, P. J., 115
McDonagh, Thomas, 110
MacFarland, Stephen, 60
McGarry, F., 6n16
McGuinness, Joseph, 98–9, 101, 102
McMorrow, Rev. P., 80
Mahon, Sir Bryan, 34, 152, 170, 189–90
Mansion House meeting, 49
Mansion House Sinn Féin Convention, 96–8, 135
Markievicz, Countess, 115, 116–17
martial law, 144, 152–3
Middleton, Lord, 45

Military Service Act, xix, 43, 44–5, 72, 126, 165, 179, 182–4, 196, 197, 214, 220
Military Service Act for Ireland, 1918, 6–7
Military Service Bill, 145, 172, 173–4, 179, 193, 218
Militia Act, revival rumour, 29–30
Milroy, John, 99
Morning Post, 24
Mount Bellew District Council, 77

National Defence Fund, 183
National Volunteers, 31, 32, 33
nationalism, 21
Nationality, 155, 199, 202–3
new historiography, need for, 10–13
New Ireland, 158, 175, 180
New York
    German Embassy raid, 51
    Second Irish Race Convention, 200
New York Times, The, 59
Nicholas II, Tsar, 3
North-Roscommon by-election, 83–9, 91

O'Connor, James, 192
O'Connor, M. T. P., 93–4, 173
O'Dowd, John, 42
O'Flanaghan, Fr, 84, 87
O'Hurley, John, 115–16
O'Leary, Jeremiah, 67–8
O'Meara, Stephan, 113–14
O'Neill, Laurence, 207–8

Page, Walter, 136, 138
Paget, Sir Arthur, 22–3, 26
Parliament Act, 20–1, 22
Parnell, Charles Stewart, 4
partition, 63–8, 78, 144, 216
    procrastination, 68–70
partition crisis, 6
Peace Conference, xviii, 6, 16, 88, 96–8, 106, 110, 114, 120, 122, 158–62, 207, 221, 222–3
Pearse, Patrick, 59
Pennell, Catriona, 185n124
physical resistance, legitimacy, 116–17
Plunkett, George, 83–9, 95, 98, 142
Plunkett, Sir Horace, 142
polarization, 19, 26–7

political culture, 4
population, 19
population decline, 217
post-war international order, 221, 222–4
Potato Famine, the, 151
Princip, Gavrilo, assassination of Archduke Franz Ferdinand, 3
Proclamation of the Irish Republic, 105–6, 221
pro-German rhetoric, 109–10
propaganda, 62
    anti-British, 36–8, 48
    counter-propaganda campaign, 210
    First World War, 34–8
    German, 41
    pro-German, 217
Protestant domination, 4
provinces, 18 (map)
public opinion
    American, 59–62
    on conscription, 168
    English, 177
    Home Rule crisis, 24–5
    and partition, 66, 67
    shift in, 135–6
    transformation of, 57–63

radicalization, 6, 8, 8n25, 15, 57–63, 71, 111, 129, 148–54
recruitment decline, British Army, 80–3
Redmond, John, 12, 22, 28, 29–34, 37, 46, 50, 89, 217
    Cambon on, 220
    and consent, 72
    danger for, 97
    death, 153, 159–60, 193
    denounced, 84–5, 116
    determination, 97
    endorsement of volunteer engagement, 31–2
    goal, 91
    the Irish Convention, 139, 140, 147
    opposition to conscription, 79, 140–1
    and partition, 64, 65, 66, 67, 69
    responsibility, 184
    speech against compulsory service in Ireland, 43
    support, 42, 76–80
    West Cork election, 1916, 78

Redmond, William, 56, 92–3, 111, 154–5
Rice, Sir Cecil Spring, 137
Roscommon Journal, 209–10
Royal Irish Rifles, 57, 176
rural population, 9, 41–2, 78, 111, 149–50, 185
Ryan, Michael J., 60

sacrifice, equity of, 170–2, 194, 195–6
St John Gaffney, Thomas, 162
St Patrick's Day parades 1916, 45
Salisbury, Marquess of, 144
Sarajevo, assassination of Archduke Franz Ferdinand, 3–4
Second Irish Race Convention, New York, 200
seditious feelings, 47
self-determination, 88, 91, 159, 161, 163, 197, 218, 221, 223
self-government, 222
separation aspirations, 209
separatist movement, first step in the revival of, 79
Shaw, General Sir Frederik, 197–8, 201
Sheehy, David, 110–11
Sherwood Foresters, 54
Shortt, Edward, 197–8
Sinn Féin, xvii, 62, 146, 153–4, 179
    address to Wilson, 207–8
    aims, 140–1, 160, 217
    anti-conscription myth, 84–5, 89, 98–9, 113–14, 115–17
    aspirations, 12
    Catholic clergy support, 123–5, 181
    causes of triumph, 10–11, 12
    consensus with IPP, 201–3
    de Valera elected president, 120
    demands, 97
    East Cavan by-election, 202–3, 204, 206, 207
    East-Clare by-election, 105–7, 108, 109–12, 109
    embarrassment of, 134–5
    emergence of, 6
    Food Committee, 152
    French concerns, 45–6, 47
    general elections, 1918, 7, 211–14
    growing popularity, 71
    hegemony, 8

increase in membership, 188
IPP narrative, 217
the Irish Convention, 139
Kilkenny by-election, 113–18
lack of popular support, 71
leaders arrested, 198–200
legitimizes Easter Rising, 83
manifesto, 1917, 141
North-Roscommon by-election, 83, 86–9
opposition to conscription, 88, 91, 96–8
opposition to the Irish Convention, 141
outlawed, 201
papal impunity, 181
and partition, 67
Peace Conference goal, xviii, 158, 207
political success, 7
popularity, 7, 151
prisoners released, 69
pro-German rhetoric, 109–10
recrudescence, 69
reorganization, 94–5
rivalry with IPP, 94
self-determination rhetoric, 15–16
South Longford by-election, 98–103
support, 46, 78, 97, 125–9, 135–6, 150, 197, 216
unconditional allegiance to Irish Republic, 120
US support, 188–9
Waterford by-election, 154, 155
Sinn Féin clubs, 126–8, 188
Sinn Féin Constitution, 120
Sinn Féin Convention, 1917, 96–8, 120–2, 135, 140
Sinn Féin sympathizers, growth in numbers, 125–9
Sligo Champion, 29
social repercussions, First World War, 73–4
socioeconomic situation, 72–4
soldiers
  local populations relations with, 119–20
  resentment to the Irish, 175–7
soldiers' wives, 101
Solemn League and Covenant, Ulster, 21

Somme, Battle of the, xix, 84–5
sources, 13–16
South Armagh by-election, 155, 156, 157
South Longford by-election, 98–103
Spring-Rice, Sir Cecil, 61
suffrage, 4, 212–13
Sweden, 162

Tangier Incident, 2
Tardieu, André, 143–4, 147–8, 158, 160
Times, The, 23, 24, 159–60, 167, 199
Triple Alliance, the, 1

Ulster, 19, 195
  dependence on agricultural produce from the south, 67
  exclusion from Home Rule Bill, 31
  revolt, 21–6
  Solemn League and Covenant, 21
Ulster National Convention, 64–5
Ulster Unionism
  and Home Rule, 19–29
  privileges undermined, 26–7
Ulster Unionists, 12, 92–3, 145, 159, 172, 219
  conscription cry, 165–70
Ulster Volunteer Force, 21–2, 23, 25, 26–7, 29, 68–9, 145, 215
  arms Importation, 27–8
  British Army enlistment, 33
Ulster Women's Unionist Council, 22n13
Unionist population, 145
United Irish League, 41–2, 77, 80, 86–7
United Irish League of America, 133
United States of America
  anti-British feelings, 133–4
  Balfour visits, 138–9
  and British procrastination, 146–8
  collective memory, 11
  counter-propaganda campaign, 210
  financial support, 51
  First World War intervention, 11, 12, 16, 129, 131–2, 133, 136–7, 146–7, 217, 219
  foreign born population, 132
  foreign policy, 13
  German Embassy raid, 51
  intervention, 131–40, 143–4, 153, 160–1, 163, 217, 218, 219, 222–3

Irish-Americans, 50–1, 60, 132–4, 143–4, 160–2, 173, 223
Labour Bureau of the American Commission on Irish Independence, 223
neutrality, 50–1, 133
and partition, 67–8
public opinion, 59–62
reaction to Easter Rising, 59–62
reaction to executions, 59–62
Sinn Féin support, 188–9

Versailles, Treaty of, 223
Vienna, 3–4
voting rights, 212–13

Waldron, 79
Walsh, Frank, 224
war economy, 39–40, 42, 152
war effort, support, 72
War Office, 22–3, 25
Washington Star, 59
Waterford by-election, 154–5
West Cork election, 1916, 78
Westport barracks, 149
Wilhelm II, Kaiser, 3
William of Orange, 4
Wilson, Woodrow, xx, 11n34, 133–4, 136, 140, 163, 189, 197, 222, 223
de Valera and, 158
and the Easter Rising, 61
Irish policy, 137, 138
opposition from Congress, 137
and partition, 67–8
Sinn Féin address to, 207–8
Wimborne, Lord, 189–90
women, and First World War, 40
Woodenbridge, 31
working classes, socioeconomic situation, 73–4
wounded demobilized men, 82

Zimmerman, Arthur, 50

www.ingramcontent.com/pod-product-compliance
Lightning Source LLC
Chambersburg PA
CBHW062128300426
44115CB00012BA/1848